Adobe
Illustrator 5.0:
The Official
Handbook For
Designers
4th Edition

ADOBE ILLUSTRATOR 5.0: THE OFFICIAL HANDBOOK FOR DESIGNERS

4TH EDITION

By Tony Bove
and Cheryl Rhodes

RANDOM HOUSE
ELECTRONIC PUBLISHING

New York

New York Toronto London Sydney Auckland

Foreword

When we started the development of Adobe Illustrator, our goal was to make a tool that would be easy to use and valuable to both the amateur and the professional artist. What we didn't anticipate was how creative users would be. They are creative in the artwork they produce, and in the ways they use the program to solve illustration problems. The users of the program continue to amaze us. They have created astounding pieces of art. They have used the program in ways that we have never contemplated, and they find applications that are new, novel, and innovative with each week that passes.

We have always thought that it would be great if someone would bottle the experience the early users have gained so that new users could benefit. *Adobe Illustrator 5.0: The Official Handbook For Designers, 4th Edition* fills such a need.

In this book, Tony and Cheryl explore the uses of Adobe Illustrator from the perspective of several of the more advanced users. This perspective gives the reader valuable insight into how various illustration problems are approached and solved. They also expose in detail the use of each tool, and describe all the new features of Illustrator 5, including new tools and menu items. All of these portions provide a valuable reference guide to the program.

If you do not own a copy of Adobe Illustrator, then this book will give you a good idea of how powerful the program is and what it can do for you.

If you have purchased the program, then this book will be a valuable reference to how the program works and how it is used, with a description of all the new features. In any event, welcome to the creative world of Adobe Illustrator.

John Warnock
Chairman and CEO, Adobe Systems Incorporated

Trademarks

Preface

Welcome to the world of computer graphics. Adobe Illustrator is a program for designers and professional illustrators that runs on Apple Macintosh computers minimally equipped with 5 MB of RAM (at least 3.1 MB of application RAM) and a hard disk, and System 6.0.7 (with 32-bit QuickDraw) or greater (System 7 is recommended), and a PostScript printer (or any Macintosh graphics imaging output device). With Adobe Illustrator you can produce high-quality illustrations and all kinds of line art. It is unique in offering a very accurate display of PostScript graphics, and a collection of sophisticated line and curve drawing and editing tools.

This is the fourth edition of this book; the first described the original version of Adobe Illustrator; the second described Illustrator 88, and the third described Adobe Illustrator 3.

What's New in Version 5

Version 5 has features tuned to make Adobe Illustrator easier to use by beginners, and this version is more intuitive and productive for both beginners and advanced users.

For both beginners and advanced users, version 5 improves tool performance and adds new tools, includes plug-in filters (to use as shortcuts to achieving professional effects fast), and layering, plus you can edit in preview or artwork views, and save up to 25 custom views (which are like snapshots of an area of detail) to switch between quickly. Palettes for Layers, Paint style, Gradient, Character, Paragraph, and more, can be hidden or displayed for easier access, and the maximum drawing size has been increased to 10-by-10 feet (from 18-by-18 inches in version 3). You can open more than one document at once, and import/export colors, text styles, paint styles, gradients, filters, and more between documents. Using Macintosh System 7 software, you can also use Publish and Subscribe commands to share and update Illustrator artwork and elements among a networked group of users.

For beginners, version 5's features that ease and improve the learning curve include: multiple levels of undo (up to 200; number limited by RAM); a brush tool, a gradient fill tool, an eyedropper tool, and a paint brush tool, which are intuitive and familiar from other applications; plug-in filters (to use as shortcuts to achieving professional effects fast); and improved tool performance for all tools, especially for the pen and type tools, as well as better access to attribute settings through improved text styling and object styling palettes. Layering can be used by beginners to effectively reduce confusion which can occur when objects are placed adjacent to each other with points that overlap, and the Info palette also improves the placement of objects.

For advanced users (and also helpful to new users), are changes that make Illustrator more intuitive. For example, using the measure tool before using the transformation tools and Move command fills in appropriate numbers to use for the movement or transformation. Gradient fills and blends depend on what output resolution setting is used to produce smooth blends and transitions between colors. Version 5 suggests optimal numbers (based on the output resolution you have specified) to use for setting smooth blends and gradients, which you can either use or replace. The gradient fill tool, gradient palette, and custom color and pattern dialog boxes give intuitive and ultimate control over coloring of objects and text. Layering and floating palettes further improve productivity.

Adobe Illustrator 5 sets a new level of performance for professional graphics application programs. Standout features are its improved text handling, new tools and new functionality for existing tools, layering features (which improve performance and provide more access to artwork elements), plug-in filters (to use as shortcuts to achieving professional effects fast), as well as improved text shaping, editing, formatting, and styling, and more. At least 40 Adobe Type 1 Typefaces are included and can be used to create editable outlines. Also included are Color matching systems files for TRUMATCH, FOCOLTONE, TOYO, and PANTONE custom color inks, and their process color equivalents, plus patterns, gradient fills and custom colors. The Adobe Separator program is included to provide control over production of color separations of Illustrator files.

Finally, the use of graphics tablets is supported, to free users from the tyranny of the mouse, or to just give them a break from using the usual bar of soap or brick (also called mouse) to draw with. Using a graphics tablet (with the brush tool) enables you to create variable width strokes, based on the amount of pressure you apply to a stylus, just as you can apply variable amounts of pressure to an ink pen to produce thin and thick stroke widths. This feature makes Adobe Illustrator suitable for a wider variety of fine art techniques, as well as easier for anyone to use.

History of Program Development

Adobe Illustrator has always been a leading application in its field. The history of development of past versions of Adobe Illustrator provides a window into the timeline of graphics software development for the Macintosh. Here then is a brief history of the added capabilities of previous versions of Adobe Illustrator:

Version 4 was released for other platforms, such as the NeXT computer and Windows equipped PCs, but was not shipped for the Macintosh.

Version 3 improved text handling, provided new variations of existing tools, and new charting and graphing features. Text could be automatically arranged to fit a shape, to follow a curve, and to wrap around graphical objects. Full typographical control over kerning and spacing, hanging punctuation, and indents was provided, as well as the horizontal scaling of characters. Typefaces compatible with Adobe Type Manager could be used to create editable outlines.

Capabilities that were added previously to version 3 included automatic tracing of scanned images, automatic color separations with Adobe Separator, the PANTONE Matching System colors, the ability to show color on any type of color Macintosh display, the blend tool for graduated fills and special effects, and the freehand tool for freestyle drawing. In addition, the DrawOver program converted MacDraw PICT graphics into PostScript.

About This Book

This book starts with a basic introduction to Adobe Illustrator and leads you on a tour through artwork created by professional illustrators. In the artists' own words are their rare insights into achieving special effects and high-quality designs.

Chapter 1 is a basic introduction to the program's features and to the Macintosh system. This chapter explains each icon you may encounter, and provides a brief tutorial on how to draw and create artwork with Adobe Illustrator.

Chapter 2 shows how maps, charts, and clip art can be prepared with the program. The artists who drew these images describe how they used Adobe Illustrator to do special effects, from building reusable graphics and drawing objects with shared borders to adding paint and the illusion of three dimensions. The artists also explain some of the techniques for placing text in graphics, and how to clone, scale, shear, reflect, rotate, and trace images. The chapter provides a tutorial on using the charting and graphing features, and it also covers page setup and printing.

Chapter 3 uses commercial art examples to show how an artist would start a large, complex illustration. Artists use multiple transformations and overlays, airbrush effects, strokes, and fills for enclosed objects, gray shades, and blends. Artists also show the most effective use of the New Window and Preview windows, how to rotate text and perform other special text effects, and how to use gray shades and colors.

Chapter 4 shows how Adobe Illustrator can scale images with or without preserving line weights. The artists explain how they used multiple rotations, reflections, and constraints for drawing complex graphics, as well as editing techniques, such as changing straight lines into curves. The chapter covers line styles, stroke widths for setting trap between color images, overprinting, and color separations.

Chapter 5 is a complete reference guide to Adobe Illustrator menus and tools. The menus and tools are presented in the order they appear in the program's display, followed by Adobe Separator.

Chapter 6 is a brief overview of PostScript, the page description language used to describe the graphics created by Adobe Illustrator. PostScript files can be used with other applications that support PostScript, and can be printed or typeset on any PostScript output device. Included is a description of the included EPSF Riders file, which is used to add PostScript fragments to customize Adobe Illustrator documents.

The appendix describes the Adobe Illustrator 88 document format, which is an optional format for saving Illustrator documents. The description is provided for users who are curious about PostScript, but it is not meant to be a complete tutorial.

We are confident that you will find Adobe Illustrator useful. By creating PostScript art you are preserving the artwork in digital form that can be used again and again without any degrading of the image. You are also preparing artwork that can be used in future graphics systems, since PostScript is the standard page description language for publishing systems.

"Only through art can we get outside of ourselves and know another's view of the universe..." (Marcel Proust). May you find inspiration with mouse (or stylus) in hand.

Colophon

This book was written and desktop published by the authors. We used the following software to produce this book: Microsoft Word 5 (Microsoft) for writing and editing; PageMaker 4.2 (Aldus) for page makeup; and Adobe PhotoShop, MacPaint (Apple/Claris), SuperPaint (Aldus/Silicon Beach Software), and Macromedia Director for preparing images of the screen and other images to use as templates in examples. We also used SmartScrap (Solutions Inc.) to keep track of icons and other graphic symbols, and Art Grabber II (MacroMind), Camera (Keith A. Esau), and Capture (Mainstay) to capture images of the screen to use in the book.

We ran this software with the following hardware: Apple Macintosh SE/30 and Macintosh LC, IIcx, Quadra 700, Centris 610, and Centris 660AV computers; Apple HDSC 80 FWB Hammer1000 and SuperMac DataFrame XP150 hard disks; the Radius dual-page monitor and the Apple Color Display monitor (with the Macintosh IIcx computer); Farallon's PhoneNet network; Apple Personal LaserWriter IINTR and Hewlett Packard PaintJet XL300 printers; Linotype Linotronic 100 and 300 imagesetters; and Apple OneScanner and Hewlett Packard ScanJet IIC/Mac color scanners.

We wish to thank the following companies for support and services in the preparation of this book: Adobe Systems, Aldus Corp., Apple Computer, Inc., Claris, Farallon Computing, MacroMedia, Mainstay, Microsoft Corp., Radius, and SuperMac Technology.

Acknowledgments

The authors wish to acknowledge the people who helped create this book, especially Fred Davis, who contributed to Chapter 5, and Steve Rosenthal and Mike Schuster, who contributed to Chapter 6 and the Appendix.

The authors thank the following artists for their artwork and assistance with this book: Gail Blumberg, Russell Brown, Louis Fishauf, Luanne Seymour Cohen, Pat Coleman, Gary Cosimini, Dean Dapkus, Laura Lamar, Keith Ohlfs, Sumner Stone, and John Warnock.

We also thank LaVon Collins, Charles Geschke, Bill Gladstone, Doedy Hunter, Michael Roney, Keri Walker, and Eric Zocher.

Table of Contents

1

Introduction to Adobe Illustrator

"Come into my parlor," said the computer to the specialist.
— Marshall McLuhan, *The Medium is the Message*

Adobe Illustrator, from Adobe Systems, is a drawing program for professional illustrators, artists, and designers that brings a new level of precision to personal computer graphics.

The program can produce an image that is not confined to the fixed resolution (measured in dots-per-inch) of laser printers. The image can be printed on almost any printer, but printers and typesetters with higher resolutions (more dots-per-inch) can do a better job of producing a smooth, yet crisp image. Because the resolution can be adjusted to such a precise degree, Illustrator graphics can also be printed onto 35mm slides, viewed on any size display found on a Macintosh, PC, NeXT, or other workstation, viewed on audience-sized display screens, or copied onto film or videotape devices. Illustrator has sophisticated curve-drawing techniques to make curves of any shape and size, as well as techniques for drawing any geometric or custom shape and using any pattern.

With Adobe Illustrator 5 for the Mac, you can instantly create text effects, charts, and graphs as well as professional illustrations. Text can be styled with different typefaces, sizes, leading, and colors, and text can be automatically arranged to fit a shape, to follow a curve, and to wrap around graphical objects. Baseline shift controls (useful for creating subscripts and superscripts) let you move type above or below the baseline to a new location on a path. Elements containing text can be selected and transformed — rotated, scaled, sheared, blended or re-flected — together, or you can transform the type alone. Full typographical control over kerning, spacing, tracking, hyphenation, hanging punctuation, and indents is provided, as well as the horizontal scaling of characters. Typefaces compatible with Adobe Type Manager — including the 40+ Adobe Type 1 typefaces included with Illustrator 5 for the Mac — can be used to create editable outlines.

You can trace lines, curves, and shapes using a rough image as a *template,* or draw freehand with or without a template for guidance. Your display becomes the equivalent of an illuminated light table, and your tracing tools are the precise functions of the program which you use by pressing keys and moving a mouse or stylus. Lines can be drawn perfectly straight, and curves can be precisely contoured by dragging a mouse with little artistic skill. However, the program is also designed for professional illustrators who understand how to use these tools to produce high-quality art and graphics. The variable brush width option supports the use of pressure-sensitive brushes, pads, pens, styluses, and tablets in place of a mouse.

To make use of a template for tracing, you can first sketch the rough image on paper and use an inexpensive desktop scanner to scan the image into the computer for use as a template. You can also use other painting and drawing programs on your Macintosh (notably Claris MacPaint, MacDraw, Adobe Photoshop, or other programs that can create black and white bitmap documents such as MacPaint documents or PICT documents) to create or modify a template for use with Adobe Illustrator.

Weather map base.
Courtesy The New York Times, *used with permission.*

Once you have the template image in a MacPaint or PICT file (either scanned or painted with a program), you can use it with Adobe Illustrator — the program displays the template as a gray-filled background image while you draw lines, curves, and shapes over it. The program offers automatic tracing over images as well.

You can change your view at any time to display what you've drawn (artwork), or see a preview of the drawing in color (provided you are using a color monitor). Or you can create an unlimited number of new windows and up to 25 custom views, showing the different points of view and magnification levels, layers, etc. that you need, and position the windows to be side-by-side or on another screen, to allow custom viewing of layers at the precise level of detail you need. You can edit in any window or view, including a preview view, and you can hide or show the template. You can even preview selected portions and layers of the artwork to see how it will look when printed.

Illustrator is popularly used for creation and editing of art for animations and videos, as well as for printed pages. Programs such as Adobe Photoshop provide effects (and filters) that are not only complementary to, but also in addition to, Illustrator's features. Adobe Photoshop and Adobe Premiere EPS image files placed in Illustrator can be replaced with updated versions of the image files, or with new art, without exiting Illustrator.

Adobe Illustrator 5 has additional features that make it easier to use than previous versions. For example, the only limit to the number of undo/redo actions that can be set is the amount of available RAM (the default is set to 10 levels of undo/redo), and the status line can be used to display the number of undo and redo actions. Version 5 features that increase capability include the ability to open multiple documents, a page size of up to 120 by 120 inches (based on available RAM), more control over document setup, an unlimited number of layers, and easily modified gradient fills with multiple colors. Features that increase *functionality* include floating palettes (for paint styles, gradient fills, layers, character and paragraph styles, and tools), new tools such as the eyedropper and paint bucket, which let you apply selected attributes of one object to another, and a brush tool which allows variable stroke widths utilizing Illustrator 5's pressure sensitive stylus/tablet support. Plug-in filters (several are included, and more are available from third-party sources) make it possible for even beginners to achieve professional results fast.

This combination — precise drawing tools, a template for tracing on the screen, automatic graphing, precise typographic control over text with special effects like using a curve as a baseline, and resolution-independent images — makes Adobe Illustrator one of the best personal computer graphics tools for professional artwork and illustration in publishing and commercial graphics. Version 5 sports a new, more intuitive interface that improves productivity for experienced users, as well as for beginners.

An excellent example of how the program can make artists more productive is at *The New York Times* art department, which uses Illustrator to prepare the daily weather map and four-day forecast. Illustrator graphics can be combined and edited to form new graphics, so that the art department can produce an image faster and still get high-quality results. The Adobe Illustrator graphics files are transferred to the various daily newspapers owned by *The New York Times* — much like a wire service distributing its news. Art director Gary Cosimini explains that his goal is "to automate some mechanical processes so that the artist can be creative without thinking about the processes."

The Role of PostScript

The reason why Adobe Illustrator can produce resolution-independent images that can be printed on laser printers or higher resolution typesetters is that it describes the graphic image in a computer language rather than in a series of spots and spaces. The language, developed by Adobe Systems co-founders John Warnock and Charles Geschke, is called PostScript.

PostScript is generally referred to as a *page description language*. It provides a standard method of describing and transferring images, and even entire pages, which contain text (in fonts) and graphics. The language is used by an application program (such as Adobe Illustrator, or Aldus PageMaker, or QuarkXPress) to send pages of text and graphics to a printer, display screen, or other output device such as an imagesetter. (The term "imagesetter" is used because, unlike typesetters, these PostScript devices can prepare halftones and color separations as well as produce typesetting and line art.)

The output device has a PostScript raster image processor (RIP) unit, which translates the PostScript language into a raster image (a series of dots) that is ideal for the resolution of the device. Programs can use PostScript to take full advantage of the resolution of the printer or imagesetter, and produce images without restrictions on resolution.

Resolution, defined by the number of dots per inch (dpi), is extremely important for high-quality graphics. The higher the resolution, the better an image will appear in print. PostScript transcends resolution by describing graphics in an algorithmic language rather than in a series of dots at a specific resolution.

As a result, PostScript makes it possible to "print" the same page on the 2540 dpi Linotronic 300 or 500 imagesetter (with vastly higher quality), that you print on an Apple LaserWriter or other PostScript laser printer at 300 dpi resolution — using the same computer, system, and software (such as Adobe Illustrator). PostScript is compatible with Macintosh system software and applications, and it is also supported on PCs by most of the page makeup and word processing programs.

Why is PostScript so important to publishing, and why does Adobe Illustrator use it to store image information? Typeset-quality text (printing with a resolution of 1000 dpi or higher) and high-quality graphics are required for most design, illustration, and publishing applications. With PostScript, it is possible to automate production from creation all the way to printing, without limiting your output to the resolution of laser printers. Pages can be sent directly to a PostScript-driven plate maker for the highest possible resolution. PostScript files can be transferred over telephone lines and networks, and PostScript can also be used to send information to color printers, film recorders, slide makers, and color electronic prepress systems.

Adobe Illustrator 5 also supports printing to non-PostScript language black and white and color printers.

Overview of Features

Adobe Illustrator is a comfortable tool for professional artists and illustrators because it uses the paradigm of drawing with mechanical tools. It is also an excellent tool for CAD/CAM and technical line art because you can draw a complex image and scale it to any size, yet preserve the line weights if you want (the lines will not get thicker when you resize the image to be larger).

Artists who have traditionally started with rough sketches may still work that way — the only difference is that "inking" the sketch is done electronically, with more sophisticated tools. The program lets you put inexpensive scanners to good use: converting a scanned bit map into an object-oriented, resolution-independent drawing. The least expensive scanner on the market may be used to scan an image at any resolution — no matter how rough — and bring it into the program.

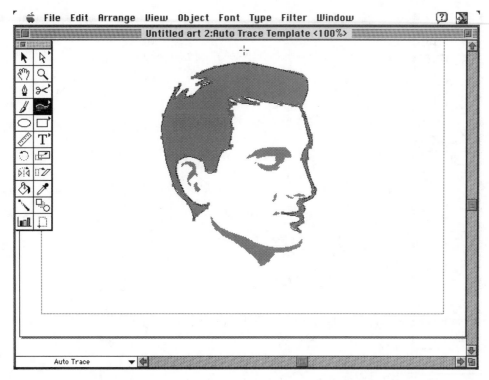

Figure 1-1.
Adobe Illustrator offers a tool that can automatically trace the outlines of scanned images to produce shapes that can be readily adjusted, added to, and redrawn as needed. Drag to the right of the freehand tool to select the auto trace tool.

Tracing and Drawing

You can turn the scanned image instantly into line art using the automatic tracing feature. Drag to the right of the freehand drawing tool (Figure 1-1) to select the auto trace tool, then click the crosshair on an edge of the scanned image (opened as a template). The program can automatically draw an outline around the image, so that you can start with shapes already drawn.

You can also draw the outlines yourself, tracing the rough scanned image with precise lines, curves, and filled areas. Illustrator offers a freehand tool for drawing curves freehand (Figure 1-2). The freehand tool responds to speed and smoothness of movement — the faster you drag, the less points are used to describe the object. If you select

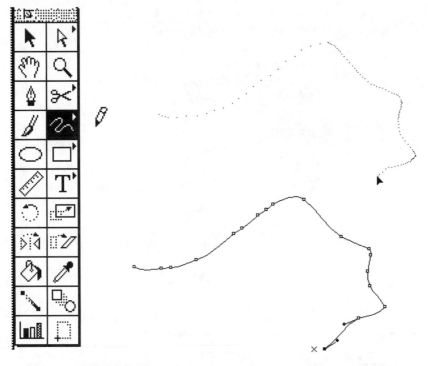

Figure 1-2.
Click to select the freehand tool. With the freehand tool you can drag the mouse to draw shapes. After sketching with the freehand tool, the program creates line and curve segments resembling your sketch. You can control the precision for freehand drawing.

Preferences-General in the File menu, you can further adjust the Freehand tolerance setting to make objects have more or less points. The resulting file can then be sent to any PostScript device with the best possible quality that device can deliver.

A graphic object in Adobe Illustrator consists of points and segments (lines or curves) connected in a *path*. A path can be a single line or curve or shape, such as a circle or rectangle, or a combination of lines, curves and shapes. A path consists of at least one *anchor point*. An anchor point defines one end of a line or curve segment; two anchor points define a segment.

To draw a curve using Illustrator's precise pen tool, start by dragging from a point in the direction of the bump in the curve you want to create (Figure 1-3). This action creates an anchor point and a direction point for the curve. Then drag from another point, this time in the opposite direction (away from the bump). This action creates another anchor

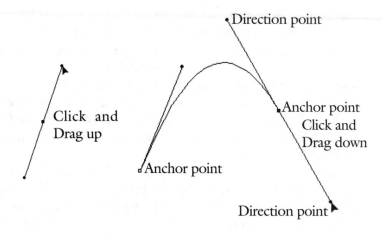

Figure 1-3.
Drawing a curve by dragging the first anchor point to create a direction point, then dragging the second anchor point to create two more direction points, defining the curve.

point with two direction points, completely defining the curve segment. You can then hold down the Command key, select an anchor point or a direction point, and reshape the curve.

Many different shapes can be drawn by manipulating anchor points, direction points, and segments. The best techniques use the fewest possible anchor points in order to get the smoothest curves.

Tool Palette and Keyboard Control

Many of the tools in the tool palette offer more than one tool (as shown before with the freehand/auto trace tool). For example, three selection pointer tools are available. To the right of the selection tool is the direct-selection tool. Dragging to the right of the direct-selection pointer tool gives you the group-selection tool.

Keyboard controls also make the program easy to use. You can switch from one drawing tool to another quickly, or bring up a dialog box for typing specifications for an operation, using combinations of the mouse button, the Option key, the Command key, the Shift key, and space bar. The keyboard controls are close to one hand, while the mouse is at the other hand. You use both simultaneously — and once you learn the tricks, you can draw complex images quickly. You hardly ever go back to the pull-down menus or the tool palette — you can keep your eyes and hands on the artwork. For example, to scroll around with the hand, press the space bar for the hand tool; to zoom in and zoom out, use the Command key, the Option key and the space bar and drag; to automatically zoom and scroll at the same time, hold down the mouse button near an edge of the screen when you are using the zoom tool.

As you draw a curve, you can go back and edit it by pressing the Command key, without leaving the drawing mode. The program remembers its state, lets you go back and change things, and then resumes without losing continuity — your hand never has to leave the mouse (which is important for an artist who is trying to concentrate on the work). To build certain types of curves you stretch the curve, press the Command key, pull back one line with the mouse, and then go on. This technique can be mastered to the point that it can become second nature; people who are proficient at it can build smooth curves much faster in this manner than by drawing freehand style.

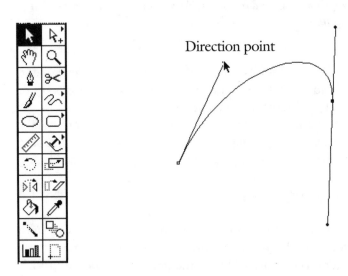

Direction point

Figure 1-4.
Selecting a point (direction points connected to the selected point control the slope and direction of the curve), and reshaping the path by moving one or more points. You can reshape a curve by moving the direction points.

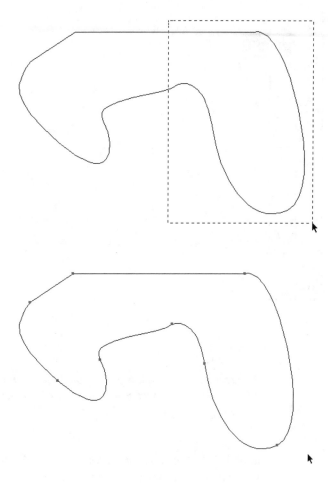

Figure 1-5.
Draw a marquee around part of the shape to select more than one point in a path. Only those points that lie inside the marquee are selected.

Selecting Paths

You select an entire path before performing many operations, such as applying paint or rotating. You can also select one or more points in a path and move them to reshape the path (Figure 1-4).

There are several useful ways to select entire objects and pieces of objects, or just points within them. The standard marquee (selection rectangle) will select every point that's within the marquee (Figure 1-5). When you select just one point, it deselects the other points unless you hold down the Shift key to extend the selection to include both the points

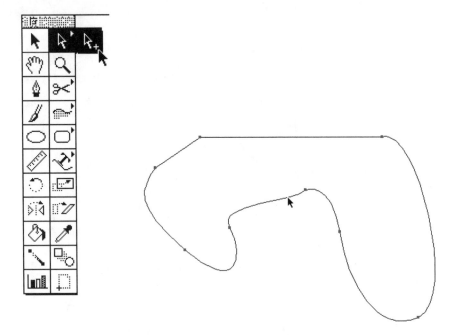

Figure 1-6.
You can select a complete path by holding down the Option key while clicking with the direct-selection tool, or by switching to the group-selection tool and clicking (without holding down Option).

already selected plus the new point. The Shift key lets you extend your selection to include a new point, or if the point was already selected, it will be deselected. With the marquee, you can extend the selection, even to another group of points.

Rather than trying to surround an entire path or large image with the marquee (especially if the path is larger than your screen's display area), you can point to the path, hold down the Option key, and click the mouse to select the entire path (Figure 1-6) with the direct-selection tool. You can then use Shift-Option-click to extend the selection to another path. This is especially useful when you have a large number of objects — you can select them in a hurry. If you plan to select only complete paths, switch to the selection tool or group-selection tool. With these tools you can select a path without having to hold down the Option key.

Using the Option key with the marquee will grab all the paths that intersect the selection rectangle (Figure 1-7). This is useful for very complex drawings — you can select everything within a certain area, and then deselect certain parts using the Shift key and clicking on them.

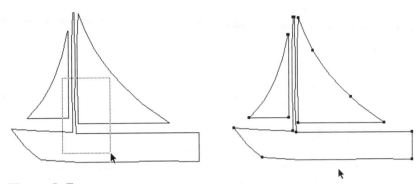

Figure 1-7.
When you hold down the Option key while dragging the marquee, the program selects all paths that intersect the marquee.

Drawing with Constraints

The Shift key can constrain movement when you are moving a group or a path. It can also constrain while drawing so that you draw perfect squares or circles. Hold down the Shift key while using the oval tool to draw a perfect circle rather than an ellipse (Figure 1-8).

You can build a circle or ellipse from center-to-edge rather than from edge-to-edge by holding down the Option key with the oval tool. By double-clicking the oval or rectangle tools you can select the center-drawing oval and rectangle tools — double-clicking toggles those tool settings between edge-to-edge and center-to-edge drawing. Ellipses are created to align to the x and y axes settings; they align to whatever degree of rotation has been set.

Also highly useful is the constrain feature that lets you set a constraining factor according to the axis you draw. If you are doing a road map, for example, and you need to indicate buildings on the map, you can draw a direction, then place graphics to be constrained to go along in that direction.

The measure tool displays the exact measurement between two points (Figure 1-9), which can help make drawings accurate. In addition, objects can be used as guides for accurate drawing.

Manipulating Objects

To paste one object between others, you can select the object, cut it, select the next object, and choose Paste In Back to paste the first

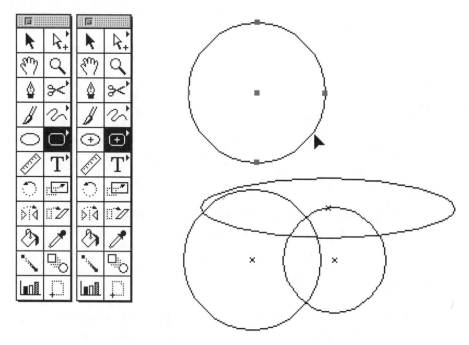

Figure 1-8.
The Shift key with the oval drawing tool constrains an ellipse to be a perfect circle. You can use the edge-drawing oval tool or the center-drawing oval tool (or hold down the Option key with the edge-drawing oval tool to draw from the center).

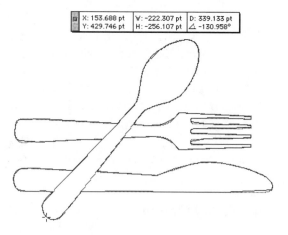

Figure 1-9.
Measuring the distance between two points with the measure tool.

object behind the selected object, but in front of a third object. Any object or group of objects can be interleaved (stacked) between any other objects (Figure 1-10).

No matter how you select a group of objects, it moves as a group until you ungroup it. This feature can be useful for moving large and complex shapes. Rectangles, ellipses and circles are grouped when you draw them, but you can ungroup them and turn them into other shapes. For example, you can select a circle and ungroup it, then select a point on the circle and cut it; the circle becomes four Bézier curves that can then be edited. You can also use the scissors tool to cut the circle into segments for precise arcs.

Selected objects can be cloned simply by holding down the Option key while dragging. You can clone a selected object and then perform a series of transformations on its shape and color.

When scaling an object or group, or pattern tiles (any object can be used as the basis for a pattern tile), you can choose uniform or constrained scaling, preserving line weights or scaling the lines. For example, you can select everything on the page and scale it down by 33 percent of the original size with preserved line weights. For technical drawings, this is better than using a stat camera. Gray shading, when enlarged or reduced, retains its exact density, because it is repainted with the specified shading percentage.

In addition to interleaving (stacking) objects, and changing their painting order, you can also use Adobe Illustrator 5's layering features. Select Show Layers from the Window menu to display the Layers palette (Figure 1-11). Choose the New Layer command from the Layers menu to add another layer.

If you choose a different selection color for each layer, you can easily tell which layer an object is on. When you select the object, its anchor points and direction points will be the selection color you choose in the Layer Options dialog box. Each layer can be set to display, preview, print, dim placed images, or lock images, or not, and you can change the selection color and layer name.

Objects can be moved from one layer to another layer, and you gain more control over editing, previewing, printing, and so on, than with stacking objects on only one layer. (However, grouped objects must be on the same layer; if you try to group objects that are on different layers, they will all be moved to the next layer, directly behind the frontmost layer.) Each layer can be deleted, the order (position) of the layers can be changed, a layer can be hidden or locked, images (EPS files) can be placed on a specified layer, and you can use the palette window, in conjunction with the Layer Options dialog box, to completely control the display of

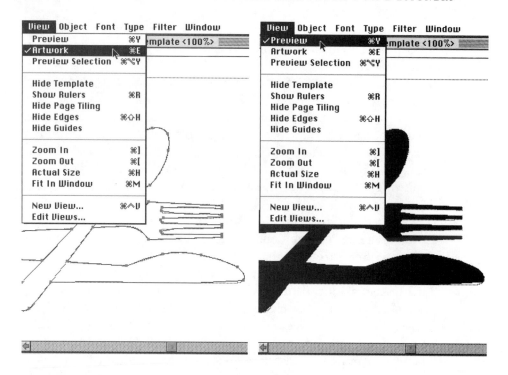

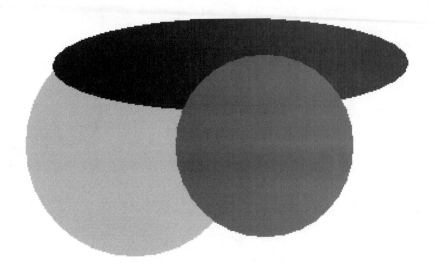

Figure 1-10.
You can edit objects in either the Artwork or Preview windows. Interleaved objects as they appear in the Preview window, after selecting the Preview command in the View menu. Interleaving (or stacking) determines the paint order of all of the objects on a layer.

artwork. You can choose to work on what looks like an empty page, if you wish, while you hide all other layers. You can even import layering settings from one document to another via the Clipboard, using Preference settings. The number of layers you can set for each document depends on the amount of memory your system has.

Custom views (up to 25 views per document) can also be created and saved to allow more control over the views you see while working. For example, you can save a view at a high magnification for finely-detailed work, another view at preview 100% size, and a third view at a low magnification for placing objects. Different views can be saved to show different layers, etc. and you can easily switch between views by selecting the named view from the View menu.

You can also display several views of the same document at once by viewing more than one window. To display more than one window and view, select New Window from the Window menu. However, only one window is the active window — the others appear to be grayer.

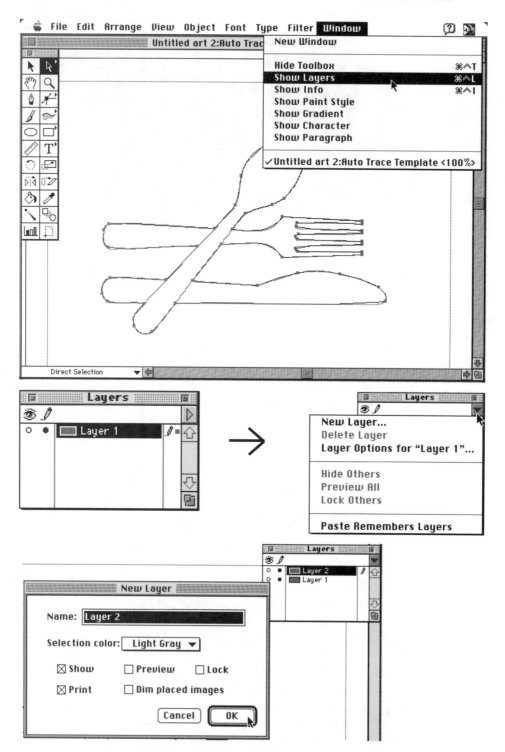

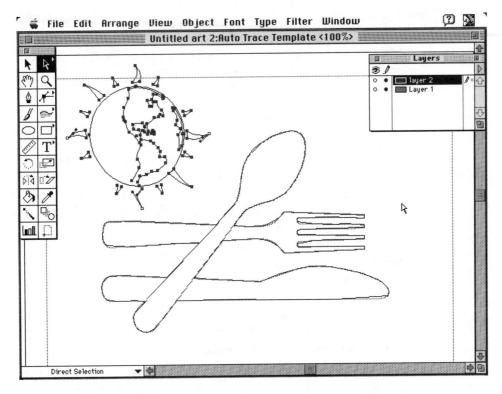

Figure 1-11.
Open the Layers palette (select Show Layers from the Window menu) to access Layer management features.

Using Colors

The program also provides the ability to assign areas of an image to have a percentage of black (gray) along with a percentage of each of the primary process colors (cyan, yellow, magenta), or a specific PANTONE MATCHING SYSTEM (PMS), FOCOLTONE COLOUR SYSTEM, TRUMATCH color swatching system, or TOYO premixed ink color or custom color. You can then produce with an imagesetter a four-color separation (one piece of film for each process color), with or without custom separations (individual film layers for each custom and premixed ink color) for the image, using the Adobe Separator program. Adobe Illustrator can display colors on a wide variety of color monitors using all of the Macintosh color capabilities.

Select Paint Style from the Objects menu, or select Show Paint Style from the Window menu to display the Paint Style palette. You can use the eyedropper tool to copy a color and its attributes (fill color/pattern and/or stroke color/pattern) to the Paint Style palette, and then use the paint bucket tool to assign exactly the same paint attributes to an object in the illustration. The Paint Style palette is updated to use the paint attributes selected with the eyedropper tool. You can also set stroke weights and line attributes from the Paint Style palette. Color selection options include None, White, Black, Process, Custom, Pattern, or Gradient.

Gradient fills are easy to create and adjust. You first assign gradient fills to objects using the Paint Style palette or the paint bucket tool. Then you use the gradient fill tool to drag across the objects. Radial fills of two colors will start light and end darker, but you can adjust the colors. Use the Gradient palette to change the gradient fill attributes (select Gradients from the Object menu, or Show Gradient from the Window menu). Select a gradient fill from the Gradient palette to use or modify, or create a named custom gradient. You can even duplicate named gradients before changing or deleting them.

To assign a gradient fill to type, you must first convert the type to outline type (Select Create Outlines from the Type menu).

If you create gradient fills of custom colors, note that gradient fills of a single custom color and white are the easiest to reproduce on press, as they can be separated onto a single piece of film without moiré patterns.

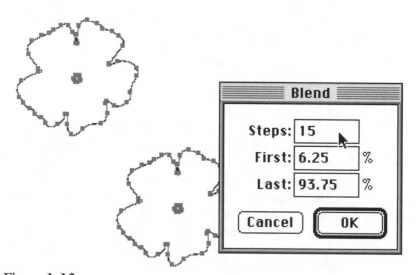

Figure 1-12.
To use the blend tool, first select a point on each path that describes the shapes at each end. The blend tool displays a dialog box requesting the number of steps, or discrete shapes, that the program should create between the starting and ending shapes.

Figure 1-13.
The blend tool automatically creates a series of objects that are a blend between the starting and ending objects. These objects are grouped so that you can move them or transform them together. Each step of the blend is a regular path you can adjust and paint.

If your gradient fill uses two or more custom colors, be sure that they use different screen angles to avoid moiré patterns on press. Alternatively, you can convert the custom colors to process colors before printing color separations to film.

Blending Shapes and Colors

 Adobe Illustrator includes a unique blend tool that helps you blend one shape (and its color) into another. First you select the two objects or paths that define the starting and ending shapes (Figure 1-12), and after selecting the blend tool, you click one point of the starting object or path and a corresponding point of the ending object or path. The program displays a dialog box asking for the number of steps, or discrete shapes, that the program should create between the starting and ending shapes. The program then creates all these shapes automatically (Figure 1-13).

You can also use the blend tool to blend one color into another to achieve an airbrush effect (see "Swan" and "Violin" in the color plates). By specifying an appropriate number of steps, you can achieve a smooth blend of two colors. You can also rotate, shear, scale, or reflect any piece of text or graphic object.

Plug in Filters

Adobe Illustrator also supports Plug in filters (some are included in the package; others are available from third parties) which can be used to create special effects, such as shadows and transparency. Filters provided with Illustrator allow you to simplify paths, create drop shadows, distort perspective along a plane, create stars, arrows, spirals, polygons and mosaics, put cropmarks within the image area, plus use color effects for text and other objects. Text filters can be used to modify, select, search, and create objects. For example, you can search for objects by stroke or fill and adjust colors globally or interactively.

Using the Type Tools

Illustrator provides a variety of text effects with three type tools: the standard type tool that places a rectangular text element in a typeface at a particular point (when you drag a marquee before typing, or alternatively you can convert a rectangle into a text rectangle by clicking it with the standard type tool), or, if you click to specify an insertion point that is not over a path or over existing type, you can create point type (type that is not bounded by or on a path), the area-type tool that sets type to fit inside an area defined by a path (such as an irregular shape), and the path-type tool that places type using a path as a baseline.

You can also import text as point type or into a rectangular or irregular-shaped area that can be linked to other irregular-shaped or rectangular areas (for example, text in columns).

Text objects created with the standard type tool or the area-type tool can be linked so that type flows from one object to another, or across several objects. Linked text is treated as one text object that flows on more than one path, and stacking order determines the flow. By changing the stacking order (either before or after flowing type), you can change the flow of type, but type always flows from the backmost object to the frontmost object.

The standard type tool can be selected from the tool palette. As you pass the text pointer across an illustration, the pointer changes from its standard shape to an area-type pointer when it falls within a closed path, and to a path-type pointer when it falls on an open path (Figure 1-14). You can use the path-type tool to set type along a path, using the path as a baseline. You can easily reposition type along a path, such as moving the type to the other side of the path, or to one end or the other, but only one text object can be placed on each path. The path and area type tools can be selected by dragging to the right of the standard type tool.

Even after text is set along a path, it can be selected and changed (Figure 1-15). You can specify a baseline shift that defines how far above or below the baseline type will be placed. Text can be styled in many different ways using different PostScript fonts and sizes.

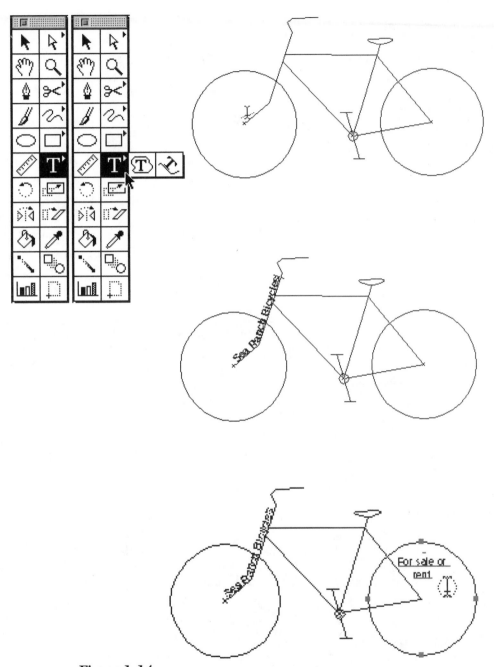

Figure 1-14.
Adding text with the type tool, which has changed to the path-type tool because the pointer is on top of an open path. The path can be used as a baseline for the type. The different type tools can also be selected by dragging to the right of the standard type tool.

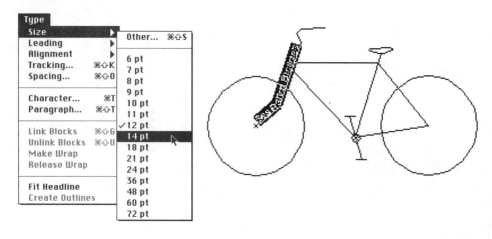

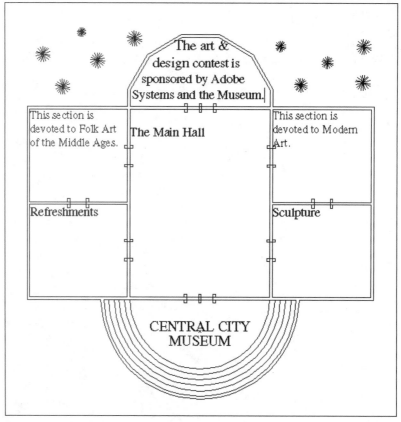

Figure 1-15.
Selecting text that is set along a path, and changing its size using the Type menu. Text can also be set inside a closed path as well as in rectangular columns.

You can adjust leading (vertical spacing between lines of text), kerning (spacing between two characters that is built in by the font designer), and tracking (adjusting the spacing between characters in a selection). Characters can be shifted vertically and scaled horizontally, indents can be set, and paragraphs aligned to the left, right, centered, or justified. You can control letterspacing and word spacing, leading before each paragraph, hanging punctuation, and hyphenation.

Type preferences can be set in the General Preferences dialog box (choose Preferences and General from the File menu). Color or shades of gray can be applied to filled characters and you can specify the color and thickness of the stroke. Individual characters within a text object can be colored different colors by selecting them with the regular type tool pointer, and selecting Paint Style from the Object menu. To apply a gradient fill of color to type, you must first convert the type to Outline format (select the Create Outlines command from the Type menu).

You can use the Rotate tool to rotate text by a percentage you specify, or you can rotate it freehand with the mouse. Text and graphics can be selected and scaled together because they are treated in the same manner. At any point you can edit the text as usual, by clicking the text element with the text tool (double-click to select a word, drag to select a block, etc.).

Once converted to outline format, the outlines of individual characters can be edited like regular curves and lines. The Create Outlines command in the Type menu converts a text object (using any Type 1 or TrueType fonts installed in your system) into a set of paths which you can then edit and manipulate with the selection tools. Letters are comprised of compound paths in which you can see through transparent areas of the path.

Outlines of characters can be modified to create logos, display type, or a variety of special effects, such as gradient color fills. Illustrator 5 includes 40 Adobe Type 1 fonts that you can modify. Note that the entire text object is converted, so you must create a text object containing only one letter if you want only one letter to be converted.

The brush tool can be used with a pressure-sensitive drawing pad to achieve variable width lines (dependent on pen pressure, just as with an ink pen), or you can use a mouse to draw variable width lines, or draw calligraphic style. For variable width lines, you can also control line caps and joins from the Brush dialog box (double-click the brush tool to display the Brush dialog box). The current color and paint style attributes set in the Paint Style palette are applied to objects created with the brush tool, but you can use the Paint Style palette to change colors and attributes.

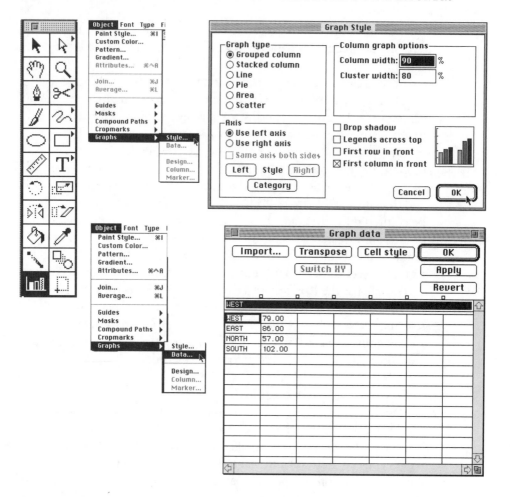

Charting and Graphing

Illustrator can automatically create a chart or graph based on numerical data. The graph tool can create column charts (grouped or stacked), line graphs, pie charts, scatter graphs, and area graphs. The default tool is the grouped column chart (also known as a bar chart). To select any other type of chart or graph, select the Graph dialog box from the Object menu. The data for the charts or graphs can be entered directly, or imported from a spreadsheet, into a table for calculations (Figure 1-16).

Graphs are created as grouped objects. As long as they remain grouped, you can change the graph's type, size, or style, add a drop shadow, display legends across the top instead of to the right of the graph, and change the order in which columns overlap (for grouped column or

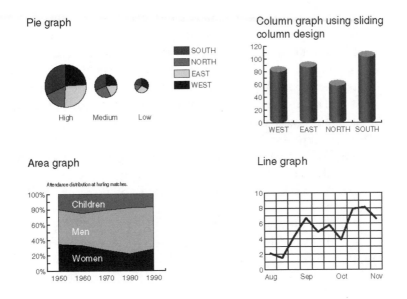

Figure 1-16.
The automatic graphing feature generates several different types of charts and graphs from data imported from a spreadsheet or typed into the data table. The charts and graphs can be changed automatically, or ungrouped into objects that can be manipulated like other objects.

area graphs) by selecting the Graph and Style commands from the Object menu. Without ungrouping the objects you can use the direct-selection tool to, for example, move a pie wedge out and away from the rest of a pie graph, to emphasis it.

Using Illustrations with Other Programs

Adobe Illustrator can create a complete PostScript page, or just the PostScript code necessary to rebuild the image when included with other page makeup, graphics, and word processing programs.

The Illustrator file format is called Encapsulated PostScript (EPS). The EPS file can include a display-only bitmap image of the illustration for viewing on a Macintosh or PC-compatible display. Illustrator offers several choices, such as including a black-and-white display image or a color display image. The original PostScript artwork contains any assigned colors, no matter which display image format you choose. The display image is just for convenience in using Illustrator files with other applications that do not display PostScript graphics. If you choose not to include a display image, be sure to choose the None option that includes the EPSF Header if you plan to print the EPS file with another program. The None option that Omits the EPSF Header saves a file that can only be opened by Adobe Illustrator and "Adobe Illustrator compatible applications."

Thus, Adobe Illustrator can save in both Macintosh and PC versions of the EPS format so that an image can be displayed on either type of system. EPS files can be used in a variety of page makeup and presentation programs. For example, you can place EPSF images in Adobe Illustrator documents.

If your Illustrator document includes a placed EPSF image, click the Include Placed Images option in the Save As dialog box (this saves the placed EPSF image file with your Adobe Illustrator artwork document), but you should also place a copy of the original source document (containing the EPSF file you placed) in the same folder as your Illustrator document that contains the placed EPSF image, so that Illustrator will always be able to find the placed image.

Those who have Adobe Acrobat installed in their system can save Adobe Illustrator files in Portable Document Format (PDF), which allows the Illustrator document file to be opened and viewed (but no changes can be made) on computer systems that do not have Adobe Illustrator installed.

Those who can program in PostScript will also find Adobe Illustrator useful. You can select any point and insert a comment, and the program inserts the comment in the PostScript file, so you can later find that area and edit the PostScript code. We recommend that you consult the *PostScript Language Tutorial and Cookbook* and other books from Adobe Systems to learn about programming in PostScript.

System Requirements

Adobe Illustrator 5 runs on any 68020 or greater Macintosh computer running Apple System 6.0.7 or greater, with at least 3.5 megabytes of RAM and equipped with a hard disk. However, we recommend 4 meg. or more of RAM and System 7.0 or greater for best performance. Illustrator can run with all of the high-resolution color monitors available for the Macintosh II models and the LC, including monitors from Apple, Radius, SuperMac Technologies and other vendors.

You don't need a color monitor, however, to assign colors to images that print in color on PostScript color printers and can be separated on PostScript imagesetters. A color monitor is useful in previewing color graphics, but it is not necessary — colors appear as different shades of gray on black and white monitors.

Adobe Illustrator displays graphics on black and white monitors faster than on color monitors. Some artists work with their monitor(s) set to black and white when working with complex images, and turn color on only to preview the artwork before printing. However, with Illustrator 5, if you use the layer management capabilities to hide all layers except the one(s) you are working on, you can maximize the speed at which you can preview artwork on color displays.

The Macintosh Desktop

The Macintosh computer displays an electronic desktop with icons for disks, files, and folders that hold files. The files may be application programs (like Adobe Illustrator) or data files (such as drawings or text).

You might see these icons on the Macintosh screen:

Adobe Illustrator™ 5.0

The Adobe Illustrator program icon. To start up the program, you point to this icon and double-click the mouse button.

The folder icon represents a group of files that are either programs (also called "applications") or "documents" (also called "data files," "image documents," "artwork files," or "graphics files") associated with those programs. A folder usually also contains other folders to further subdivide the files. Folders are useful for organizing the icons for files on the Macintosh desktop.

Folders are the equivalent of *subdirectories* on other computer systems. When you create a new folder, it is automatically named "Empty Folder." Folders usually contain a group of related items, so you should rename your folder to describe the folder's contents. (See your Macintosh manuals for a description of how to create and rename folders, and move files into and out of them.)

bike.art

Bicycle Art

These icons represent Adobe Illustrator artwork documents (or "artwork files"), which should be named to describe their contents. The Tutorial folder supplied with the Adobe Illustrator files includes Adobe Illustrator 3 format artwork documents named "Lesson1.start," and "Balancing Act.start."

An Adobe Illustrator document is a text file which contains the PostScript description of the artwork. An Illustrator document can be opened by either the Adobe Illustrator program, or it can be opened by a word processing program if you want to edit the PostScript code.

If you point to an Illustrator document icon and double-click the mouse, the Adobe Illustrator program is automatically started and it opens the Adobe Illustrator artwork document and any template document associated with that artwork document.

Bicycle

This icon represents a Macintosh Encapsulated PostScript document. This file format is used when you want to use Illustrator-created artwork with another Macintosh program such as a page layout program. For more information about creating a Macintosh Encapsulated Post-Script file (or PC Encapsulated PostScript file for use with PC applications) see the File menu's Save As command description in Chapter 5. See Chapter 6 for a detailed discussion of Adobe Illustrator and Encapsulated PostScript.

This icon represents a MacPaint file containing a graphic image. MacPaint and PICT files are the only type of documents that can be used as templates for tracing over with Adobe Illustrator. MacPaint files have similar icons to files of other painting programs that also save images in the MacPaint format, such as FullPaint and SuperPaint. If you plan to use a paint program other than MacPaint with Adobe Illustrator, it must be able to save its files as either MacPaint files or PICT files; virtually all painting programs allow you to do this. MacPaint files have a fixed resolution of 72 dpi (dots per inch), which matches the Macintosh display resolution.

This icon represents a MacDraw graphics file saved in the PICT format. Files in the PICT format and MacPaint files are the only files that can be used as templates for tracing over with Adobe Illustrator. If you plan to use another drawing program, you must save its files as either MacPaint files or PICT files; virtually all of the drawing programs allow you to do this. MacDraw PICT documents have a resolution of 72 dpi when used as templates with Adobe Illustrator.

A Guided Tour of Adobe Illustrator

You start the Adobe Illustrator program by double-clicking its icon. The familiar Apple icon and other Menu titles appear at the top of your screen, but no tools or windows (other than the opening screen) are displayed, because no documents have been opened.

Most Adobe Illustrator commands are not available unless a document is open. Unavailable commands appear as gray text in the menus; available commands appear as black text. The only commands you can use from the Adobe Illustrator desktop are New, Open, Preferences, and Quit from the File menu, and Show Clipboard from the Edit menu. No commands can be selected from the other menus.

Choose Open from the File menu (the three dots after Open indicate that a dialog box will appear to request further information). Use the Open option from the File menu to either resume work on an existing Illustrator document or to create a new Illustrator document by tracing over an existing MacPaint file or PICT file that you want to use as a template. Use the New option to create a new Illustrator document with or without a template image to trace.

After you choose Open from the File menu, a dialog box appears (see Figure 1-17). Drag the scroll box if necessary to select an Adobe Illustrator document, MacPaint document, or PICT document. If you select an Illustrator document that already has a template associated with it, the template is automatically opened. If you select a template document (MacPaint or PICT file) a new, untitled Illustrator document is opened on top of the template, and the template becomes associated with that document.

Select the document you want to open, then point to the Open button in the dialog box and click the mouse button. In Figure 1-17, the Illustrator document named "Airplane Art" is opened. The template document named "Airplane Template" is a MacPaint file created by using a scanner to digitize sketches or photographs.

When the Illustrator document and its associated template are first opened you see both the artwork and the template. Since Adobe Illustrator is often used for tracing over scanned images, the background

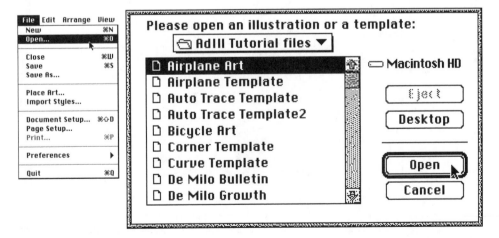

Figure 1-17.
After selecting the Open option from the File menu, a dialog box appears with an Open option for selecting a document.

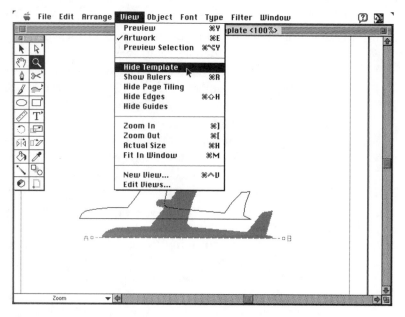

Figure 1-18.
The program displays the artwork in black and its background template in gray so that it is easier to trace.

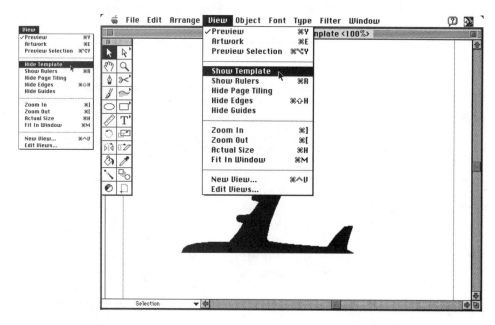

Figure 1-19.
Adobe Illustrator offers a variety of viewing options.

template is displayed in gray rather than black (see Figure 1-18). The default Illustrator document size (Artboard) is letter size (8 1/2 inches by 11 inches), but can be changed to a maximum size of 120 inches by 120 inches. Due to the small size of the Macintosh Classic and SE screens, it is often impossible to fit the entire image in the active window when the document is viewed at its actual size. Larger video screens — available for the various Macintosh models — let you see more of the Illustrator document at once and save scrolling time.

To find out what view is displayed in the active window, check the View menu. In Figure 1-18, the check mark in front of the Artwork option and the Hide Template option mean that the Illustrator document (the artwork) and the MacPaint document (the template) underneath it are displayed in the active window. (If your screen shows more than one window, only one window is the active window; click the mouse in any window to make it the active window.)

Other views of the active window can also be selected from the View menu. To hide the template, select the Hide Template option from the View menu (see Figure 1-19). Likewise, to display the Illustrator artwork with the template, select Show Template from the View menu (see Figure 1-20).

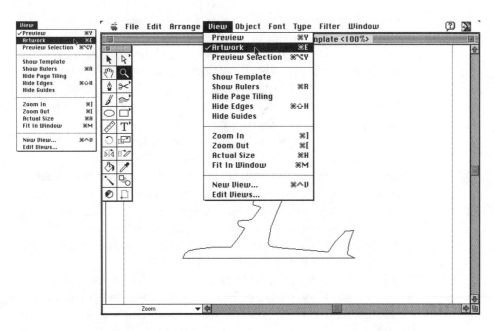

Figure 1-20.
You can hide or show the template.

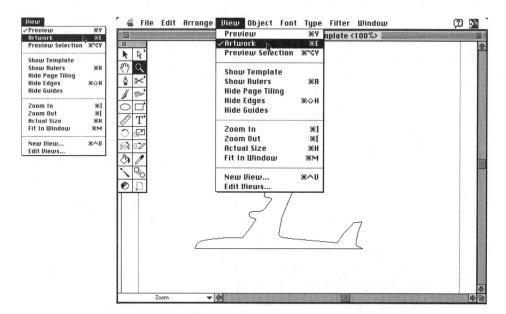

Figure 1-21.
Displaying the artwork by itself, without the background template.

Adobe Illustrator also provides a zoom tool to "zoom into" the artwork and magnify your view to see the smallest details. To zoom into (magnify) an area of the artwork, click on the zoom tool (the magnifying glass) in the toolbox palette, position the zoom tool over the area you want to inspect more closely, and click the mouse button (see Figure 1-21).

Each click of the mouse magnifies your view of the artwork and template. Zooming doesn't change the actual size of your artwork, just your view of it. In Figure 1-22 the mouse button was clicked twice, doubling magnification from 100 percent to 200 percent.

The + disappears from the magnifying glass when you have reached the maximum enlargement (1600 percent). You can hold down the Option key and click the mouse button to zoom out (a minus sign in the magnifying glass indicates you are zooming out to reduce the view).

The program offers reduction levels up to 6.25 percent and magnification levels up to 1600 percent.

The Artwork view displays the points, lines, and curves created with the Adobe Illustrator program. These points, lines, and curves do not exactly match the printed artwork because the Artwork view does not display line weight, gray-scale values, color values, and other characteristics of the printed artwork.

To see a better approximation of the printed artwork, select the

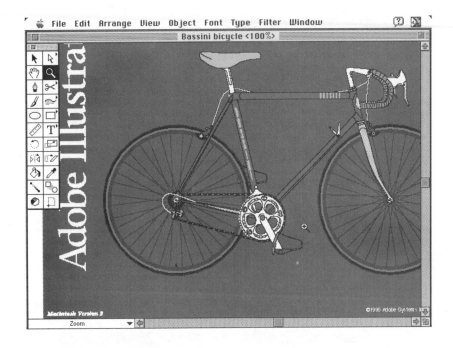

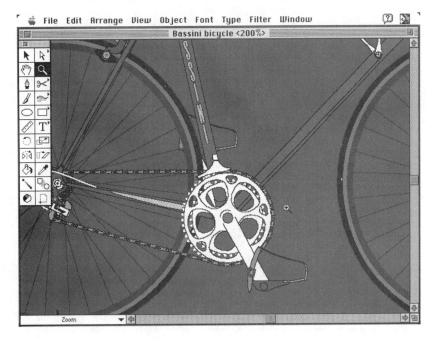

Figure 1-22.
Using the zoom tool (magnifying glass) to enlarge your view to see more detail. The zoom tool magnifies the image to be twice as large as before without changing the size of the graphics.

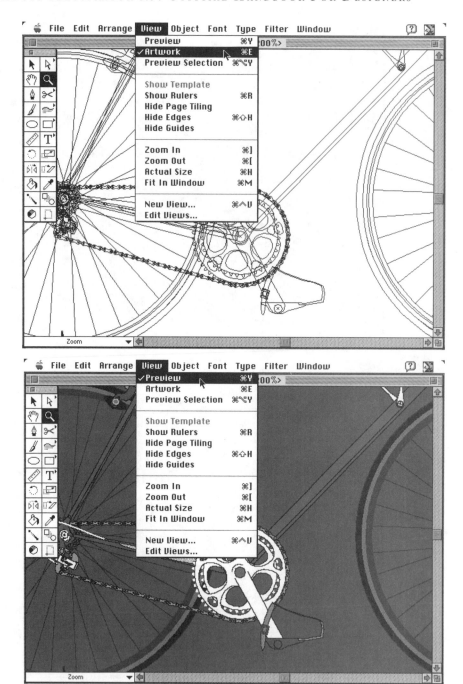

Figure 1-23.
The Preview display comes closer to showing how the printed output will appear, using actual line weights and patterns (and colors if you are using a color monitor).

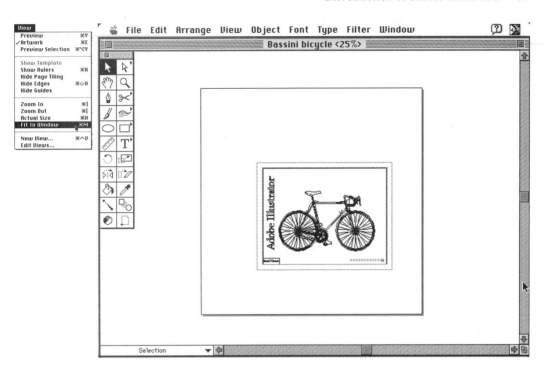

Figure 1-24.
The Fit In Window viewing option displays the entire artwork.

Preview option from the View menu. You can even quickly preview a selection (select the Preview Selection option) rather than preview the entire illustration. However, even the Preview display is not exact.

For an accurate view of the printed artwork, you must actually print it on a PostScript printer or imagesetter (laser typesetter).

In Figure 1-23 the Preview option displays line weights different from the Artwork view; the heavy line weights were specified when the artwork was drawn.

Not only can you view the Illustrator document and template in a variety of ways, you can also view them in a variety of sizes. If you want to reduce the entire 120-by-120-inch Adobe Illustrator document in order to fit it in the active window, you can either select Fit In Window from the View menu (Figure 1-24), or you can select the hand tool in the toolbox palette, and double-click the hand tool.

To end this quick tour of Adobe Illustrator, select Quit from the File menu to exit from the program. If any changes have been made since the last time the document was saved to disk, the program asks if you want to save the changes you made, and you can either save them or leave the artwork in its original state.

2

Maps, Charts, and Clip Art

The best way to learn Adobe Illustrator is to practice. Dean Dapkus, an artist from San Jose State University, knew nothing about computers when he started: "The rate with which you increase your efficiency is incredible. I began by doing simple symbols such as the men and women on bathroom doors and other international sign symbols. For my first drawing, I spent about three days doing a simple coffee cup.

"By the time I did the Gallery artwork, I was able to complete those drawings in 10 to 20 hours. By now, I could cut the time it took to do those images by half again. You build skills as you go along, and you can apply the techniques you learn to each new drawing."

Learning how to use Adobe Illustrator is different from learning most computer programs because it has so many features. Illustrator can be difficult to learn at first, but it is not difficult to master over time with practice. You learn how to become more productive with the program, and you find out that once you know how to do something, you don't have to keep reinventing the solution. Pat Coleman, a freelance graphic designer at Adobe Systems, is well adapted to using what is readily available: "Once you create an image, it can become a piece of clip art and you can borrow from it to create new images."

Although the freehand and brush tools in Adobe Illustrator are similar to the drawing tools found in other graphics programs, the curve manipulation tools are not the same. The pen tool does not draw lines — you use it to establish points for the program to draw with precision the line or curve segment to connect the points. The process of drawing with the pen tool is more like a connect-the-dots puzzle. Click to establish points, or click and drag to establish curve segments, and also depress the Shift key if you want to constrain the line or curve angles to 45 degree increments (relative to the Constrain angle [0 is default] set in the General Preferences dialog box in the File menu).

You can switch from the pen tool to the selection tool (press the Command key to switch between the pen tool and the selection tool) or direct-selection tool in order to move the points, lines, and direction pointers to change the shape of a curve, then switch back to the pen (depress the Command key while clicking the mouse outside the selected object) and continue establishing more points.

When you click to establish points with the pen tool, your path is open (and new points will be connected to points already established), until you either click the first point established (called an anchor point) to close the path, or end the current open path in one of these ways: reselect the pen tool or select any other tool in the toolbox; click while depressing the Command key outside the selected path or object; or choose Select none from the Edit menu (Command-Shift-A). The anchor points at the ends of an open path are called endpoints. A line is an example of an open path, and a triangle or circle is an example of a closed path. There are no endpoints in a closed path, only anchor points. Anchor points (including endpoints) display as solid squares when selected, and as hollow squares otherwise. Direction points appear as circles.

The pen tool pointer (click the pen tool and move it onto the artboard to see the pointer) includes an x, an o, or nothing to tell you what it will do with the next point you click. Before starting a new path, it includes an x. It displays the plain pen icon when it is set to continue a path, and it includes an o when it is in position to close an open path. (Turn on or off the Snap to point option in General Preferences [File menu] to improve control over path closing.)

The freehand tool creates a straight line or curve based on the actual movement of the mouse — you actually draw with the mouse as if it were a pencil or paintbrush, even though the shape of the mouse makes it very hard to draw with precision (as John Warnock, one of the inventors of Adobe Illustrator, described the process, "It's like drawing with a brick.").

Illustrator's freehand tool can be adjusted to be less sensitive to variations in your hand movement, so that sketching with a mouse can be a more natural activity than it usually is. Set a higher number of pixels for the Freehand tolerance in the General Preferences dialog box (select Preferences General from the File menu), to adjust the freehand tool to be less sensitive, and you'll get smoother lines with less points.

If you use as few points as are necessary to describe an object at the level of detail that is appropriate for your use, you can conserve the amount of disk space required for the file, and avoid printing problems. (The complex drawing of a U.S. map illustrated later in this chapter demonstrates the importance of using the tools appropriately. For complex drawings, you will need to conserve file space.)

If you want to draw more naturally, you should investigate using a pressure sensitive drawing pad and pen — the pen can be wireless or not. Using a pressure-sensitive drawing pad and pen, you can select a variable width brush stroke for the brush tool, and the stroke thickness will vary with the amount of pressure — thick strokes for heavy pressure, and thinner strokes for lighter pressure. Set the Freehand tolerance in the General Preferences dialog box to be a lower number to increase sensitivity of the freehand tool.

The auto trace tool creates a tracing of a template, with a level of accuracy you can set in the General Preferences dialog box (select Preferences General from the File menu).

Set the Auto Trace gap distance to the number of pixels that you want. Set the gap to be higher for not very detailed tracings, or when accuracy isn't important in a highly detailed tracing. A low gap number won't guarantee more accuracy, but will result in a larger file size, because more points will be created. If you set the Auto Trace gap distance to be higher, your template will be traced faster, and your file size will be smaller. You can then use the pen and freehand tools to adjust the tracing and capture finer details with precision.

You can switch freely among the selection tool, the pen tool, the freehand tool, the auto trace tool, the brush tool, and other tools while drawing an object, making Adobe Illustrator more powerful than most drawing programs.

Building Reusable Graphics

Besides drawing with the freehand tool and using the auto trace tool, you can build an illustration by establishing the points along a path with the pen tool, linking those points with straight lines (by clicking without dragging) or curves (by dragging).

You can also draw rectangles and ovals (including perfect squares and circles when you hold down the Shift key) in much the same manner as other graphics programs — dragging the rectangle or oval tool to describe the area to be enclosed. Other polygons and arbitrarily enclosed shapes are really just paths of points.

The fewer points you use, the less choppy the shape appears because the program computes the smoothest curve. By adding more points you gain more control over the shape. Add too many points, however, and you might have printing problems (such as limitcheck error messages).

A map is an excellent example of the type of line art that can be manipulated easily with Adobe Illustrator. You can quickly scale a complete map to any size and either keep the line weights the same (each line remains exactly the same width, but changes length to accommodate the resizing), or let the line widths change with the same ratio as everything else.

A newspaper, for example, can take a large weather map and reduce it for use as a background for a four-day forecast, reducing the line weights as well, so that the smaller versions of the map do not have heavy lines. The map could also be made very large (the size of a poster), but with all of the lines left at the same width as the actual size.

Maps or portions of maps can be reused for other purposes, and patterns (for example, rain and snow weatherfront patterns) can be overlayed on top of a copy of the map to produce a different weather chart for each day. The benefit over manual methods is that once a state map is drawn, it never has to be drawn again — it can be scaled to any size and reused by itself or as part of the entire weather map.

Drawing Objects With Shared Borders

Pat Coleman drew the United States map found in Gallery Disk #1 of Adobe Illustrator version 1.1. Figure 2-1 shows the map template ready for use as a drawing aid, and Figure 2-2 shows how she drew more precise curves in areas where the template did not show enough detail (the drawing is magnified by the zoom tool).

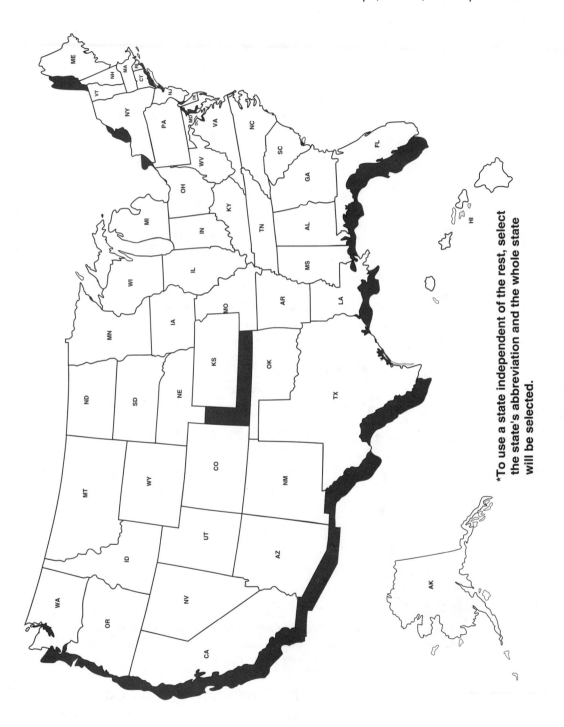

*To use a state independent of the rest, select the state's abbreviation and the whole state will be selected.

Figure 2-1.
A MacPaint file containing a scanned image is brought into Adobe Illustrator as a template for drawing the U.S. map.

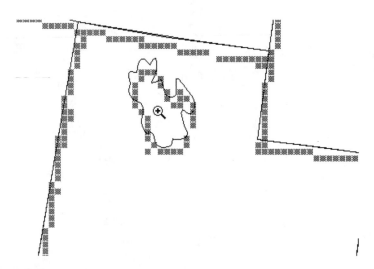

Figure 2-2.
The Great Salt Lake is a pattern of dots in the MacPaint template that can be dramatically improved by drawing precise curves with the pen tool after using the zoom tool to magnify the area of the image.

To start drawing the map, Pat concentrated on each state and drew its outline separately. California, for example, combines curved segments with straight segments (Figure 2-3). Each state was drawn with segments that connect, so that the state is one closed path (Figure 2-4). It takes a

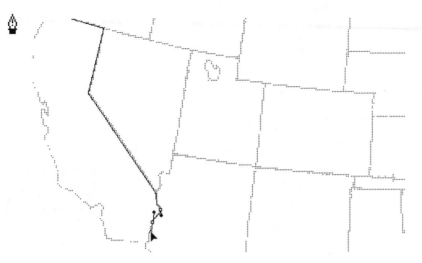

Figure 2-3.
You can use the pen tool to draw both straight line and curve segments to form a complete outline.

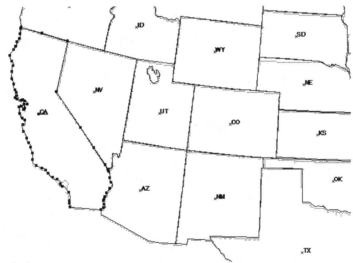

Figure 2-4.
Each state is drawn as a complete path that can be selected and moved or transformed without affecting other states.

lot of small curved segments to draw the outline of the Bay Area, so she used the zoom tool to zoom into the area and see more detail (Figure 2-5). You can use the zoom tool to magnify the page to the largest magnification level and still use all of the other tools to draw the smallest segments.

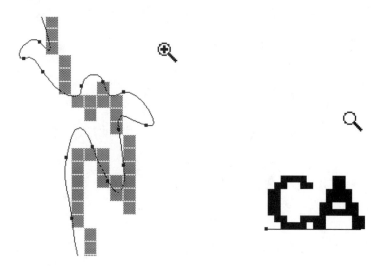

Figure 2-5.
Using the zoom tool to see more detail; the magnification can be as high as 1600 percent of the actual size.

To form a border where two states join (and thereby start the outline of the next state), Pat first selected the anchor points that defined the segments of the common border, and copied the segments to the Clipboard (Figure 2-6). Then she used the Paste In Front command, which placed the segments in the Clipboard in the same location and on top of the segments copied. She switched to the pen tool to continue drawing the rest of the state (Figure 2-7). "I used that technique for all of the common borders, so I had a head start in creating each new state, and it went fairly quickly."

Each state's border overlapped other state borders, so she made it easier to select a state by using the state's abbreviation as a handle. She typed the abbreviation inside the state area with the type tool, specifying the appropriate font, style, and size. Then she selected the outline path by holding down the Option key while pointing to a segment of the outline, and held down the Shift key to point at and include the state abbreviation in the selection. Finally she used the Group command in the Arrange menu to combine the selected items into one group. Anyone can now point at the state's abbreviation and click the mouse button to select the entire state (Figure 2-8).

Colorado is another example of using Paste In Front. First she drew all of the states that border it and added the Colorado state abbreviation in the proper place; then she selected the segments for the borders (holding down the Shift key to add segments to the selection), copied the

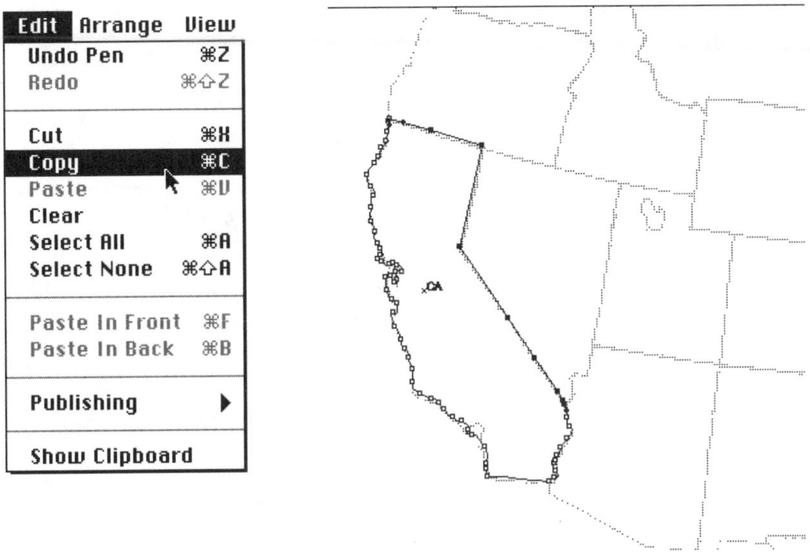

Figure 2-6.
To copy a state border, select the segments of the border (hold down the Shift key to include another segment in the selection), and Copy to the Clipboard.

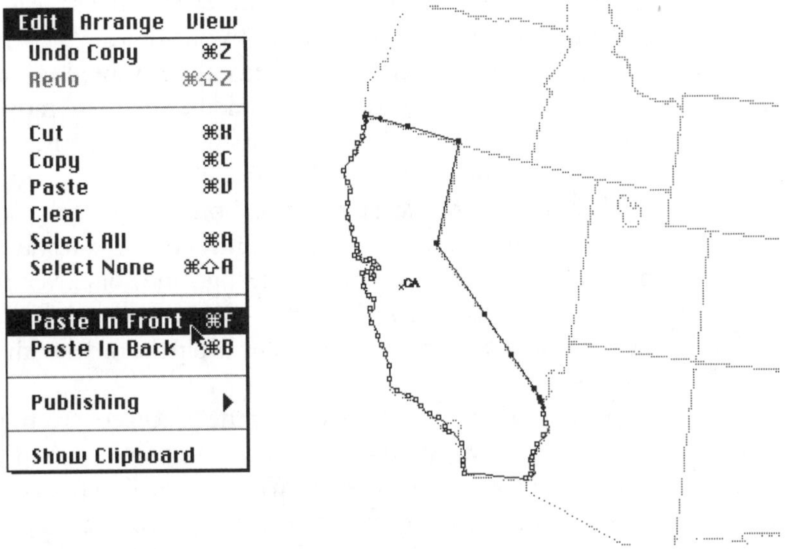

Figure 2-7.
After using the Paste In Front option to paste the copied border on top of the existing border, you can continue to draw the borders of the adjoining state.

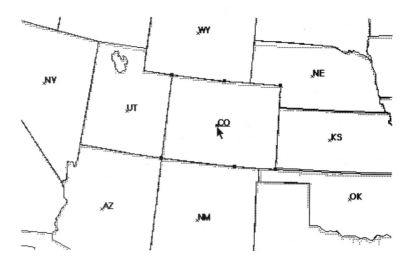

Figure 2-8.
Selecting the path for the entire state by selecting the state abbreviation, which is grouped to the path for the border outline of the state.

borders to the Clipboard, and used Paste In Front while the borders were still selected (Figure 2-9). The borders joined to form an enclosed path; she selected it by holding down the Option key while pointing to a segment, and then held down Shift and selected the state abbreviation (CO), and finally grouped them to form one unit.

Pat explains why she chose this method: "I wanted to demonstrate that each state was independent and could be lifted out, moved around, and used as an independent state. So each state is a path by itself."

It is very convenient to select the state abbreviation and get the entire state. However, if you select a common border and get the neighboring state by accident, you can paste it behind the one you want by typing Command-B. (The key with the Apple logo and/or cloverleaf design is also known as the Command key.) You can then select the state you want because it would be on top. You can always flip the order of the segments with this shortcut.

Important Tip: At any time during the process of creating the map, you can save your work, so that if a power outage occurred you would not have to redo the work. Save the map continually while you work, but when it is finished and you want to edit a copy while leaving the original intact, use the Save As command to create a new illustration based on the original. The illustration's name changes to the new name (leaving the original name and illustration untouched), and subsequent Save commands save the work under the new name.

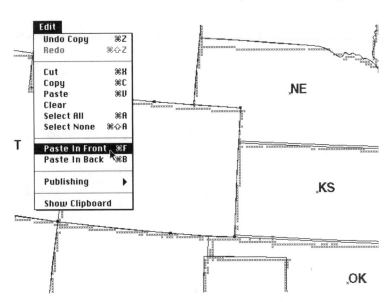

Figure 2-9.
Select the border of the other states and copy them to the Clipboard, then Paste In Front the contents of the Clipboard to make Colorado's border.

Adding Paint and Depth

To give the map a three-dimensional look, Pat Coleman added a shadow behind it, painted in gray. The outline of the entire country consisted of so many anchor points that the program could only move and duplicate the outline slowly. Thus, Pat decided to cut the shadow outline in half: one for the East Coast and one for the West.

The outline is in two halves, so that someone could use only half of the country for a map, or apply shading to only half of the country. It is also easy to dissect the partial outline and create regions, such as New England or the Midwest, if you want to use shading to differentiate them.

On the map there are many segments meticulously defining coastline features, so Pat decided to draw another, less detailed outline using just the map's template. First she closed the artwork file and saved it, then she opened the template by itself, creating a new artwork file, and drew one outline around the West Coast, and one around the East Coast (Figure 2-10). To join the endpoints of the East Coast shadow (to keep it separate from the West Coast shadow), she clicked with the pen tool on a point on top of the first endpoint, then clicked on top of the other endpoint —

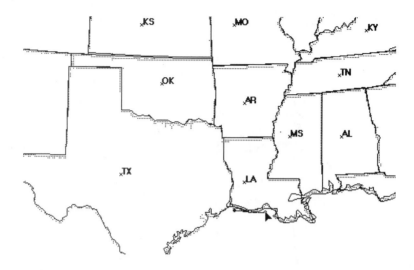

Figure 2-10.
Using the same template, the artist draws a separate outline of the entire country to be used as a shadow behind the map (this shadow outline has less detail than the state borders that form the regular outline).

Illustrator drew a straight line. Another way to accomplish this is to select the endpoints and use the Join command in the Object menu.

She created the same type of line for the West Coast shadow by copying it to the Clipboard, then using the Paste In Front command to place the copy on top of the original line.

After finishing the outlines, she selected the first one by holding down the Option key while selecting a segment (which selects an entire path); then while holding down the Shift and Option keys, she selected the other path. The Group command combined the two paths, defining the shape of the country into one unit (Figure 2-11). She then used the Copy command to copy the entire group into the Clipboard, and the Save command to save the new art file containing the U.S. profile.

Using the Open command (from the File menu), she opened the original U.S. art file without its template, and used the Paste In Back command to paste the group of paths from the Clipboard behind the U.S. map (Figure 2-12). The group remains selected, so she took the opportunity to specify the shadow using the Paint Style command in the Object menu — an 85% shade of black (dark gray) for the pattern, and no stroke (no outlining of the paths), as shown in Figure 2-13.

Returning to the art window, she started dragging the selected paths defining the shadow and then held down the Shift key while

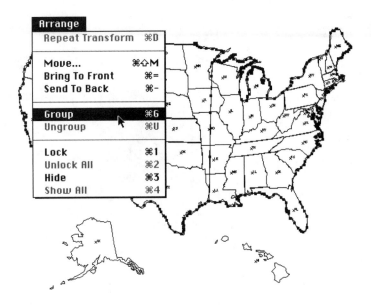

Figure 2-11.
The shadow outline consists of two paths; to combine them in a group, select one path with Option-click, and hold down the Shift key as well as the Option key to select the other path, and then choose the Group option from the Arrange menu.

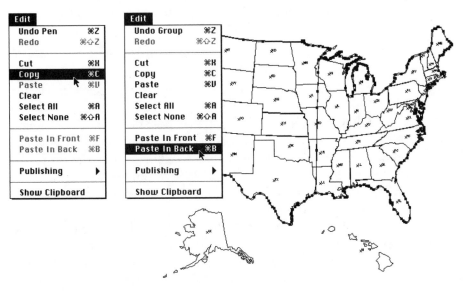

Figure 2-12.
Using the Paste In Back option to place the shadow outline (stored in the Clipboard) behind the map.

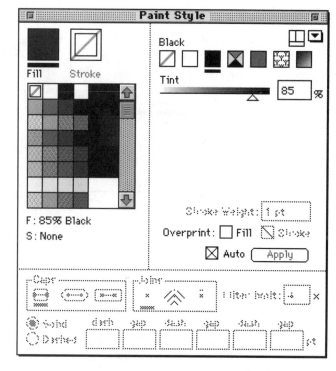

Figure 2-13.
Painting the selected closed path or group (in this case, the shadow outline) with 85 percent black for the fill, which is printed as a shade of gray. The Paint option is found in the Object menu.

dragging. When she released the mouse and then released the Shift key, the shadow's outline had moved in a 45-degree angle below and to the right of the U.S. map (Figure 2-14).

The final step was to select a state, then hold down the Shift key and add all of the states to the selection, so that she could use the Paint Style command again and apply the setting to all of the states at once. She switched the shade from black (the default setting) to white (Figure 2-15). The white shade makes the enclosed path white so that nothing underneath shows through.

To see what the map and shadow would look like if printed (and to see an approximation of the shadow's pattern), use the Preview option in the View menu (Figure 2-16). Preview displays the closest view of what the artwork will look like when printed, but takes longer to perform on complex artwork. You can use the drawing or editing tools while using Preview — you don't have to switch back to Artwork view to draw or edit the artwork.

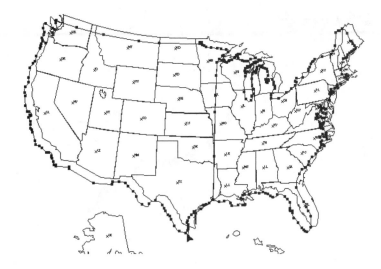

Figure 2-14.
Moving the grouped shadow outline paths by selecting and dragging.

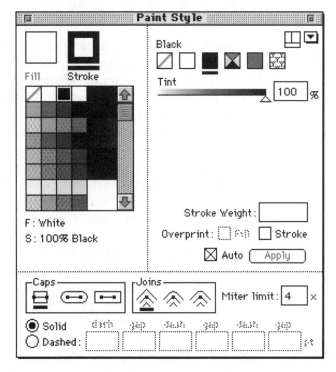

Figure 2-15.
Painting the selected states with white fill and black strokes so that the shadow outline does not show through the states.

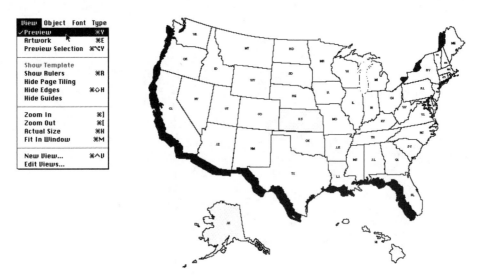

Figure 2-16.
Using the Preview option to see (as best as the screen can display) how the image will look when printed. Color monitors can display in color, and gray-scale or color monitors can display true gray scale.

To save time, you can create custom views of your work in both Artwork and Preview views, and select the desired custom view from the View menu. After setting the desired magnification level (magnify tool), and setting the view to Artwork or Preview, select the New View command from the View menu to create a named custom view. Custom views (up to 25 of them) are listed at the end of the View menu, and can also be selected by using Command-Shift-number key (1-25) shortcuts.

Another time-saving method for viewing complex artwork is to place portions of the artwork onto different layers. Then you can select specific layers for previewing and also create custom views to save time and gain more flexibility. For example, Pat Coleman could have placed the shadow objects for the U.S. map onto a new second layer, behind the first layer containing the individual states.

To create a new layer, first select the Show Layers palette from the Windows menu (Command-Shift-L) as shown in Figure 2-17, and then click the arrow icon in the upper right to display the Layers menu and select the New Layer command. In addition to naming the new layer, you can select a different selection color for objects placed onto that layer, and you have the option of showing, previewing, printing, locking, and dimming placed images, or not, for all objects on that layer. To change the order of layers, drag them higher or lower in the list in the Layers palette. You can cut, copy, and paste objects from one layer to

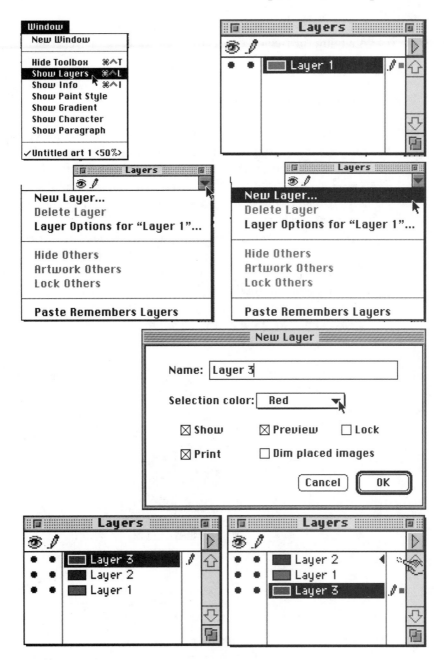

Figure 2-17.
*Selecting the Show Layers command from the Window menu to display the
Layers palette, menu of Layers commands, and layering options. Drag
layers up or down in the list to change the order of layers. The colored square
on the right, which represents selected items on layer 3, can be dragged to the
destination (layer 2), to move selected items between layers.*

another, and you can move selected objects from one layer to another by dragging their colored dots up or down in the Layers palette.

Text and Its Background

Dean Dapkus borrowed the U.S. map to create a weather chart. First he ungrouped each state and deleted the state's abbreviation; then he added small black circles and city names for the prominent cities in the country. The circles are easily drawn by selecting the Oval tool and dragging from edge to edge, while holding down the Shift key to constrain the oval into a perfect circle.

Dean explains how he placed city names on top of state lines: "I wanted the black text of the city names to go over existing state lines, but rather than having a white box behind the name to cover the state line, I wanted a white outline of the text behind the text of the city name. To do this I typed the name of the city, gave it a line thickness of three, painted the stroke white, and painted the fill white." (See Figure 2-18.)

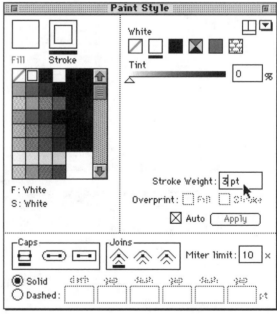

Figure 2-18.
Creating a white outline behind a word by assigning a white fill and thick stroke to the word, using Copy and Paste In Front to place a new version of the word on top of the white version, and painting the new version with a black fill and no stroke.

"I then copied the name to the Clipboard, then used Paste In Front to paste the copied name on top of the white name, and changed the copy to have no stroke and a black fill. I then had the city name in black, with a white outline around it. That's something you can't do with other graphics programs — they don't let you treat text as graphics."

Using any Type1 or TrueType font outlines you may have installed on your system to specify type, you can create a text object (consisting of a single character or more), and convert it into an editable outline (to then treat as a graphic object). First select the regular type tool and specify the font (Font menu) and any type attributes (using Type commands), then type the text, then select the type with the selection tool, and select the Create Outlines command from the Type menu to convert the type from a text object into an editable outline (Figure 2-19). If you specify

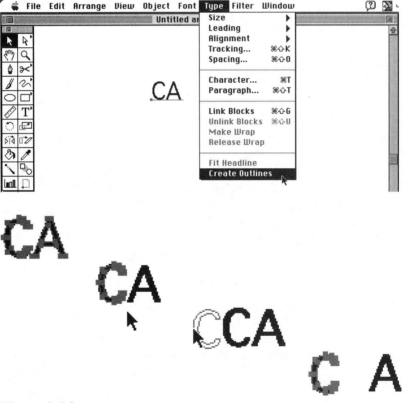

Figure 2-19.
Creating outlines from type, by first selecting the text object with the selection tool, and then selecting the Create Outlines command from the Type menu. Each character is now a separate, editable outline object, which can be moved or transformed, filled with a pattern, and so on.

paint attributes (using Paint Style from the Object menu) for the type, the outlines will retain those attributes. For example, type filled with a pattern will convert to an outline filled with the same pattern. All of the text in a text block is converted to individual outlines for each character by the Create Outlines command.

Cloning and Rotating

Dean Dapkus also designed the curved weather front that overlays the weather chart. The curved weather front comprises a lot of small triangles whose baselines are matched to a long curve. Dean started the weather front by first making a triangle, then cloning it. To make the triangle, Dean used the pen tool to define three points and link them with straight lines (Figure 2-20). The enclosed path is automatically filled with black as the default shade (visible in Preview, but not in Artwork view), and its stroke is also black.

To duplicate the triangle, Dean selected the first triangle by holding down the Option key while selecting a segment; this action selects the entire path. He started to drag the path, then held down the Option key so that he would create a copy (Figure 2-21), and held down the Shift key so that the movement would be constrained horizontally. When he had the second triangle next to the first and touching at the baseline, he let go of the mouse, then let go of the Option and Shift keys. He could then repeat the duplication many times by pressing Command-D (or selecting the Repeat Transform command from the Arrange menu) for each duplication.

Figure 2-20.
Drawing a triangle path that will be cloned and rotated to form a weather front pattern to place on top of the map.

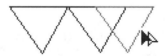

Figure 2-21.
Cloning the triangle to form a series of triangles.

Dean had drawn a string of triangles, but they were in a straight line. To make curved weather-front graphics, Dean drew a curve to simulate the weather pattern, and selected all of the triangles. Dean then used the rotation tool to rotate the triangles into position to match the curve. He first selected the rotation tool, then clicked one end point of the first triangle to be the center of rotation (sometimes called the locus point), then dragged the corner of the baseline of any triangle up to the curve (Figure 2-22).

After releasing the mouse and finishing the rotation, Dean held down the Shift key and clicked a path of the first triangle to remove it from the selection of triangles to be rotated. This left the subsequent triangles still part of the selection, which could then be rotated into place (Figure 2-23), removed from the selection, and so on. "I just rotated every time I needed a curve," said Dean, explaining his technique for treating a group of paths as one object, and rotating it.

To draw the part of the weather front around the Great Lakes, Dean drew a half circle next to a triangle, then selected both the half circle and triangle and cloned them by dragging and holding down both the Shift and Option keys, as described above when cloning the triangle, then

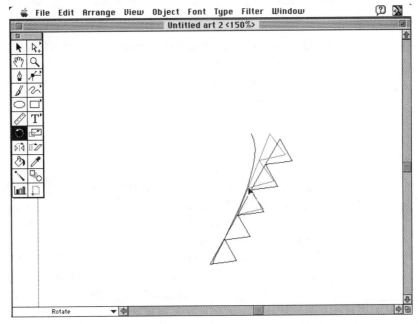

Figure 2-22.
Rotating the series of triangles, so that each triangle aligns with a curve representing the weather front.

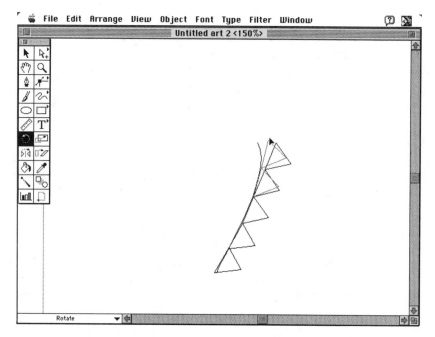

Figure 2-23.
As each triangle is aligned to the curve, you can deselect the triangle and continue rotating the rest of the series to match the next triangle.

using Command-D (Repeat Transform) to repeat the duplication. To align the string of half circles and triangles, Dean used the same rotation technique described above, removing from the selection each triangle and half-circle that was properly aligned with each rotation.

Page Setup and Printing

The drawing area (called the artboard) in Adobe Illustrator is 120-by-120 inches, which is larger than a standard 8 1/2-by-11-inch page or tabloid sized page printed by laser printers. Linotype's Linotronic imagesetters, however, can print an image the width of the paper or film path — that is, less than 12 inches in one dimension (Linotronic 100 and Linotronic 300), or 18 inches in one direction (Linotronic 500). Images larger than your printer's imageable area can be tiled for printing. Adobe Illustrator lets you control how large a page size to use, and where the image falls on the page or pages.

Illustrator divides the drawing area into pages that match the page dimensions set for the page size in the Page Setup dialog box (in the File menu) and the dimensions set in the Document Setup dialog box (File

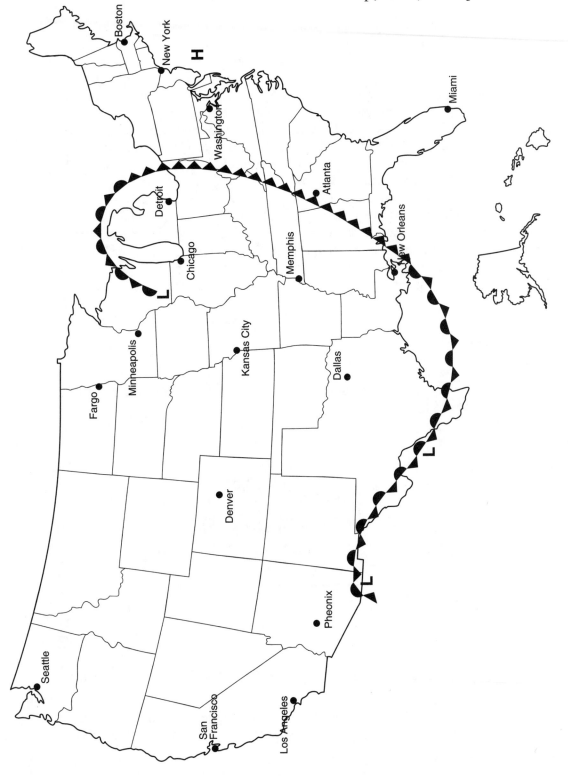

menu). The program assumes you want a vertical page, also called portrait mode, where the longest edge of the page is vertical. Figure 2-24 shows the page boundary for a standard tabloid laser printer page. If you changed the Page Setup to portrait orientation, the artwork (titled Henry's Trip) would print vertically if you just used the Print command, and only a portion of the art would print on one page.

With the page tool you can move the page dividers to control how much of the image prints on the page. You can change the page orientation in the Document Setup and Page Setup dialog boxes to be horizontal or landscape mode.

Before printing, you can open the Document Setup dialog box to set the artboard size, including dimensions for a custom artboard size, and page orientation, or check the Use Page Setup option to automatically set the artboard size to match the Page Setup dialog box options.

You can use the Page Setup dialog box to change the page orientation to horizontal (Figure 2-25), and then use the page tool in the Fit In Window view (View menu) to fit the entire chart on one page (Figure 2-26). In the Document Setup dialog box (Figure 2-27), you can set the

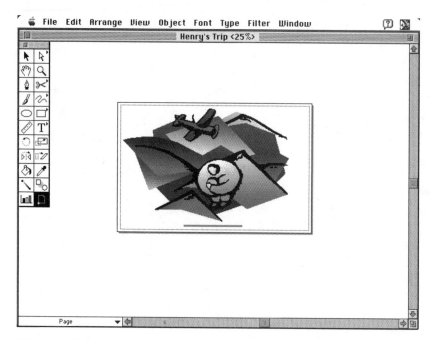

Figure 2-24.
The drawing area is larger than a standard page, and you can move the page boundary with the page tool to control how much of the image prints.

page to one of three views. Single full page is the default, but you can instead tile imageable areas or tile full pages.

These other options, described in Chapter 5, enable you to print tiled (overlapping) pages for images larger than the page size of the printer. Adobe Illustrator numbers the pages (but does not print the page

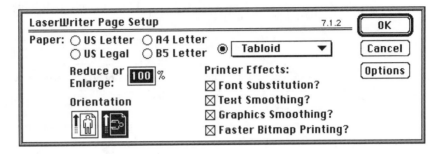

Figure 2-25.
Changing the page orientation to horizontal (landscape mode) in the Page Setup dialog box. You can also specify a percentage enlargement or reduction.

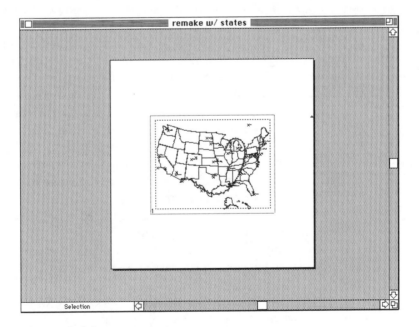

Figure 2-26.
After changing the artwork to landscape mode you can still adjust the page boundaries with the page tool.

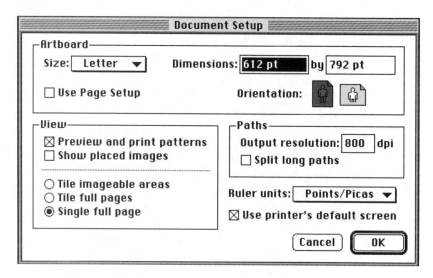

Figure 2-27.
Set artboard and page dimensions in the Document Setup dialog box, or check the Use Page Setup option to match the Page Setup dialog box options.

numbers), so that you can specify one page or a range of pages when printing. The program will print only those pages that contain part of the graphic image or its bounding box (the area that represents the smallest rectangle surrounding all points of the graphics). If your shape has curved edges, for instance, the bounding box that encloses the shape could extend across an extra page that will print as a blank.

If a direction point extends across a page boundary, the printer could print a blank page for that reason. (The direction point determines the shape of a curve, and is connected to an anchor point.)

The Page Setup dialog box lets you specify a percentage reduction or enlargement. You can specify a percentage in the range of 25 percent reduction to 400 percent enlargement.

No laser printer can print all the way to the edge of the paper. The imageable area is less than the page size.

Linotronic imagesetters do not have this limitation since you can run wide film or paper and print large images in landscape or portrait mode.

The program saves the page setup settings you chose for your artwork file, so that when you open the artwork file again, it will use the same settings if the same printer is chosen with the Chooser desk accessory. If, however, you have chosen a different printer, the program adopts the default settings for that type of printer.

Scaling, Rotating, and Cloning

Keith Ohlfs, a freelance artist and a student at San Jose State University, drew "Skier" and "Horse and Rider," as well as several other pieces on the Gallery disks. We use "Skier" as an example of how you can take one image, change its shape and size by scaling, change its orientation by rotating, and then duplicate it many times to form a succession of images suggesting movement.

Keith started the skier illustration by scanning a photograph of a skier, then tracing its basic shape. This can be done easily with the automatic tracing feature (Figure 2-28). First select the auto trace tool, then click a starting point near the edge of the scanned shape to be traced. The program draws an outline around the shape and returns to the starting point. The automatic tracing tool works best with closed shapes, but it may treat a line as a closed shape rather than as a line.

Keith drew the spokes of the ski poles by zooming in to see the detail of the template. After drawing several paths to make the image of the skier and poles, he selected all of them and grouped them so that the rest of the operations worked on the entire group.

Figure 2-28.
Using the automatic tracing tool to trace the outline of a scanned image of a skier.

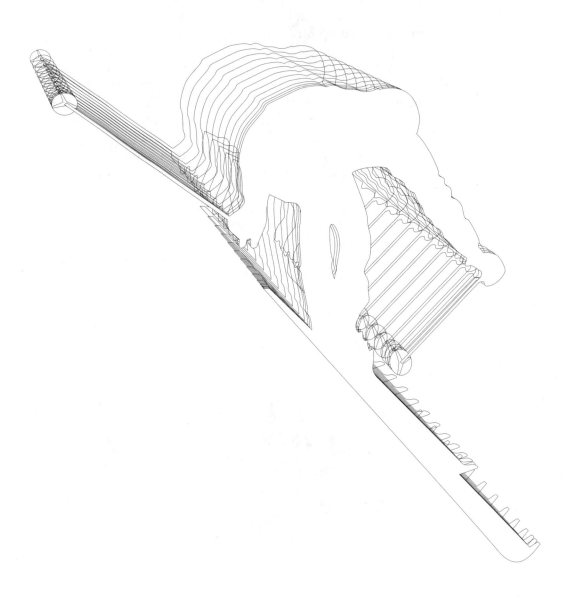

The image was too big for the LaserWriter page, so Keith used the scaling tool to manually rescale the artwork. He scaled it by clicking on a focal point for the reduction that was below and to the left of the image (Figure 2-29), and dragging to the left and down, holding the mouse button while watching the outline of the graphic change shape. He let go when he liked the way the image had been slightly stretched and contorted (Figure 2-30). Keith then selected the rotate tool, clicked on

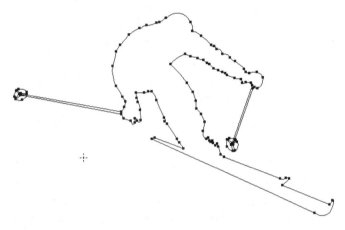

Figure 2-29.
After selecting the object and the scaling tool, click a focal point for scaling, then drag in a direction toward (reducing) or away (enlarging) from the focal point.

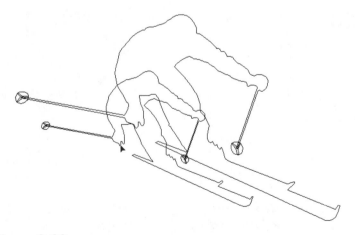

Figure 2-30.
You can stretch or compress an object with the scaling tool, or scale proportionately by holding down the Shift key.

a focal point for the rotation, and dragged downward clockwise. He then changed his display to view artwork only, to touch up the curves and lines and make the image look better.

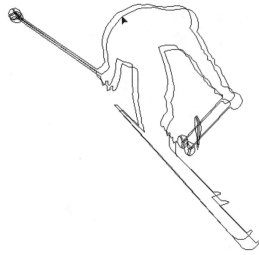

Figure 2-31.
Dragging the selected outline while holding down the Option key so that a duplicate is made that is offset from the original. This operation is a simple transformation.

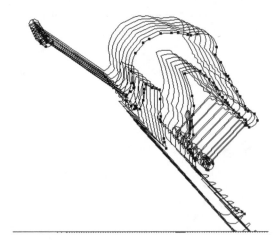

Figure 2-32.
Immediately after performing a transformation of any kind (such as the simple transformation in the previous figure), you can repeat the transformation over and over to create many clones by selecting the Repeat Transform command in the Arrange menu, or by typing the Command-D shortcut.

To create the first duplicate skier, he started dragging the selected group up and away from the original position, then held down the Option key (while dragging) so that he would be moving a copy of the image, not the original. He also held down the Shift key (while dragging), so that the copied outline moved in a 45-degree angle (Figure 2-31). Having done this simple transformation (actually just a move and copy) once, he could repeat it over and over very quickly (Figure 2-32) by pressing Command-D or selecting the Repeat Transform command in the Arrange menu. The result is an image that simulates movement when the outlines are properly painted. The skier image and its copies are painted black by the default setting.

If you wanted to be more precise about the movement, you could select the Move command from the Edit menu, or hold down the Option key while using the selection tool (after selecting all of the segments of the outline), and bring up a Move dialog box (Figure 2-33) which lets you specify a measure of space in points (there are 72 points, or 6 picas, to an inch).

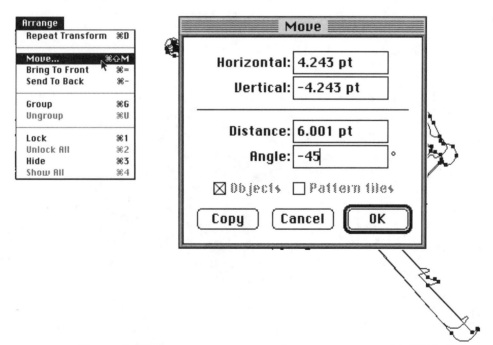

Figure 2-33.
After selecting the group of paths comprising the skier, choose the Move option, which lets you enter precise measurements for distance and angle. The distance is in points because the measuring unit was set to picas/points in the Preferences General dialog box (File menu).

Shearing

"Horse and Rider" shows how you can create a slanted shadow of an object. You can slant an image along an x and y axes by using the shearing tool. "Horse and Rider" started as an automatic tracing of a template (Figure 2-34), which took only a few minutes.

To create the slanted shadow, Keith drew a marquee around the entire object by clicking the selection (arrow) tool and dragging from one corner of the object to the other corner (Figure 2-35). Everything inside the marquee's dotted lines is selected, even though the paths are not grouped. You can group the paths after they are selected by using the Group command in the Arrange menu.

Then Keith clicked the shear tool, and the pointer turned into a crosshair. He moved the pointer to the horse's hind foot to define the intersection of the x and y axes for shearing (Figure 2-36). The pointer changed from a crosshair to an arrowhead, and he then dragged horizontally away from the intersection of the x and y axes, and held down the mouse button to wait for the program to redraw the sheared image. He then held down the Option key to make a duplicate image for shearing (leaving the original image unsheared), and

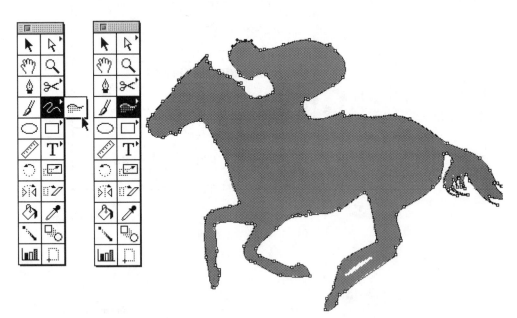

Figure 2-34.
After clicking the automatic tracing tool and a starting point for tracing, the program takes a minute or less to trace the scanned image.

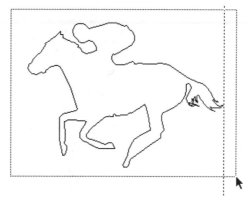

Figure 2-35.
Selecting the entire object by drawing a selection marquee with the selection (pointer) tool. Every point and segment inside the marquee's dotted lines becomes part of the selection.

Figure 2-36.
Clicking a focal point for the shear tool to establish the x and y axes for shearing.

continued dragging back and forth slightly to adjust the shearing. When he had the image properly sheared, he released the mouse button, then released the Option key (Figure 2-37).

Shearing is best understood if you imagine that there is a horizontal (x) or vertical (y) axis that is either parallel to the sides of the window (the usual case), or angled from that position (if you've changed the axes to be other than 0° with the Constrain angle option in the General Preferences dialog box in the File menu, described in Chapters 4 and 5). You pick the intersection of the x and y axes, and you drag in either the horizontal (x) or vertical (y) direction parallel to an axis to shear the image in the direction of that axis. All points in the image that lie along the

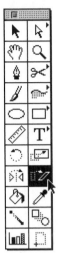

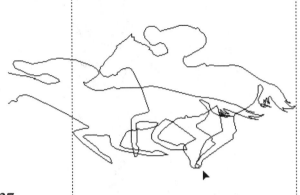

Figure 2-37.
Dragging horizontally shears the object along the x axis, and holding down the Option key creates a duplicate object for shearing, leaving the original unchanged. Remember to release the mouse button first, then the Option key, to create a sheared copy.

chosen axis do not move; all other points in the image move in the direction of that axis. So, as you drag horizontally, the image is slanted horizontally (along the x axis); as you drag vertically, the image is slanted vertically (along the y axis).

If you have trouble with the shear tool — for example, if the shearing is too drastic, flattening the image into a line — you can start your dragging farther away from the intersection point of the x and y axes, and have finer control over the shearing so that the changes are not so drastic.

After shearing in one direction, the pointer turns back into a crosshair so that you can establish another x-y intersection and drag along the x or y axis to shear the object again. You can also shear along angles that are multiples of 45 degrees (relative to the x and y axes) by holding down the Shift key while dragging the arrowhead pointer.

To specify the exact shear angle in degrees rather than dragging the arrowhead pointer, double-click the shear tool to select the Shear dialog box (the center point of the object will be used as the point of origin), or hold down the Option key while clicking the shear axis point, and Illustrator displays the Shear dialog box for specifying the shear angle and the type of shear (horizontal, vertical, or angled by a specific degree, as in Figure 2-38). A positive shear angle slants the image clockwise, and a negative shear angle slants the graphic counterclockwise (as in "Horse and Rider"), both relative to the original position. (This differs from other functions, such as rotation, where a positive angle produces a counterclockwise rotation.)

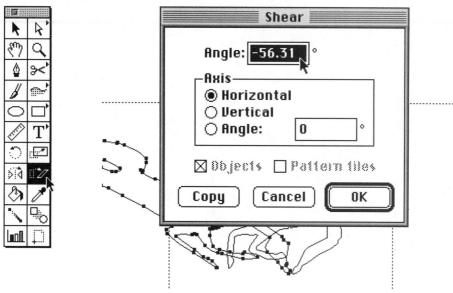

Figure 2-38.
Double-click the shear tool (or hold down the Option key when clicking the shear tool's focal point) to use the Shear dialog box to specify the shear angle in degrees rather than dragging.

If you click the OK button, the program uses the specifications to perform the shear. To shear a copy of the image rather than the original image, click the Copy button rather than the OK button in the dialog box. (You can also shear a copy rather than the original by holding down the Option key while dragging the shear.)

Reflecting

For the final transformation, Keith used the reflect tool to produce a mirror image of the sheared copy. First he selected the reflect tool, then he clicked a point of reflection on the same hind foot that served as the point of shearing. Dragging downward away from the reflection point caused the image to be reflected into a shadow (Figure 2-39). In this case Keith did not hold down the Option key, since he was not making a duplicate image — he wanted to keep only the reflected version.

The "Horse and Rider" image and its sheared and reflected copy are both painted black, which is the default setting.

Reflection creates a mirror image across an invisible axis defined by clicking a focal point (Figure 2-40). You can reflect directly across a

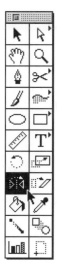

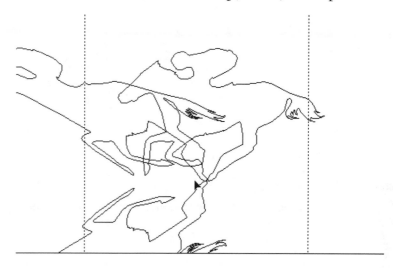

Figure 2-39.
Using the reflect tool to make a reflection of the object; the focal point for the reflection is the point where the objects touch.

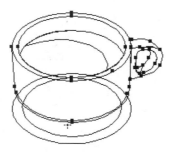

Figure 2-40.
Clicking a focal point for reflecting an object across a horizontal axis.

horizontal or vertical axis by first clicking the focal point (the crosshair turns into a pointer) and then clicking along another point on the invisible axis (Figure 2-41). Hold down the Option key while clicking to create a duplicate shape (Figure 2-42).

To reflect across a diagonal axis, click the focal point, then drag the invisible axis in order to rotate it at an angle (Figure 2-43).

You can constrain this angle to 45-degree increments by holding down the Shift key. When you let go of the mouse button (and the Shift key if constraining is used), the reflection is complete.

You can also specify the angle of the axis by holding down the Option

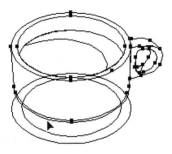

Figure 2-41.
Clicking along the invisible horizontal axis in order to reflect directly across the axis.

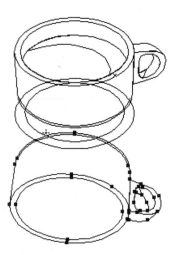

Figure 2-42.
The reflect tool creates a mirror image of the cup across the horizontal axis.

key while clicking the reflect tool's focal point (Figure 2-44).

For example, in the coffee cup clip art (from T/Maker's ClickArt EPS series), two mirror reflections are adjusted to make a shadow effect appear on the coffee cup's saucer.

When you are adjusting objects and you want to quickly preview the change (and you can use the Undo command [in the Edit menu] to experiment), first select the New Window command from the Window menu, which creates a second window on the artwork. You can resize the two windows to be displayed side-by-side, and turn Preview on for one window, then click in the other window and turn on the Artwork view.

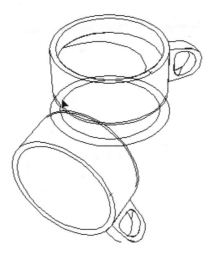

Figure 2-43.
After clicking the focal point, you can drag in order to rotate the invisible axis and reflect the object across a diagonal axis rather than a horizontal or vertical axis.

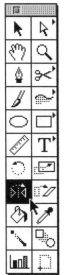
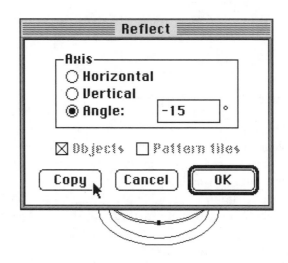

Figure 2-44.
Specifying a precise angle for the reflection axis by holding down the Option key while clicking the focal point.

The result is that you can adjust objects in the Artwork window and preview every move in the Preview window (Figure 2-45).

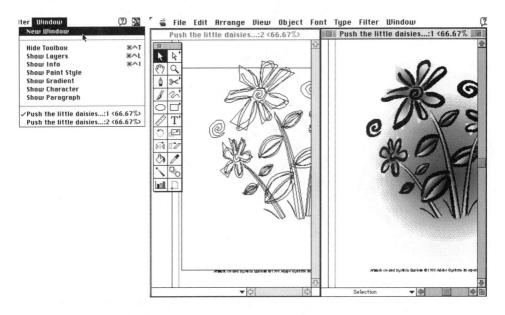

Figure 2-45.
After choosing New Window and resizing the two windows to fit side-by-side, you can set one window to be a Preview window so that it shows a preview of every move.

Blending

The blend tool creates a series of shapes between two objects. If both objects are patterned, they must use the same pattern, but you can use different fill colors, or gray values, and stroke widths. The blend tool can blend process and custom colors, gray values, and stroke widths to achieve special effects, such as an airbrush effect or a contour with different line weights.

For a simple example of blending, you could take a standard clip art symbol (the man symbol from T/Maker's ClickArt EPS series) and blend it with another shape, such as an oval. First you select both objects, then choose the blend tool and click a point on the first object (Figure 2-46) and a corresponding point on the second object (Figure 2-47). The program displays the Blend dialog box, where you can specify the number of steps (Figure 2-48). The program calculates the first and last blend percentages, which you can change if you wish. For example, if you specify 19 steps, the first and last blends will be at 5 and 95 percent, which means that the first blend is at 5 percent of the starting object, and the last blend is at 95 percent.

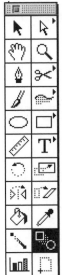

Figure 2-46.
After selecting two objects for a blending operation, select the blend tool and click a point on the first object.

Figure 2-47.
Click a corresponding point on the second object for the blend operation.

Blend

Steps: 5

First: 16.67 %

Last: 83.33 %

Cancel   OK

Figure 2-48.
The Blend dialog box appears, letting you specify the number of steps. The starting and ending percentages of the new steps are calculated for you, but you can change them.

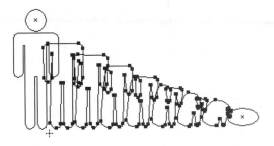

Figure 2-49.
The blend tool produces the steps grouped and preselected for further transformations.

Figure 2-50.
The blending of patterns, fills, and strokes are shown in the Preview window.

When you click OK, the program performs the blending operation, creating a group of steps that are already selected (Figure 2-49). You can see the fill and stroke blend in the Preview window (Figure 2-50).

The blend tool interpolates between two points you select and calculates the steps. You can select more than two points (such as two entire paths) to have more control over the results. Paths must both be either open or closed. Paths must be ungrouped first before blending. To blend between open paths, select an endpoint on each path. You can create up to 1000 steps; the more steps you specify, the finer the gradation will be between the starting and ending shapes. For examples of blended process colors, see Plate 7 and Plate 8 in the color plates.

Drawing Freehand

Some artists prefer to draw images freehand, then adjust and refine them to get to the final result. Adobe Illustrator 5 provides a freehand tool for this purpose. First you select the freehand tool, then position the x marker where you want to start drawing. As you drag, the marker turns into a pointer and leaves behind a dotted line. The faster you drag, the fewer dots are created.

The freehand tool responds to shakiness or other slight variations in your drawing motion, creating bumps. You can set the freehand tolerance level to reduce (or increase) the number of bumps by choosing the Preferences General option from the File menu (Figure 2-51).

You can erase any part of the dotted line while you are drawing by holding down the Command key and redrawing back over the line

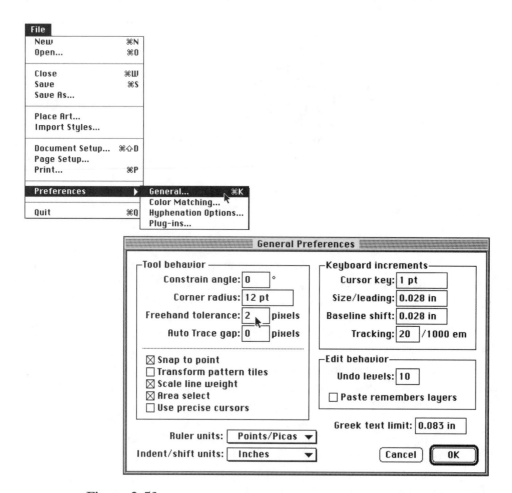

Figure 2-51.
The Preferences General dialog box lets you specify, among other things, the freehand tolerance level to the number of pixels of variance in your drawing — more pixels means more bumps will be ignored by the freehand tool.

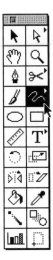

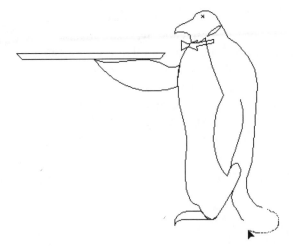

Figure 2-52.
With the freehand tool you can drag from a starting point and draw a shape; you can also hold down the Command key to go back over the shape and erase it.

(Figure 2-52). However, you can only erase the line if you have not yet released the mouse button. You can always delete a line or curve segment by selecting it and pressing the Delete or Backspace key, or by selecting Undo from the Edit menu.

You can stop drawing freehand at any point, and continue drawing freehand or using the pen tool to continue the path, by starting at the endpoint. To create a closed path, keep drawing with the freehand tool (or establishing points with the pen tool) until you reach the starting point of the path.

Creating Graphs Automatically

Adobe Illustrator 5 provides six different styles of automatic graphs: grouped column, stacked column, pie, line, area, and scatter. Your choice depends on the content of the information and how you want to present the information.

Illustrator lets you experiment with different graph styles and combine them in one illustration. You can use colors and designs, including PostScript drawings, to customize graphs, and you can continue to edit the information. Graph data can be typed into a table provided by Illustrator, or imported as text from a spreadsheet, word processing, or database program.

You can choose a graph style (grouped column is the default style) either by selecting the Graph and Style commands in the Object menu, or by double-clicking the Graph tool in the tool palette.

To create a graph from scratch, select the graph tool and drag diagonally across the drawing area to define the size of the graph (Figure 2-53) from edge to edge. Hold down the Option key while dragging diagonally to define a graph from the center to the edge. A table appears for entering the data for the graph. The first line is

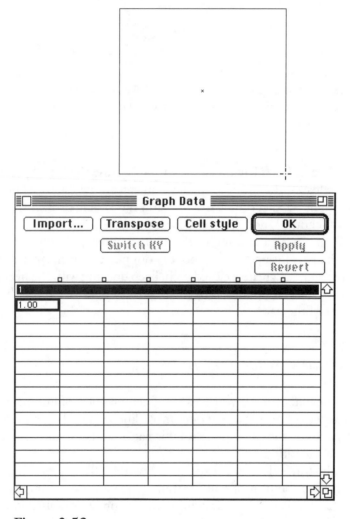

Figure 2-53.
Selecting the graph tool and dragging to define the size of the graph. A table appears for entering the graph data.

the entry line for typing values directly into a cell. You can click on any cell and then enter a value on the entry line.

Start by entering labels in the first row of the table (Figure 2-54). You

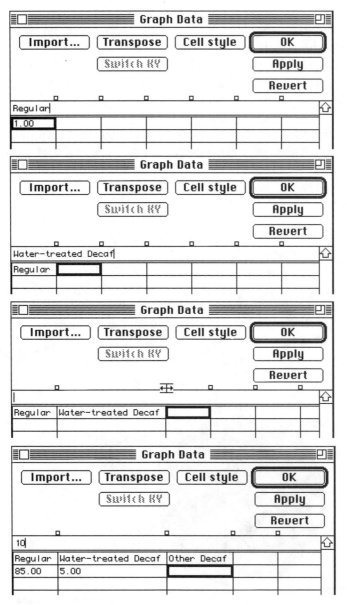

Figure 2-54.

Entering labels and data in the table for the graph. You can stretch a column to be wider by dragging on the column handles above the table.

can use the Tab key to jump from one cell to the next. Then enter the values in the second row. You can drag the column borders to widen the columns if necessary. Click OK when you are finished entering labels and values, double-click the graph tool or select the Graph and Style commands in the Object menu, and select Pie for the Graph type. The result is a pie graph automatically shaded and supplied with legends to indicate different columns in the table. You can see how the graph will look when printed in the Preview view (Figure 2-55).

You can change the data in the graph while the graph is selected by choosing the Graph Data option from the Object menu (Figure 2-56). The graph changes with new data, and you can see the changes in the Preview view.

Other aspects of the graph can be changed automatically. With the graph still selected, you can change the type size of all the text in the graph by choosing Size from the Type menu. You can also edit different parts of the graph, changing the size of some text, or changing the pattern or paint style of a section of the graph. Illustrator provides the direct-selection tool for selecting parts of a graph without having to ungroup the graph. You should leave the graph grouped so that automatic changes can be applied.

For example, to change one of the pie slices to a different color, you can choose the direct-selection tool (located to the right of the selection tool), and select one of the slices while holding down the Option key (to select a path). Option-click the same slice again, and related objects in the graph (such as the slice's legend) are automatically selected (Figure 2-57). Graphs are organized into "subgroups"

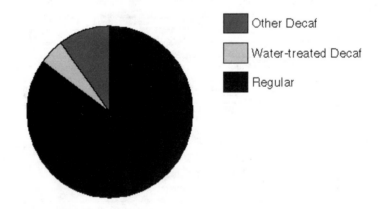

Figure 2-55.
The result is an automatic pie graph with appropriate paint styles for each pie section and a legend for each section.

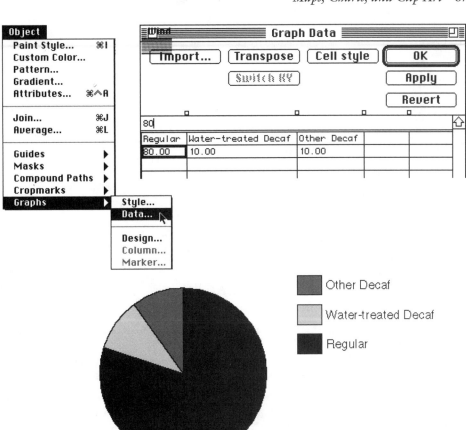

Figure 2-56.
You can change the data for the graphs with the Graphs Data command, and the graph automatically changes.

that can be selected by Option-clicking on an object twice. Changes can be made to the entire subgroup or to individual selections of the graph. The direct-selection tool is the key to selecting individual objects and subgroups.

Illustrator combines powerful drawing tools with automatic data graphing tools, so that professional-looking graphs can be created quickly and easily. Although you can ungroup and manipulate the line and curve segments of any graph, the ungroup operation throws away the cohesive nature of a graph that allows automatic updating with new information. Instead, the program offers an automatic method of assigning a graphic object or design to a graph to create sophisticated graphs.

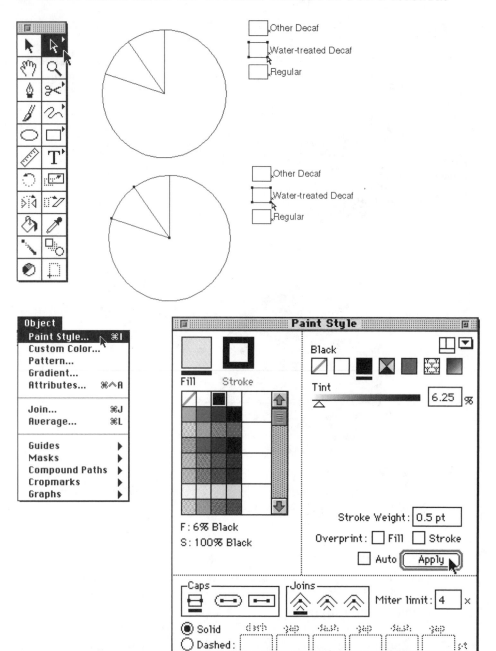

Figure 2-57.
Select a segment with the direct-selection tool, holding down the Option key to select a path. Option-click the path again in order to select other parts of the graph attached as a subgroup. Any change affects all elements of the subgroup.

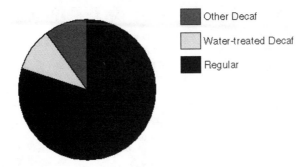

Adding Graphics to Graphs

You can use a drawn object, such as the coffee cup used in earlier examples, to fill columns of a graph or use as markers in line and scatter graphs. The object can be simple or complex, and Illustrator can scale the object uniformly or stretch it vertically using a sliding design boundary.

For example, you can create a bar graph using coffee cups. To start, the pie graph created in the previous example can be changed to a bar graph simply by selecting the graph with the selection tool (*not* the direct-selection tool) and choosing the Graphs Style option from the Object menu. A dialog box appears showing various options and styles for graphs (Figure 2-58).

The next step is to create three versions of the coffee cup to represent the three columns in the graph. Each cup should be grouped to itself, but not to the other cups (Figure 2-59).

Now you can draw the bounding rectangle around the first cup. This rectangle (Figure 2-60) defines the entire image to use as a column or marker design. Or, you can select one of the columns from the column graph to use as your bounding rectangle, to be sure that the object will be sized appropriately. Paint the rectangle to have no fill and no stroke, and use the Send to Back command to send it behind the graphic object.

Draw a selection rectangle around the bounding rectangle in order to select the graphic object with its rectangle, and group them together (Figure 2-61). Then choose the Graphs Design command from the Object menu. Click the New button to create a new design. A small preview of the design appears, and you can give the design a name.

To use a specific column design with the graph, first use the direct-selection tool with the Option key to select a column's legend block, and

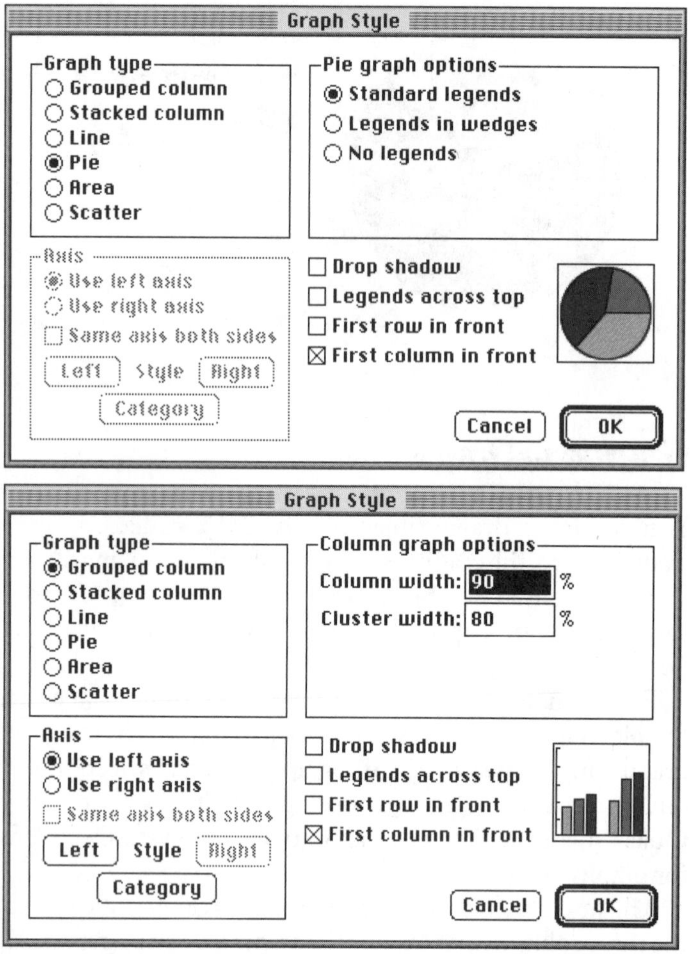

Figure 2-58.
Choosing the Graphs Style option from the Object menu. A dialog box appears showing options for graph types, and for pie graph options. Changing the style to a grouped or stacked column bar graph displays other options.

click again with the Option key to select the subgroup (Figure 2-62). Then choose the Graph Column Design command in the Object menu, and pick the design you want for the selected column subgroup. You can choose to scale the design vertically, to scale it uniformly, to repeat the design, or to set up a sliding design (to reduce or enlarge the design to fit). For the coffee cup graph, choose to repeat the design, and set the Repeated design increment (the amount each design represents) to 10.

After choosing a column design for each column, check the results by choosing the Preview view (Figure 2-63). Column designs are scaled, so

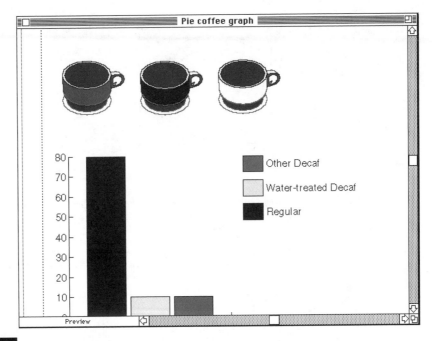

Figure 2-59.
Creating three versions of the coffee cup to represent the three columns in the graph. Each cup should be grouped to itself.

that the entire design fits within the column. You can experiment by choosing different graphics effects from the Graph Column Design dialog box.

Whether the graph remains grouped (so that automatic recalculations can be made) or ungrouped, you can use Illustrator's drawing and selection tools to modify the artwork and customize the graph. The direct-selection tool lets you select one or more objects and subgroups

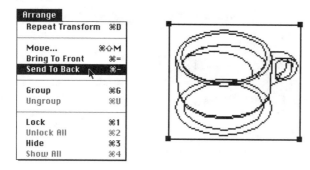

Figure 2-60.

Drawing the bounding rectangle around the first cup, and using the Send to Back command to send it behind the graphic object.

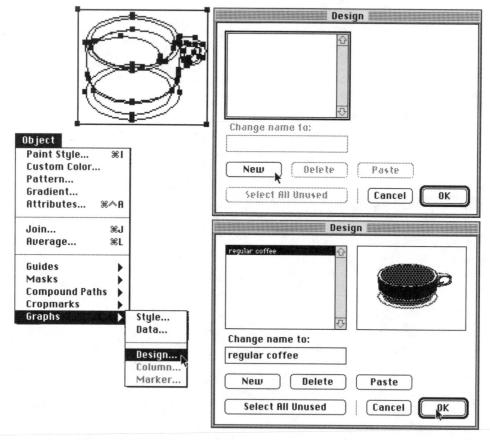

Figure 2-61.

Selecting the graphic object with its rectangle, grouping them together, and choosing the Graph Design command from the Object menu. Click the New button to create a new design.

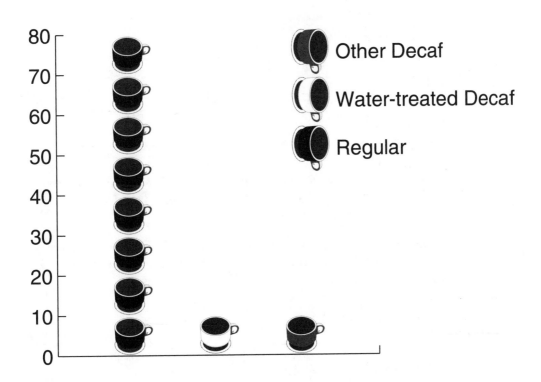

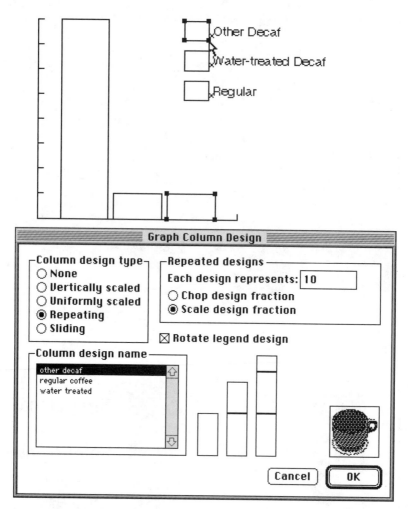

Figure 2-62.
Using a column design for the selected subgroup in the bar graph. The option is selected to repeat the design for every increment of 10 units.

within a grouped graph so that you can make modifications or change the graph style. As described in Chapter 5, the graph commands and options allow you to change all attributes of the graphs.

Summary

With "U.S. Map," Pat Coleman showed how to draw objects that have common borders; how to copy and paste a line and curve segment, path,

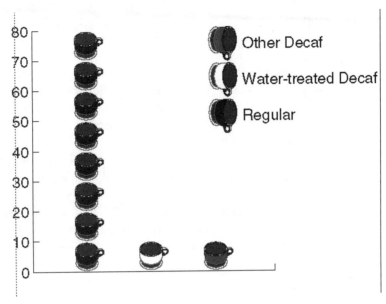

Figure 2-63.
A Preview of the bar graph with the coffee cup designs for the columns set to repeat every 10 units.

and group of paths; and how to set up a shadow behind an object to make it appear three-dimensional. She also explained how she grouped the path outlining each state with the state's abbreviation, for easy selection of individual states. She drew a map that could be used whole, or in part; each state or group of states could be used individually and with other artwork files.

Dean Dapkus took Pat's map and created a weather chart. Dean showed how he made clones of an object and used the rotation tool to form a weather front. He also explained how he used the text tool with a white stroke and fill to place text that extends over areas of the image. Dean changed the page setup to horizontal (landscape) in order to print the entire chart on one LaserWriter page, and discussed how you might scale a complete illustration by a percentage reduction or enlargement in the Page Setup dialog box.

Keith Ohlfs showed his technique for transforming and then cloning an image in the "Skier" illustration. Keith showed how you can repeat a duplication (or any transformation) over and over to achieve a special effect such as the skier that appears to be moving. Keith also showed a simple example of shearing and then reflecting a duplicate of an image (the horse and rider) to make a shadow.

The T/Maker ClickArt EPS graphics, stored in Encapsulated Post-Script files, were manipulated by the reflect and blend tools, and you learned to use two windows to show a preview window simultaneously with the artwork window.

This chapter also described how to create a pie graph and a grouped bar graph, and how to use a graphic design for the bar graph columns. It also showed how you can direct-select objects within a grouped graph and make changes to them without affecting the ability to recalculate a graph with new data.

A wide range of tools for creating graphics were described in this chapter, including tools for selecting, scaling, zooming, rotating, reflecting, blending, and shearing an object. The Type and Paint dialog boxes, and the pen, freehand, auto trace and oval-drawing tools were also shown. The chapter introduced nearly all the commands and options in Illustrator's menus. The next chapter shows more sophisticated graphics techniques using these tools and options.

3

Graphic Design and Illustration

The largest category of artwork produced using Adobe Illustrator is graphic design and illustration. Andy Warhol is one artist who would have especially liked the program; his Campbell Soup cans would have been an excellent project. He could have outlined the cans quickly, added text for the label, and specified exact shades of gray and process colors.

Adobe Illustrator gives you a better chance of getting high-quality results because it is a versatile program for cloning, scaling, and transforming graphic objects to form illustrations. The effects take some time to create, but once they are created, they can be reused over and over, and modified very quickly for custom work. Keith Ohlfs, a freelance artist who drew many of the Gallery pieces, compared the use of Adobe Illustrator for the images he drew with conventional methods: "These effects could be done in an ink drawing, but Illustrator makes them much easier, and you can vary copies of them again and again for use in other drawings, which saves a lot of time and effort."

Illustrator 5 includes several plug-in filters (additional filters are available from third-parties and user group forums), which can save you additional time while creating effects.

Filters supplied with the program simplify the creation of such effects as stars, arrowheads, spirals, polygons, mosaics, calligraphy, drop shadows, adding trim marks (crop marks) to the artwork (for example, trim marks for several nametags or business cards on a single page), and distorting perspective along a plane.

Text filters assist you in exporting and finding text.

Color filters can help you customize blends as well as adjust, invert, saturate, and desaturate colors.

Object filters can be used to add anchor points, and scale, rotate, move, and align objects.

Other filters include Distort filters (such as the Tweak filter, which moves points randomly), Stylize filters (such as Bloat and Punk), and Select filters (such as Same Fill color, which selects all objects of the same color, Same Stroke Weight, Select Masks, and Select Stray Points (usefully finds all isolated single points so you can delete them).

In addition, PathFinder filters (which run only on computers equipped with math co-processors) supplied by Adobe Systems can be used to create a hand-painted look, see-through shapes, transparent paint effects, and more. For example, combining two objects can require many steps in Illustrator to subtract parts of the objects from each other, or to use lines to slice through the objects. PathFinder filters such as Back Minus Front, Exclude, Intersect, Unite, Crop Fill, Merge Fill, Crop Stroke, Merge Stroke, and so on, provide useful shortcuts. Other PathFinder filters are available from third parties.

You can experiment with Filter effects, and undo the results, and try other filter effects, to produce more professional results quickly. See the Filter menu section in Chapter 5 for more information about Filters.

Starting a Large Illustration

"The Golfer," by Luanne Seymour Cohen, a graphic designer for Adobe Systems, is an excellent example of the type of commercial art that is easily

ARTWORK CREATED USING ADOBE ILLUSTRATOR. ADOBE ILLUSTRATOR IS A TRADEMARK OF ADOBE SYSTEMS INCORPORATED.

rendered by using Adobe Illustrator. Luanne started with a scanned image of a photocopy of an old advertising poster. She scanned a photocopy because the original, which was in color, scanned too dark. The goal was to get as much detail out of the poster as possible, and not to worry about the quality of the scanned image (Figure 3-1).

Luanne started the artwork by drawing the background because, she says, "I think of [Illustrator artwork] as layers of paper." She drew the background square first, then the circles for the clouds, then the lines on top of the circles, then the golfer's clothing, and finally the overlays, such as the golfer's bracelet. She worked on the face before the hair because she knew the hair would cover the head, and therefore she didn't have to draw a perfect head shape (Figure 3-2).

Luanne explains how she drew the face: "When it was scanned, a lot of detail disappeared. I wanted the golfer to have a modern face, so I sketched my office mate, but changed her hair." Figure 3-3 shows that although the scanned image has very little facial and hairstyle detail, Luanne used the image as a guide to help draw a new face and hairstyle. "There was no eye, or any facial detail in the scanned image, so I drew the eye from a sketch, and moved it around by selecting, until I had it where I thought it should be." The selection tool lets you draw a marquee by dragging; you can drag the marquee around the part of the image you want to select, and the program selects any path intersected by the marquee (Figure 3-4).

Figure 3-1.
Starting with a low-quality scanned photocopy may be better for tracing than a direct scan of the color image because the contrast is sharper in the photocopy.

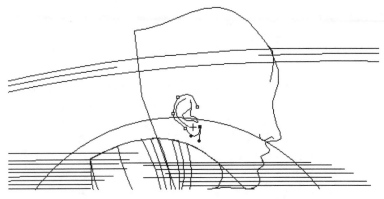

Figure 3-2.
Drawing the front part of the head without regard to the back part, since the back part will be covered by an object representing hair.

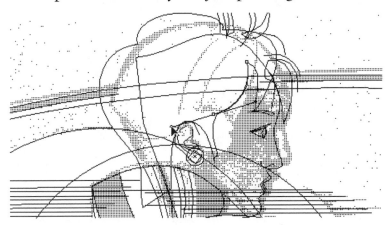

Figure 3-3.
Drawing a new face and hair using the scanned image as a template.

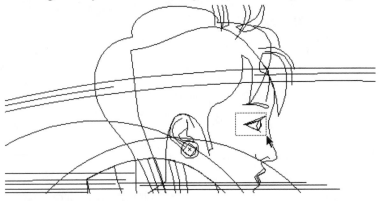

Figure 3-4.
Selecting the eye object by dragging a selection marquee.

Transformations

To draw the belt, Luanne drew one square and sheared it into a diamond shape by using the shear tool. To shear, she clicked a point defining the x and y axes for the shear on the lower left corner of the square, and dragged upwards along the y axis (Figure 3-5). The axes point and the vertical drag keeps the left side of the rectangle from moving as the other points of the shape are sheared into a diamond.

Luanne created a copy of the shape by holding down the Option key while dragging, then using the rotation tool to rotate the copy slightly (Figure 3-6). She repeated the copy with several Command-D (Repeat Transform) commands, and moved them into place using the selection tool and then the rotation tool.

Strokes and Fills

To draw the folds in the tunic, Luanne drew lines and turned their strokes to white (Figure 3-7). She drew them last, so that they would be placed on top of the 100 percent black tunic (she could also have used Copy and then Paste In Front to place the line in front of the selected objects). To get the soft fold in the golfer's skirt, she drew

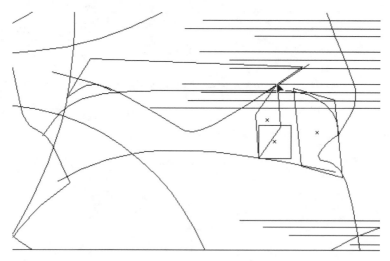

Figure 3-5.
Shearing a square into a diamond shape by selecting the shear tool, clicking a point to define the x and y axes for shearing, and dragging upward along the y axis.

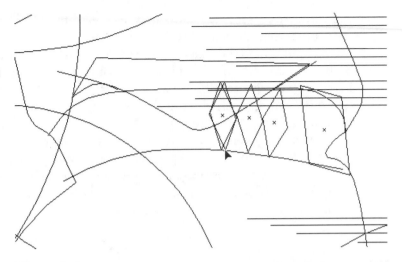

Figure 3-6.
Drawing the belt by cloning the diamond shape and rotating each clone to fit the belt outline.

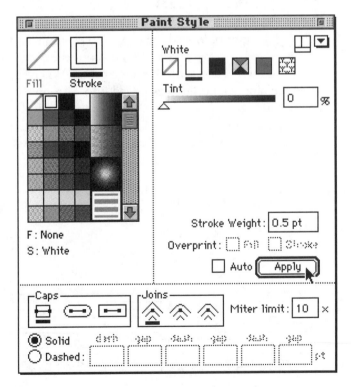

Figure 3-7.
Painting strokes white to represent folds in the golfer's tunic.

lines with strokes set to a shade of gray. However, the white line on the bracelet is a white-shaded shape, not just a line.

The cloud behind the golfer comprised many circles filled with white that have no stroke, so they blend together without seams. She drew one circle and set the Paint attributes (white, no stroke), then those attributes were used automatically for the shapes drawn afterwards (until she changed the Paint Style settings).

The white circles are drawn on top of a large rectangle for the entire page, which is set to have a 10 percent black screen (gray), and a 100 percent black stroke whose weight is one point. Another box was drawn on top of the gray box with the same dimensions, but with a heavier line (three points) and no fill.

Overlaying Graphics

The lines on the clouds were drawn first, and then pasted in back of the clouds (first she copied the lines to the Clipboard, then she selected the clouds, then used the Paste In Back command). Luanne drew a few lines of random length, moved them into position, grouped them, then copied the group, moved the copy into position, and grouped the first group with the copy. She could then copy the bigger group, move this copy into place, and form one large group. When she was finished, she had seemingly random lines joined into a group that could be moved anywhere on the page.

Luanne added the sailboats on top of the sea pattern at the bottom of the page by drawing one sailboat, painting it white with no stroke, and

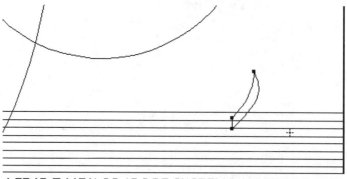

Figure 3-8.
Clicking a focal point for the scale tool to reduce the sailboat shape.

copying it while scaling the copy to a smaller size. First she selected the sailboat and the scaling tool, then she clicked the scale focal point (Figure 3-8), and finally she dragged while holding down the Option key to make a clone that is scaled down (Figure 3-9).

The last object drawn to complete the figure of the golfer was the sleeve, which covered some of the rough edges of the other objects. The sleeve was given a fill of 20 percent black (gray) with a 100 percent black stroke with a weight of 0.2 points. The fill makes it a solid shape; no fill would have made it transparent. "I really think of drawing with Illustrator as layers of paper," says Luanne, "perhaps a collage of objects. I think about things as being in front, or behind... When you are working with a complex drawing with a lot of lines and pieces, you might not be able to keep track of what's in front and what's behind. You can use Cut and Paste In Front or Paste In Back to move things behind or in front of other selected objects. There are times when, even if you know the order to draw things, circumstances dictate that you can't follow that order. I have to draw the golf club in front of her head, but I can cut and paste to layer it in the correct order."

Although Luanne drew all her objects stacked onto a single layer, and managed to keep track of the order of objects, this complex project could be made simpler to work on by placing objects onto different layers, and using Illustrator's layer management features available from the Layers palette (select Show Layers from the Window menu). For projects that are more complex than this one, you will want to use Illustrator's layering features. Layering information can even be passed from one document to another via the

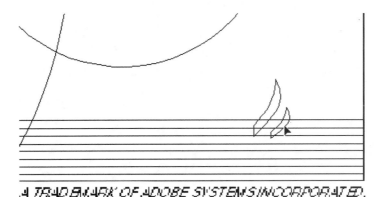

A TRADEMARK OF ADOBE SYSTEMS INCORPORATED.

Figure 3-9.
Cloning the sailboat while reducing it, by holding down the Option key while dragging with the rotate tool.

clipboard, if you've selected the Paste remembers layers option in the General Preferences dialog box (from the File menu).

Techniques For Calligraphy

Adobe Illustrator can turn the skill of calligraphy into a piece of cake. The original calligraphy for the Artifactory logo was drawn by hand using calligraphy techniques by Sumner Stone. Pat Coleman scanned the hand-drawn image to use as a template for drawing (Figure 3-10). Although she could have used the automatic tracing tool, she wanted to draw them so that she would have more control over the creation of line and curve segments.

To get the thick and thin lines of calligraphy, Pat treated each pen stroke as an enclosed polygon, not as a single pen stroke, and drew around the characters to get the filled paths. Pat describes how Illustrator compares to a calligraphy pen or brush: "The program fills any enclosed space. It's a different technique than calligraphy, but you actually have more control than with a calligraphy brush or pen, and you can zoom in to get the thick and thinness of each stroke exact." (Figure 3-11 shows how she could zoom into the artwork and work on the serifs and strokes.)

Pat cloned an already-drawn pen stroke and used the copies to make other strokes, making the strokes consistent. She could also point to a stroke and adjust its direction points to change the curve.

To create the reduced versions, Pat selected all of the paths in the logo

Figure 3-10.
Starting with a scanned sketch of the logo as a template, the artist drew outlines of the characters to represent calligraphy strokes.

by using the selection tool and drawing a marquee around the image (Figure 3-12). She then selected the scaling tool, clicked a focal point for the scale (upper right corner to scale downwards), and dragged down and to the right in a diagonal. "Scaling is another feature that makes Illustrator useful for calligraphy and logos. The image doesn't lose quality when it's reduced, and it doesn't fill in and get muddy, like bit-mapped graphics do when they are reduced."

Calligraphic effects can also be achieved by checking the Calligraphic Style option in the brush tool dialog box, and then using the brush tool

Figure 3-11.
After using the zoom tool to increase magnification, you can adjust the strokes and points to make smoother or sharper characters.

Figure 3-12.
Selecting the entire logo (comprised of many individual paths) by dragging the selection marquee.

to create objects to form the logo. Or, for paths already drawn, you can use the Calligraphy filter to vary the width of strokes and the pen angle of selected filled or stroked paths (but not text). If you have a pressure-sensitive drawing tablet and pen, change the brush width to Variable, and the width of strokes you draw will vary based on the amount of pressure you apply.

Gradation, Shadow, and Airbrush Effects

Keith Ohlfs' "Grapes" shows how you can create a gray or color gradation and airbrush effect. Keith created one grape using concentric circles on the grape to simulate gradations in shading. Although he could have used the blend tool to create the steps for the gradations, Keith drew the concentric circles by drawing one circle, selecting the scaling tool, clicking the edge of the circle as the focal point for scaling, and holding down the Option key while dragging the circle. This transformation created a second circle that still touched the first circle at the focal point. He repeated this transformation (cloning and scaling) by typing Command-D (or selecting Repeat Transform). He then went back to adjust each circle for positioning.

Each circle has no stroke and a fill of a percentage of black (or of a color) relative to its position on the grape; for example, one of the inner circles (Figure 3-13) has a fill of 40 percent black and no stroke (Figure 3-14), which makes it easier to blend the circles into a pattern. The innermost circle is white.

After creating one grape, Keith cloned it by using Copy and Paste In Front or Paste In Back, so that some grapes were overlapping others.

To create the more pronounced gradations of gray in the branch (Figure 3-15), Keith painted the branch path with a 10 percent gray fill, then drew white-stroked and black-stroked lines and white shapes on top to intersperse white and black in the gray pattern.

Keith saved a grape in a separate file by using Copy, then selecting New (from the file menu), then using Paste. The new file could then be opened whenever he needed a group of concentric circles with a gradation of shades. Eventually Keith had made several of these files containing pieces of graphics with well-defined gray scales. He could then use these pieces to make new illustrations simply by transforming them into new shapes.

To see how the artwork will look when printed, at the same time that you are editing the overlaid graphics, create another window display of the same artwork with the New Window command in the Window menu, then select the Preview command to make the new (active) window the preview. You can resize both windows to fit side-by-side on

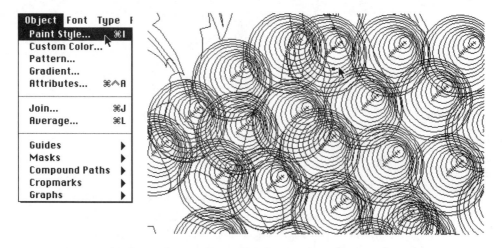

Figure 3-13.
Selecting the middle oval in the grape to display or change its paint attributes.

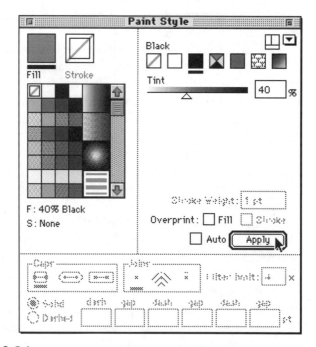

Figure 3-14.
The paint attributes of the oval selected in the previous figure: 40 percent black fill (gray), and no stroke (so that each oval blends into the adjoining oval without a visible line).

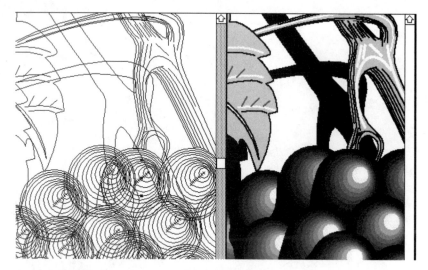

Figure 3-15.
The branch was painted with a 10 percent black (gray) fill, then white-stroked and black-stroked lines and white shapes were drawn on top to make shadows and highlights (the second Preview window was created by using the New Window and Preview commands, then resizing both the preview and artwork windows to fit the screen).

Figure 3-16.
Adjusting the leaf shadow using two views: an artwork window and a preview window.

the screen (see Figures 3-15 and 3-16), and either window can be the preview window.

Using the New Window and Preview commands, Keith set up two windows in order to adjust the background shadow (Figure 3-16). To create the leaf shadow, Keith selected the path of the outline of the leaf and held down the Option key while dragging it to create a duplicate outline. Keith then painted the duplicate 100 percent black, cut it from the artwork, selected the path of the outline of the leaf again, and used the Paste In Back command to place the 100 percent black outline behind the leaf. The branches and the grapes were just as easy to create.

Dean Dapkus' "Abe Lincoln" is an example of an image that would ordinarily be drawn with a paint-type graphics program because it has so much irregular detail that could only be drawn with dots. (Paint-type graphics are called "bit-mapped graphics" because they comprise many single pixels of the display, which correspond to specific dots on paper when printed.) However, since paint-type graphics cannot change in resolution (the number of pixels and the number of dots per inch can't be reduced to achieve higher resolution), artists have always wanted a program that could be as precise and flexible as Adobe Illustrator for defining very tiny line and curve segments that are independent of the screen's resolution.

Dean drew "Abe Lincoln" using large black silhouette shapes. He then magnified areas and drew segments with very thin line weights and white strokes. First he drew one segment and changed the default paint specifications (with the Paint Style command in the Object menu, or Command-I) to have no fill, a white stroke, and a thin line weight (Figure 3-17). After clicking OK, those specifications were used for drawing subsequent segments until he changed them again with the Paint Style command.

Figure 3-18 shows a magnified view of segments Dean drew in Lincoln's beard. Dean explains: "This technique is similar to one that a lot of artists are familiar with, called scratchboard. You start with a black artboard, and you scratch or etch in white shapes."

For the tie, the effect of a simulated halftone with gray shades can be done by drawing paths close together and using increments of gray shading for fills (for example, 5 percent), and no strokes.

The strawberries in the label of "Jar of Preserves" (by Gail Blumberg, a graphic designer for Adobe, and Keith Ohlfs) were drawn with one basic shape (Figure 3-19) that was cloned and scaled (Figure 3-20). You can quickly clone and scale an object by repeating the first clone-and-scale transformation with Command-D or Repeat Transform.

The artists assigned a different percentage of black (gray) to fill each shape, and set no stroke (Figures 3-21 and 3-22). Small ovals were drawn to look like seeds on top of the layers of gray.

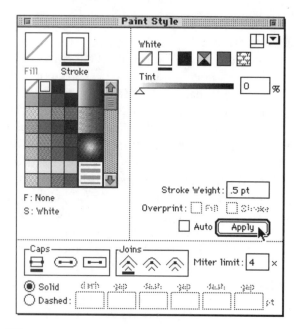

Figure 3-17.
Changing the default paint attributes in the Paint dialog box to make paths with no fill and with very thin white strokes (line weight at 0.5 points).

Figure 3-18.
Drawing white-stroked curve segments in the black silhouette of Lincoln's beard.

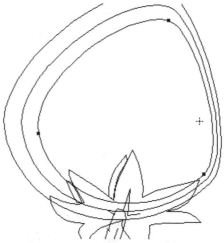

Figure 3-19.
Each strawberry in "Jar of Preserves" is a series of scaled clones of a basic shape, with the scale focal point set to make the cloned shapes closer to the basic shape on one edge.

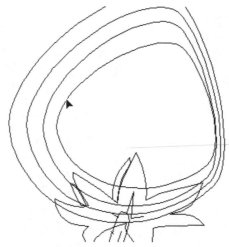

Figure 3-20.
Cloning and scaling the shape by holding down the Option key while dragging with the scale tool. Repeat this transformation with the Transform Again option or Command-D.

Keith created a file of standard gray shaded objects that can be scaled in any direction and used for filling areas of other illustrations (Figure 3-23). The shaded circle and the top grayscale band are designed for 300 dpi laser printers (such as the LaserWriter) and have 33 steps, each with a different percentage

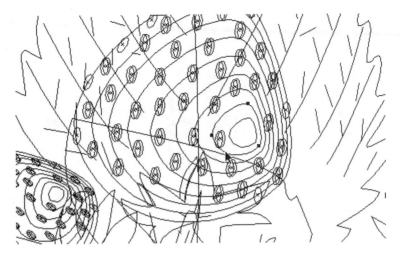

Figure 3-21.
Selecting one of the shapes to paint it with a shade of gray.

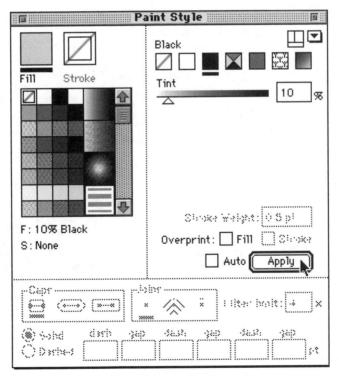

Figure 3-22.
Each scaled shape is filled with a different percentage of black (gray) and has no stroke so that the gray shades blend together.

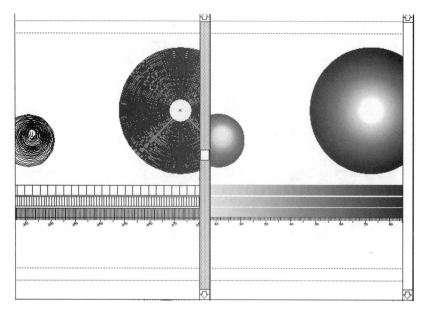

Figure 3-23.
A file of standard shapes that can be copied and pasted into other documents and adjusted to fill different shapes.

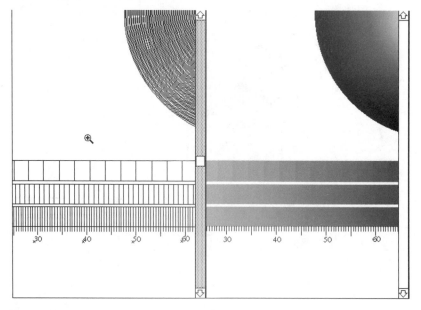

Figure 3-24.
The gray shade bands are designed for use with the 300-dpi LaserWriter (top), the Linotronic 100 at 1270 dpi (middle), and the Linotronic 300 at 2540 dpi (bottom).

of black to simulate a gray shade (Figure 3-24).

The middle band is designed for 1270 dpi imagesetters (such as the Linotype Linotronic 100), and has 100 steps.

The bottom one is designed for 2540 dpi imagesetters (such as the Linotype Linotronic 300) and has 200 steps.

"Although each one takes up a lot of disk space," says Keith, "when I want to have an airbrush effect, I can copy and paste the appropriate shape and then stretch it to whatever size I need."

The shaded objects can be adjusted properly because they consist of grouped paths — Keith can select anywhere on the object and get the entire object.

He used Copy and Paste to copy the shade to another document, where he could drag direction and anchor points until the shades (Figure 3-25) lined up with the shape, then used the reflect tool to mirror it to the other side of the jar.

He added points to segments with the scissors tool in order to bend them. "Using the shades reference saves a lot of time," he says, because he can use them over and over in many different illustrations, no matter what the final shape is.

Figure 3-25.
Adjusting direction and anchor points to fit gray shaded paths in the shape of the artwork.

Arranging Type

There are several ways in Illustrator to arrange type so that its baseline conforms to a shape, such as the label on the jar of strawberry preserves. Illustrator offers an automatic method using the path-type tool to place text along a path. Once placed, you can change attributes and positioning until you are satisfied with the result.

However, sometimes the manual method of moving each character provides a feeling of more control and greater flexibility. Gail Blumberg used the rotate tool with individual characters to arrange the text on the label of the jar of strawberry preserves.

To add the text to the label, Gail used the default type tool and clicked a starting point for the first letter, typed the letter, and set its type characteristics (Figure 3-26). Then she selected the rotate tool, clicked the point of rotation at the center of the label (Figure 3-27), and dragged with the Option key to create a rotated copy of the first letter. To rotate

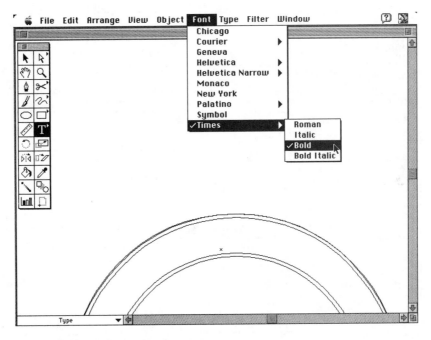

Figure 3-26.
After clicking a starting point with the type tool, you can set the text's typesetting attributes using options in the Type and Font menus, including the font, style, size, leading, and spacing values. Afterwards, the text can be treated as a graphic object.

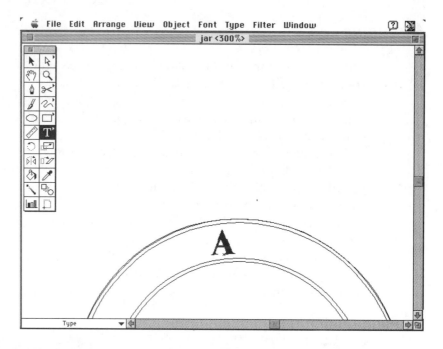

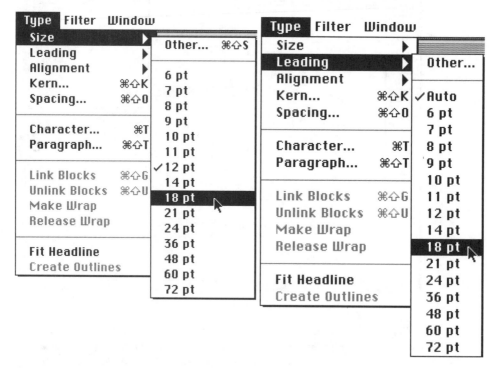

Figure 3-26.
Continued.

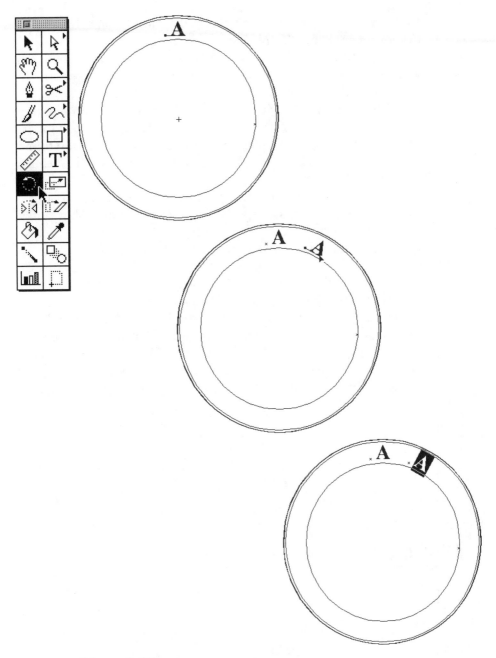

Figure 3-27.
Clicking a focal point for rotation, and then rotating a character into position manually while holding down the Option key to clone the character. Command-D or Repeat Transform repeats the transformation to form more characters rotated the same distance and angle. The characters can be edited with the type tool.

more letters to form a word, she repeated the transformation by pressing Command-D (Repeat Transform).

After rotating the same letter around the label into the positions she wanted, she went back and selected each letter with the type tool to change it to the appropriate letter for that word.

An automatic way to set text along a path is to use the path-type tool (Figure 3-28). Select the path-type tool by dragging to the right of the type tool. Move the pointer to the path you want to attach the text to and click an insertion point. Type the text, and it appears with its baseline attached to the path.

With leading, spacing, tracking and kerning options, and other type attributes you can set in the Type menu, as well as a Baseline Shift setting (in the Type Character dialog box) which can be a negative or positive value, you can make the text look exactly the way you want.

Illustrator 5 makes the process of setting type above and below a circle even easier than the two methods just described. Chapter 6 of the Adobe Illustrator user manual describes how in just a few steps.

Through careful use of the Paste In Back and Paste In Front commands, Gail was able to place the strawberries in front of the text on the label, while the stems of the berries are behind the label, providing the illusion of three dimensions. It is helpful to work with two views (Figure 3-29) when overlaying complex images.

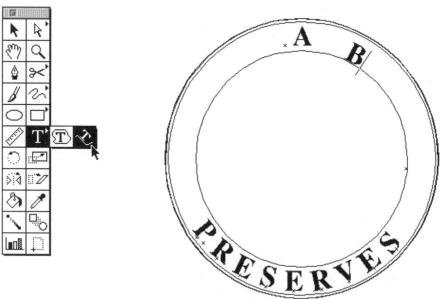

Figure 3-28.
Using the path-type tool to place the text baseline along a path.

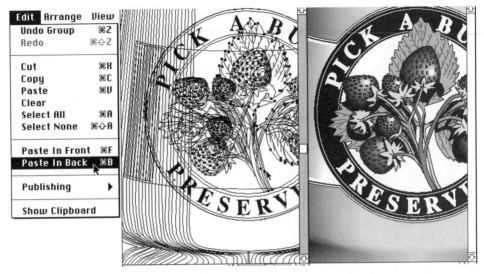

Figure 3-29.
Using the Paste In Front and Paste In Back options (with the help of a preview window) to paste strawberries in front of the label and paste stems behind for a three-dimensional effect.

Painting With Color

Adobe Illustrator lets you assign colors to paths in an image whether or not you are using a color display. You need a color display to see the color assignments, but you don't need a color display to print the image, nor do you need it to produce color separations for publishing. However, to be able to predict the results better, a color display is most helpful, as is a knowledge of how color is reproduced on the printing press.

If you are not familiar with color printing and separations, we recommend that you consult with the print shop or printer whose press will be used for your publication. This is because there may be major differences in appearance between the colors you assigned and the color inks that are printed, and you may want to take certain factors into consideration and adjust your color assignments before producing a color separation.

A color rarely appears in print in exactly the same way as it appears on film or on the video display. In addition, no two displays are exactly alike, and the appearance of the same color on the same screen can be different depending on factors such as the ambient lighting of the room and the presence of other objects that are within your vision while you are looking at the display.

There is also a disparity in the color models used in printing presses and displaying devices. For displays, video monitors use the red, green, and blue (RGB) primary additive colors that are combined with direct light to form any color on the screen.

Printing presses use cyan, magenta, and yellow (CMY), primary subtractive colors in inks that can be applied to a white (or pre-colored surface and combined with black ink. This color model, referred to as CMYK (for cyan, magenta, yellow, and black), corresponds to the process color inks available with all full-color printing presses. Premixed color inks, like PMS (Pantone Matching System) premixed inks, are often run in a single pass together with the four process color inks on color presses, or these premixed inks can also be run on a color press in place of process (CMYK) color inks.

Although some Macintosh programs let you specify colors using the RGB model, publishing on paper requires that you convert these specifications to the CMYK model so that you can choose proper ink mixes. Adobe Illustrator lets you directly assign percentages of CMYK to the image, so that color assignments closely reflect process color inks. The program automatically displays your CMYK assignments using the proper RGB values so that you don't have to make wild guesses about how the colors will appear.

Illustrator also lets you adjust this conversion from time to time for your particular display, so that colors will appear the same under different lighting conditions.

To calibrate your display to match a sample progressive color bar printed by your color printer or printing press, select Preferences and Color Matching from the File menu, and select CIE calibration in the Color Matching dialog box.

To calibrate displayed ink colors to match their printed counterparts, choose from the list of color PostScript printers, standard web offset print (SWOP), and a paper type, such as coated, uncoated or newsprint, for SWOP printing presses, Toyo inks, even large presses such as Ad-Litho newspaper presses (Figure 3-30).

Adobe Illustrator also offers the ability to assign more than 700 PMS printing inks which are also available with all printing presses. The premixed PMS colors are chosen by consulting the PANTONE MATCHING SYSTEM, developed by Pantone, Inc. You specify a specific PMS color and the printing press uses an ink formula provided by Pantone, Inc. Unlike process colors, which can be mixed by your printer to make different shades of color, PMS colors can't be mixed — you simply select one that looks right.

There are two kinds of color you can assign to artwork: a mix of the process colors (cyan, magenta, yellow, and black), or custom colors, such as premixed PMS, TOYO, FOCOLTONE and TRUMATCH colors, and named combinations of process colors, which are custom colors, such as TOYO91 colors, and PANTONE Process Color System colors.

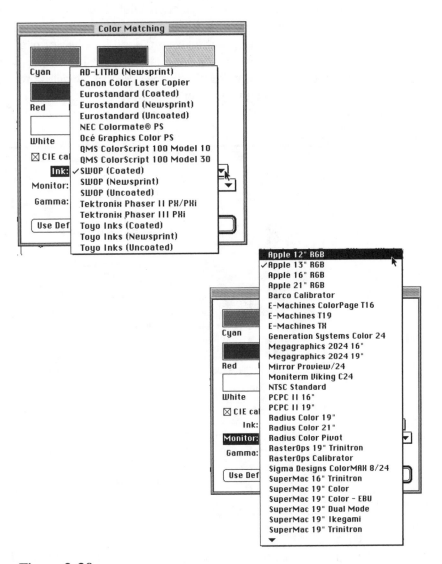

Figure 3-30.
Using the Preferences command and Color Matching dialog box (from the File menu) to calibrate the displayed colors to match specific display monitors and ink matching standards, using the CIE calibration option.

Process colors are specified by percentages in the Paint Style palette (Figure 3-31).

To assign PMS colors, you must also have open a document with PMS colors already specified; Adobe Systems provides several documents containing all of the PMS, TOYO, FOCOLTONE and TRUMATCH colors, (including ones for specific color printers). You can open one of these documents and leave it open while coloring objects in other documents (Figure 3-32). PMS colors are specified by clicking the Custom Color button to display a scrolling list of color names. As you select a color, it appears in the fill rectangle in the Paint Style palette. You can select a different color for an object's stroke by clicking the stroke rectangle and selecting another color from the list.

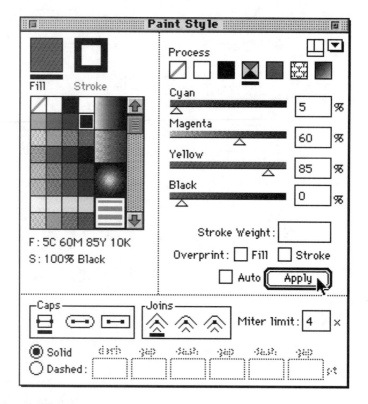

Figure 3-31.
Assigning 5 percent cyan, 60 percent magenta, and 85 percent yellow to make a bright orange shadow for the flowchart (Plate 1). Colors appear as patterns on black and white monitors, or dithered (as shown) on eight-bit color displays.

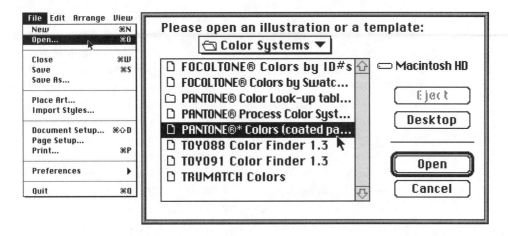

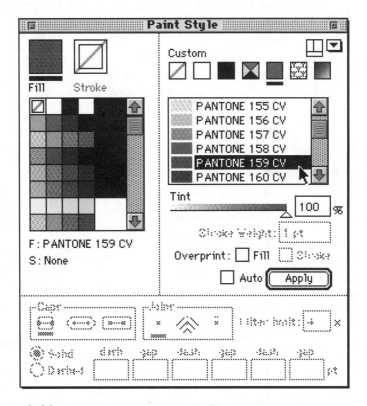

Figure 3-32.
Opening a document containing PMS colors, and then assigning a PMS color to another document (while the PANTONE document is open). You can open multiple documents with Illustrator.

As you assign a PMS color to an object in a document, that particular color name is saved with the document, appearing whenever you open that document. You can also create custom mixes of process colors, that can also be listed by name along with the PMS (and TOYO, FOCOLTONE and TRUMATCH) colors in this scroll box. First create the custom color with the Custom Color option in the Paint Style palette (from the Object menu). You can simply create a custom name for a PMS color (Figure 3-33), or mix process colors into custom color that you can use by name (Figure 3-34).

As you begin to use colors regularly, you will want to create custom color mixes using familiar names, and perhaps have specific PMS colors ready for use in any new document. To make it easy to call up these colors, create a document that contains all of these colors. As long as this document is open, you can assign those colors to objects in any other open documents. You can easily switch between open documents by selecting their names from the Window Menu.

PMS colors are often used for spot color to highlight a graphic image, and the use of PMS ink is usually in addition to process color inks in order to achieve a color effect not possible with a mix of process colors. It is helpful to consult with your printer before choosing PMS colors, since

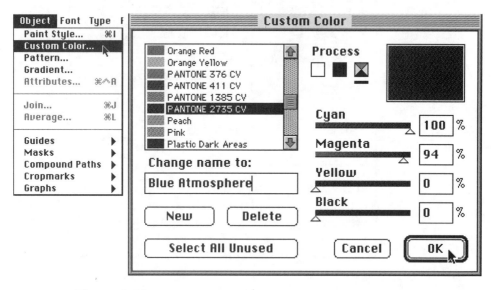

Figure 3-33.
Using the Custom Color option to change the name of a PANTONE color as it will appear in the Custom Color list in the Paint Style palette.

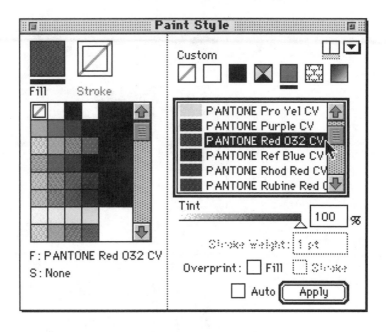

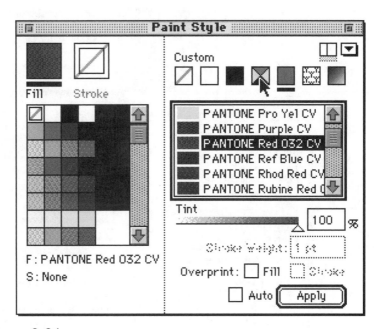

Figure 3-34.
*Using Custom Color to premix process colors under a name that will
appear in the Custom Color list in the Paint Style palette (on an eight-bit
display).*

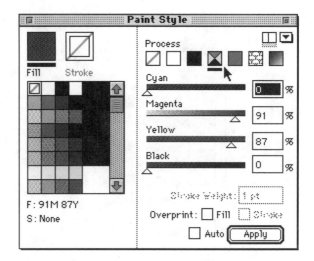

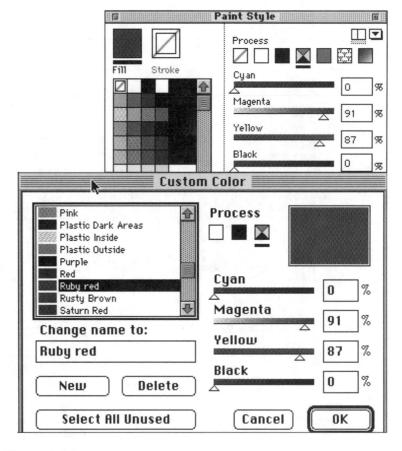

Figure 3-34.
Continued.

they can add to the cost of your press run. You may want to simulate a PMS color by mixing process colors precisely, following a guideline such as the PANTONE Process Color Simulator available from Pantone, Inc. Open the PANTONE Process Color System colors document to assign these colors to your artwork document.

Whenever you mix or use new colors, you should print a test page to be sure that the result is printable without any problems. For example, TOYO process color matches marked with one or two asterisks (*, **) are not precise matches to the TOYO premixed colors, and should therefore only be used sparingly for spot color. The FOCOLTONE document contains 763 process colors that help you avoid pre-press trapping and registration problems. The TRUMATCH Colors document contains over 2000 computer generated colors, but you should print a test page to be sure that the colors you select can be printed without moirés.

The color plates included in this book were produced entirely with process colors. "The Nurse" (Plate 2) began as a black and white sketch and then was colorized in the Roy Lichtenstein comic book style, with strong primary colors — red lips of 100 percent magenta, with 80 percent yellow added to produce the warm ruby red, and hot spots of white light

Figure 3-35.
White hot spots are added to ruby red lips to make them appear wet (see Plate 2).

to make them look wet (Figure 3-35). The fingernails are 30 percent magenta with 25 percent yellow, producing the effect of a comic book pink color, with warm red dots. The skin of the hands and face are colored 10 percent red to achieve the palest pink, which enhances the white tear in the eye. Also, to enhance the white tear, the background is painted darkly in 100 percent cyan, giving the effect of nighttime. Her blouse and hat stripe are 80 percent cyan to distinguish them from the background.

You can print color images in color on the QMS ColorScript color printer or similar PostScript color printing or recording device (see Figure 3-30 for a partial list of color printers supported). You can also make films for color separations using black-printing Linotronic imagesetters and other high-resolution devices.

Adobe Systems supplies a separate program, Adobe Separator, for producing professional-quality film-based color separations with Adobe Illustrator artwork. The program can produce four-color or custom-color separations (such as a separation for each PMS color) for a selected printer type (printer type can be changed, provided you have installed the PPD folder included with your Illustrator program). It offers control over the page size and orientation, settings for emulsion type and halftone screen ruling, and the ability to produce custom color separations or to convert custom colors to the four process colors for a four-color separation. Before using Adobe Separator, you should first set crop marks (select Cropmarks and Make from the Object menu), which can then be adjusted by either Illustrator or Separator. We describe color separation details in the next chapter.

Summary

This chapter showed examples of using nearly every tool in Illustrator's arsenal and provided tips and techniques for drawing almost any type of illustration, including the use of gray shades and color.

"The Golfer" started with a photocopy scan as a template and Luanne Seymour Cohen, the artist, used numerous overlaying graphics to hide all the rough spots. She was able to select all of the paths that make up an object (the golfer's eye) by dragging across the object with the pointer tool, creating a marquee rectangle that selected everything inside it and every path it intersected. Luanne also showed how to perform simple transformations — shearing and rotating — to draw the diamond-shaped belt. To repeat a transformation, you can use the Repeat Transform command or type Command-D. She used the scale tool to transform several sailboat images.

"The Golfer" provided examples of drawing white-stroked lines and pasting them on top of a black-filled shape using the Paste In Front command. White-filled circles (with no stroke) were used to simulate clouds, and a 10 percent black screen was applied to the background.

The "Artifactory" example showed how you can simulate calligraphy by drawing lines that enclose the pen strokes to form individual shapes that can be manipulated to simulate the thick and thin of the calligraphy stroke. The zoom tool comes in handy for working on details. The example also demonstrated how an image that has been worked into perfection can be copied and used for other areas in the artwork. Illustrator calligraphy can be reduced or enlarged without any loss in quality.

The "Grapes" artwork demonstrated an airbrush effect you can achieve by drawing one shape, scaling it slightly, and using Repeat Transform (Command-D) to repeat the transformation many times, then assigning to the shapes a gradual range of percentages of black or color (and no stroke, for smoothness). By drawing paths closer together and using a more gradual range of percentages of black or color for fills, you can make the airbrush effect smoother.

You can also draw white-stroked lines to place on top of black areas, or black-stroked lines and white shapes on top to intersperse white and black in the gray pattern. To see two views of the artwork while working — a preview and a view of the artwork — you can use the New Window command (from the Window menu), and select different views (from the View menu) for the two windows.

The "Abe Lincoln" portrait was drawn by mimicking a conventional process called scratchboard, where an artist scratches or etches white shapes on a black artboard. After setting up white strokes for lines with a certain line weight, those specifications are used for drawing subsequent segments until changed again with the Paint Style command.

"Jar of Preserves" demonstrates many features, from quickly performed successive transformations to the use of Paste In Front and Paste In Back to simulate three-dimensional graphics. Artist Gail Blumberg also used the rotate tool with individual letters to rotate them around the jar's label. Another technique is to use the path-type tool to set the baseline of text according to the shape of a path.

The example also includes the use of a file of standard gray shaded images that can be scaled in any direction and used for filling areas of other illustrations. Gray shading was accomplished with a one-time use of the airbrush technique with finer gradations used in gray-shade templates designed for the LaserWriter printer and the Linotronic 100 and 300 imagesetters.

Painting with color is introduced at the end of this chapter, with a description of "The Nurse" (Plate 2) by artists at Adobe Systems. Adobe Illustrator can show colors on a color monitor, which can be adjusted for room lighting and individual characteristics to match printed colors (see Preferences, Color Matching, File menu, in Chapter 5). On black and white monitors, the program displays different colors as patterns. You can use either type of monitor to assign colors to paths. Process colors can be freely mixed, or you can select a PMS color if you open a document that has PANTONE color assignments (such as the supplied PANTONE documents). You can also premix process colors under a new name to be listed in the Custom Color list, and rename PMS colors for this list.

For more on using color and Adobe Illustrator's color tools (blend, gradient fill, paint bucket and eyedropper), creating color separations, trapping, and printer preparations, read on through Chapter 4. See also the tool sections in Chapter 5.

4

Advanced Techniques

Adobe Illustrator can make art departments and publishing efforts far more productive than they have ever been. In addition to the power to trace scanned images, the program also provides the flexibility to incorporate pieces or entire drawings in other drawings, to produce color separations, and to make the archival recording of drawings routine and therefore less prone to casualties.

Artists can start with an automatic trace or use the freehand tool, then transform shapes with the mouse or with the precision of the dialog boxes. When specifying a uniform scale for the artwork, you have the option of scaling or preserving the line weights of strokes.

Combine these capabilities with the ability to trace templates that can be scanned images or sketches, and the ability to add formatted text in fonts and perform PostScript effects, and you have a fantastic tool for artists, designers, and illustrators.

Technical publications departments will especially like the feature of automatically tracing scanned images, because this method may be the best way to convert old images into Illustrator graphics. All of the previous examples were based on scanned templates. However, you can also draw without using a template simply by measuring points in your sketch or original image and using the ruler to precisely place those points.

Dean Dapkus drew "Eyeball" from thumbnail sketches derived from biology texts. "Once you know how to use the zoom tool to analyze and edit details, and the shortcuts for drawing [the reflect, rotate, shear, and scale tools], there isn't anything difficult about working without a template."

Scaling or Preserving Line Weights

In traditional technical art drawing, artists have to draw diagrams and illustrations at a large scale and then reduce the art photographically. Line weights are automatically scaled with the rest of the art. This means that you have to take the final reduction percentage into consideration before drawing a single line.

With Adobe Illustrator, you can scale either one path, a group of paths forming an object (or part of an object), or an entire illustration, and have the choice of scaling or preserving the line weights. Artists especially appreciate the choice of preserving line weights on drawings with hairlines so that when the art is reduced, the lines don't disappear. On the other hand, with a finished drawing that looks good the way it is, scaling the line weight with the art will preserve the look of the drawing. The thinnest line your printer may be able to reproduce is a .25 point line, but you can enter a line weight of as little as 0 pt (which produces a line that is one pixel wide), in the Paint Style dialog box. You can access the Paint Style dialog box by selecting either Paint Style from the Object menu, or Show Paint Style from the Window menu.

When you drag to scale, the line weights are preserved (not scaled). To get the option of scaling or preserving line weights, you must use the Scale dialog box rather than the drag method of scaling. After selecting the object you want to scale and the scale tool, hold down the Option key

The Eye

1. Lens
2. Conjuctiva
3. Iris
4. Pupil
5. Cornea
6. Sclera

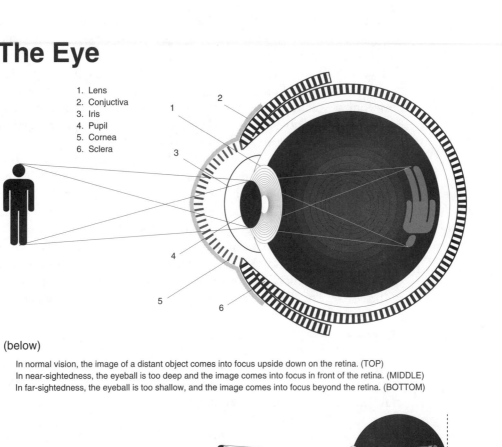

(below)

In normal vision, the image of a distant object comes into focus upside down on the retina. (TOP)
In near-sightedness, the eyeball is too deep and the image comes into focus in front of the retina. (MIDDLE)
In far-sightedness, the eyeball is too shallow, and the image comes into focus beyond the retina. (BOTTOM)

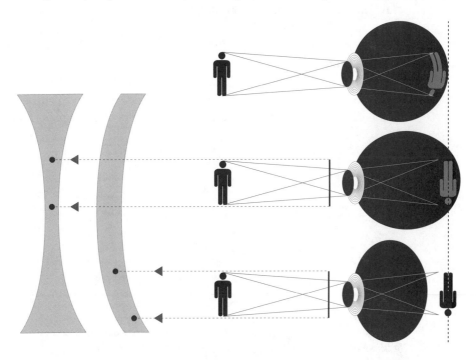

while clicking a scale origin point. Alternatively, you can double-click the scale tool to choose the scale dialog box, and use the center point as the scale origin point.

The Scale dialog box lets you enter a scale factor as a percentage for uniform scaling (scaling in proportion), and gives you the choice of preserving or scaling line weights by the same percentage. You can't scale line weights with non-uniform scaling, in which the image is scaled in uneven proportion for deliberate distortion.

Dean Dapkus started "Eyeball" by drawing concentric circles, and repeating a transformation that used a precise scale percentage. First he used the oval tool while holding the Shift key to draw a circle, then he selected that circle, clicked the scale tool, and held down Option while clicking the focal point (Figure 4-1) to get the Scale dialog box.

In the Scale dialog box, he typed a percentage under 100% for a uniform reduction (Figure 4-2), and unchecked the option to scale line weights. He then clicked Copy to produce a reduced copy and preserve the first circle. The reduction percentage was consistent for the remaining circles, so Dean could use Command-D to repeat the transformation to make each subsequent circle.

Dean used the same technique to draw the lens of the eye: first he drew an ellipse for the outer edge of the lens using the oval tool, then he reduced a copy of the ellipse and repeatedly pressed Command-D to draw the concentric ellipses (Figure 4-3).

Line Caps and Joins

Dean drew the human symbol based on the American Institute of Graphic Arts (AIGA) symbol used by the Department of Transportation

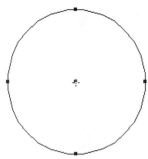

Figure 4-1.
Clicking the focal point for the scale operation, while simultaneously holding down Option to get the Scale dialog box (next figure).

for men's bathrooms and other signs. (The Man symbol is included in T/Maker's ClickArt EPS Series.) He used round line caps and joins which can be set in the Paint Style dialog box (Figure 4-4).

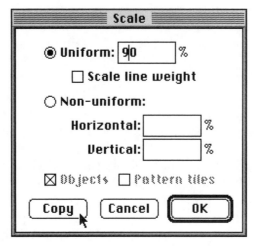

Figure 4-2.
Scaling precisely with the Scale dialog box, which provides the option to scale line weights (default settings are shown, with a change in the scale percentage).

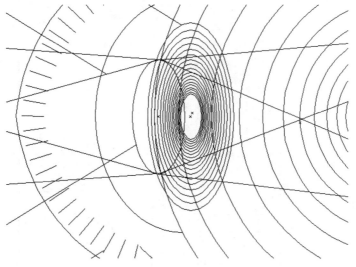

Figure 4-3.
The lens of the eye is made up of many concentric ellipses drawn using Repeat Transform to repeat a scaling and cloning operation.

The line cap choices affect the endpoints of open paths and dashed lines. The line join choices affect the corners of paths that are stroked (it has no effect on unstroked paths or points where paths intersect). Figures 4-5 and 4-6 show examples of line caps and joins.

The default setting for line cap is the butt cap (at the top). If you don't change it, the butt line cap uses squared-off ends perpendicular to the path. The middle choice, round cap, creates a half-moon cap in which the diameter equals the line width. The projecting cap (bottom) offers square ends that extend half of the line width beyond the end of the line.

The default line join is a miter join (at top), in which the edges of the intersecting strokes are extended until they meet in a point. The middle choice is the round join, which connects corners in a circular arc with a diameter equal to the line width. You would use both round caps and round joins because round joins do not fit well with squared-off butt caps. The bottom choice is the bevel join, which connects corners with squared-off ends.

Miter joins can be modified by the miter limit setting, which is active if you select the miter join choice (Figure 4-7). When two lines intersect at a sharp angle, a miter corner extends a spike that is controlled by the miter limit ratio. The higher the ratio, the sharper the corner (Figure 4-8). You can select a ratio between 1 and 500, depending on the weight (Width) of the lines, with the default of 4x corresponding to a square

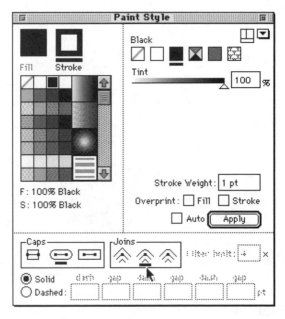

Figure 4-4.
The line cap and join styles are set to round for the human icon.

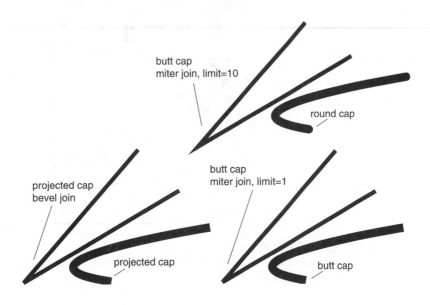

Figure 4-5.
Examples of line cap and join styles.

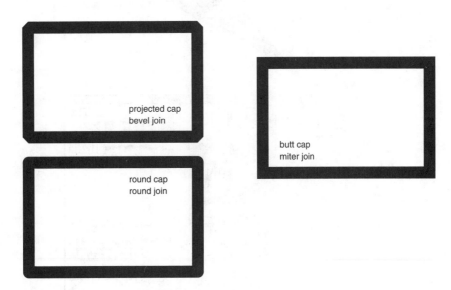

Figure 4-6.
Bevel joins with projecting caps work best with rectangular corners.

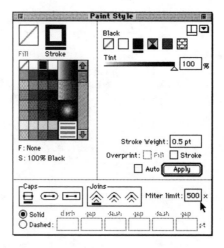

Figure 4-7.
After selecting a miter join, you can set the miter limit to 500, which is the sharpest miter limit ratio.

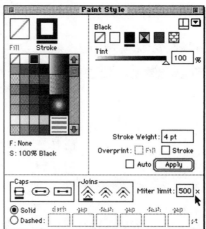

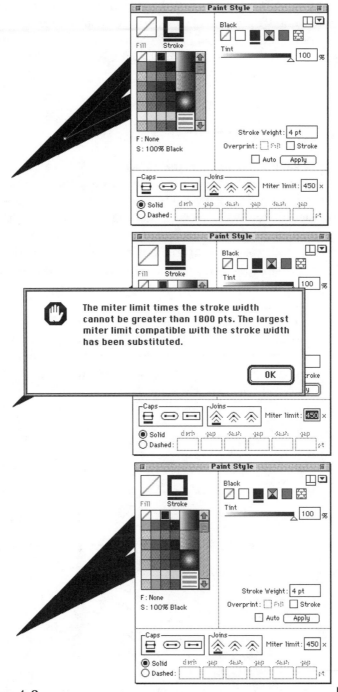

Figure 4-8.
A preview of a miter corner with two four-point lines and a miter limit ratio of ten.

corner (bevel join) when the length of the point reaches 4 times the line weight. If the length of the point is less than 4 times the line weight, a miter join is used. A miter join set to a limit of 500x would result in very long spiked corners for lines joined at small angles. A miter join set to a limit of 1 results in a bevel (squared-off) corner.

Multiple Transformations

To draw the many lines that look like spokes of a wheel that make up the outside edge of the eyeball, Dean drew the first line (see Figure 4-9), then selected it for rotation. He chose the rotate tool and held down the Option key while clicking the point of rotation at the center of the concentric circles, in order to use the Rotate dialog box. An alternative method is to first select the object to be rotated, and then double click the rotate tool, in order to use the Rotate dialog box.

In the Rotate dialog box (Figure 4-10), he specified a fractional percentage based on the number of lines divided into the 360 degrees total. He left the Pattern tiles option unchecked, since he was not using a pattern. This option lets you specify whether or not the pattern tiles (if any) used in a shape should also be rotated. To rotate only the pattern tiles, without rotating the object, you would check the Pattern tiles option and uncheck the Objects option. We describe pattern tiles later in this chapter.

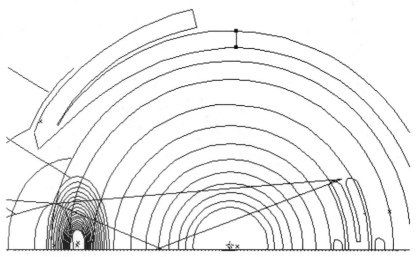

Figure 4-9.
The first line to clone and rotate to make the outer edge of the eyeball.

Dean clicked the Copy button to produce a duplicate while rotating and preserving the first line. The result was a duplicate line rotated slightly to the left (counterclockwise) of the first line. Positive-degree rotations are counterclockwise; to specify a clockwise rotation, subtract the degree of rotation from 360 degrees and use this figure as the degree of rotation.

After clicking the Copy button, the program remembered the transformation so that Dean could repeat it quickly by pressing Command-D (Figure 4-11) to repeat the transformation. After pressing Command-D about one hundred times, Dean had completed the ring of lines.

To bend the human icon to fit the curves of the concentric circles, Dean reflected the shape directly across a horizontal axis to create a mirror clone of the shape that was turned upside down, then changed the lines of the shape to curves while moving points to adjust the curves.

With the reflect tool, you can click to establish a focal point on the axis of reflection, or drag in a circular motion around the focal point to establish an area in which the program can calculate the axes by bisecting the angle between the starting position of the drag and the ending position. By holding down the Option key while dragging, you create a clone that is a mirror image of the original, reflected along the axis.

You can also reflect an image quickly over a horizontal or vertical axis, or an axis defined as a degree relative to the current x and y axes. After selecting the image to reflect, choose the reflect tool and hold down the Option key, or choose the reflect-dialog tool by dragging to the right of the reflect tool, and click a focal point for the reflection.

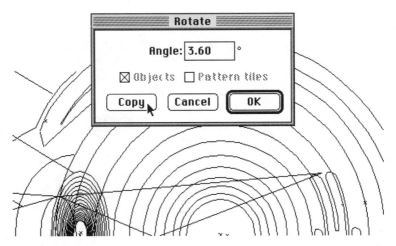

Figure 4-10.
The Rotate dialog box lets you specify a precise angle, and the Copy button creates a clone as part of the transformation.

The Reflect dialog box appears (Figure 4-12), and you can select a horizontal, vertical, or angled axis, and click the Copy button to make a copy of the reflected image.

You can also specify whether or not the pattern tiles (if any) used in the shape should also be reflected.

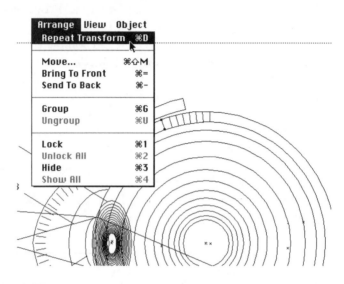

Figure 4-11.
Repeating the transformation with Repeat Transform (Command-D) to create the outer layer.

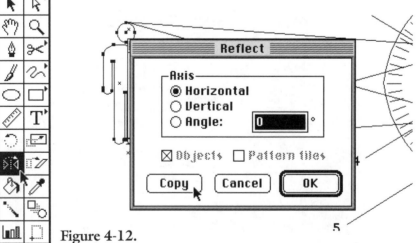

Figure 4-12.
The Reflect dialog box lets you specify a horizontal, vertical, or angled axis of reflection as well as the option to reflect pattern tiles and objects, or just pattern tiles.

If you uncheck the Objects box, and you check the Pattern tiles box, then only the pattern tiles will be refelected. We describe pattern tiles later in this chapter.

The reflection does not change the shape. To bend the human icon shape to the curves of the concentric circles, Dean had to replace line segments with curved segments. Fortunately his method of drawing the human icon made this editing change easy. "I tried to use as few points as possible to draw the human icon. With the exception of the head, hands and balls of his feet, and his shoulders, he was made of straight lines, and each of these lines had two definition points. I made the straight reflected image, then selected the straight lines, and drew them over as curves."

Figure 4-13 shows the reflected human shape placed in the inner eye image. Dean first selected the line segment, then deleted it and drew the segment as a curve. Figure 4-14 shows how he fine-tuned the curves to match the curves of the concentric circles — by dragging the direction points.

Drawing With Perspective

Normally when you draw shapes such as rectangles and circles, you are drawing along standard x and y axes parallel to the sides of your display.

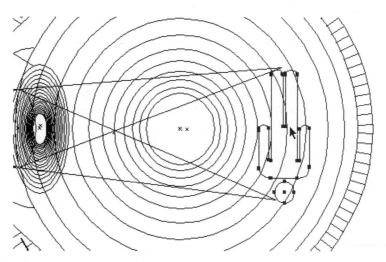

Figure 4-13
The human icon shape after the reflection, placed in the inner eye before editing.

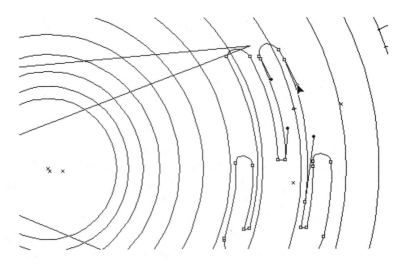

Figure 4-14.
The human icon shape, composed of straight lines, is edited to be composed of curves that are adjusted to the concentric circles.

By holding down the Shift key, you can move or transform shapes straight up or down, sideways, or constrained to increments of 45 degrees — these are based on the standard x and y axes.

However, you can also change the axes orientation that determines these angles by changing the constrain angle in the Preferences General dialog box, available in the File menu. The horizontal and vertical (x and y) axes are usually parallel to the sides of your window, but you can change them to any orientation, then constrain all movements to that orientation. For example, you can rotate the axes so that when you draw rectangles (or squares), ovals (or circles), text objects, gradient vectors (drawn with the gradient tool) and graphs, and when you constrain movements or transformations, the result is angled according to the new axes. Objects already drawn remain at the axes orientation they were created at.

The constrain angle does not affect rotation, blending, or drawing with the auto trace or pen tools.

To add to the "Mazda" artwork, Keith Ohlfs changed the constraining axes in the Preferences dialog box, in which he could specify an angle that is counterclockwise from the standard x and y axes (Figure 4-15). He could then draw a rectangular shape constrained along the new axes (Figure 4-16), and shear it to match the shape already used in the drawing (Figure 4-17). By holding down the Shift key while drawing, the rectangle would be constrained to an angle that was a 45° multiple relative to the new constrain angle.

General Preferences

┌─Tool behavior ────────────────┐
Constrain angle: `124` °
Corner radius: `12 pt`
Freehand tolerance: `2` pixels
Auto Trace gap: `0` pixels
─ ─ ─ ─ ─ ─ ─ ─ ─ ─ ─ ─ ─ ─ ─ ─
☒ Snap to point
☐ Transform pattern tiles
☐ Scale line weight
☒ Area select
☐ Use precise cursors

Ruler units: `Points/Picas ▼`
Indent/shift units: `Inches ▼`

┌─Keyboard increments─────┐
Cursor key: `1 pt`
Size/leading: `0.028 in`
Baseline shift: `0.028 in`
Tracking: `20` /1000 em

┌─Edit behavior─────────────┐
Undo levels: `10`
☐ Paste remembers layers

Greek text limit: `0.083 in`

(Cancel)   (OK)

File Edit Arrange View

New ⌘N
Open... ⌘O

Close ⌘W
Save ⌘S
Save As...

Place Art...
Import Styles...

Document Setup... ⌘⇧D
Page Setup...
Print... ⌘P

Preferences ▶ General... ⌘K
Color Matching...
Quit ⌘Q Hyphenation Options...
Plug-ins...

Figure 4-15.
Changing the constrain axes counterclockwise from the standard x and y axes by setting a new Constrain angle, so that all constrained movements and transformations follow the new constrain axes.

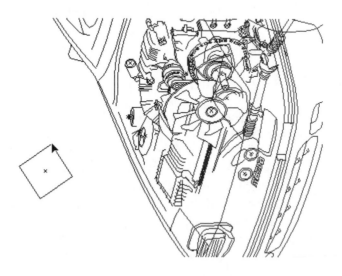

Figure 4-16.
Drawing a rectangle with the new constrain axes.

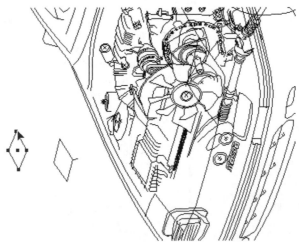

Figure 4-17.
Shearing the rectangle with the Shift key to use the new constrain axes for control.

Plate 6 ("The Car") shows extensive use of constraining for perspective drawing, which helped the artist draw the lines in the seat cushions, the lines defining the car body, the shapes for the open car doors (changing the constraining axes to change the perspective), and drawing the ovals for the tires.

By using slanted constraining axes, you can draw a complex image to perspective and keep your geometric shapes accurate. You can also use the shear tool to slant the image along different axes. The constraining axes also affect the angle of the baseline of text typed with the text tool.

Drawing in Layers

When an illustration has a lot of detail and cut-away views of interior construction, as with Keith Ohlfs' "Mazda," you have to dissect the image into layered objects. "You begin to think of things as all being layered on top of each other," says Keith about starting a complex illustration, "so you draw the background first, then draw the layers you want to be on top."

PostScript automatically masks objects that overlap one another, so that the part of an object that is underneath another object does not print. It is like painting with non-transparent pieces of paper for each shape (even though the shapes in the artwork view are transparent). If you ever have any doubt that two shapes overlap, choose the Preview option to see what will happen when the illustration is printed.

Illustrator also lets you draw two paths that intersect to form a "hole"

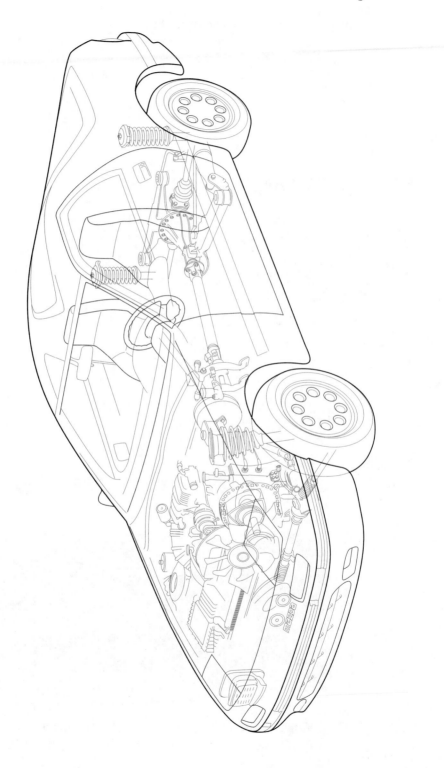

in which the underlying layer shows through. Such paths are called *compound* paths. You create compound paths by drawing two paths, so that the intersection of the paths forms the hole (Figure 4-18). Then

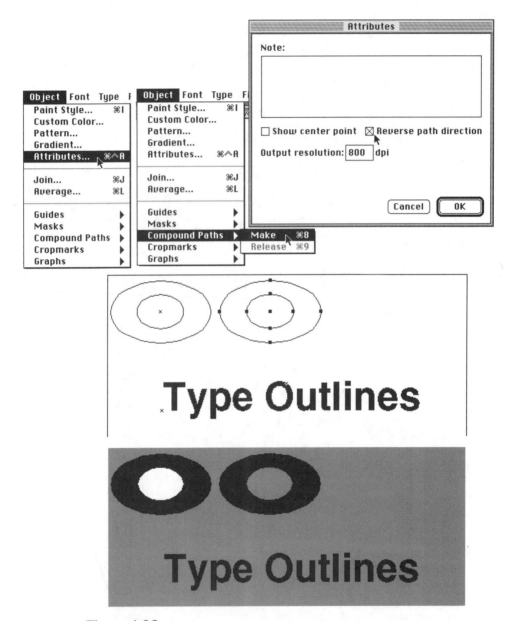

Figure 4-18.
Using Make Compound to turn the right doughnut into compound paths that intersect to form a hole. Note that type outlines contain compound paths.

select the two paths and choose Compound Paths and Make from the Object menu.

When drawing on a single layer, sometimes it helps to be able to hide or lock some of the artwork while drawing. You can hide objects temporarily so that they do not appear in the artwork view and can't be selected. Hiding objects can speed up performance if you are working on a large or complex project. You can also lock objects. This technique is useful if an object is too close to where you are drawing and you don't want to accidentally select it.

To hide objects, select the objects (usually one or more paths or groups), and choose the Hide command from the Arrange menu (Command-3). If you select some anchor points or segments (only part of a path), or only some paths of grouped objects, the entire path or group will be hidden. Alternatively, if you hold down the Option key while choosing Hide, all *unselected* objects are hidden, leaving only the selected objects showing. Hiding does not change an object in any way. Hidden objects do not display or print, but the objects do not remain hidden if you close and reopen the document.

To show all objects, use the Show All command in the Arrange menu (Command-4).

To lock objects, select the objects (usually one or more paths or groups), and choose the Lock command from the Arrange menu (Command-1). Alternatively, if you hold down the Shift key while choosing lock, all *unselected* objects are locked, leaving only the selected objects unlocked. Locking does not change an object in any way. Locked objects cannot be moved or transformed, but the objects do not remain locked if you close and reopen the document.

To unlock all objects, use the Unlock All command in the Arrange menu (Command-2).

Note: The Show All and Unlock All commands show and unlock all objects in the artwork. To show or unlock only the selected objects, hold down the Option key and select Show All (Option-Command-2), or Unlock All (Option-Command-4) from the Arrange menu.

Drawing Complex Illustrations

Complex illustrations usually require precision as well as detail. Illustrator provides various methods of aligning objects, measuring distances, and moving objects.

For example, when you use the measure tool, the measurement is remembered and supplied as the default measurement for the next Move, so that when you choose the Move command, the numbers are already entered in the dialog box.

The distance and angles measured by the measure tool are displayed in the Info palette (Show Info command in the Window menu), which you can hide, or position anywhere on your display screen.

However, if you use Copy or Paste, or another command that moves or copies a selection, before doing a Move operation, the distance and angle values measured with the measure tool will not be remembered.

You can change the ruler origin point (where the zero appears on each ruler) by dragging the crosshairs in the right bottom corner where the rulers intersect to a new location. You can drag non-printing ruler guides from the ruler (horizontal and vertical dotted lines) to help align objects. When Snap to Point is activated (in the Preferences General dialog box), you can attach objects or points to the guides by coming within a few pixels of the guide.

You can also turn any object into a guide object, so that the object itself acts as a guide. Select the object and choose Make Guide from the Object menu (Command-5). To lock the guides, select Guides and Lock from the Object menu (Command-7). To release guides, choose Release All Guides from the Object menu (Command-6).

Technical illustrators usually have to choose a line weight that will be scaled when the entire image is scaled, but Keith discovered that he could draw the entire "Mazda" artwork using one line weight (and no fill). He then fine-tuned the image and changed some of the lines, such as the outer edges of the car body, to a thicker line weight. "It was really simple [to change line weights], and it's a great example of how a technical illustration can be done without worrying about line weights."

Keith found it easier to work on "Mazda" in sections, then join the sections as the last step. He started with the background detail, and the last object he drew was the outline. To work out the detail, Keith used the zoom tool to magnify the drawing. "You can zoom in [to the artwork] to make a little, very complicated part of a drawing almost a drawing by itself."

The "Mazda" artwork took about 12 to 16 hours to finish (using an earlier version of Adobe Illustrator). Although this may seem a long time, it would take a lot longer using conventional methods.

It may take a while to learn all the tricks and techniques of using Adobe Illustrator, but these techniques can be utilized over and over, and pieces of the artwork can be reused, scaling or preserving line weights. As Keith described his efforts, "I would never try to do these illustrations with a pen and ink. Only Illustrator makes it possible to do them."

Color Separations

Adobe Separator™ 5.0

Adobe Illustrator files can be separated by the Adobe Separator program (supplied in the Separator & Utilities folder). You can produce four-color and custom separations, and choose various options including the page size, orientation, type of emulsion, positive or negative, and the halftone screen ruling in lines per inch. Adobe Systems provides PostScript Printer Description (PPD) files for various printers and imagesetters, so that separations are produced with the best possible control settings.

When designing color artwork, you first need to understand the printing process you will use, so that your artwork can be properly reproduced by a printing press. To assure success before producing final film, ask your printer to look at a color proof and tell you whether the piece can be reproduced without problems on press. The benefit of using Adobe Illustrator is that if your printer tells you the artwork won't reproduce well and describes the changes needed (such as larger or bold type), you can quickly modify the artwork before producing the negatives, and the final art will print properly, saving time, money, and aggravation.

For Plate 1 ("Flowchart") a separation consisting of four pieces of film (one for each process color) was produced by the Adobe Separator program. Each piece of film contained the necessary elements to ensure proper registration and color control on press.

When you start Adobe Separator, a dialog box asks for the name of an Encapsulated PostScript file (Figure 4-19). Illustrations saved by Adobe Illustrator are PostScript files, and you can also select PostScript files from other applications.

Adobe Separator offers the capability to preview the Illustrator image, but this capability works only with Illustrator files that have been saved with a preview format. Illustrator offers five different preview format options when you use the Save or Save As command, including two formats for the Macintosh. Use the Color Macintosh Preview option for the best results with the Separator preview capability. You can also use the Black & White Macintosh Preview option with Adobe Separator.

After choosing the PostScript file, the program asks for a Post-Script Printer Description file. The PPD file contains specific device information for Adobe Separator including the resolution, available page sizes, color support, and acceptable screen rulings. You should always use the appropriate PPD file for the device you are using.

After clicking OK for the PPD file, Adobe Separator displays a

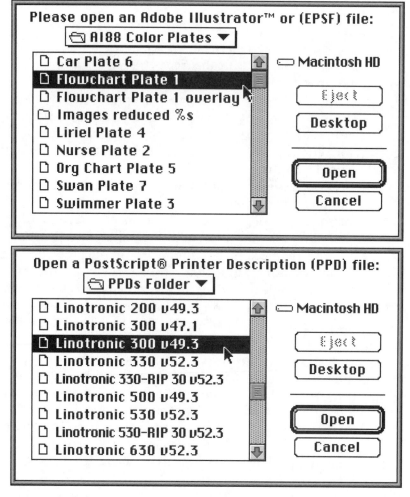

Figure 4-19.
*Opening an Encapsulated PostScript file (an Illustrator document) with
the Adobe Separator program, and choosing a PostScript Printer Description file for the device you are using to create the separations (Linotronic
300 chosen).*

preview image and various output settings and choices (Figure 4-
20). You can switch PPD and PostScript files for convenience in
producing multiple separations.

The program displays a dotted line representing the dimensions of
the artwork's bounding box. The bounding box is defined in
PostScript units (points), and represents the outside dimensions of
an illustration (the smallest rectangle that could be dragged over all

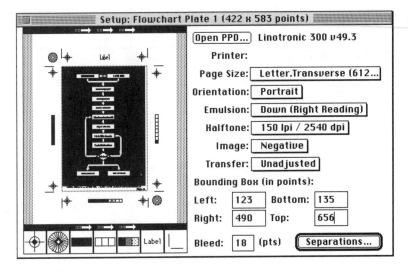

Figure 4-20.
*Adobe Separator displays a preview image for changing the bounding box,
setting crop marks and registration targets, and changing other settings
and various options for output (Linotronic 300 defaults shown).*

printing pieces of the artwork). You can adjust this bounding box by
dragging on the dotted line from any edge or corner, or by typing the
desired values in the Left:, Right:, Bottom:, and Top: boxes.

Crosshair register marks, trim marks (crop marks), labels, color
and gray bars, a black overprint color bar, and star targets are
provided as icons that can be dragged onto the preview image. These
bars, targets, and marks are printed just outside the bounding box,
so that printers can align the pieces of film and position the image on
the page. They should always appear outside the trim area, are
required by most print shops, and should be left on the film.
Crosshair register marks (the most common type of mark) are usually
placed two at each corner of the page. The star target is also a type of
register mark. Although harder to match up than crosshair register
marks, star targets are more accurate, and at least two should be used (as
well as crosshair register marks, which printers prefer) whenever the
tightest registration possible is necessary.

You can get information about the illustration by choosing the Get
Info command from the File menu (Figure 4-21). You can also print this
information, which is useful when sending files to an imagesetting
service. Included is information about the fonts, placed EPS illustrations,
patterns (if any), and bounding box.

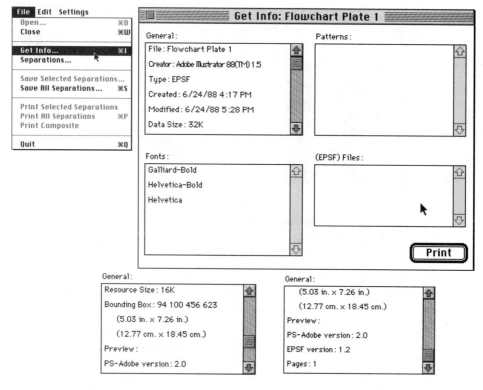

Figure 4-21.
The Get Info box shows information about the illustration to be separated, including the bounding box dimensions, the fonts, any patterns or placed EPS files, and the date it was last modified.

The page size option includes the dimensions (in points) of the page (Figure 4-22). Page sizes are listed by name or by dimensions, which define the printable area for the separation (including space for trim marks and registration targets). For some devices you can specify a custom page size and an offset to move the page away from the right edge of the printed sheet. The maximum page size you can use depends on the imageable area setting of the target print device, and also the resolution setting (halftone line screen) if your image is very large or complex. For example, the Linotronic 300 can accommodate a larger page size (up to the maximum imageable size) if the resolution is lowered in a very large or very complex image.

The page orientation can be set to Portrait or Landscape. Portrait is the usual setting for illustrations in which the top should be parallel with the short side. Landscape orientation prints the illustration's top in parallel with the long side.

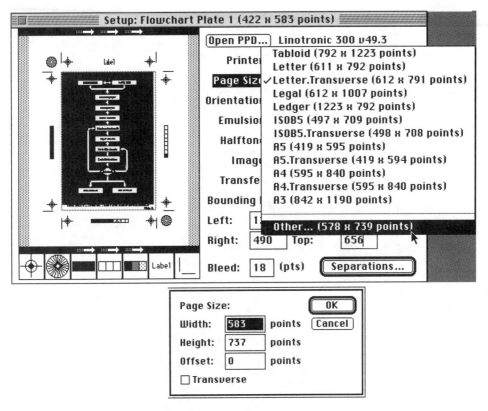

Figure 4-22.
Changing the page size in Adobe Separator.

The emulsion type you choose (Figure 4-23) depends on your printer's requirements. Emulsion, the sensitive layer on film or paper, can be up (readable when facing at you) or down (readable when facing away from you). Illustrations printed on paper are usually set to have emulsion side up, and film separations are usually set to have emulsion side down. You can also choose to print a positive or negative image (usually set to negative for film separations). If you need to produce separations, you should use film since it cuts out one step in the production process and avoids image degradation problems that may occur by shooting screened images.

The halftone screen ruling (Figure 4-24) defines the number of halftone dots per inch, referred to as lines per inch (lpi). A higher screen ruling (usually produces a better separation, but requires a high resolution device such as a Linotronic 300 set to 2540 dpi. Not all presses can hold a 150 lpi halftone screen produced by the Linotronic 300 set to 2540 dpi. If you use a halftone screen that is too fine for the press to

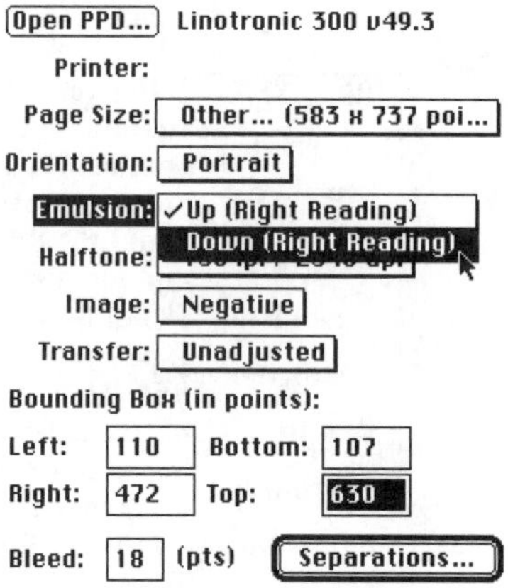

(Open PPD...) Linotronic 300 v49.3

Printer:

Page Size: [Other... (583 x 737 poi...]

Orientation: [Portrait]

Emulsion: [✓Up (Right Reading)]
　　　　　　 [Down (Right Reading)]

Halftone:

Image: [Negative]

Transfer: [Unadjusted]

Bounding Box (in points):

Left: [110] 　 Bottom: [107]

Right: [472] 　 Top: [630]

Bleed: [18] (pts) 　 (Separations...)

Figure 4-23.
*Adobe Separator offers two emulsion choices for Linotronic 300 film
separations: emulsion side up or down (both right reading).*

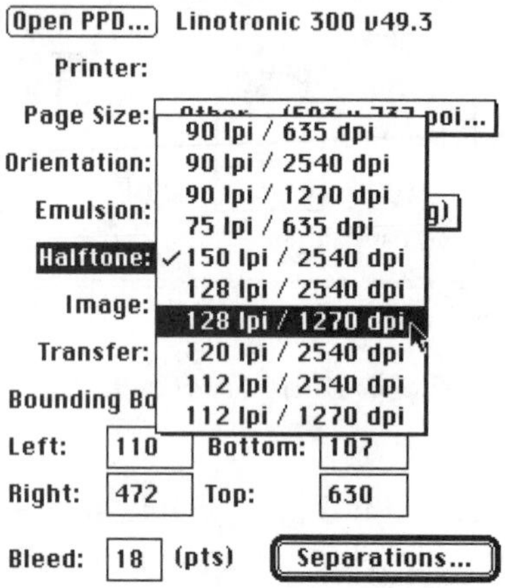

(Open PPD...) Linotronic 300 v49.3

Printer:

Page Size:
Orientation:
　　　　　　 90 lpi / 635 dpi
　　　　　　 90 lpi / 2540 dpi
Emulsion:　 90 lpi / 1270 dpi
　　　　　　 75 lpi / 635 dpi
Halftone: ✓150 lpi / 2540 dpi
　　　　　　 128 lpi / 2540 dpi
Image:　　 128 lpi / 1270 dpi
　　　　　　 120 lpi / 2540 dpi
Transfer:　 112 lpi / 2540 dpi
Bounding Bo 112 lpi / 1270 dpi

Left: [110] 　 Bottom: [107]

Right: [472] 　 Top: [630]

Bleed: [18] (pts) 　 (Separations...)

Figure 4-24.
*Setting the halftone screen ruling in lines per inch to 128 (most print shops
can't print rulings finer than 150 lpi).*

reproduce, your image may lose highlights and contrast on press. Lost
contrast is due to dark areas plugging up with ink. Highlights may fade
away, due to the lightest dots being too small to reproduce. A laser printer
or other lower resolution printer reproduces a smaller number of grays,
and a coarser halftone screen (60-85 lpi) is best. In some cases, you have
a choice of resolutions for a particular line screen. Be sure that you choose
a halftone screen value that also uses the resolution value used by your
printer.

You can specify a bleed area, which is an area of the image outside the printed area used as a margin, so that colors are filled to the edge properly, after the page has been trimmed to its final size.

Bleed can be used only when the bounding box of the image is smaller than the actual image. The bounding box is used as the margin for adding crop marks (also called trim marks). The page bleeds if the image goes at least 1/4 inch or so beyond the crop marks on one or more sides. For example, an image which extends beyond the bounding box on three sides is called a three-sided bleed. Adobe Separator allows a minimum bleed of 0, and a maximum of 72 points (1 inch), with a default bleed of 18 points. Ask your printer to specify how much of a bleed margin is needed for your particular type of press, before you print to film.

Illustrator should be used to set crop marks, which you can then delete and reset in Adobe Separator. Illustrator places crop marks just outside the bounding box. You can release these (Cropmarks and Release in the Object menu) and make new ones by drawing a rectangle to define your trimmed page size, and then using the Make Cropmark command in the Object menu in Illustrator. Illustrator allows only one set of cropmarks. Adobe Separator allows you to reposition the crop marks farther from or closer to the artwork when you change the amount of bleed, without changing the bounding box and trim size/position. To set more than one set of crop marks, without affecting the bounding box and crop marks, use the Trim Marks filter in Illustrator.

Adobe Separator can also print other printer marks, such as crosshair register marks, star targets, progressive color bars, gradient tint bars, black overprint color bars, and labels. You can place and position these printer marks by dragging their respective icons into the preview window. To customize the text on a label, use the Separations button to access the Separations dialog box and the Label text field, where you can type the desired label text that will print on each piece of film. By default, the filename is used as the label text.

To reposition or delete printer marks, drag them to a new position, or off the page. However, if you drag the label off the page before printing color separations, your printer's prepress shop (and stripper) may not be able to tell which piece of film is for which color, because in addition to the filename or text you specify, the label prints the separation color and screen angle (plus line screen) for each piece of film.

The transfer function (Figure 4-25) lets you adjust tint values so that you can adjust Separator's output based on densitometer readings taken from the imagesetter. With appropriate settings, the transfer function helps ensure that the tint values in your separation will closely match the tint values you originally assigned to the illustration. To use the transfer

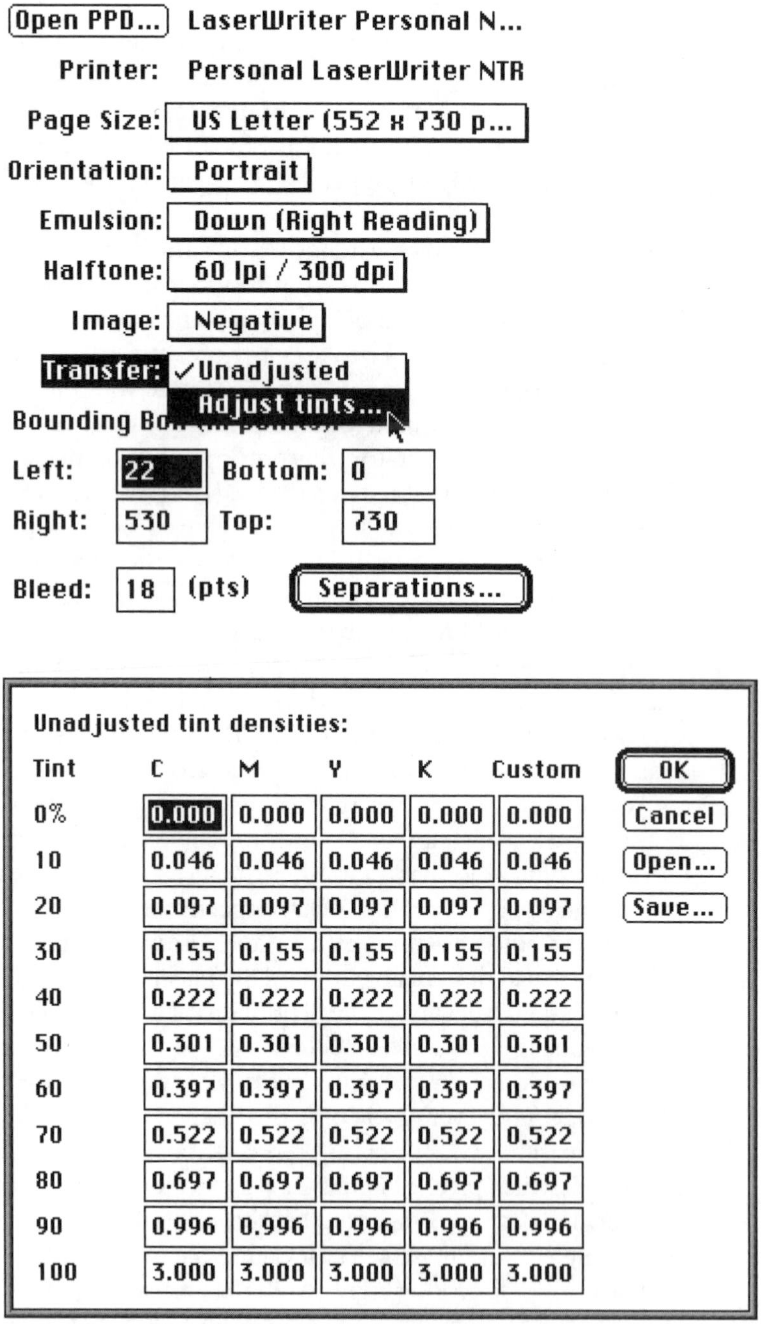

[Open PPD...] LaserWriter Personal N...

Printer: Personal LaserWriter NTR

Page Size: [US Letter (552 x 730 p...]

Orientation: [Portrait]

Emulsion: [Down (Right Reading)]

Halftone: [60 lpi / 300 dpi]

Image: [Negative]

Transfer: ✓ Unadjusted
Adjust tints...

Bounding Box (in points)

Left: [22] Bottom: [0]

Right: [530] Top: [730]

Bleed: [18] (pts) [Separations...]

Unadjusted tint densities:

Tint	C	M	Y	K	Custom	
0%	0.000	0.000	0.000	0.000	0.000	[OK]
10	0.046	0.046	0.046	0.046	0.046	[Cancel]
20	0.097	0.097	0.097	0.097	0.097	[Open...]
30	0.155	0.155	0.155	0.155	0.155	[Save...]
40	0.222	0.222	0.222	0.222	0.222	
50	0.301	0.301	0.301	0.301	0.301	
60	0.397	0.397	0.397	0.397	0.397	
70	0.522	0.522	0.522	0.522	0.522	
80	0.697	0.697	0.697	0.697	0.697	
90	0.996	0.996	0.996	0.996	0.996	
100	3.000	3.000	3.000	3.000	3.000	

Figure 4-25.
Adobe Separator provides a transfer function for adjusting the tint values according to densitometer readings of actual imagesetter output.

function, you must first print a separation negative of the Densitometer Control Chart EPSF file included with Separator. This file contains percentages of all four process colors, plus a custom color you can add — first open the file with Illustrator, assign percentages of the custom color to the designated areas of the chart, and save the file with a new name to open with Adobe Separator. After printing the chart negative to film, use a transmission-type densitometer to take a reading of each percentage square on the chart negative. Enter the densitometer readings into the Tint Adjustment chart that is displayed when you select the Transfer: Adjust tints option. If your service bureau has fresh chemistry in their developer and has calibrated their imagesetter for the day before running your film, you do not need to use the transfer adjustment option.

Adobe Separator lets you print all of the process color separations (cyan, magenta, yellow, and black) in one operation, or separately, or as a color comp to a color printer, or color comps are translated to grays. The Print All Separations command in the File menu lets you print separations for all four process colors and one for each custom color. Alternatively, custom colors and PMS colors can be converted into percentages of process colors automatically and included in the separations for the four process colors.

To convert a custom (including PMS, etc.) color to appropriate process color percentages, click the Convert To Process box next to that color's name in the list of custom colors, to toggle between the No and Yes options. The program automatically converts the custom or PMS color into process color percentages; to reverse the process click that color's Convert To Process box again.

Although custom colors should be converted since they are comprised of process colors, PMS colors may not appear the same after conversion to process colors, since process colors can only approximate PMS colors. Since the results differ depending on the imagesetting device, you must experiment or use a custom separation for each PMS color, or use Illustrator's Import Styles command to access the Pantone Process color system, that loads over 3000 CMYK combinations that can be used to generate Pantone color equivalents.

Importing the styles of the TRUMATCH color swatching system provides over 2000 computer created colors that cover the visible spectrum of the CMYK gamut in even steps, or the TRUMATCH COLORFINDER, including four-color grays, and 40 tints and shades of each hue.

The TOYO 88 Color Finder 1050 contains 1050 TOYO ink colors, some of which may not reproduce exactly — such colors are marked with one or two asterisks, and should be used sparingly (and for small areas of spot color), if at all.

Setting Type in Color

Many of the registration problems that occur with color separations are related to the fact that fast presses sometimes print slightly off-register. Type can be a problem if it is too thin. Black type prints best (sharp and crisp) on any type of press, and is usually the best color choice for small type sizes and for thin-stroked characters. However, web offset presses can have problems trying to register type that is too fine, or one pixel wide lines produced by an imagesetter.

Color Plate 1 ("Flowchart") has black type for the copyright notice and bold blue type in the flowchart boxes. It also has type (for "yes," "no," and "maybe") reversed-out from the background color which is larger than the copyright notice, and set in bold. Reversed type should be large and bold enough to avoid printing problems, such as characters breaking up or plugging up. Bold type is also easier to register on press and to read when the type or the background of reversed type is composed of more than one process ink color.

Color Plate 5 ("Organizational Chart" by Laura Lamar) also shows the use of colored text. The title, "ORGANIZATIONAL CHART," is not stroked (outlined), but is filled with color — 50 percent yellow, 35 percent magenta, and 90 percent cyan (Figure 4-26).

Type settings can be chosen directly from the Type menu, or you can set all characteristics in two dialog boxes by choosing the Character (Command-T) and Paragraph (Command-Shift-T) commands (Figure 4-27). (You can also choose to Show or Hide the Character and Paragraph palettes in the Window menu.)

Illustrator offers *tracking*, which is a method of inserting uniform spacing between more than two characters to space them further apart. You can specify a negative number for spacing to move characters closer together. Spacing is measured in 1/1000 of an em space, which is relative to the current font size.

Type attributes can be set before typing text and changed after typing text, and you can set attributes for several blocks of type simultaneously (if they are all selected).

If your type requires a special look or modification to its shape or serif, you should create outlines from type and then modify the characters, or draw the characters with the pen, brush, or freehand tool, perhaps starting with an automatic trace of scanned characters. Color Plate 4 ("Liriel" by Luanne Seymour Cohen) has a title composed of characters that were drawn rather than typed (Figure 4-28). The path created for each character has a fill of 40 percent magenta and 100 percent yellow and no stroke. Another reason for drawing text characters rather than

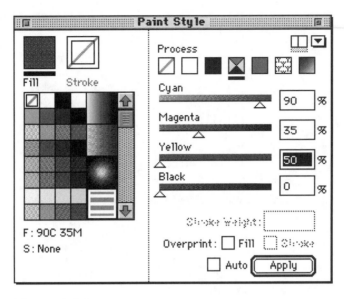

Figure 4-26.
*The Paint Style dialog box for the text "Organizational Chart" for Plate 5,
set to 90 percent cyan, 35 percent magenta, and 50 percent yellow for its fill
and no stroke.*

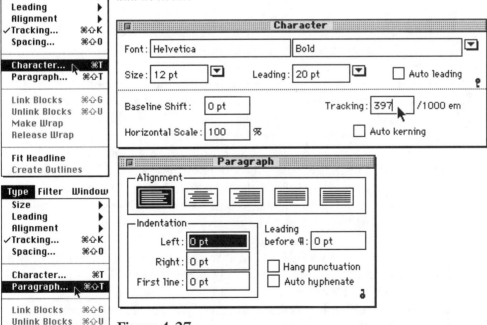

Figure 4-27.
*The Character and Paragraph palettes for the text "Organizational
Chart" for Plate 5, set to 12 point Helvetica Bold with 20 points of leading.
Tracking is also applied.*

Figure 4-28.
The title "Liriel" (Plate 4) was drawn rather than typed so that the characters have a unique shape.

typing the text with the text tool is that drawn character shapes can blend into other shapes, but you can't use the blend tool with typed characters. You can convert text into outlines with the Create Outlines command in the Type menu, and then use the outlines with the blend tool.

You don't have to draw the characters if you want to perform transformations such as rotating, scaling, shearing, or reflecting. Text placed with the type tool can be transformed, and its baseline will conform to whatever angle the x and y axes are set to in the constrain field of the General Preferences dialog box (Command-K). You can also change the line cap and join styles in the Paint Style palette (Command-I) for typed text. If you get long, sharp corner points with letters such as "M," "A," "V," and "W," change the join style to something other than a miter join, or lower the miter limit.

The white text below the title of "Liriel" was placed with the type tool, set to a specific point size and leading, and painted with a white fill and stroke. When "Liriel" was scaled down for color separations, the entire illustration was uniformly scaled, and the size of the type was also scaled. As a result, the type font size is defined in fractional points (Figure 4-29). If your illustrations will be scaled before printing them, choose text and line weights that will still print well after the image has been scaled.

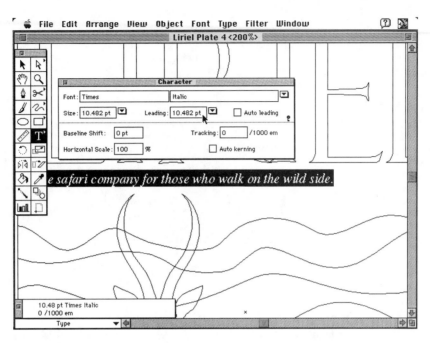

Figure 4-29.
Typed text can be scaled along with the rest of an illustration, and the actual point size may be fractional.

Trap and Overprinting

Adobe Illustrator provides precise control over the coloration of paths and strokes so that you can fine-tune images for print jobs on different presses. There are a host of problems that can occur in a press run, including registration problems in which the dots of ink do not fall precisely where they should and cause white to appear between two colors. Illustrator's overprint feature and black strokes can be used to "create trap" and prevent some of these problems.

When you draw painted objects that will overlap each other, you should draw the background first, then draw the layers you want to be on top. Alternatively you can draw the layers in any order, then use the Paste In Front and Paste In Back options to place layers on top of or underneath other layers.

PostScript automatically masks painted objects that overlap one another, so that the color that is underneath another color does not print. Color Plate 4 ("Liriel" by Luanne Seymour Cohen) shows

Figure 4-30.
The bright red path in "Liriel" (Plate 4) extends behind other paths colored to be reddish-purple and purple. When colored paths overlap, the color of the path on top is the color printed and displayed, unless you use the overprint feature.

how colors do not mix when they overlap. The path for the bright red hilltops (Figure 4-30) extends behind other colored paths (the reddish-purple and purple areas), which are on top of the bright red path. The bright red does not mix with the colors of the other path, unless you use the Overprint option in the Paint Style menu, but in most cases you will not want to mix the colors of two or more paths.

An exception to this guideline is that you should overprint 100 percent black strokes and fills with a four-color process black to prevent underlying or adjacent process ink colors from showing through. Your printer can tell you what percentage of each process color to use to compose the four-color black for a particular press type.

When there is a high probability that registration problems will occur and cause white to appear between two colors, you can use several different techniques to "create trap" to compensate for anticipated registration problems. One way is to apply a stroke with a heavy weight, as shown in "The Swan" (Color Plate 7) around the swan figures. Whenever colors meet at solid black lines, Adobe Separator automatically

Figure 4-31.
The swimmer shape (Plate 3) is stroked and filled with black, with color-filled shapes placed in front. Trap is automatically created between shapes due to the solid black lines.

creates the necessary trap. "The Swimmer" (Color Plate 3) is one interesting way to ensure trap with black lines: the basic swimmer shape is a path (Figure 4-31) that is stroked and filled with 100 percent black, then colored shapes are pasted in front of the swimmer shape.

Without black lines, you ensure trap by providing a bit of overlap. To create trap for a shape within another shape, specify a stroke for the inner shape in the same color as its fill. Usually a stroke line weight between 0.3 and 1 point is useful for creating trap, and Illustrator allows stroke widths between 0.6 and 2.0 points, which create traps of between .3 and 1 point. Then click the Overprint: Stroke box in the Paint Style palette (be careful — there is another Overprint box for the Fill that you should not click).

Although nothing appears different in the preview display, the overprint option allows color underneath the object to mix with the color of the object, thus creating a color somewhere between the two for the overlapping area. An overprinting stroke mixes its color with the color beneath it, preventing any separation between the two objects in print even if the registration is slightly off.

If two colored objects meet flush along a straight line, you can select the top-most object and check the Overprint option in the fill part of the Paint dialog box, then stretch the topmost object slightly, so that it overlaps the other object. If the objects don't meet in a straight line, you can create trap by specifying a stroke with overprint. If, however, an object needs trap only on a segment that overlaps another object, use the masking feature described later.

You don't need to use the overprint feature for 100 percent black lines, because Adobe Illustrator automatically overprints black. However, stroke tints of black must be overprinted if used for trapping. When a colored object is overprinted, the process colors that are common to it and the objects behind it are not affected and print normally; only the colors that are not in common are mixed.

Shapes that are 100 percent black are automatically overprinted by Adobe Separator over all other colors. If a large black area has two or more different colors behind it, you should add 15 to 30 percent cyan, magenta, and yellow to the black area. When two objects contain all four process colors, overprint does not affect them, but trapping is usually not necessary with such objects. In fact, when you have two objects that contain the same color, you probably don't need to create trap between them. When a lightly-colored object overlaps a darker object, create trap using strokes of the lighter object's color.

The eyedropper and paint bucket tools, as well as plug-in filters, can help you examine and adjust the colors in your artwork, and create both spread and choke traps. A spread trap enlarges the topmost object by stroking it with the fill color. The lighter object overprints a darker background. A choke trap strokes a dark object with the lighter background color.

Blending Colors and Tints

Adobe Illustrator can blend colors and tints as well as shapes. Plates 7 and 8 are examples of color and tint blending as well as shape blending, all created with the blend tool.

Blending works between two objects painted with process colors or custom colors, and between a PMS or custom color and a process color. Process colors are used for all intermediate shapes between any two colors. Tints are blended by percentage in the same color, whether it is a process or custom color.

In Color Plate 7 ("The Swan"), the outline "S" (from the Adobe Collector's Edition of non-text characters and other PostScript clip art

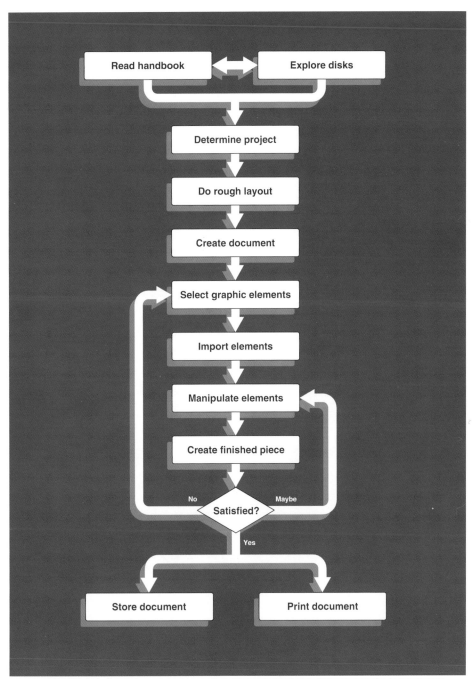

Plate 1.

Plate 2.

Plate 3.

The safari company for those who walk on the wild side.

Plate 4.

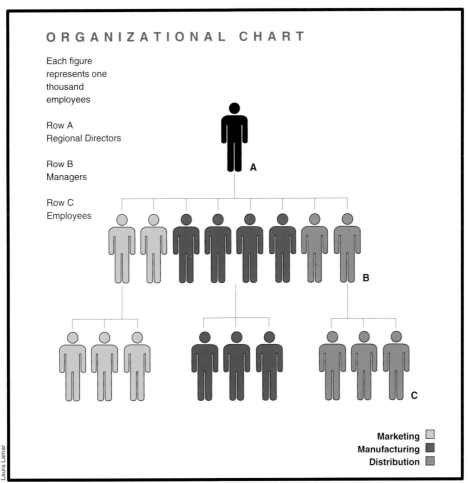

ORGANIZATIONAL CHART

Each figure represents one thousand employees

Row A
Regional Directors

Row B
Managers

Row C
Employees

A

B

C

Marketing
Manufacturing
Distribution

Plate 5.

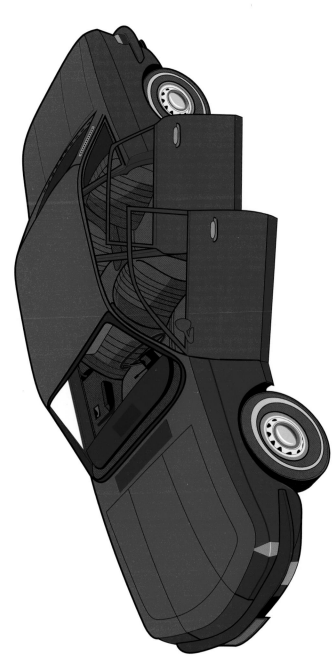

Plate 6.

Plate 7.

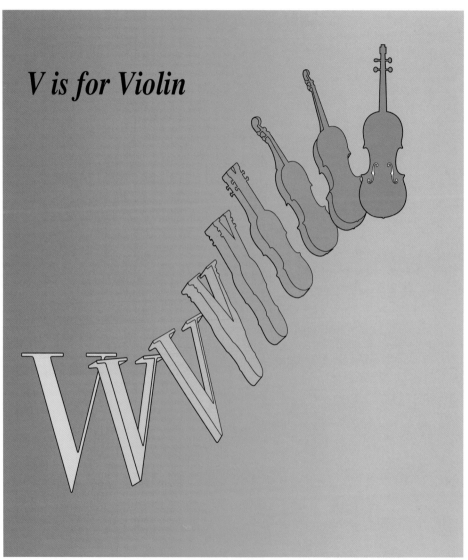

V is for Violin

Plate 8.

objects) is blended into the swan shape. Both object shape and color (fill) were blended. The outline of the letter has a beak shape overlaying its upper serif to correspond to the beak shape that appears at the other end of the blend.

The outline's fill is 100 percent cyan, 90 percent magenta, and 20 percent yellow, and it blends in four intermediate steps to a swan shape with seven percent cyan and no other colors. The first intermediate step is 81.4 percent cyan, 72 percent magenta, and 16 percent yellow, and the next is 62.8 percent cyan, 54 percent magenta, and 12 percent yellow. The third step is 44.2 percent cyan, 36 percent magenta, and eight percent yellow, and the fourth and last intermediate step is 25.6 percent cyan, 18 percent magenta, and four percent yellow.

The blend tool was also used to create the gradual color blend from left to right behind the "S" and the swan. In 194 steps, an ungrouped rectangle (Figure 4-32), painted 30 percent cyan, 40 percent magenta, and 50 percent yellow, was blended to another rectangle at the other end of the illustration painted with 1.4 percent cyan, 13.8 percent magenta, and 50 percent yellow (the yellow stayed at 50 percent for all intermediate steps).

Plate 7

Figure 4-32.
The color gradation background for "The Swan" (Plate 7) was created by blending the process colors of two rectangles; the "S" was blended into the swan shape and their colors were also blended.

The Blend dialog box displays the recommended number of steps to use for the blend, but any number (from 1-1000) you specify in the Blend dialog box for the number of steps determines the color and tint blending percentages. You can also change the percentages of the first and last intermediate steps in order to fine-tune the blending or produce special effects.

The cover of this book was designed using Adobe Illustrator by Louis Fishauf of Reactor Art & Design (Toronto, Canada), using mostly the blend tool to create the special effect with the number 5. Louis first used Adobe Dimensions to get the beveled look he wanted for the number 5. The 5 was then converted to an outline, and a black outer rectangle was created behind it. Points were then added to the rectangle by Louis to coincide with points on the number 5. The rectangle and number 5 were then blended, the points were adjusted, and the blend was tried again until the points were positioned exactly where he wanted them. See chapter 5 for more information on using the blend tool.

Paint bucket and Eyedropper

Adobe Illustrator lets you specify which paint style attributes to apply with the paint bucket tool, or to pick up with the eyedropper tool (see figure 5-84). Double-click either tool in the toolbox to display/change the attributes selected for both tools.

Clicking at a point in the artwork with the eydropper tool samples the point, as if you were drawing ink into an eyedropper, and updates the Paint Style palette to use the new Paint Style attributes for all new objects, until you either click with the eyedropper tool again to sample a new point, or change the Paint Style attributes.

Clicking at a point in the artwork with the paint bucket tool applies the current Paint Style attributes to the object or point you click.

To switch between these two tools quickly, hold down the Option key when using either tool to switch to the other tool.

To examine paint style attributes for many objects, first select the objects with a selection tool, or use Select All (Edit menu) and deselect unwanted objects. Use the Show Paint Style command in the Window menu to display the Paint Style palette. The attributes in common for the selected objects are displayed, and those not in common are displayed with Question marks and the description mixed, or are blank (see Figure 5-86).

To change the specified attributes for all selected objects at once, use the eyedropper tool to click a point which uses the desired attributes, then double-click at the point.

Gradients

Adobe Illustrator lets you fill paths (but not stroke paths) with gradients (blended shades of two or more colors), using the paint bucket tool or the Paint Style palette to assign either a radial or linear gradient fill. You can also use the gradient tool to adjust the colors, add colors, etc.

Use the Gradient command in the Object menu, or double-click on a gradient color name in the Paint Style dialog box to display the Gradient color bar, where you can set parameters for the gradient fill colors.

Assign the gradient fill color to objects that you have selected, or draw new ones that use the gradient fill. Then use the gradient fill tool to modify the gradient fill. For example, you can give a circle a 3-D ball effect by adjusting a radial fill to simulate a light source, by moving the highlights (light color) away from the center of the circle. The gradient fill tool is also useful when you want to spread a gradient across a word that has already had its individual characters filled with a gradient.

See the gradient tool section, the Gradient command (Object menu) section, and the Gradient palette (Window menu) section of chapter 5 for more information about assigning and adjusting gradient fills.

Custom Patterns

Adobe Illustrator lets you fill and stroke paths with a custom pattern. You can even stroke and fill type with a custom pattern. A pattern can be transformed with the shape, transformed separately, or remain the same while the shape is transformed. You can also move a shape and have the pattern move with it or have the pattern stay in the same place while the shape moves (as if the shape was a window exposing the stationary pattern).

A pattern is available for a document if it has been defined in that document or in another document that is open at the same time. A custom pattern is always stored with the document in which it was defined and in any document that uses the pattern as a fill or stroke. You can see the list of custom patterns stored with the documents that are currently open by choosing the Paint Style palette and clicking the Pattern button for either the fill or stroke. You can also see the pattern list by choosing the Pattern command from the Object menu.

Any pattern in the list can be used in any open document. If a pattern you want is not in the list, open a document that uses it, leaving your other document or documents open at the same time. The pattern name should appear in the list if it was saved with the newly opened document.

For example, if you want to use the pattern Meadow 1 in the "Pennsylvania" document, but Meadow 1 is so far saved only in the "California" document, simply open both documents and assign the Meadow 1 pattern to a shape in the "Pennsylvania" document. The result is that Meadow 1 is stored in both documents.

Alternatively, you can use the Import Styles command in the File menu to open the Patterns folder (stored in the Gradients and Patterns folder, supplied with Illustrator) and add patterns to your file.

To manage the use of many different patterns, it may help to create a document that contains all patterns (perhaps called "Patterns"), that you can leave open while opening other documents and applying patterns. Patterns remain stored with a document unless they are explicitly deleted in the Pattern dialog box. Another option is to create a document that contains all patterns, colors, and graph designs and name it *Adobe Illustrator Startup,* and place it in the same folder as the Illustrator program. Extensive use of complex patterns may cause printing problems, plus patterns require a lot of storage, so you should delete all unused patterns from your final art.

To create a pattern, simply draw an element of the pattern using Adobe Illustrator in a document (Figure 4-33). Paint the element as you would like it to appear in the pattern — we used 80 percent cyan and 90 percent yellow for the fill (a strong green), and no stroke.

Next, clone the element several times and place the clones in appropriate places (Figure 4-34). The placement of these elements is critical for achieving a uniform pattern — you may want to use the Shift key to constrain the movement of clones so that they are at specific angles from the main element. You can draw these elements at any size, then scale them later when you decide how large the pattern elements should be.

The next step is to define the pattern tile with a rectangle. The pattern tile acts as a masking object (more on masking later) that shows only the part of the pattern that is inside it. The rectangle must have perpendicular corners (be sure that the corner radius is zero in the Preferences dialog box). You can draw the rectangle with the rectangle tool or with the pen tool as long as the constraint angle set in the General Preferences dialog box is set to zero.

Pattern tiles are placed next to each other in the pattern, so draw a pattern tile rectangle so that the edges will match smoothly. You should make the pattern tile as small as possible to contain a few carefully placed elements (Figure 4-35). When you are drawing the pattern tile rectangle, imagine how the pattern will appear if the tiles are placed next to each other and in rows above and below it.

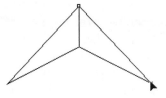

Figure 4-33.
Creating an element of a custom pattern just as you would create any other artwork. It is painted with a green fill and no stroke.

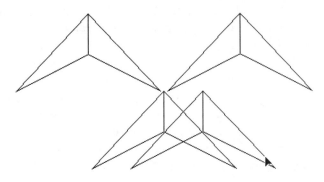

Figure 4-34.
Cloning the pattern element and placing the clones in appropriate places to create a custom pattern.

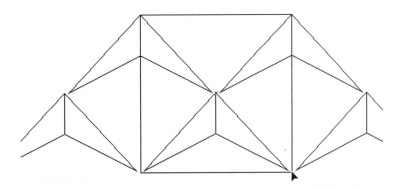

Figure 4-35.
Drawing the pattern tile rectangle to define the custom pattern; this rectangle acts like a masking object that shows only what is inside it.

The pattern tile rectangle must be behind the other objects in the pattern, so after drawing the rectangle, Cut it and use the Paste In Back option to paste it in back of the other objects. You should also paint the rectangle — whatever fill you apply to the rectangle becomes the pattern's background. If you specify no fill, the background will have no fill. You should always specify no stroke for the pattern tile rectangle, unless you want the pattern tile lines to be visible in the pattern.

We painted our pattern tile rectangle to have a slight yellow-green tint (the elements themselves are painted green) and no stroke. This fill becomes the color of the background of the pattern. We then Cut the rectangle and use Paste In Back to paste it behind the pattern elements.

The next step is to scale our pattern tile and pattern elements to the size we want for the defined pattern (Figure 4-36). You must select all pattern elements and the pattern tile rectangle and scale them together. You can do this by holding down Option while dragging a selection marquee with the selection tool. Scale the pattern tile and elements in any way you like, stretching, condensing, or scaling uniformly.

Finally, you can define the pattern by choosing Pattern from the Object menu (Figure 4-37), and click the New button. The name New Pattern 1 appears in the pattern list and in the change name field, and you can rename it by typing over this name (Figure 4-38). A preview of the pattern appears in the Pattern dialog box.

It sometimes helps to preview the artwork before scaling or before defining the artwork as a pattern. We drew another custom pattern of ovals and used the Preview option to see how they would appear in a pattern tile before defining the pattern (Figure 4-39). If you intend

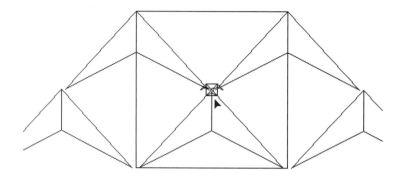

Figure 4-36.
Scaling the pattern tile and pattern elements at once to the size they should appear when defined as a pattern.

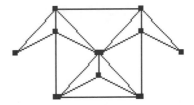

Figure 4-37.
With the pattern tile and elements still selected (after scaling them down to actual pattern size), choose the Pattern option.

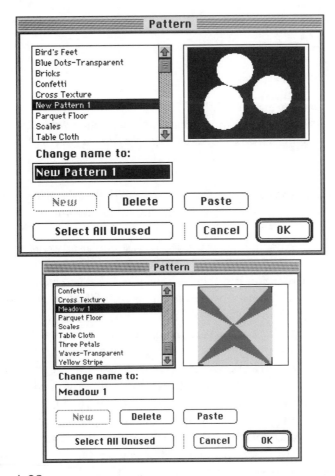

Figure 4-38.
After clicking the New button in the Pattern dialog box, the New Pattern 1 name appears, which you can change by typing over a new name. A preview of the pattern appears in the dialog box.

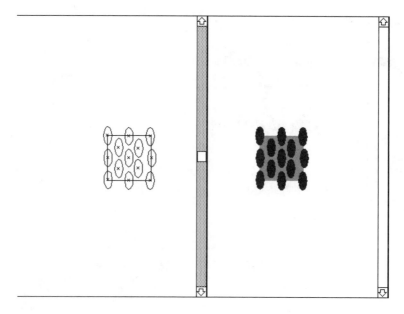

Figure 4-39.
Using Preview to preview new artwork to be defined as a pattern (the pattern tile rectangle is behind the pattern elements).

to use a lot of patterns, it helps to define them in one document which can be left open while opening other documents and applying patterns.

When you have defined a pattern, you can paste it into another document so that it is treated as regular artwork, not as a pattern. Use the Paste button in the Pattern dialog box after selecting a pattern by name. You can then use the artwork to create another pattern.

To assign a pattern to an object's fill, click the Pattern button in the Paint Style palette (for the fill area) and click on the name of a pattern. A preview of the pattern appears in the preview window (Figure 4-40). You can also choose a pattern for an object's stroke. The pattern appears in the artwork when you choose the Preview option (Figure 4-41). The pattern itself starts at the current ruler origin, which is at the lower left corner. You can change the ruler origin (the point where zero appears on both rulers) by moving the ruler intersection square to the new position. You can alternatively move the pattern itself, as described later.

An object painted with a pattern fill can be transformed (that is, moved, scaled, rotated, reflected, and sheared) and the pattern can either be transformed in the same fashion, or left alone. You can also transform the pattern itself without transforming the object.

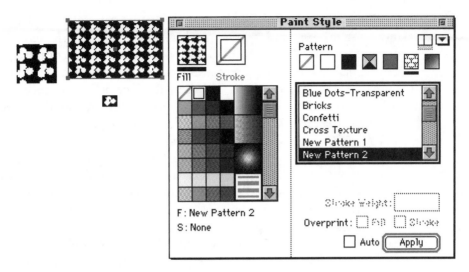

Figure 4-40.
The new pattern is selected by clicking its name, and a preview appears in the fill preview window.

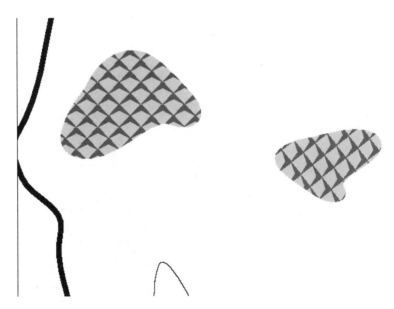

Figure 4-41.
The Meadow 1 pattern displayed with the Preview view.

When moving or transforming an object with a pattern, if you drag to move or transform (and you haven't checked the Transform pattern tiles box in the General Preferences dialog box, or in the Move or transformation dialog box), the pattern is not moved or transformed with the object. If, however, you check this box in the General Preferences dialog box, the pattern tiles are always moved or transformed with the object when you drag to move or transform the object (Figure 4-42).

You can also choose to transform (or not to transform) the pattern tiles and/or object in a transformation dialog box, such as the Rotate dialog box (Figure 4-43). Whenever you turn this option on or off, it automatically updates the Transform pattern tiles option in the General Preferences dialog box to your latest choice. Each transformation dialog box and the Move dialog box has an option to transform or move the pattern tiles alone, pattern tiles with the object, or the object alone.

To transform the pattern by itself, without transforming the object, first select the centerpoint of the object or path, and hold down the P key as you drag with the transformation tool (Scale tool, rotate tool, reflect tool, shear tool, or blend tool). You can similarly move the pattern without moving the object, using the Move command in the Arrange menu.

When you transform a pattern, the operation doesn't change the definition of the pattern, nor does it change the pattern as it is used in other parts of the document or other documents.

Figure 4-42.
Transformed objects are filled with patterns that are also transformed.

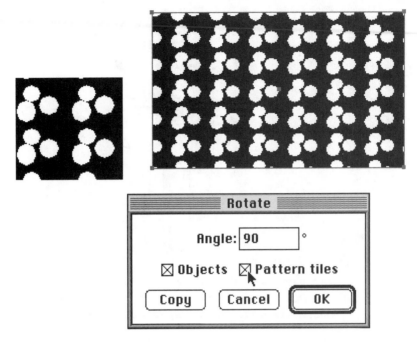

Figure 4-43.
The Rotate pattern tiles box is already checked because the Transform pattern tiles box was checked in the General Preferences dialog box. Turning this option on or off (in any dialog box) automatically turns the Transform pattern tiles box off in the General Preferences dialog box.

You can blend two objects that have the same pattern, but not objects with different patterns unless one of the patterns is defined with artwork that is a transformation of the other pattern (the blend produces intermediate shapes with intermediate transformations of the pattern).

Masking

You can prepare an object so that it is filled with whatever artwork lies behind it. The object in front, called the masking object, defines the boundaries and treats everything it touches (that is pasted in back of it, including objects on layers in back of the masking object) as part of a pattern for the mask. With this neat trick you can compose an object that looks like a window on top of a piece of art. You can also use masking to create trap between two irregularly-shaped objects where stroke-style trapping would be noticed in inappropriate areas of the artwork.

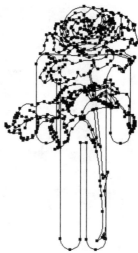

Figure 4-44.
After placing the masking object ("Man" icon) on top of the objects to be masked ("The Rose"), and selecting both, choose the Masks and Make commands (Object menu) to complete the masking operation.

To create a masking object, draw and select the path (for the mask) and be sure it is ungrouped. You should use a single object for your masking object, and one masking object per set of objects to be masked. You can't use a blend as a masking object (although each intermediate step could be a masking object for a set of masked objects). Then choose Paint Style from the Object menu, and set paint and stroke attributes. Select all of the objects, after first checking that the mask object is on the frontmost layer and is the frontmost object. Then select the Mask and Make commands from the Object menu to make this object a masking object. The selected objects behind the masking object are revealed only through the mask.

Figure 4-44 shows the masking object, which in this case is the Man icon from T/Maker's ClickArt EPS Series of PostScript clip art. The artwork to be masked is "The Rose" which is supplied in the Adobe Illustrator 3 Tutorial folder. After selecting both objects (and checking that the masking object — the Man icon — is in front of the masked object), the Mask and Make commands in the Object menu are selected. This completes the masking operation, and the Preview view shows the result (Figure 4-45).

You can use the blend tool to create a blend that could be used as a set of masked objects. With the combination of the blend tool and masking, you can mask a gradation of colors or shades of gray.

Figure 4-45.
The Preview view shows the result of masking the flower with the man icon as the masking object.

For example, we blended two rectangles shaded at five percent and 95 percent black with 99 intermediate steps, and used the Paste In Back option to paste the blend object behind the Man icon used as a masking object (Figure 4-46). The Preview window shows how the masked blend appears in print.

Another use of the masking feature is to set trap for a colored object that overlaps another colored object (only partially enclosed). In such cases, a heavy stroke would be noticed in the areas where the trap is not needed. However, a masking object limits the exposure of the objects behind it. You can set the object on top to be a masking object, and clone the other object and place the clone behind the masking object, and paint the clone with no fill and a stroke that is heavy enough to act as a trap (usually 0.6 to 2.0 points). The masking object limits the exposure of the clone's stroke to the area within the masking object, which is the area where trap is needed.

Use the selection tools to select objects to add or delete from masks. To add an object to a mask, select the object and drag it in front of the mask. Cut or copy the object, then use the direct-selection tool to select an object in the mask to paste the new object in front of or behind. Use the Paste in Front or Paste in Back command (Edit menu) to paste the object, which becomes part of the mask. To delete an object from a mask, use the direct-selection tool to select it and then use the Cut command (Command-X). Use the selection tool to select an object outside the

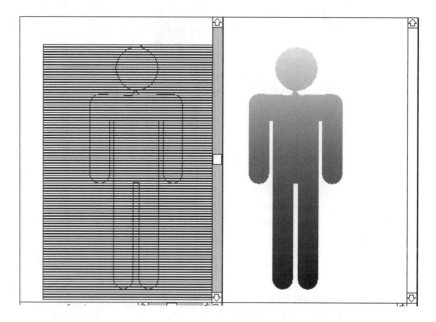

Figure 4-46.
Masking a blend of gray shades with the man icon, and a Preview window showing the result.

mask, and use the Paste in Front or Paste in Back command to paste the object in front of or behind the selected object, and it will no longer be part of the masked artwork.

Summary

Professional illustrators gain productivity by using the automatic tracing feature, the blending feature, constraining, multiple transformations, patterns, gradients, masks, paint brush and eyedropper tools, measuring tools and rulers.

Adobe Illustrator lets you scale either one path, a group of paths forming an object, or an entire illustration, and have the choice of scaling or preserving the line weights. This choice comes only with the use of the Scale dialog box and uniform scaling (using the dialog-scale tool, or the scale tool with the Option key, to click a scale focal point). If you drag to scale, the line weights are preserved (not scaled). The line weights are also preserved with non-uniform scaling. The Scale dialog box lets you type a percentage for a uniform scale (scaling in proportion), with the choice of preserving or scaling line weights by the same percentage, or for a non-uniform scale.

The "Eyeball" illustration demonstrated the use of multiple rotation transformations, the use of the reflect tool to create an upside-down image, the use of alternate line caps and joins, and the techniques for editing lines into curves.

The "Mazda" illustration showed how you can change the axes for constraining drawing and movement in the General Preferences dialog box. You can draw a complex illustration in perspective with accurate geometric shapes, and use the shear tool to slant the artwork along an angled axes. The axes also constrains the angle of the baseline of text typed with the text tool.

When an illustration has a lot of detail and cut-away views of interior construction, as with "Mazda," you have to dissect the image into layered objects. PostScript automatically masks objects that overlap one another, so that the part of an object that is underneath another object does not print. You can create compound paths that intersect to form holes that show the underlying layer. To help with alignment of objects, you can reset the ruler's origin point, and use ruler guides and objects as guides for attaching points. You can also hide objects and show them later.

To produce color separations, use the Adobe Separator program, which can produce four-color and custom separations. You can change the bounding box, page size, orientation, emulsion type, positive or negative, and the halftone screen ruling in lines per inch. PostScript Printer Description (PPD) files supply information for various printers and imagesetters. You should always use the appropriate PPD file for the device you are using.

To assure success before producing final film, ask your printer to look at a color proof and tell you whether the piece can be reproduced without problems on press. You can use Adobe Illustrator to change things like stroke weights, type point sizes, and process color percentages to adjust your illustration for specific press conditions.

Adobe Separator can print all process color separations in one operation, or separately, or as a color comp to a color printer. Custom colors (including PMS colors) can be converted into percentages of process colors automatically and included in the separations for the four process colors, or you can specify custom separations.

Color Plate 1 ("Flowchart") shows how you can reverse type out from the background color as long as the type is large and bold enough to avoid printing problems. Color Plate 5 ("Organizational Chart") also shows the use of colored text and the use of the tracking value for spacing out type characters. Color Plate 4 ("Liriel" by Luanne Seymour Cohen) has a title composed of characters that were drawn rather than typed.

Illustrator's overprint feature and black strokes can be used to create trap between colored objects and prevent registration problems on high-speed presses. Whenever colors meet at solid black lines, Adobe Separator automatically creates the necessary trap (Color Plates 3 and 7). Without black lines, you ensure trap by providing a bit of overlap and using the overprint feature. The overprint option allows color underneath the object to mix with the color of the object, thus creating a color somewhere between the two for the overlapping area. Shapes that are 100 percent black are automatically overprinted by Adobe Separator over all other colors.

You can blend between two objects painted with process colors or custom colors, and between a PMS or custom color and a process color. Process colors are used for all intermediate shapes, and tints are blended by percentage in the same color (Plates 7 and 8).

The program lets you fill and stroke paths and type with a custom pattern. A pattern can be transformed with the shape, transformed separately, or remain the same while the shape is transformed. Patterns are created as regular artwork, then defined with a pattern tile using the Pattern command. A custom pattern is always stored with the document in which it was defined and in any document that uses the pattern as a fill or stroke.

Finally, this chapter covered the masking feature. You can select an object to be a masking object that defines a boundary of exposure for printing (and previewing) any artwork that lies behind it. You can use this feature to create a window on top of a piece of art, to put a gradation of color or gray shapes inside an object, and to create trap between two objects where a partial stroke is required.

The next chapter takes Adobe Illustrator apart and describes every tool and menu option. You can use it as a handy reference to the program's features.

5

Adobe Illustrator Dissected

This chapter provides a complete description of each Adobe Illustrator tool, each menu item, including dialog boxes, and keyboard command shortcuts.

The tools are discussed in sequence (from the top to the bottom of the toolbox). Use the toolbox palettes in the left margin of each page to find tool descriptions. Each tool description is followed by a summary list of tool actions and keyboard command options.

The menus are then discussed in sequence. Dialog boxes and keyboard command shortcuts are included in the descriptions of the menu items.

Using the Mouse

The arrow cursor is also referred to as the pointer. You move the pointer by dragging the mouse, and you click the mouse button to select menu items, dialog box options, objects, line segments, and so on. The mouse can also move and resize windows. Moving the mouse (or any other input device such as a trackball, graphics tablet stylus, etc.) moves the pointer around so that you can point to things on the screen for the purpose of selecting or manipulating them. The ratio between the amount the pointer moves and the amount the mouse moves can be adjusted in the Control Panel (see Figure 5-1).

There are basically five actions to perform with a mouse:

Point. When you move the mouse, a pointer moves across the display.

Click. You click a point on the display by quickly pressing and releasing

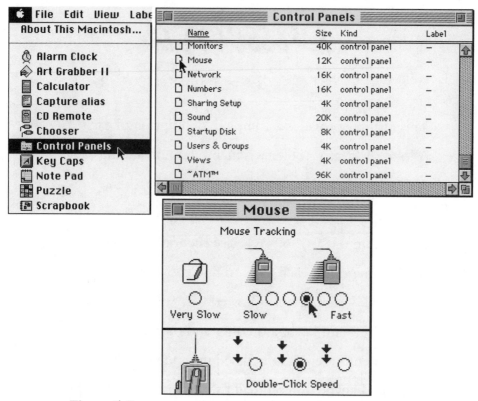

Figure 5-1.
Adjusting the mouse tracking option will change the ratio between the amount the pointer moves and the amount the mouse moves.

the mouse button. You do this to establish a point in an illustration, or to select an option in a dialog box (such as a check box or button).

Double-click. You double-click a point (such as a file or program icon) by quickly pressing and releasing the mouse button twice. By double-clicking a file or application program, you automatically run the program associated with that file.

Drag. You drag something (such as a graphic object or icon) by pointing the mouse, holding down the mouse button, and moving the mouse so that the pointer (or object) moves to a new position. Then you release the mouse button.

Select. To select a menu option or command, drag down a menu (which drops down to show you the options or commands) until the command or option you want is highlighted, then release the mouse button.

The Macintosh employs drag-down menus and displays dialog boxes after you select a command or option. In the dialog boxes you can select items by clicking boxes or buttons displayed on the screen, and sometimes there are scroll bars for scrolling items in a small window.

To operate the scroll bar, click below the white box in the gray area, or click the up or down arrow, or drag the white box up or down.

Dialog boxes often have text boxes for typing numbers or text, scrollable menus of options, and check boxes or buttons.

Whenever any pointer is moved outside the active window, it changes into the arrow pointer in order to let you select tools, issue commands, or move windows.

The Status line at the bottom left of the active window displays the name of the tool you are using (current tool), or optionally you can view the date and time, available (free) memory, or number of undos and redos you can perform.

Resizing, Zooming, and Moving Windows

You can move and change the size of Adobe Illustrator windows. For example, to change the size of a window, point to the window's size box (see Figure 5-2), hold down the mouse button, and drag with the mouse until the window is the size and shape you want it to be. When you release the mouse button, the window will change size.

A shortcut for enlarging the window is to point to the zoom box in the window's title bar (Figure 5-3). The zoom box is located in the upper right-hand corner of the window. Click the zoom box, and the window

Figure 5-2.
In the bottom right corner of the active window is the size box; drag it with the mouse to change the window size.

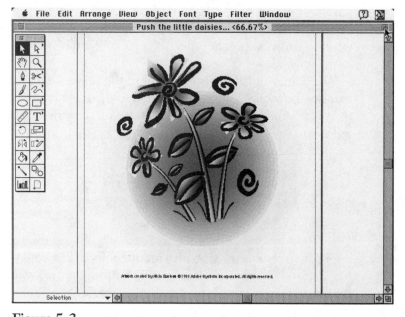

Figure 5-3.
The title bar at the top contains the name of the document (and template, if any). At the left end of the title bar is the close box, and at the right end is the zoom box.

will enlarge until it fills up the Macintosh's screen. Click it again and it returns to the size it was before.

If you want to move the window, point to any place on the window's title bar (except the close box at the left end of the bar and the zoom box at the right end of the bar), hold down the mouse button, and drag the window to a new location on the Macintosh's screen (or onto an additional monitor if you are using two monitors that work together). If you move a window with this technique, it will become active if it was previously inactive.

If you want to move an inactive window and have the window remain inactive after it is moved, use the previous technique except first depress the Command key and hold it down while dragging the window to its new location.

On the other hand, to make an active window inactive, point to the title bar of the window, hold down the Command key, and click the mouse button; this will deactivate the window and send it to the back, behind any other windows that are displayed.

Selection Tools

The arrow icon in the top left slot of the toolbox is the selection tool. To get the selection tool you can either click on the selection tool in the toolbox or use the tool temporarily by holding down the Command key while using another tool. (If your view is set to an inactive window, the pointer will remain an arrow, the first click will make the window active, and the second click will select something.) You can select objects using the Preview view, the Artwork view, or the Preview Selection view; selected from the View menu.)

Once you have drawn a path, you can use the selection tool to move the path to a new location, or the direct-selection tool to manipulate the path to change its shape. The selection tool is used to select an entire grouped or ungrouped object or path, by selecting any point on the path.

The direct-selection tool selects a single path (segment) or point on a path, whether or not it is part of a group. To move an object (a path) with the direct-selection tool without changing it, the entire object (and all its connecting lines and points) must be selected; otherwise you may accidentally alter the artwork, since moving any anchor points, direction points, lines, or curves without moving all of them can change the shape of the paths.

The Area Select option in the General Preferences dialog box (select Preferences General from the File menu), which is on by default,

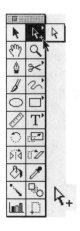

mitigates this problem by selecting an entire filled object whenever you click anywhere inside it.

To prevent objects from being changed when you move them, use the Group command on the Arrange menu to group the points, lines, and curves in the object into a single unified object. The grouped object is not only resistant to accidental changes, it is also easier to select, because pointing and clicking anywhere on the object with the selection tool selects the entire object.

You can use the direct-selection tool to select a single point or path in a grouped set of objects without ungrouping the set.

The group-selection tool is used to select groups of objects by clicking an object in the group, and then successive clicks select successive subsets of grouped objects. After you select the first object with the group-selection tool, you can select additional objects that are part of that group by clicking the selected object again to add them to the selection. They are added to the selection based on the grouping hierarchy, as in the following example.

You can also use the group-selection tool to determine whether or not an object is part of a group by selecting the object with this tool and then clicking again to see if any other objects are added to the selection.

For example, if group A and group B are grouped together, and then that group is in turn grouped with group C, you have nested groups, and a group hierarchy.

If you click to select group A with the group-selection tool, and then click again, you add group B to the selection. A third click adds group C to the selection.

If you click to select group B with the group-selection tool, and then click again, you add group A to the selection. A third click adds group C to the selection.

If you click to select group C with the group-selection tool, and then click again, you add both group B and group A to the selection.

To select an object to move, you select all the items that comprise the object. You can select all the items by dragging a selection marquee (see Figure 5-4) completely around an object, being careful not to include any other objects. To select an entire path, point to any location on the path and click while holding down the Option key. If you hold down Option while dragging the marquee, the marquee selects all paths that intersect it.

You can select one component of an object by pointing to it and clicking (or by using the selection marquee), and then select another component by pointing and clicking while holding down the Shift key. If you hold down the Shift key before you click on or drag over an item, the item is added to the group of selected objects. If you hold down the

Shift key after you start dragging, the program constrains movement of the arrow to increments of 45 degrees, relative to the constrain angle you set in the General Preferences dialog box. Constraining movement with the Shift key makes it easier to move objects vertically, horizontally, or diagonally at a 45 degree angle.

If you plan to select only complete paths, use the selection tool. You can select several paths by holding down the Shift key while clicking to select additional paths with the selection tool.

If there are several objects on top of each other, you can select the top object with the selection tool, then move it by dragging the object to a new location. If you hold down the Option key while you drag an object, it will create a duplicate of the object for moving, and the original will be left in its place. This duplication technique is extremely useful for cloning items to reuse in your artwork.

Another way to move objects without changing them is to use the Move dialog box to specify movement precisely. To move an object with the Move dialog box, first select the object, then point to the selection tool in the toolbox and hold down the Option key while clicking to

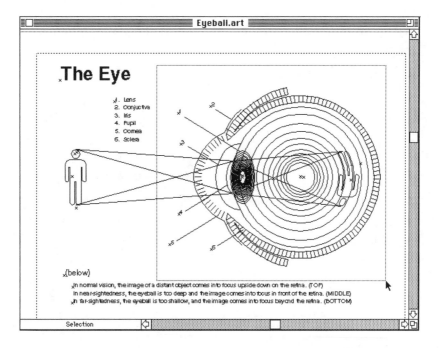

Figure 5-4.
Dragging the selection marquee around a set of objects to select everything inside the marquee.

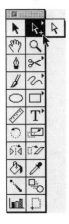

activate the dialog box (Figure 5-5). After you release the mouse button, the Move dialog box appears (Figure 5-6). The dialog box contains the values of the last move, or measurement (with the measure tool), if any, during the current program session; if no move or measurement has yet taken place, the values are set to a move distance of zero and horizontally.

To specify the distance to move the selected object(s), click inside the entry box for Distance and type the distance. The measure you use depends on the measurement chosen for the rulers in the General Preferences dialog box (available from the File menu). By default the measure is inches, and you can type a fraction of an inch by using decimal notation. You may want to switch the measurements to points (one point = 1/72 of an inch).

Next, specify the direction of the movement by clicking inside the entry box for Angle and type the angle as a percentage. The Horizontal and Vertical entries are automatically filled in, calculated by the distance and angle values. Change any value and the others also change accordingly.

Specifying a positive measure for a horizontal move will move selected

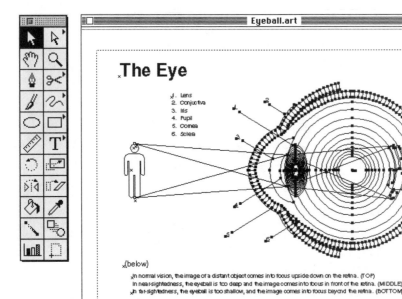

Figure 5-5.
With one or more objects selected, you can activate the Move dialog box by holding down the Option key while clicking the selection tool in the toolbox.

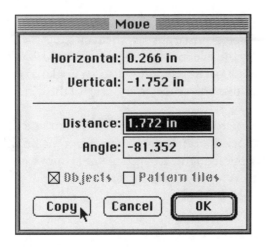

Figure 5-6.
The Move dialog box lets you specify in points (or other measures) how far to move the selected object or objects; you can choose a horizontal, vertical, or angled move and specify the angle in degrees. You can also click Copy to create a clone.

objects to the right, and a negative measure moves them to the left. Likewise, specifying a positive measure for a vertical move will move the selected objects up, and a negative measure will move the objects down. Negative numbers specified for an angled move will move the objects clockwise from the horizontal origin, rather that counterclockwise.

After you have specified the amounts, you can either click the OK button to initiate the move (the double line around this button indicates that it will be selected if you press the Return key); click the Cancel button to abandon the move and return to the active window; or click the Copy button to create and move a duplicate while leaving the original in its place. The Pattern tiles check box, if checked, will move any pattern associated with the object or objects, or will move only the pattern(s), if the Objects checkbox is unchecked.

If you have altered the x and y axes in the Constrain angle field in the Preferences dialog box, then movement of the object or objects will be relative to the altered x and y axes. For example, if you have rotated the x and y axes by 20 degrees by changing the angle in the General Preferences dialog box, any objects that you move will be moved at an additional 20-degree angle: specifying a horizontal move would result in a 20-degree move and specifying a 30-degree move would result in a 50-degree move. If you are moving objects and they seem to be moving in

a tilted or exaggerated direction, check the alignment of the x and y axes by looking at the dialog box that appears after you select the Preferences General option from the File menu (or type Command-K). If there is a number other than zero, the axes are set to an angle. To restore the original x and y axes that are parallel to the sides of the window, set this field to zero.

To move objects in front of or behind other objects, use the Paste In Front and Paste In Back options in the Edit menu, or the Bring To Front and Send To Back options in the Arrange menu. To move an object into the center of the active window, use the Paste command.

Changing Segments and Moving Points

In addition to using the selection tool for moving an entire object without changing it, you can use the selection tool with any ungrouped object, or the direct-selection tool with any grouped set of objects, to change or modify an object or path by moving one or more of its component parts (i.e., anchor points, endpoints, corner points, smooth points, direction points, straight line segments, curve segments, and direction lines). The program gives you a great deal of flexibility to change objects — you can draw shapes roughly with the freehand tool and come back later and fine-tune the drawing with the other tools.

Adobe Illustrator lets you reshape an object a variety of different ways, depending on how the object is selected (see Figures 5-7, 5-8, and 5-9). An object must be selected before it can be manipulated or modified. Objects can be selected in the artwork, preview selection, or preview windows. The first view (artwork) displays changes you make in the shortest amount of time, and the last (preview) takes the longest to redraw your screen.

Normally, if you point within two pixels of an object or several objects (pixels are dots on the screen), the topmost object will be selected and all other objects will be deselected. If you point to a location more than two pixels away from any object and click the mouse, all objects will be deselected. If you want the feature that selects anything within two pixels of the arrow to be turned off, deselect the Snap to point feature in the General Preferences dialog box (described with the File menu later in this chapter).

The main techniques used for manipulating objects with the selection or direct-selection tool are moving points or segments. You can move anchor points, endpoints, corner points, smooth points, direction points, direction lines, and straight line and curve segments. For making

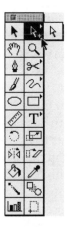

Figure 5-7.
A path consisting of curve segments that are not selected.

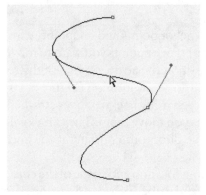

Figure 5-8.
Selecting a curve segment with the direct-selection tool. Illustrator displays endpoints, smooth points and direction points for manipulating the curve.

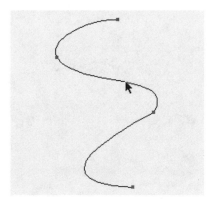

Figure 5-9.
The path selected as a whole using the selection tool, or using the selection tool and holding down the Option key while clicking on the path. Anchor points, corner points, and endpoints are shown, but not direction points.

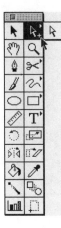

adjustments, the Join and Average commands on the Object menu are useful in addition to the selection tool, since these two commands let you move anchor points or endpoints together and join any two of them with a line segment. Join and Average are described later in this chapter with the Object menu.

The scissors tool is also helpful — it lets you cut segments in two. The add-anchor-point tool and the delete-anchor-point tool (both are located to the right of the scissors tool) let you add anchor points to a segment, and delete anchor points from a segment, without cutting the segment. Any segment, or group of segments, can be modified with the scale, rotate, reflect and shear tools. The combination of these tools, commands, and techniques allows excellent control over very precise modifications of the artwork — a luxury not provided with traditional pen and ink.

To move anchor points and endpoints with the direct-selection tool, first select the point or points you want to move with the direct-selection tool, then position the arrow on one of the selected anchor points and drag the point to a new location (Figure 5-10). As you drag the mouse you will notice that any lines or curves attached to any points moved will also change as you move them. The curves will change in a way that will keep the curve directions constant at the anchor points that are being moved.

The previous location and shape of the curve is displayed as well as the new location and shape. To move direction points with the selection tool, first select an anchor point (or an adjacent segment) whose direction

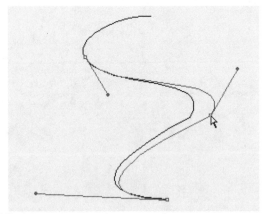

Figure 5-10.
Dragging an anchor point alters the shape of the curve without changing its direction; its original shape remains displayed until you release the mouse button.

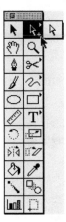

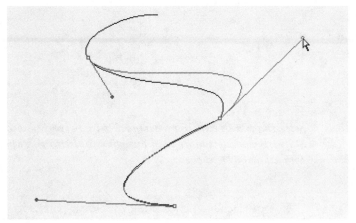

Figure 5-11.
Dragging a direction point alters the shape of the curve without changing its points.

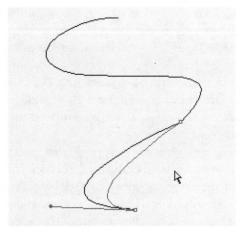

Figure 5-12.
Selecting and moving a curve segment without changing its points.

point you want to move. Next, point to the direction point that you want to adjust and drag the direction point with the mouse to change the curve of the segment or segments that are connected to the anchor point whose direction point you are moving (Figure 5-11).

To move the line or curve segment itself, select the segment you want to modify, point to an area on the selected segment that is between its anchor points, and drag the segment. As you drag the segment you will notice that any other selected segments also change shape, and the associated direction points move in accordance with the drag, but the selected segments' anchor points remain fixed (see Figure 5-12).

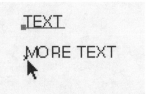

Figure 5-13.
Selecting text by clicking the x mark with the selection tool; holding down Shift lets you select more than one object. Selected text appears with baselines and an alignment point.

If you select an anchor point by clicking on it, you will also select any segments that are connected to it. If two anchor points are on top of each other, only the topmost anchor point will be selected by clicking on it.

To select an anchor point and all the points underneath it, drag the selection marquee around the points. When an anchor point (or endpoint) is selected, it appears as a solid black square, and all the other anchor points in the object are also displayed. Anchor points (or endpoints) that are not selected appear as hollow squares.

If you select a curved segment, no anchor points will be selected, but the direction points associated with the curved segment will appear as solid black circles (see Figure 5-8). If you select a straight line segment, the direction points will not be displayed since they would be on top of the segment's anchor points.

When you select an entire path (click on it using the selection tool, the group-selection tool, or use the direct-selection tool and drag a selection marquee), all the anchor points will be selected, and no direction points will be displayed (see Figure 5-9, a selected path). To select type, point to the "x" symbol in the baseline of the text and click (see Figure 5-13). If several blocks of type are on top of each other, the topmost block of type will be selected. If you use the selection marquee to select type, all the type blocks whose baselines fall even partially within the marquee will be selected.

Selection Tool Summary

 + click

Selects the entire object or path you are pointing at. The path can be a single point, a line, a curve, an open or closed path, or a group. You can't select part of a group, only the entire group.

Use the direct-selection tool and the group selection tool to select part

of an object or group. In Artwork view, you must select a path segment or anchor point or endpoint of an object to select it. In Preview or Preview selection views, you can click inside a filled object to select the entire object, if the Area select option is checked (default) in the General Preferences dialog box. If the Area select option is turned off, you must select a path segment or anchor point or endpoint of an object to select it in Preview or Preview selection views.

If the path or object you are pointing at is already selected, the click will deselect it.

+ Shift key + click

If you hold down the Shift key while you are clicking the mouse or before you start to drag with the mouse, it will extend (or reduce) your selection.

+ Option key + point to path + click

If, while holding down the Option key, you point to a path and click the mouse, the entire path will be selected.

Option key + click in toolbox

Gets Move dialog box for specifying precise movement.

+ drag

If you click and hold down the mouse button, and move the mouse, you will drag a selection marquee (dotted rectangle) around the path or object. The entire path or object or group will be selected, even if you drag over only part of the object, path or group.

+ Shift key + drag

If you hold down the Shift key after you have started to drag something with the mouse, it will constrain the motion of the object or objects being dragged to horizontal movement (movement along the x axis), vertical movement (along the y axis), or movement in 45-degree increments (relative to the x and y axes).

+ Option key + drag

Clones (creates duplicates of) all selected objects.

+ click

The direct-selection tool selects only the point or path segment you are pointing at, whether or not it is included in a group. The item remains grouped.

+ Shift key + click

If you hold down the Shift key while you are clicking the mouse or before you start dragging with the mouse, it will extend (or reduce, if you deselect an item) your selection.

+ Option key + point to path + click

If, while holding down the Option key, you point to a path and click the mouse, the entire path will be selected, even if it is part of a group.

+ drag

If you click and hold down the mouse button, and move the mouse, you will drag a selection marquee (dotted rectangle) around the path or object. Only the portion of the path, object or group that is enclosed by the selection marquee will be selected.

+ Shift key + drag

If you hold down the Shift key after you have started to drag something with the mouse, it will constrain the motion of the object or objects being dragged to horizontal movement (movement along the x axis), vertical movement (along the y axis), or movement in 45-degree increments (relative to the x and y axes).

+ Option key + drag

Clones (creates duplicates of) all selected segments, or paths (and objects).

+ click

The group-selection tool selects the entire path you are pointing at. Successive clicks select additional groups of objects, based on the grouping hierarchy. If no additional objects are added to the selection by a successive click, then the object is not grouped with other objects.

+ drag

If you click and hold down the mouse button, and move the mouse, you will drag a selection marquee (dotted rectangle) around the path or object. Only those objects that are enclosed by the selection marquee will be selected.

Command Key

Temporarily converts the tool you are using into the last used selection tool.

Hand Tool

 The hand tool is primarily for scrolling an illustration within an active window. Although you can also scroll the document with the scroll bars on the right and bottom sides of the window, the hand tool gives you more precise control over scrolling.

To use the hand tool, select the hand tool icon in the toolbox. The pointer turns into a hand when you move it back into the active window (Figure 5-14). Next, place the hand over the illustration and drag in the direction you want to move it. The artwork doesn't move, but the active window does move to show the object.

Another way to use the hand tool is to press the space bar while using any other tool. Whatever tool you are using changes into the hand tool while you are holding down the space bar, then changes back to the appropriate tool as soon as you release the space bar. This shortcut is handy for moving the window since you don't have to go back to the toolbox and switch tools.

Hand Tool Summary

 + drag

Moves the document around within the active window.

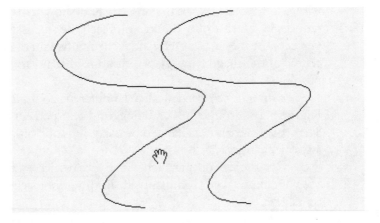

Figure 5-14.
You can move an illustration within the active window with the hand tool.

Space bar + drag

Temporarily converts the current tool into the hand tool for moving the document within the active window.

Double-click in toolbox

Displays the entire document in the active window regardless of window size. This is a shortcut for the Fit In Window option in the View menu.

Zoom Tool

The zoom tool is for zooming into or out from the actual size view of the active window. Zooming in lets you inspect the detail of your artwork; zooming out lets you take a step back and see the big picture.

To zoom into an area of your artwork, click the magnifying glass icon in the toolbox. The pointer changes to a magnifying glass with a plus sign (+) in its center when you move it into the active window. The plus sign indicates that the zoom tool will enlarge your view when you click it anywhere in the active window, showing more detail. This is called zooming in. Be sure to place the magnifying glass on top of the area of the artwork that you want to see. Each click enlarges your view of that area until you reach the largest possible magnification level (1600 percent of the actual size). When you reach that point, the plus sign disappears from the center of the magnifying glass.

To zoom out, hold down the Option key after selecting the zoom tool. The plus sign changes to a minus (-) sign, indicating that the tool will reduce your view of the artwork and show less detail. Each click reduces by a factor of two until you reach the smallest reduction (6.25 percent). At the smallest reduction, the minus sign disappears from the center of the magnifying glass indicating that no further reduction is possible.

A document can be viewed at 17 different zoom levels as shown in Figures 5-15 through 5-30, ranging from 6.25 percent to 1600 percent. The artwork size is not changed by the zoom tool, only your view of the artwork changes.

To view the artwork at its actual size, either select Actual Size from the View menu, or type Command-H. Both methods change the view to actual size.

To fit the entire document in the active window, you can select the Fit In Window option from the View menu, type Command-M, or double-click the hand tool. Any of these commands also center the drawing space

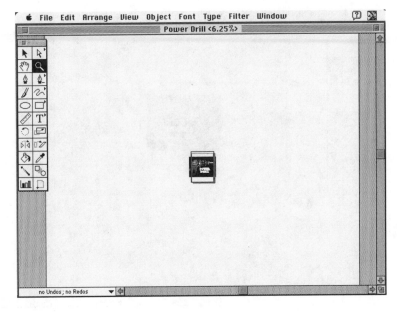

Figure 5-15.
A document viewed at the most reduced zoom level, which is 6.25 percent of the artwork's actual size. Zooming in or out does not change the size of the artwork, only the view.

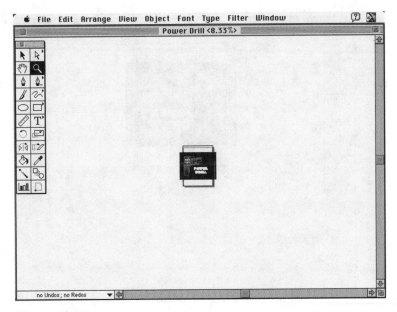

Figure 5-16.
Zooming into the document from the previous figure, now viewed at 8.33 percent of the artwork's actual size.

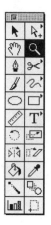

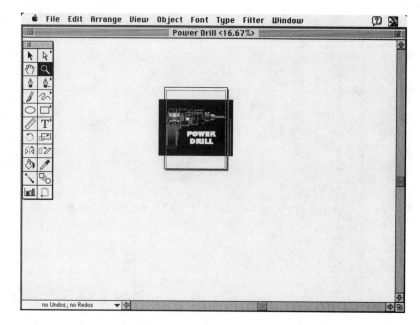

Figure 5-17.
Zooming into the document from the previous figure, now viewed at 16.67 percent of the artwork's actual size.

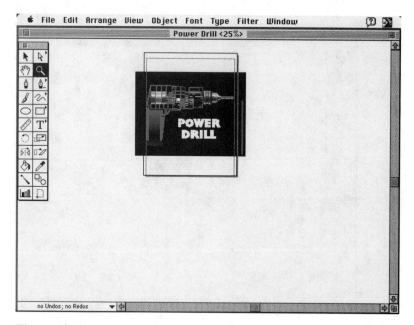

Figure 5-18.
Zooming into the document from the previous figure, now viewed at 25 percent of the artwork's actual size.

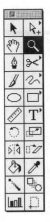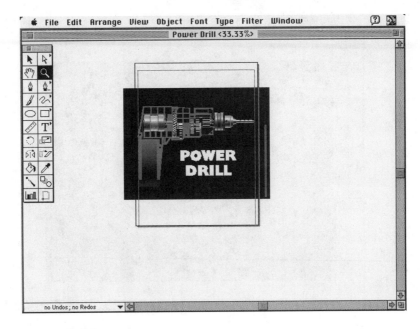

Figure 5-19.
Zooming into the document from the previous figure, now viewed at 33.33 percent of the artwork's actual size.

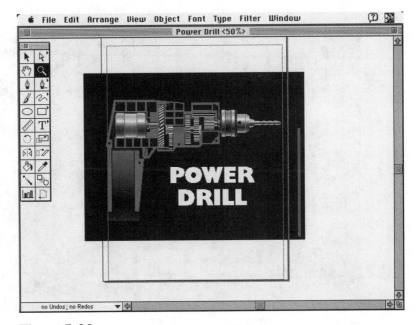

Figure 5-20.
Zooming into the document from the previous figure, now viewed at 50 percent of the artwork's actual size.

Figure 5-21.
Zooming into the document from the previous figure, now viewed at 66.67 percent of the artwork's actual size.

Figure 5-22.
Zooming into the document from the previous figure, now viewed at the artwork's actual size (100%).

Figure 5-23.
Zooming into the document from the previous figure, now viewed at 150 percent of the artwork's actual size.

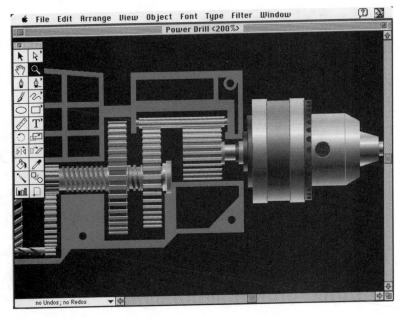

Figure 5-24.
Zooming into the document from the previous figure, now viewed at 200 percent of the artwork's actual size.

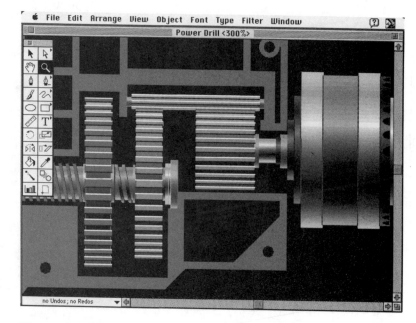

Figure 5-25.
Zooming into the document from the previous figure, now viewed at 300 percent of the artwork's actual size.

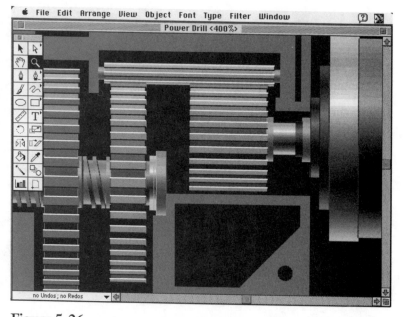

Figure 5-26.
Zooming into the document from the previous figure, now viewed at 400 percent of the artwork's actual size.

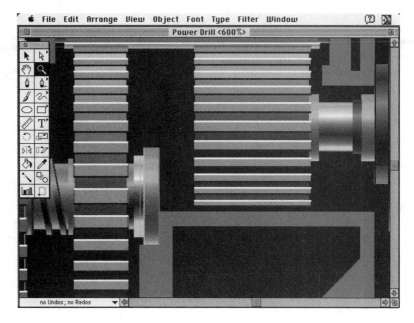

Figure 5-27.
Zooming into the document from the previous figure, now viewed at 600 percent of the artwork's actual size.

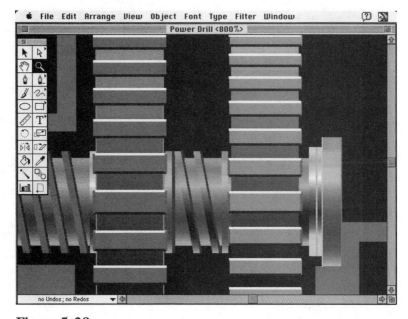

Figure 5-28.
Zooming into the document from the previous figure, now viewed at 800 percent of the artwork's actual size.

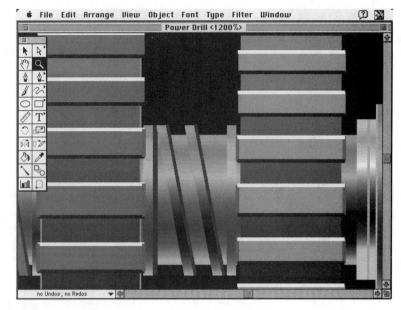

Figure 5-29.
Zooming into the document from the previous figure, now viewed at 1200 percent of the artwork's actual size.

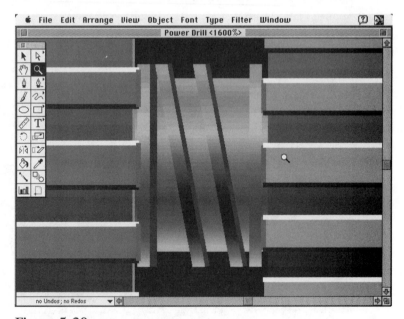

Figure 5-30.
Zooming into the document from the previous figure, now viewed at 1600 percent of the artwork's actual size. Each square is equal to one pixel of a MacPaint document (at 72 pixels per inch).

in the window, although your artwork may not be in the center of the drawing space. If you open a template but don't see the image in your active window, try the Fit In Window option, then use the zoom tool to zoom into the template image.

The zoom tool also affects the rulers that can be displayed in a window. To display rulers, select the Show Rulers option from the View menu, or type Command-R. Two rulers will appear — one along the bottom of the active window and the other on the right side of the window (Figure 5-31). As you zoom in or out, the ruler tick marks change to provide a more detailed or less detailed ruler. To remove the rulers from view,

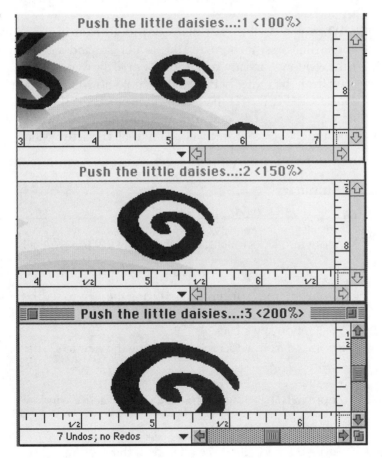

Figure 5-31.
The Show Rulers option in the View menu displays rulers that are calibrated to the measure selected in the Preferences dialog box (by default, inches, but the default can be changed to picas, etc. in the General Preferences dialog box).

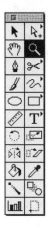

choose Hide Rulers from the View menu (the Hide Rulers option takes the place of Show Rulers when the rulers are displayed). You can also type Command-R again, which acts as a toggle switch for turning the rulers on or off.

The program offers a quick way to zoom in or out while you are using another tool (without having to go back to the toolbox to switch tools). Hold down the Command key and the space bar simultaneously when using another tool. Whatever tool you are using changes into the zoom tool while you are holding down the Command key and space bar. You can click to zoom in, or use another finger to hold down the Option key (as well as the Command key and space bar) to zoom out. The tool changes back to the original tool as soon as you release the Command key and space bar.

When you double-click the zoom tool's icon in the toolbox (the magnifying glass), it zooms to 100 percent size, and centers the artboard in the window. Similarly, to quickly zoom all the way out (to 6.25 percent view) from the center of the window, hold down the Option key while double-clicking the zoom tool icon in the toolbox. If you need to zoom in to see a portion of the artwork, you can drag a marquee with the zoom tool, and the selected area will zoom to fill the active window.

Zoom Tool Summary

 + click
Zoom into a document, enlarging the view to see details.

  + click
Zoom out from a document, reducing the view to see the big picture.

  + Option key + click =
Zoom out from a document, reducing the view to see the big picture.

  + drag
Zoom in to have the selected area fill the active window.

  + drag
Zoom out and center the artwork in the window.

  + Option key + drag =
Zoom out and center the artwork in the window.

Double-click in toolbox
    Zoom to 100 percent view in the window.

Option key + Double-click in toolbox
    Zoom out from the center of the window to 6.25 percent view.

Command key + Space bar
    Temporarily converts the current tool into the zoom tool for zooming into the document while using another tool.

Command key + Option key + Space bar
    Temporarily converts the current tool into the zoom tool for zooming out from the document while using another tool.

Command key + Space bar + drag
    Temporarily converts the current tool into the zoom tool and selects an area with a marquee for zooming into to fill the active window while using another tool.

Pen Tool

You use the pen tool to create points, curves, and lines. Although the freehand tool also creates points, straight lines, and curve segments, and is similar to the drawing tools found in other graphics programs, the pen tool is not the same. The pen tool is used to establish points for the program to precisely draw the straight line or curve segments necessary to connect them.

The process of drawing with the pen tool is more like a connect-the-dots puzzle. Rather than drawing freehand so that the lines and curves reflect the actual mouse movement while drawing (as with the freehand tool), you click points and the program draws the lines and curves accurately between them. To control the directions and shapes of curves, you drag with the pen tool while establishing points, and you can later select points or curve segments with the selection tool.

You can switch from the pen tool to the selection tool (depress and hold down the Command key to switch between the pen tool and the selection tool) in order to move the points, lines, and direction points to change the shape of a curve, then switch back to the pen (by releasing the Command key) and continue establishing more points.

You can build an entire illustration by establishing the points along a path with the pen tool, linking those points with straight lines (by clicking without dragging) or curves (by dragging). Since the pen tool does not literally translate your mouse movements into lines and curves in a freehand style (which may produce a lot of bumps if you have an unsteady hand), you can use the pen tool to make accurate lines and curves without any drawing skill.

Anchor Points

The pen tool is mostly used to place points that link together straight line and curve segments or define the ends of paths. These points that the pen tool can establish are called *anchor points*. An anchor point determines the starting and ending point of any straight line or curve segment.

Anchor points are invisible unless any segment of the path formed by the segments is selected. Anchor points, including anchor points that have no line or curve segment attached to them, display as solid squares when selected. Anchor points that have a line or curve segment attached display as hollow squares when they are not selected but a line or curve segment attached to them is.

A single point displays as an x in Artwork view when it is not selected. (Adobe supplies a filter called Select Stray Points that displays and selects all single anchor points in your artwork document, so that you can then delete them from your final artwork file. Do this as a last step to eliminate all stray points at once.)

Endpoints are a special case of anchor points, defining the beginning and end of a path, which can consist of straight line and curve segments linked by anchor points. For example, a triangle is a closed path object that has no endpoints. A line is an example of an open path object, with endpoints at the beginning and end, and possibly some anchor points in between. Endpoints are anchor points that appear as solid squares when selected, otherwise they appear as hollow squares (as do anchor points).

Direction points, which seem to sprout from anchor points that define an end of a curve segment, control the direction that a curve segment is going from the anchor point. Each anchor point has two direction points associated with it, although if the anchor point links a straight line to a curve, one of those points is not visible (it is behind the straight line). When you select a curve segment, a direction point at each end becomes visible (as shown in Figure 5-8, in the description of the selection tool). When you select the next curve, the other direction point associated with the common anchor point is displayed (see Figure 5-12, also in the

section on the selection tool). The shape of the curve can be changed by moving those direction points with the direct-selection tool.

A *smooth point* is an anchor point that connects two curve segments whose direction points point in the same direction (there is no sharp turn in direction). The convert-direction-point tool converts corner points to smooth points (see the description later in the Scissors tool section).

A *corner point*, on the other hand, is an anchor point that connects two curve segments, two straight line segments, or a curve and a line segment in such a way that the direction points point in different directions, forming a sharp turn. The convert-direction-point tool converts smooth points to corner points (see the description later in the Scissors tool section).

Lines, Curves, and Paths

There are two types of segments in Adobe Illustrator: straight lines and Bézier curves. All artwork is fashioned from these segments. Ovals and circles are actually drawn with curve segments and can be ungrouped into individual segments. Segments start and end with anchor points.

Unless the segment is a straight line, the segment's curvature is determined by two direction points connected to the anchor points by tangent lines. Direction points and associated tangent lines are invisible when not selected (they also do not print).

A path is either a single anchor point, a single segment, or a group of connected segments.

A path is open if it starts at a distinct endpoint and ends at another distinct endpoint.

A path is closed if the starting and ending point are the same point. The difference between a closed and an open path is important when painting paths; you can get unexpected painting (fill color) of an object if the path is not properly closed because the program draws an imaginary line from the two endpoints of an open path in order to paint the path. When placing text inside an open path with the area-type tool, the imaginary line acts as a text boundary.

When you click to establish points with the pen tool, your path is open (and new points will be connected to points already established), until you either click the first point established (called an anchor point) to close the path, or end the current open path in one of these ways: reselect the pen tool or select any other tool in the toolbox; click with the pen tool while depressing the Command key outside the selected path or object; or choose Select none from the Edit menu (Command-Shift-A).

Drawing With the Pen Tool

To begin drawing a segment, click the pen tool icon in the toolbox. The pen tool pointer displays an x when you move it into the active window. Next, click an endpoint in your drawing space to start the segment (Figure 5-32). The pointer no longer displays an x, indicating that a path is under construction.

To draw a straight line, click another point where you want this line segment to end. The program automatically draws a straight line (Figure 5-33). You can click another point and draw another straight line, which is added to the path. Each point is an anchor point, and you have one endpoint on the path, until you end it.

If you drag rather than click a point, the program draws a curve. As you begin dragging the mouse, the program creates an anchor point, the

Figure 5-32.
After clicking the pen tool, the pointer displays an x. Click an endpoint to start the line segment, and the pointer turns into an arrowhead briefly, then into a pen when you release the mouse button to indicate that a path is being created.

Figure 5-33.
After clicking the second point (an anchor point), the program draws a straight line between the two points. You can continue to add line segments to the path by clicking more anchor points.

pointer changes to an arrowhead, and direction points appear in the direction of your dragging (Figure 5-34). The curve changes shape as you drag the direction points (Figure 5-35).

When you release the mouse, the pointer changes back to the plus (+) sign to indicate that you can add more segments to the path. You can continue to add curve segments to the path by dragging new points; each time you drag an anchor point, a curve is drawn with direction points attached to the anchor points (Figure 5-36). Each anchor point is a smooth point.

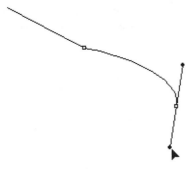

Figure 5-34.
As you drag, a curve is drawn to link that point with the previous anchor point, the pointer changes to an arrowhead, and direction points appear in the direction of your dragging.

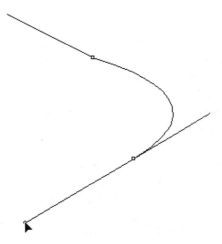

Figure 5-35.
The curve changes shape as you drag the direction points.

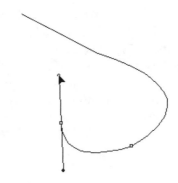

Figure 5-36.
Extending the path with another curve segment by dragging to establish another anchor point. The anchor points in this path are smooth.

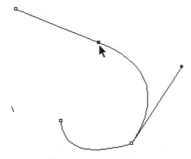

Figure 5-37.
The anchor point between the straight line and curve segments does not have a direction point because it is a special form of a corner point, dedicated to the direction of the straight line.

Note, however, that the anchor point between the straight line and curve segments does not have a direction point (Figure 5-37). This is because that point is a special form of a corner point, dedicated to the direction established by the straight line. To start drawing a curved path, you should start by dragging the first endpoint (Figure 5-38), so that the first point also has direction points (Figure 5-39).

You need to create corner points to make an angled or sharp turn of direction between curves or to join a straight line to a curve. To add a corner point and change the direction sharply for the next curve, hold down the Option key and either drag (to create another curve segment) or click (to create a straight line segment) to start the segment from that anchor point (Figure 5-40). When you release the mouse and Option key, the anchor point turns into a corner point.

Figure 5-38.
To start a path with a curve going in a particular direction, drag the first endpoint in that direction to establish the direction point for the endpoint.

Figure 5-39.
Drag the next anchor point in the same general direction, but in reverse order, moving the direction point to alter the shape of the curve. You can continue to add curve segments by dragging more anchor points.

Figure 5-40.
To establish a corner point, hold down the Option key and drag from the anchor point in a new direction.

Figure 5-41.
The next curve is shaped by the direction point attached to the corner point as well as the direction point of the new anchor point.

If you drag the next anchor point (Figure 5-41), the curve is shaped by the corner point's direction point. Hold down the Option key while clicking or dragging an anchor point if you want the point to act as a corner point.

To close a path and make it a solid object, click or drag the last anchor

point of the path onto the same location as the first endpoint, completing a loop. The pointer displays an o when it is in position to close an open path. (Turn on or off the Snap to point option in General Preferences [File menu] to improve control over path closing.) After you click to close the path, the x then reappears to show that a path has been completed and the tool is ready to create another path.

To stop drawing an open path, click the pen tool or any other tool in the toolbox, and the pointer changes. If you click the pen tool, the pointer displays an x so that you can start drawing a new path. You can also click with the pen tool while depressing the Command key outside the selected path or object, or choose Select none from the Edit menu (Command-Shift-A) to stop drawing an open path. Or, click the first point established, to close the path.

To extend an existing open path, click (to extend with a straight line) or drag (to extend with a curve) an endpoint of the path, holding down the Option key if you want the point to act as a corner point, or without Option to create a smooth point. Then click or drag another anchor point to make a new segment. The new segment and further segments connected to it become part of the path.

When drawing straight lines with the pen tool, if you hold down the Shift key when clicking the anchor point it will constrain the line being drawn horizontally, vertically, or in increments of 45 degrees. If you change the Constrain angle in the Preferences dialog box, the degree of constraining is relative to the new x and y axes.

If you are using an extended keyboard, you can switch from the pen tool to the freehand tool, or from the freehand tool to the pen tool, by holding down the Control key. For example, if you are drawing with the freehand tool and want to switch to the pen tool, hold down the Control key and the freehand tool turns into the pen tool. If you are drawing with the pen tool and you want to use the freehand tool for a segment, hold down the Control key and the pen tool turns into the freehand tool.

Pen Tool Summary

The pen tool puts down anchor points (including endpoints, corner points, and smooth points) for linking segments, and direction points for curve segments. The program draws the straight line or curve segments.

 + click

Creates the first anchor point for a straight line if starting a new path or extending a path; or creates a second anchor point and a straight line segment in the new path or in an extension to an existing path.

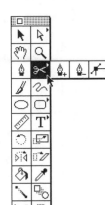

＋ drag

Creates the first anchor point for a curve if starting a new path or extending a path; or creates a second anchor point and a curve segment in the new path or in an extension to an existing path.

＋ Shift key ＋ drag

If you hold down the Shift key while drawing with the pen, it will constrain the line being drawn horizontally (i.e., along the x axis), vertically (along the y axis), or in increments of 45 degrees (relative to the x and y axes set (Constrain angle) in the General Preferences dialog box).

＋ Option key ＋ drag

Creates a corner point and establishes a new direction for the next segment, thereby changing the direction of the path you are drawing.

＋ Control key

Switch to the freehand tool (extended keyboards only).

Scissors and Points Tools

The scissors tool is used to cut a segment into two segments. You can either cut an open path into two open paths, or break a closed path into one open path. The add-anchor-point tool can be used to add anchor points to a segment. The delete-anchor-point tool lets you delete an anchor point while retaining the path (so that the path is not cut into two paths, as it would be if you simply deleted the anchor point with the Delete key or with Cut). The convert-direction-point tool can change corner points into smooth points, and vice-versa. Commands such as Average and Join (Object menu) can be used in conjunction with these tools to manipulate paths.

The scissors tool cannot be used to split endpoints of an open path, nor will it work on paths with text. If you want to use the scissors tool on a grouped object you must first select the object and ungroup it by selecting Ungroup from the Arrange menu (or by typing Command-U as a shortcut).

To use the scissors tool, first click the scissors icon in the toolbox. The pointer turns into a plus sign (+) when you move it into the active window (Figure 5-42).

To cut a segment into two segments, position the (+) pointer where you wish to cut the segment and click the mouse button. The segment is split into two segments where you clicked (Figure 5-43). Two new

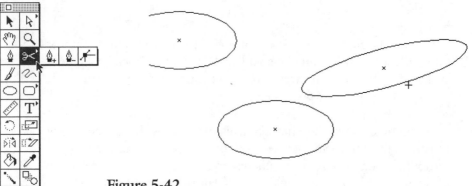

Figure 5-42.
Before clicking the scissors tool on an ungrouped path.

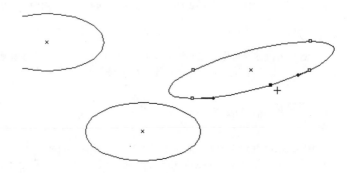

Figure 5-43.
After clicking the scissors tool, the segment is divided into two segments joined by a new anchor point.

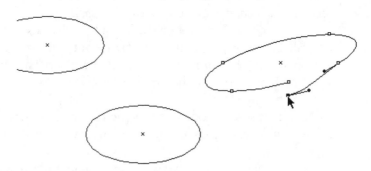

Figure 5-44.
Separating the new endpoints created by clicking the scissors tool.

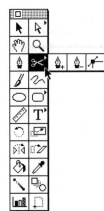

endpoints appear, although it appears that there is only one anchor point because the two new endpoints are directly on top of each other, and they are both selected. Since you can't tell from looking at the screen that there are actually two endpoints on top of each other, it's a good idea to move the endpoints apart right after you make the cut (Figure 5-44).

To move the two new endpoints apart, first change to a selection tool either by clicking the selection tool in the toolbox, or by holding down the Command key. Then point to the endpoints, hold down the Shift key, and click to deselect the endpoint on top while leaving the one beneath it selected. You can then move the bottom endpoint by positioning the pointer over it and dragging the endpoint to a new location.

The procedure for cutting an open path into two new open paths is quite similar. The only difference is that you can either cut a path in the middle of a segment to create two new endpoints, or you can cut a path on an anchor point to turn the existing anchor point into an endpoint and create a new endpoint on top of it.

Since you'll be faced with the same problem of having two endpoints on top of each other, you'll either want to move an endpoint as described above, or you may want to move one of the new paths. In order to move a path, first switch to a selection tool. Then point somewhere in the active window (but away from any artwork) and click to deselect all the objects in the artwork. Next, hold down the Option key, and click on the path that you want to move (or use the direct-selection tool). Move the path to the new location by dragging it there.

Breaking a closed path into an open path is much like the previous procedure except that you wind up with only one path instead of two. Whether you cut the closed point in the middle of a segment or at an anchor point, it's a good idea to move the two endpoints away from each other right after you cut them, since the screen shows them overlaying each other, and it is impossible to see that there are two endpoints at that location.

You can use the add-anchor-point tool to add new anchor points to any line segment in a path without cutting or breaking the path. Since adding anchor points does not add any new endpoints or break any paths, a single open path remains a single path, and a closed path stays closed. However, adding new anchor points gives you a greater degree of control over the shape of a path or object, since you can change the shape of the line segments where the new anchor points are added. This technique is very useful for fine-tuning small details in a complex piece of artwork, and for adding or deleting anchor points in an object that was traced with the auto trace tool.

To add new anchor points to a path, curve, or line segment, first select

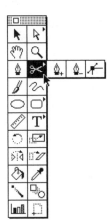

the add-anchor-point tool (a pen with a plus sign) by dragging to the right of the scissors tool in the toolbox. Next, click the (+) pointer where you want the new anchor point to be located. A new anchor point will appear, and it will be the only selected point. You can also use the scissors tool with the Option key held down to perform the same function.

You can use the delete-anchor-point tool to remove an anchor point without cutting the path. Removing an anchor point without cutting the path is useful for changing the shape of a path, and for reducing the number of points in a curve (for greater printing efficiency and smoother curves). Using the delete-anchor-point tool to remove an anchor point leaves the path connected, unlike the Delete key or the Cut command.

To remove an anchor point from a path, first select the delete-anchor-point tool (a pen with a minus sign) by dragging to the right of the scissors tool in the toolbox. Next, click on the anchor point to be removed.

The convert-direction-point tool can change a corner point into a smooth point, and vice-versa.

A smooth point is one where both direction points lie on a straight line and the curve flows smoothly through the point; a corner point is one where there are no direction points, and the curves or lines extend in different directions from the point. Converting from one type of point to another is useful for changing the shape of a path without disconnecting the path segments.

To change from one type of point to another, first select the convert-direction-point tool by dragging to the right of the scissors tool in the toolbox. Next, click on the point to be converted.

Scissors and Points Tools Summary

 + click

The scissors tool cuts a segment into two segments, cuts an open path into two open paths, or breaks a closed path into one open path.

  + click

The add-anchor-point tool adds a new anchor point to a path, creating two segments but not cutting or breaking the original path.

  + click

The delete-anchor-point tool removes an anchor point from a path without cutting or breaking the path.

 + click

The convert-direction-point tool converts a corner point into a smooth point, or a smooth point into a corner point.

Brush Tool

The brush tool is used to draw variable-width lines or calligraphic lines that are objects, using a brushstroke motion for a brush-like effect. You can set a stroke width and optionally select a calligraphic style, or you can vary the stroke width with specified minimum and maximum line widths for a pressure-sensitive drawing pad using the Brush preferences dialog box. The current color and paint style attributes set in the Paint Style palette are applied to objects created with the brush tool, and you can use the Paint Style palette to change colors and attributes. The brush tool can be used with a pressure-sensitive drawing pad to achieve variable width lines (dependent on pen pressure, just as with an ink pen) and draw as with a real calligraphic pen.

To use the brush tool, first click the brush icon to select it in the tool palette. The pointer still resembles a brush when you move it into the

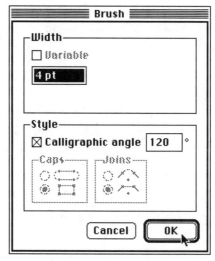

Figure 5-45.
The Brush dialog box is where you set a stroke width for the brush. Choose the Variable width option for a Pressure-sensitive drawing pad. The Calligraphic-style brush option can be used for drawing with a mouse or a Pressure-sensitive drawing pad.

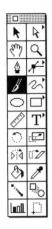

active window. To change the brush width or style before drawing, double-click the brush tool to open the Brush preferences dialog box (Figure 5-45) and specify a brush width. You can optionally select the calligraphic style option and set an angle.

To use the brush tool with a pressure-sensitive drawing pad, you must select the Variable width brush option, and specify minimum and maximum line widths. You can optionally select the calligraphic style option and set an angle.

Drag to draw with the brush tool, and a closed path object is created, which appears selected with anchor points visible. You can change the paint style attributes while the path is selected, or later use the selection tools to select and adjust the paths and change the paint style attributes. In addition, you can use the scissors tool, the add-anchor-point tool, the delete-anchor-point tool, or the convert-direction point tool to adjust the paths.

You can select cap and join styles, except for the calligraphic brush style. If you are drawing with the calligraphic style option on, then you do not have a choice of the style of caps and joins.

Brush Tool Summary

✦ + click

Draws a closed path object, using current paint style and cap and join style settings.

✦ + drag

Draws a closed path object that could vary in width if a pressure-sensitive tablet is being used, or with a specified width (if not using a pressure-sensitive tablet), or in a calligraphic style.

✦ + Command key

Temporarily changes to the direct-selection tool until the Command key is released.

✦ + Command key + Option key

Temporarily changes to the group-selection tool until the Command and Option keys are released.

Freehand Tool

The freehand tool is used to draw curves with a free hand, without constraints of any kind. The freehand tool in Adobe Illustrator is similar to the drawing tools found in other graphics programs. You can switch freely among the selection tool, the pen tool, and the freehand tool while drawing an object, making Adobe Illustrator more powerful than most drawing programs.

The freehand tool creates a straight line or curve based on the actual movement of the mouse (or stylus or trackball) — you draw with the mouse as if it were a pencil or paintbrush. Use the Control Panel to adjust the mouse to be less sensitive to variations in your hand movement when sketching, to make it a more natural activity, or use a pressure sensitive tablet and stylus.

To draw with the freehand tool, first select the freehand tool by clicking its icon in the toolbox, then position its pencil pointer at the place where you want to start drawing. As you drag this marker, it remains a pencil pointer and leaves behind a dotted line. The faster you drag, the fewer dots are created (Figure 5-46). The tool creates a normal path with points and curve segments that you can manipulate with the selection tools (Figure 5-47).

The freehand tool responds to shakiness or other slight variations in your drawing motion, creating bumps.

Figure 5-46.
Drawing with the freehand tool around a template. The faster you drag, the fewer points are created.

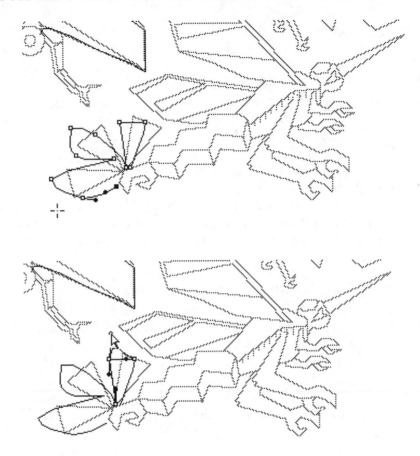

Figure 5-47.
The freehand tool turns a sketch into a path with points and curve segments that you can manipulate with the direct-selection tool or the selection tool.

You can set the freehand tolerance level to reduce (or increase) the number of bumps by choosing the General Preferences option from the File menu. The default setting for the freehand tolerance level is two pixels, which means that a variation of two pixels will not create a bump.

You can erase any part of the dotted line while you are drawing by holding down the Command key and dragging back over the line (an eraser pointer appears when you hold down the Command key). However, you can only erase the line before you release the mouse button.

You can always delete a straight line or curve segment by selecting it and pressing the Delete or Backspace key.

You can stop drawing freehand at any point, continue drawing freehand, or use the pen tool to continue the path by starting at the endpoint. To create a closed path, keep drawing with the freehand tool (or establishing points with the pen tool) until you reach the starting point of the path.

You can switch from the freehand tool to the selection tool to edit the curve segments by holding down the Command key.

You can switch to the zoom tool by holding down the Command key and the space bar, and zoom in or hold down Option as well to zoom out. You can also hold down the space bar alone to switch to the hand tool for scrolling while drawing.

You can switch from the pen tool to the freehand tool, or from the freehand tool to the pen tool, by holding down the Control key.

For example, if you are drawing with the freehand tool and want to switch to the pen tool, hold down the Control key and the freehand tool turns into the pen tool. If you are drawing with the pen tool and you want to use the freehand tool for a segment, hold down the Control key and the pen tool turns into the freehand tool. The combination of tools is the most versatile method of drawing, and these shortcuts greatly increase productivity, once you learn them.

Freehand Tool Summary

The freehand tool is used to draw curves with a free hand. The freehand tool creates a line or curve based on the actual movement of the mouse — the faster you drag, the fewer dots are created in the path.

✏▶ + Command key
Temporarily converts the freehand tool into the selection tool.

✏▶ + Space bar + drag
Temporarily converts the freehand tool into the hand tool for moving the document within the active window while drawing.

✏▶ + Command key + Space bar + click
Temporarily converts the current tool into the zoom tool for zooming into the document while using another tool.

✏▶ + Command key + Option key + Space bar + click
Temporarily converts the current tool into the zoom tool for zooming out from the document while using another tool.

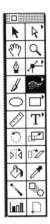

+ Control key
Switch to the pen tool.

Command key + K
Activate the General Preferences dialog box to set the freehand tool's tolerance level (default is two pixels).

Command key + drag over previous drawing
To erase any part of the dotted line while you are drawing.

Auto Trace Tool

The auto trace tool automatically traces outlines of shapes in a scanned image used as a template, so that you can start with shapes already drawn. To select the auto trace tool, drag to the right of the freehand tool.

To make use of a template for tracing, you can first sketch the rough image on paper and use an inexpensive desktop scanner to scan the image into the computer for use as a template. You can also use other painting and drawing programs on your Macintosh (such as Adobe PhotoShop, Claris MacPaint, Letraset's ImageStudio or ColorStudio, Silicon Beach Software's SuperPaint or Digital Darkroom, or other programs that can create MacPaint documents) to create or modify a template for use with Adobe Illustrator.

Once you have the template image in a MacPaint file (either scanned or painted with another program), you can display the template as a gray-filled background image while the program traces straight lines, curves, and shapes. You can at any time display only what you've drawn, or the template and what you've drawn. You can hide or show the template (Hide Template and Show Template commands in the View menu). You can see a preview of exactly how the artwork will look when printed, or of a selected portion of the artwork.

To use the auto tracing feature, first click and drag across the freehand tool to the auto trace tool icon in the toolbox, then click a starting point near the edge of the scanned shape to be traced. The program draws an outline around the shape and returns to the starting point (Figure 5-48). The automatic tracing tool works best with closed shapes, but it may treat a line as a closed shape rather than as a line.

Scanned images sometimes have gaps that are visible when you enlarge your view with the zoom tool. To control the accuracy with which the auto trace tool creates shapes, you can set the auto trace gap distance in

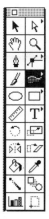

the General Preferences dialog box. The auto trace tool ignores gaps that are equal to or less than the number of pixels you specify for the distance.

The auto trace tool can draw entire paths or parts of a path. To automatically trace a partial path, drag across from the starting point to the desired ending point (Figure 5-49) rather than clicking a starting point. If you are having trouble, you can change the Auto trace gap

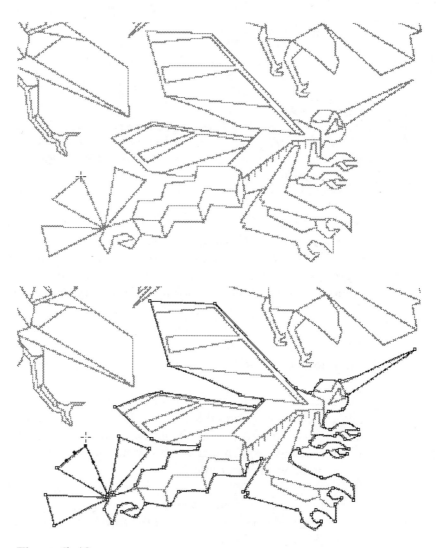

Figure 5-48.
With the auto trace tool selected, you can click a starting point to begin an automatic trace.

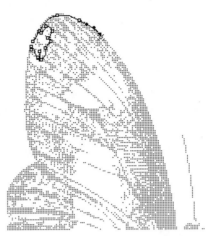

Figure 5-49.
With the auto trace tool selected, you can drag across an area to establish starting and ending points of the automatic trace, rather than tracing the entire shape. The result of dragging across the butterfly's wing tip is a series of curve segments.

setting in the General Preferences dialog box (File menu). You must start and end dragging within 0, 1, or 2 pixels of the edge of the template you want to trace. You can also draw a corner with the auto trace tool by clicking on an anchor point of an existing path where you want the corner point to be, and while holding down the Option key, dragging to the area where you want the path to end.

Auto Trace Tool Summary

The auto trace tool automatically traces outlines of shapes in a scanned image used as a template. When you click a starting point, the program draws an outline around the shape and returns to the starting point. When you drag across an area to establish starting and ending points, the program draws a partial outline.

+ click anchor point + Option key + drag
Automatically draw a corner with the auto trace tool, establishing a corner point at the anchor point.

Command key + K
Activate the General Preferences dialog box (File menu) to set the auto trace gap distance to 0, 1, or 2 (default is zero pixels).

Oval Tool

The oval tool is used to create ovals and circles. Although you can construct ovals and circles by using the pen tool to create a series of connected curves, the oval tool is much faster and easier to use because it also creates a center point for the oval or circle and groups it all together as a single object. You can't delete the center point, but you can hide it if you first select the object and then the Attributes command in the Object menu, and uncheck the Show center point box. Select the Attributes command in the Object menu, and check the Show center point box to make the center point visible again.

To draw an oval, click the oval tool in the toolbox. The arrow pointer changes into a plus sign (+) when you move it into the active window, signifying that you are about to begin drawing an entire path rather than placing an endpoint.

Position the (+) pointer where you want one side of the oval to begin. Drag left or right, up or down, or diagonally, until the oval is the size and shape you desire. The + pointer is positioned at the edge of the oval; the x indicates the center point (Figure 5-50), and the oval forms starting at the point where dragging began. The pointer moves as you drag across to the edge on the opposite side; thus the width or height of the oval is the distance between where you began dragging and the current pointer position (Figure 5-51).

You can also draw an oval from the center point to an edge with the centered-oval tool. Double-click the standard oval tool to select the center-oval tool, or press the Option key while using the oval tool. The

Figure 5-50.
Starting to draw an oval from edge to edge with the oval tool. Use the center-oval tool to draw an oval from center to edge.

Figure 5-51.
Dragging the edge of the oval (to make a perfect circle, hold down the Shift key while dragging).

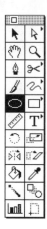

point at which you start dragging becomes the center point, and the point at which you release the mouse button becomes an anchor point at the edge of the oval.

If you hold down Option and then click a center point instead of dragging an oval, a center point is placed where you clicked, and the Oval dialog box appears (Figure 5-52), allowing you to specify dimensions for height and width of the oval or circle. If the unit of measure is not the one you want, Cancel, and change it in the General Preferences dialog box available from the File menu (Command-K) to points/picas, inches, or centimeters. (Changing the unit of measure only affects new objects you draw. It does not change the size of objects previously drawn using another Ruler unit setting.)

Ovals or circles created with the oval tool consist of four curved segments connected by four anchor points and a center point. The center point looks like an x when it is not selected, and like a regular small square anchor point when it is selected. The center point is created by the program as a reference point for aligning or manipulating an oval.

Selecting the center point also selects the lines and vice-versa. You can cut the oval or circle with the scissors—first select the oval with a selection tool and then select the scissors tool. You can also use the add-anchor-point, delete-anchor-point, and convert-direction-point tools to modify the oval or circle, after first selecting the ellipse with a selection tool, however, you cannot delete or change the center point (but you can hide the center point).

You create a circle the same way you create an oval except that you hold down the Shift key (to constrain the oval into a circle) while dragging up or down, left or right, or diagonally, to form a circle from edge to edge. Hold down the Shift key and drag the center-oval tool to construct the

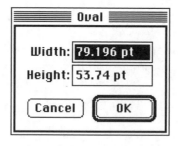

Figure 5-52.
The Oval dialog box lets you specify the dimensions of an oval or circle in width and height. Use the same number for both entries to specify the diameter of a circle.

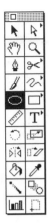

circle from center to edge. To create a circle with the Oval dialog box (activated by clicking rather than dragging with the oval tool), specify the same numbers for both height and width.

As a shortcut, no matter whether you click or drag to draw an oval or circle, if you want to clone it, click at the center point desired for positioning the duplicate object, and then press the Return key or click the OK button when the dialog box appears, and the size settings you last used are used again to draw the new object, which appears selected and slightly offset from the first. If you click to specify the size for a circle or oval, draw a second circle or oval by dragging, and then click to create a third, the dimensions in the dialog box represent the size of the second object, and not the first.

The four sides of any oval or circle that you draw are aligned with the coordinates of the program's current x and y axes. However, if you have altered the x and y axes by changing the Constrain angle setting in the General Preferences dialog box (select the Preferences and General commands from the File menu, or use Command-K), the circle or oval is drawn aligned to the new angle of constraint of the x and y axes. If you have altered the x and y axes, the diagonal dragging of the mouse (and therefore the construction of the oval or circle) is relative to the new x and y axes.

When you change the Constrain angle setting, the new angle only applies to new objects you draw. This means that if you have rotated the x and y axes by 30 degrees, any ovals and circles you then create with the oval tool will be drawn at a 30-degree angle (Figure 5-53). Ovals, circles, rectangles, squares, and type are placed at whatever angle of constraint is specified. If you aren't getting circles when you hold down the Shift key, check the alignment of the x and y axes by looking at the Constrain

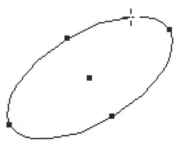

Figure 5-53.
The Constrain angle set in the General Preferences dialog box determines how ovals and circles are drawn. This oval has been drawn at a 30-degree angle of constraint.

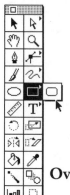

angle setting in the dialog box that appears after you select the General Preferences option in the File menu (Command-K). The default setting is zero. (NOTE: You may notice the effect of a constrain angle other than 0 degrees when drawing ovals, but may not notice the constrain angle when drawing circles. However, the constrain angle determines the placement of anchor points on circles.) To change the angle of constraint on an already drawn oval or circle, use the rotate tool.

Oval Tool Summary

+ drag

Draws an oval from edge to edge as you drag.

+ drag
+ Option key + drag

Draws an oval from its center to its edge as you drag instead of drawing it from edge to edge.

+ Shift key + drag

Draws a circle from edge to edge by constraining an oval.

+ Shift key + drag

Draws a circle from its center to its edge as you drag instead of drawing it from edge to edge.

+ click
+ click

Establishes a center point and displays a dialog box where you specify precise dimensions for height and width. Use the same number for height and width to create a circle.

Rectangle Tools

The rectangle tools are used to create rectangles and squares. Although it is certainly possible to construct rectangles and squares by using the pen tool to draw a path consisting of four straight lines, the rectangle tools are much faster and easier to use for this task, because they also create a center point for the rectangle or square and group the object's components together as a single object. (You cannot delete the center point, but

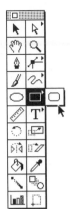

you can hide it if you first select the object and then the Attributes command in the Object menu, and uncheck the Show center point box. Select the Attributes command in the Object menu, and check the Show center point box to make the center point visible again.)

Illustrator offers two rectangle tools: the standard rectangle with sharp corners, and a rounded-rectangle tool. Both come in two flavors: one for drawing from the edge, and one for drawing from the center.

To begin drawing a rectangle from the edge, click the standard rectangle tool in the toolbox. The arrow pointer changes into a plus sign (+) when you move it into the active window, signifying that you are about to begin drawing an entire path rather than placing an endpoint.

Position the (+) pointer where you want one of the corners of the rectangle to be placed. Drag left, right, up, down, and diagonally, until the rectangle is the size and shape you desire. The + pointer is positioned at the edge of the oval; the x indicates the center point of the rectangle (Figure 5-54), and the rectangle forms starting at the point where you began dragging. The pointer moves as you drag across to the edge on the opposite side; thus the width and height of the rectangle are the distance between where you began dragging and the current pointer position (Figure 5-55).

To draw the rectangle from the center, double-click the standard rectangle tool to select the centered-rectangle tool, or press the Option key while using the rectangle tool. The point where you start dragging becomes the center point, and the point where you release the mouse button becomes an anchor point at the edge of the rectangle.

If you hold down the Option key and click a center point instead of dragging a rectangle, a center point is placed where you clicked, and the Rectangle dialog box appears so that you can specify dimensions for height and width, and a corner radius (Figure 5-56).

Figure 5-54.
The starting point of a rectangle as it is drawn with the standard (drawing from the edge) rectangle tool.

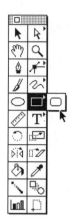

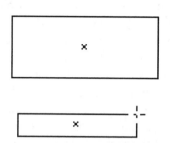

Figure 5-55.
Dragging the rectangle to the size and shape desired.

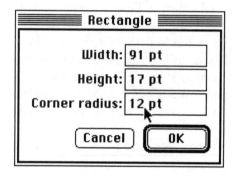

Figure 5-56.
Clicking with the Option key and center-rectangle tool brings up the Rectangle dialog box, which lets you specify dimensions and the corner radius.

The Rectangle dialog box allows you to specify dimensions for height and width of the rectangle, rounded-rectangle, square or rounded-square, but if the unit of measure is not the one you want, Cancel, and change it in the General Preferences dialog box available from the File menu (Command-K) to points/picas, inches, or centimeters. Then select the rectangle tool and Option-click a center point to get the Rectangle dialog box, where you can specify height, width, and a corner radius, using the newly specified unit of measure. (Changing the unit of measure only affects new objects you draw. It does not change the size of objects previously drawn using another Ruler unit setting.)

If you specify a corner radius, that radius is applied to all new squares or rectangles you draw, until you change it again in the Rectangle dialog box, or in the General Preferences dialog box (select Preferences and General from the File menu, or use the Command-K shortcut). Which-

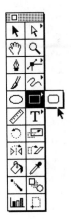

ever dialog box (Rectangle or General Preferences) you use to change the corner radius, the other dialog box is automatically updated to be the same corner radius.

The default corner radius is 12 points. A corner radius of 0 gives you square corners. If you are using the rectangle tool and you specify a corner radius greater than 0, then the rounded-rectangle tool is invoked. Conversely, if you are using the rounded-rectangle tool, and you specify a corner radius of 0, the rectangle tool is automatically invoked. Always specify the corner radius before drawing the rectangle, because you can't apply a new corner radius to an existing rectangle.

Rectangles created with the rectangle tool consist of the four straight line segments connected by four anchor points and a center point. Rounded-rectangles created with the rounded-rectangle tool consist of the four curved segments, which are connected by four anchor points and a center point. If the rounded-rectangle is too small for the corner radius specified a circle is drawn.

Rounded-rectangles can alternatively consist of the four curved segments and two line segments, which are connected by six anchor points and a center point, or four curved segments and four line segments, which are connected by eight anchor points and a center point (Figure 5-57). The center point is created by the program as a reference point for aligning or manipulating a rectangle. The center point looks like an x when it is not selected, and like a regular filled square anchor point when it is selected (Figure 5-58).

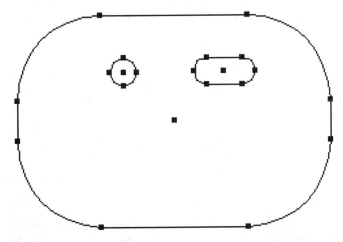

Figure 5-57.
Round-cornered rectangles, drawn with a 12 point corner radius are selected, showing corner points, anchor points, and center points.

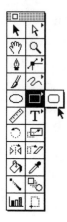

Selecting the center point also selects the four lines and vice-versa. You can cut the rectangle or square with the scissors — first select the rectangle with a selection tool and then select the scissors tool. You can also use the add-anchor-point, delete-anchor-point, and convert-direction-point tools to modify the rectangle or square, after first selecting the object with a selection tool, however, you cannot delete or change the center point (but you can hide the center point, as described earlier).

You create a square, or rounded-corner square, the same way that you create a rectangle except that you hold down the Shift key (to constrain the rectangle into a square) while dragging, or you can use the Rectangle dialog box and specify the same number for width and height, and set a corner radius (Figure 5-59). To

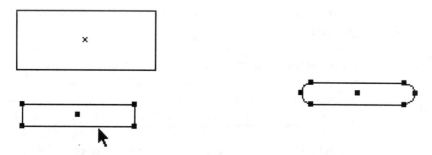

Figure 5-58.
The specified corner dimensions in the Rectangle dialog box draw a round-cornered rectangle. Both the round-cornered rectangle and a 0-corner-radius rectangle are selected, showing corner points and center points.

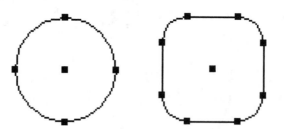

Figure 5-59.
Rounded-corner squares drawn using the Rectangle dialog box to specify dimensions and a cornerradius. The square on the left has a 2-point corner radius, and the square on the right has a 1-point corner radius.

construct a square from center to corner, hold down the Shift key when dragging with the center-rectangle tool or center-rounded-rectangle tool, or click to invoke the rectangle dialog box, and specify the same dimensions for height and width.

If you have created a rectangle, rounded-rectangle, rounded-square, or square and want to clone it, no matter whether you dragged or clicked to create the first object, you can click where you want the duplicate object's center to be, then press the Return key or click OK when the dialog box appears, and the same size settings you last used are used to draw the new object. If you click to specify the size for a rectangle or square, then you draw a second rectangle or square by dragging and click to create a third, the dimensions in the dialog box represent the size of the second rectangle, not the first. However, the corner radius you set remains in effect for all new rectangles or squares, until you change the setting again in the Rectangle dialog box or General Preferences dialog box.

If the square or rectangle you draw is small, and the corner radius specified is large, and the circle radius is too big for the object, the program draws the largest circle that can fit inside the square. This effect produces a circle or oval for certain sizes, until the square or rectangle reaches a large enough size to use the specified corner radius. From that point, no matter how large a square or rectangle you draw, the specified corner radius is used.

The four sides of any rectangle or square that you draw are aligned with the angle of the current constraining x and y axes, set in the General Preferences dialog box. If the Constrain angle setting in the General Preferences dialog box in the File menu (Command-K) is not 0 degrees the diagonal dragging of the mouse (and therefore the construction of the square or rectangle) is relative to the new x and y axes.

When you change the Constrain angle, the new angle only applies to new objects you draw. For example, if you have rotated the x and y axes by 30 degrees (in the Preferences dialog box, setting the Constrain angle to 30 degrees), then all rectangles and squares will be drawn at a 30-degree angle. If you can't get right angles on your parallelograms, check the alignment of the x and y axes by looking at the Constrain angle setting in the Preferences dialog box (the default setting is zero).

Neither the size nor the angle of constraint for a rectangle or square can be changed after it's drawn. Set the desired angle of constraint before drawing, and don't stop dragging until the size is right. To change the angle of constraint on an already drawn rectangle or square, use the rotate tool.

Rectangle Tool Summary

+ drag
Draws a rectangle from corner to corner as you drag.

+ Option + drag
+ drag
Draws the rectangle from its center to its corner as you drag, instead of drawing the rectangle from corner to corner.

+ Shift key + drag
+ Shift key + drag
Draws a square by constraining a rectangle to equal dimensions for height and width as you drag from corner to corner or center to corner.

+ click
+ click
Establishes a center point and displays the Rectangle dialog box where you specify precise dimensions for height, width, and corner radius. Use the same number for height and width to create a square. Dimensions remain the same for the next rectangle unless you drag to draw a different-sized rectangle or change the settings in the dialog box, or change the corner radius in the General Preferences dialog box.

+ drag
Draws a rounded rectangle from corner to corner as you drag.

+ Option + drag
+ drag
Draws the rounded rectangle from its center to its corner as you drag, instead of drawing it from corner to corner.

+ Shift key + drag
+ Shift key + drag
Draws a rounded square (a circle) by constraining a rounded rectangle to equal dimensions for height and width as you drag from corner to corner or center to corner.

+ Option + click
+ Option + click
Establishes a center point and displays a dialog box where you specify precise dimensions for height, width, and corner radius for a rounded-

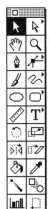

rectangle. Use the same number for height and width to create a rounded square. The corner radius minimum is 0 (which invokes the corresponding rectangle tool), and the maximum is 12 points (default). Dimensions remain the same for the next rectangle unless you drag to draw a different-sized rectangle or change the settings in the dialog box.

Measure Tool

The measure tool measures the distance between any two points or two areas in your drawing space, and displays the dimensions in the unit of measure selected in the General Preferences dialog box in the File menu or in the Document Setup dialog box (the default Ruler units are in inches, or click to use picas/points, or centimeters). You can use the measure tool in any window view, including the Preview view.

To measure distance, click the measure tool icon in the toolbox. The measure tool displays a + pointer when it moves into the active window. Then click the first point (Figure 5-60). The Info palette appears with x and y distance measures for the location of the first click, from the x and

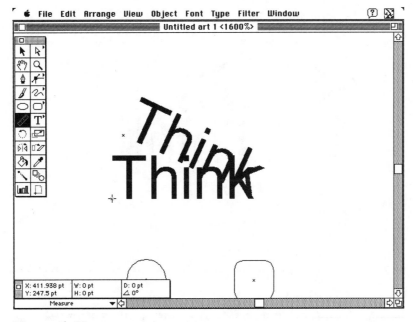

Figure 5-60.
Clicking the first point in the artwork (in Artwork view) with the measure tool.

y axes. Click the second point (Figure 5-61), and the Info palette displays x and y distance measures for the location of the second click, the angle of an imaginary line connecting the two points, and the distance along the horizontal and vertical axes between the two points (the dimensions of a triangle).

The Show Info command in the Window menu also brings up the Info palette, which can be used to show dimensions of an object you select with a selection tool, or to show the point size and typeface of text, and tracking values (Figure 5-62), when you are using the text tools.

Whether you use the measure tool and click, or you select the Show Info palette from the Window menu, the Info palette remains displayed until you click its close box, or select Hide Info from the Window menu.

When you use the measure tool to measure an object, the measurements are used to update the Move dialog box, so that you can easily move the object precisely, but the measurements change whenever you perform an action that moves or copies a selection, so be sure to perform the move right away.

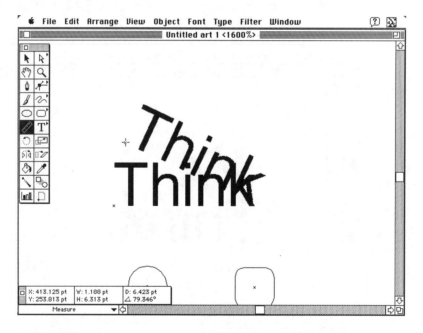

Figure 5-61.
The Info palette with distance and angle information. The angle describes the line between the two points clicked and the distance along the horizontal and vertical axes.

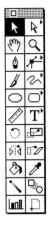

If you have turned on Snap to point in the General Preferences dialog box (Command-K), the measure tool will snap to the nearest anchor point or guide object, giving an imprecise result. For more about the Snap to point option, see the section on the Preferences and General commands (File menu).

You can constrain the measurement to an angle that is a multiple of 45 degrees by holding down the Shift key when clicking the second point. If the second click is snapped to an anchor point, the Shift key does not constrain the measure. If the second click is at a 45-degree angle, then measurement is constrained to where the path intersects the imaginary 45-degree axis running through the second point.

Measure Tool Summary

+ click first point

Displays the Info palette with the x and y distance measures for the location of the first click, from the x and y axes.

+ click first point + click second point

Displays the Info palette with the following information: the x and y distance measures for the location of the second click, the angle of an imaginary line connecting the two points, and the distance along the horizontal and vertical axes between the two points (the dimensions of a triangle).

+ click first point + Shift key + click second point

Constrains the measurement to the x and y axes, or to an angle that is a multiple of a 45-degree offset from the x and y axes. If the second point is an anchor point, measuring will not be constrained.

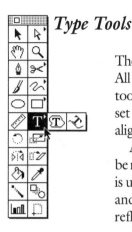

Type Tools

The type tools let you incorporate text and typography into your artwork. All PostScript (Type 1) fonts work with the type tools. You use the type tools to add new text and to select and edit text, and the Type menu to set or change the type specifications (font, size, leading, etc.) and alignment settings.

Adobe Illustrator treats an element of text as a single object that can be manipulated in the same way as any other artwork. Type manipulation is useful for creating such things as typographic design elements, logos, and special headlines. Special effects can be achieved by rotating, reflecting, scaling, shearing, painting, or stroking text elements.

All of the characters within a text block, or individual characters isolated into their own text block, can be manipulated as artwork and blended with the blend tool after conversion into outlines with the Create Outlines command in the Type menu. (Plate 7, "Swan," and Plate 8, "Violin," use outlines created from the "S" and "V" characters that are blended into a swan and violin, respectively.)

Illustrator offers the standard (default) type tool (or rectangle type tool) that places text at a specified point or inside a rectangle, the area-type tool that places text so that it fits inside (or outside) an area defined by an open or closed path, and the path-type tool that places text using a path (which can be open or closed) as a baseline. You can also link one rectangle or path to another so that text flows from one element to the next (for example, text in columns).

Illustrator creates four different types of type, and uses three different type pointers or cursors.

Point type is created when you use the standard type tool (which uses an I-beam cursor surrounded by a box) to click a starting point (away from other objects) for placing text. Point type is not attached to any other objects.

To create *rectangle type*, you drag a marquee (dotted-line box) using the standard type tool (which again displays an I-beam cursor surrounded by a box) to first create a rectangle, and then you type the text, which is contained within the rectangle. Alternatively, you can use the rectangle tool to create a box, using the rectangle dialog box to specify dimensions. Then choose the standard type tool, click inside the rectangle at one of the corners, and type the text. Do not press return at the end of each line— the text will be word-wrapped to fit the rectangle. Press the Return key only at the ends of paragraphs.

To create *area type*, you use the area-type tool and click when the area-type cursor is positioned over a path. Area type can be placed inside the

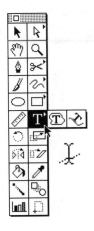

closed path, to fill the object, or, by adjusting the Baseline Shift to a negative value, it can be positioned to follow the outside edge of the object (to wrap around the object). Click the lever in the lower right corner of the Character dialog box to display (or hide) the Baseline Shift setting. To invoke the Character dialog box, select the Character command from the Type menu, or select the Show Character command from the Window menu.

To create *path type*, first select the path-type tool, and then click when the path-type cursor is positioned over an open or closed path. Path type can be placed inside the closed path, by adjusting the Baseline Shift to a negative value, or it can be positioned to follow the outside edge of the object (to wrap around the object), using zero or a positive value for the baseline shift setting. Both the position and the direction of path type can be changed, using the selection tool.

The type tools can place text anywhere. You can create type at a point, within a rectangle, inside (or outside) an area defined by an open or closed path, and using a path (which can be open or closed) as a baseline. You can drag the standard type tool to create the rectangle to hold the text, or you can click inside an existing rectangle.

No matter which method you use to create the type, you can type new text or select any number of text objects (Figure 5-62), and edit the text or change its font by selecting a new font from the Font menu, or change its characteristics with commands in the Type menu. You can't set text styles, such as Underline, Strikethru, Outline, Shadow, and Reverse, but you can achieve these effects and more using Illustrator's tools, commands and filters. Selecting the Character and Paragraph commands from the Type menu display the Character and Paragraph dialog boxes for making multiple changes at once. For more about type attributes and type characteristics, see the Type menu section later in this chapter.

When you drag the standard type tool to create a rectangle (a column), the rectangle itself does not have a fill or stroke; it does not appear in print or in Preview. If you want the rectangle to appear, you must select it and use the Paint Style command in the Object menu to fill and/or stroke it. You can also create a rectangle first, then use the type tool to place text inside it if you want the rectangle to be visible. If you are using the standard type tool, be sure the type cursor snaps to the left side of the rectangle (or to another side, depending on the Constrain angle set in the General Preferences dialog box), or the type created will be point type, not attached to the shape. You can also use to the area-type tool to easily create area type inside the object.

The type tool changes into the area-type cursor when you move it over a selected closed path (Figure 5-63). It changes into the path-type cursor

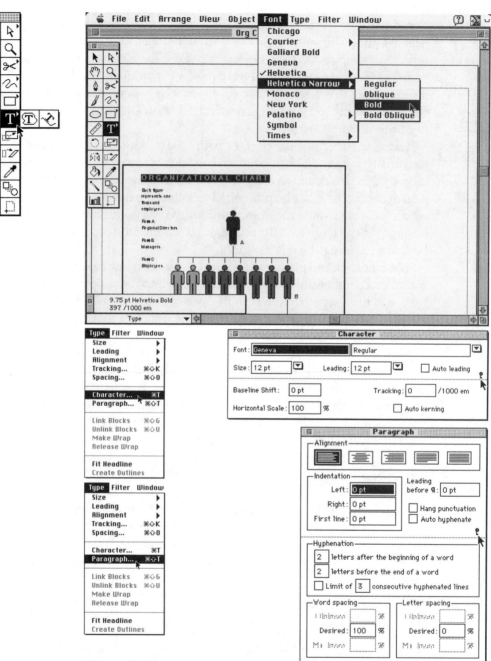

Figure 5-62.

Typing and then selecting the text with the type tool, and changing the font, size, spacing, alignment, and other settings using the Type menu commands. The selected type's size, font, and tracking values are displayed in the Info palette at the bottom left corner of the window.

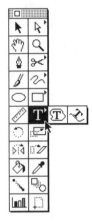

when you move it close to an open path. Thus, you can use the standard type tool for all three operations, or you can switch tools. The area-type tool lets you enter text only inside areas, and the path-type tool lets you enter text only to be aligned along a path.

Select either the area-type tool or the path-type tool by dragging to the right of the type tool. Click inside a closed path with the area-type tool. Click near a path to use the path-type tool (Figure 5-64). Type the text, and it appears with its baseline attached to the path. You can place text along a closed path's outline, rather than within the closed path, by using the path-type tool rather than the area-type tool.

If you enter more text than the amount that can fit inside the area, a plus sign appears. To display more of the text element you can adjust the path enclosing the text, lengthen the open path to which the text is attached (see Figure 5-63), or link the text object to another object.

To link a text object to another duplicate object, so that the text overflow from the first object appears in the second, use the group-selection tool and the Option key to drag a copy of the object to the new location. Text flows from the first to the second automatically.

To link blocks of rectangle type and/or area type, including irregular objects containing text, use the direct selection tool to select the blocks, and then select the Link Blocks command from the Type menu. A single text element can then fill several columns or irregularly shaped objects. Select the Unlink Blocks command from the Type menu to unlink selected text blocks.

To change the order in which text flows from one object to another, use the Send to Back and Bring to Front commands (from the Arrange menu) or Paste in Back and Paste in Front (from the Edit menu) to change the stacking order of the objects either before or after linking the objects. Type always flows from the backmost object to the frontmost object.

Any path can be used as an area for enclosing text. The path is set to be without a stroke or fill, although you can paint the path to have a stroke and fill after adding the text. Regular text paths (unstroked and unfilled) can be placed on top of other paths without obscuring them. This is the typical method for precisely aligning text within a shape.

Text within an area (rectangle or area type) can be made to wrap around an irregularly shaped object within the area. However, the object within the area must be in front of the object containing the text (use the Bring to Front command from the Arrange menu or the Paste in Front command from the Edit menu), and if the text is grouped, it must be ungrouped. (To see if the text is part of a group, use the group-selection tool to first click the text to select the text, and then click again to select any objects grouped with it.) To wrap text around an object,

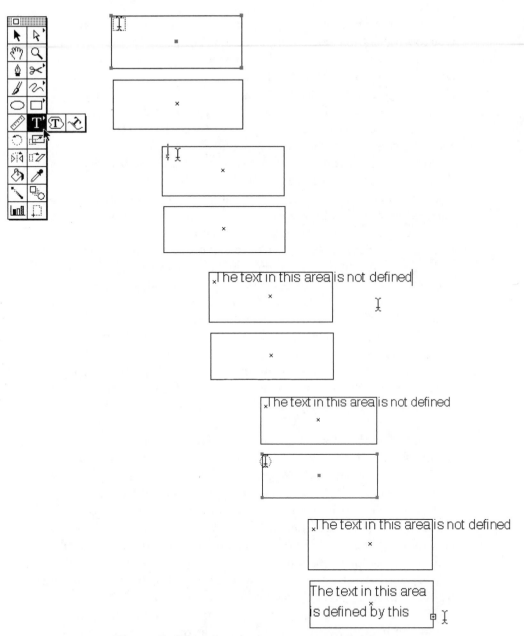

Figure 5-63.

The type and area-type tools flow text within a rectangle. You can enter text inside a closed path with the area-type tool. By positioning the type tool over a selected closed path, you can enter text inside the closed path. If you position the type tool within, but not touching the path, you create point type, which is a separate object, not bounded by the closed path object. You can also link text elements.

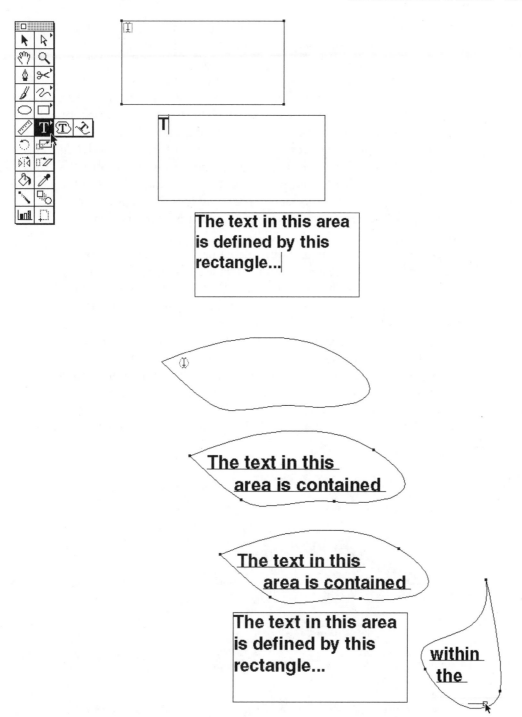

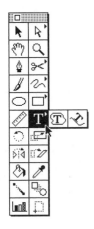

select the text object and the graphic object using the selection tool, and choose Make Wrap from the Type menu. The Release Wrap command separates the text object from the graphic object.

For the most precise of wraps, you can use the drawing tools to create an unfilled, unstroked object to use (as a sort of boundary box) for a precise text wrap to fit a particular shape, then select the text object and boundary box object using the selection tool, and choose Make Wrap from the Type menu. Adjust the wrap using the direct-selection tool and other tools, and then place the graphic object in front. The advantage to using a new object as a boundary box is that anchor points can be added and deleted to the boundary box object, and its shape can be adjusted to form a precise wrap of the text, without making any changes to the graphic object placed in front of the text.

You can attach the baseline of text to a path (one text element per path). You can flip the direction of the text along the path by dragging the text pointer across the path, or by double-clicking the pointer (Figure 5-65). To move text across a path without changing its direction, use the Baseline Shift option in the Character dialog box.

The baseline for text elements not aligned on a path (area type, rectangle type and point type) are aligned with the coordinates of Illustrator's current x and y axes, so if you have altered the x and y axes by setting a Constrain angle, the baseline of the text is aligned relative to the new x and y axes. Activate the Preferences and General dialog box to check or change the constrain angle that governs the angle of the type

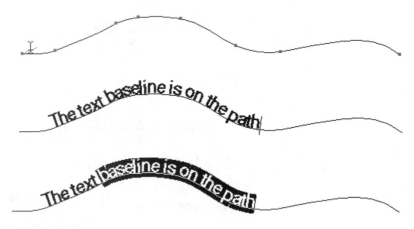

Figure 5-64.
Entering type with the path-type tool along an open path, then selecting the text to be edited. When path type is added to a path, the path becomes a text path (with no stroke and no fill, until you specify them).

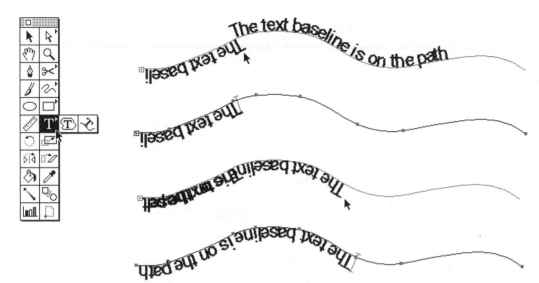

Figure 5-65.
Dragging the alignment point of path type across the baseline of an open path with the selection tool to reverse the type's direction. Path type can also be repositioned by dragging its alignment point to a new position on the path.

baseline, and adjust the Baseline shift increments setting (also in the General Preferences dialog box), which determines how much the baseline is shifted up when you press Option-Shift-Up Arrow, or how much the baseline is shifted down when you press Option-Shift-Down Arrow.

An alignment point appears in the baseline of the type at the left end if the type is left-justified (Figure 5-65), at the right end if it is right-justified, or in the center if it is centered (Figure 5-66). This alignment point can be moved by the selection tool (along with the attached baseline) so that you can align the type to an exact point in the artwork.

The Fit Headline command in the Type menu fits blocks of rectangle type and/or area type across the width of an object. If the type font used is one of the Adobe multiple master fonts, the type is fitted by adjusting the weight of the font and the tracking value. For other fonts, such as TrueType fonts, only the tracking value is adjusted.

You can even import text, using any type tool to first click an insertion point, and then use the Import Text command from the File menu to select a text document to import. Each line of text is wrapped around to fit inside the defined area. Use a Return only to define the ends of

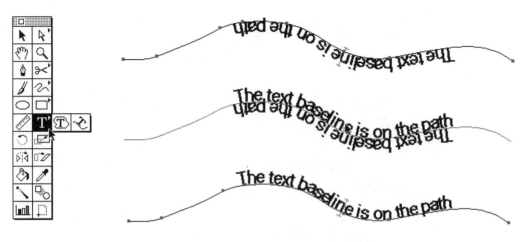

Figure 5-66.
In Center-aligned text, the alignment point is in the center of the path text, but not necessarily in the center of the open path it is attached to.

paragraphs. However, if the text is word-wrapped, and it is imported as point type, each line of imported text ends only when a Return is encountered, which means each paragraph is only one line long.

Text objects can be transformed using the rotate, scale, reflect, or shear tools.

If text objects are linked, and you don't want to transform them all, use the group-selection tool to select only the objects that you want to transform, and then select the desired transformation tool. For example, you can rotate text by a percentage you specify with the rotate tool, or you can use the Rotate tool to rotate the type freely with the mouse. Text and graphics can be selected and scaled together because they are treated in the same manner. At any point you can edit the text as usual, by clicking the text element with the text tool (double-click to select a word, drag to select a block, etc.).

Once converted to outline format, the outlines of individual characters can be edited like regular curves and lines. The Create Outlines command in the Type menu converts a text object (using any Type 1 or TrueType fonts installed in your system) into a set of paths which you can then edit and manipulate with the selection tools. Letters are comprised of compound paths, in which you can see through transparent areas of the path.

Outlines of characters can be modified to create logos, display type, or a variety of special effects, such as gradient color fills. Illustrator 5 includes 40 Adobe Type 1 fonts that you can modify. Note that the entire text

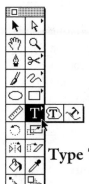

object is converted, so you must create a text object containing only one letter if you want only one letter to be converted.

Note: See also the Type menu section (later in this chapter) for more information on type attributes and shortcuts for setting type characteristics.

Type Tools Summary

You use the type tools to add text, edit text, and set the type specifications and alignment, and you use the Font and Type menus for access to type fonts, specifications, and special effects.

Graphical text effects can be achieved by using the rotate, reflect, scale, and shear tools, and painting and stroking type in the Paint Style dialog box. If you altered the x and y axes by setting a Constrain angle, the baseline of the new text is aligned to the new x and y axes.

T (pointer is ⟦Ⅰ⟧) + click outside path or shape
The type tool can place text anywhere on the page.

T (pointer is ⟦Ⅰ⟧) + drag
The type tool can create a rectangular column of text anywhere on the page.

T (pointer changes to (Ⅰ)) + click inside closed path
The type tool can place text inside a closed path.

T (pointer changes to Ⅰ) + click outside closed path
The type tool can place text along the outside of a closed path.

T (pointer changes to Ⅰ) + click on open path
The type tool can place text along an open path.

⟨T⟩ + click inside closed path
The area-type tool places text inside a closed path.

⤳ + click outside closed path
The path-type tool places text along the outside of a closed path.

⤳ + click on open path
The path-type tool places text along an open path.

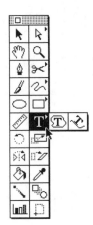

Command key + K

Activate the Preferences and General dialog box to check or change the constrain angle that governs the angle of the type baseline, and adjust the Baseline shift increments setting (also in the General Preferences dialog box), which determines how much the baseline is shifted up when you press Option-Shift-Up Arrow, or how much the baseline is shifted down when you press Option-Shift-Down Arrow (see shortcuts below).

Command key + T

Activate the Character dialog box (from the Type menu) to change the font, type size, leading, baseline shift, horizontal scale, and tracking, and to turn on or off auto leading and auto kerning.

Command key + Shift + T

Activate the Paragraph dialog box (from the Type menu) to change the alignment, indentation, hyphenation, and word spacing and letterspacing specifications. Also set the leading before paragraphs, and turn on or off hanging punctuation and auto hyphenation.

+ Option key + (Shift key — optional) + drag

Create a duplicate shape, linked to the original, with type flowing to the new shape.

Select a block of rectangle type or area type with the group-selection tool, begin dragging, and hold down the Option key (also hold down the Shift key to constrain the shape to match the original) while dragging, until the duplicate shape is in the position you want it in. Keep the Shift and Option keys depressed until you let go of the mouse button, and a duplicate shape is created, with text automatically flowing into the new object. The two objects are automatically linked.

+ drag

Moves path type along a path, into a new position on the path.

First click at the beginning of the path type with the path-type tool to position an I-beam text entry cursor at the beginning of the path type. Next, select the path type with the selection tool. (Note: the I-beam cursor will be repositioned when you select the path type with the selection tool, depending on the alignment setting. For this example, we assume the text is left-aligned. In your case, drag the I-beam cursor, whatever its position in the line of type.)

Click and drag the I-beam cursor at the beginning of the line of type until the type is where you want it to be. Drag in the direction you want

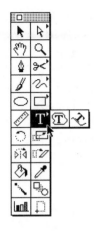

the type to move, but be careful not to drag across the baseline of the path (see next shortcut), or the direction of the type will also be changed.

↖ + drag, or,

↖ + double-click mouse

Moves path type across a path, into a new position on the path, and changes the direction of the type.

First click with the path-type tool to position an I-beam text entry cursor at the beginning or at any position in the line of the path type. Next, select the path type with the selection tool. (Note: the I-beam cursor will be repositioned when you select the path type with the selection tool, depending on the alignment setting. In this example, we assume the text is left-aligned. In your case, drag the I-beam cursor, whatever its position in the line of type.)

Click and drag the I-beam cursor at the beginning of the line of type up or down across the baseline of the path to change both the direction and position of the type.

Alternatively, you can double-click the I-beam cursor at the beginning of the line of type to change the direction of the type, and use the same starting position. To change position, but not the direction of the type, see next shortcut.

T + Option key + Shift key + Up-arrow key

⟨T⟩ + Option key + Shift key + Up-arrow key

⤳⟨ + Option key + Shift key + Up-arrow key

Baseline shift shortcut. After using any of the type tools to select the text, you can quickly adjust the baseline shift of point type, rectangle type, area type and path type up by holding down the Option and Shift keys and then pressing the Up-arrow key until the type is in the position you want, above the baseline. To adjust the increments shifted with each up-arrow key, change the Baseline Shift Keyboard increments setting to be bigger or smaller in the General Preferences dialog box in the File menu (Command-K).

T + Option key + Shift key + Down-arrow key

⟨T⟩ + Option key + Shift key + Down-arrow key

⤳⟨ + Option key + Shift key + Down-arrow key

Baseline shift shortcut. After using any of the type tools to select the

text, you can quickly adjust the baseline shift of point type, rectangle type, area type and path type down by holding down the Option and Shift keys and then pressing the Down-arrow key until the type is in the position you want, below the baseline. To adjust the increments shifted with each down-arrow key, change the Baseline Shift Keyboard increments setting to be bigger or smaller in the General Preferences dialog box in the File menu (Command-K).

Note: See the Type menu section (later in this chapter) for more information on type attributes and shortcuts for setting type characteristics.

Rotate Tool

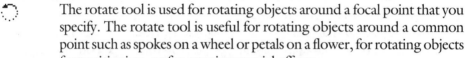

The rotate tool is used for rotating objects around a focal point that you specify. The rotate tool is useful for rotating objects around a common point such as spokes on a wheel or petals on a flower, for rotating objects for positioning, or for creating special effects.

Before you use the rotate tool you must first select the path or any other object that you want to rotate (you can select multiple segments and paths). To select more than one object to rotate, either drag a selection marquee around the objects or select one object first by clicking it, and then hold down the Shift key as you click to select each remaining object. Once you have selected the object or objects that you wish to rotate, you can either rotate the selected object by dragging, or you can request the Rotate dialog box for specifying precise amounts of rotation.

If you want to rotate the selected object by dragging, first click the rotate tool in the toolbox. The pointer will turn into a plus sign (+) when you move it into the active window. Next, click at the point you wish to establish as the point of rotation; the axis around which the selected object will be rotated. Clicking establishes the center of rotation (see Figure 5-67).

The pointer changes from a plus sign to an arrowhead to indicate that the center point has been established. When you hold down the mouse button and drag the mouse in a circular motion around the center point, the selected objects will rotate around the center point (see Figure 5-68).

If you need more control over the rotation, begin dragging at a point that is farther from the center of rotation.

Alternatively, you can use the center of the object as the center of rotation. Simply click and drag the selected object with the rotate tool.

While dragging, you will see both the original object you selected and

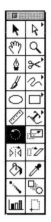

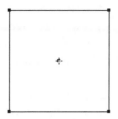

Figure 5-67.
To rotate the square, position the pointer over the axis of rotation (in this case, through the center) and click to establish the rotation focal point.

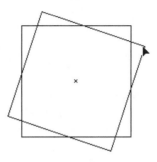

Figure 5-68.
You can rotate the object freely with the mouse after clicking the focal point; holding down the Shift key constrains the rotation to 45-degree increments, offset by the constrain angle. Set or change constrain angle with Command-K shortcut.

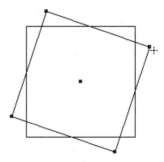

Figure 5-69.
Holding down the Option key while dragging with the rotate tool. Dragging at a point far from the focal point gives finer control over movement.

the rotating counterpart. When you have finished rotating the selected object, release the mouse button and the original object will be erased, leaving only the rotated object. However, if you hold down the Option key while dragging, a duplicate will be created and rotated, leaving the original in its place (Figure 5-69).

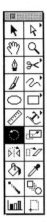

You can repeat the rotation as often as you want by selecting Repeat Transform from the Arrange menu or by pressing Command-D as a shortcut (Figure 5-70). You can achieve special effects by using Repeat Transform over and over (Figure 5-71).

Even if rulers are displayed, rotating objects by dragging a precise amount can be difficult. For better control over rotation, hold down the Shift key while dragging; this constrains the rotation angle to multiples of 45 degrees. For precise control over the angle of rotation, use the Rotate dialog box.

To use the Rotate dialog box for rotating objects by a precise amount, first click the rotate tool in the toolbox. The arrow pointer will turn into a plus sign (+) whenever you move it into the active window. Next, position the pointer over the spot that you want to become the axis around which the selected object will be rotated, hold down the Option key, and click once to establish the center of rotation. As soon as you hold down the Option key, the (+) pointer changes into a (+...) pointer, indicating that the Rotate dialog box is ready to be requested; when you click the mouse, the Rotate dialog box will appear (Figure 5-72).

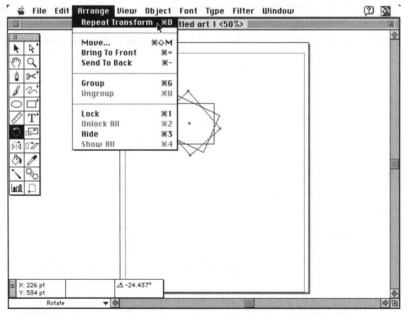

Figure 5-70.
Using the Repeat Transform command to repeat the transformation (in this case, a rotation). You can repeat the transformation over and over with this menu command, or with the Command-D shortcut.

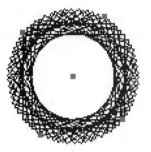

Figure 5-71.
The result of many Repeat Transform commands to continually rotate and duplicate the square.

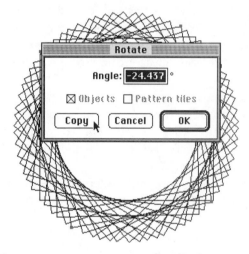

Figure 5-72.
Hold down Option when clicking the focal point with the rotate tool to activate the Rotate dialog box, or double-click the rotate tool to use the center point of the selected object as the focal point. You have the option to rotate objects and/or pattern tiles if the object is painted or stroked with a pattern. You can rotate a clone (and leave the original in place) by clicking the Copy button.

If you intend to rotate objects exclusively by means of the Rotate dialog box, using their center points as the point of rotation, you can select the object(s) to be rotated and then double-click the rotate tool. This way, you don't have to hold down the Option key to bring up the dialog box—whenever you double-click the rotate tool, the Rotate dialog box automatically appears.

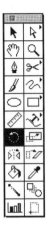

The Rotate dialog box retains the settings from the previous rotation. If this is the first use of the rotate tool since you started up the program, the rotation angle is set to zero.

Specify the desired angle of rotation in degrees. The angle of rotation that you specify is applied relative to the x axis, and objects are rotated around the center point (which is the intersection of the x and y axes). You can specify angles from 360 degrees to -360 degrees. Positive numbers will rotate the selected object counterclockwise and negative numbers will rotate the object clockwise. By specifying a 180-degree rotation, the item will be reflected across the x axis; however, for better control over reflecting, use the reflect tool (described later, after the scale tool).

Once you have specified the angle of rotation, and whether or not you want to rotate pattern tiles and/or objects, you can either click the OK button in the dialog box to perform the rotation; click the Cancel button to abandon your specifications and return to the unaltered active window; or click Copy to create a rotated copy while leaving the original in its place.

You can also rotate type that has already been defined with the text tool. Simply select the text, click the focal point with the rotate tool and drag, or double-click the rotate tool to get the Rotate dialog box. Then, with the Repeat Transform command, you can produce special effects with text (Figure 5-73).

If you aren't getting the results you expect, check the Constrain angle setting in the General Preferences dialog box in the File menu. The

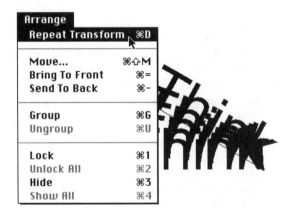

Figure 5-73.
Rotating text that was selected, and using Repeat Transform (Command-D) to create an effect.

rotation of the selected object is relative to the current x and y axes. For example, if you had set the Constrain angle for the x and y axes to 30 degrees using the General Preferences command in the File menu (Command-K), when you select objects to rotate with the rotate tool, they will be rotated at the angle you specify, plus the additional 30-degree constraint angle. If you are unsure about the alignment of the x and y axes, you can check their settings by looking at the Constrain angle setting in the dialog box that appears after you select the Preferences and General commands on the File menu (or type Command-K as a shortcut for requesting the Preferences dialog box).

Rotate Tool Summary

+ click on axis + drag
Rotates any selected objects around a focal point that you specify.

+ click on axis + Shift key + drag
Constrains the rotation angle of the selected object to increments of 45 degrees (relative to the x and y axes).

+ double-click tool
+ Option key + click on axis
Displays the Rotate dialog box for specifying precise amounts of rotation.

+ click on axis + Option key + drag
Creates a rotated duplicate while leaving the original object in place.

Command-D
Repeat the previous transformation, which may be a rotating operation, or a combination of rotating and cloning and movement.

Scale Tool

 The scale tool is used for stretching or shrinking objects. You can scale objects horizontally (i.e., along the x axis), vertically (along the y axis), or a varying amount of both. The scale tool can also be used as a built-in "stat camera" that allows you to enlarge or reduce your artwork to fit into an allotted space in a page layout, or to fit in with some other graphic design element. Using Adobe Illustrator as a substitute for a stat camera

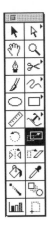

involves stretching or shrinking objects in equal amounts both vertically and horizontally; this is best accomplished through use of the Scale dialog box, which offers a Uniform scaling option.

Objects are scaled relative to a focal point you specify, so that you can scale an object from different vantage points to produce different effects. Scaling a path or other object is the only way to alter its size; zooming in and out with the zoom tool, or setting the enlargement or reduction options in the Page Setup dialog box in the Print menu does not affect the actual size of paths or objects.

Before you use the scale tool you must first select the path or object you want to scale (you can select multiple segments and paths). To select a grouped object to scale, simply click on the object; alternatively, you can hold down the Command key to temporarily change the scale tool to the selection tool, and drag a selection marquee around any object or objects you wish to select.

Once the item that you wish to scale is selected, you can either use the mouse to scale the selected object by dragging, or you can click to request the Scale dialog box and specify precise amounts of enlargement or reduction, including whether to scale line weights (if you don't scale them, they will remain the same weight, no matter if the art is enlarged or reduced) for uniform scaling, non-uniform scaling and other scaling options, such as the Copy option. And, if you don't get the result you expected, you can immediately use the Undo command at the top of the Edit menu, then try again.

If you want to drag to stretch or shrink the selected object, first click the scale tool in the toolbox. The pointer will turn into a plus sign (+) when you move it into the active window (Figure 5-74).

Click at the spot you want to use as a focal point for the scaling operation, and the plus sign pointer changes to an arrowhead to indicate that the focal point, or *point of origin*, has been established (see Figure

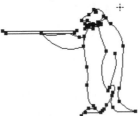

Figure 5-74.
The scale tool displays a plus (+) sign for the pointer. You select a focal point for the scale, which is the point of origin from which a transformation begins.

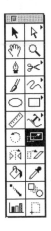

5-75). The focal point or point of origin is the point where the transformation starts; the direction you drag in from that point determines the size and shape of the object.

Next, drag from the focal point in the direction that you want the selected object to be scaled in (Figure 5-76). While dragging, both the original object you selected and the scaled counterpart are visible on the screen as the counterpart changes size and shape.

If you want to stretch the object, move the mouse away from the focal point; if you want to shrink the object, move the mouse towards the focal point. The direction in which you drag the mouse also affects the dimension in which the selected object is scaled; if you move the mouse horizontally, the object will be stretched (or shrunk) horizontally; if you move the mouse vertically, the object will be stretched (or shrunk) vertically; and if you move the mouse diagonally, the object will be stretched (or shrunk) both vertically and horizontally (useful for creating perspective views).

For example, to create a rectangle of half the size and to the right of a selected rectangle, click the scale tool and then click a focal point to the right of the selected rectangle. If you drag away from the focal point, the shape will be scaled up; drag toward the focal point and the shape is scaled down.

The closer your second point is to the focal point, the less mouse movement is required to alter the size and shape of the selected object. In order to get better control of the scaling process, it's a good idea to select a second spot that is as far away from the focal point as practical. You can select a second spot at the far edge of the active window if you are shrinking the selected object. However, when stretching an object by dragging from a second point that is far away from the first (perhaps at the edge of the active window), your view of the object may scroll about as you stretch the object, and the scrolling can be quite distracting.

You may notice that while scaling you can also create a reflection of the object by dragging to the left of or above the focal point. However, it is easier to use the reflect tool to create reflections.

When you have finished stretching or shrinking the selected object, release the mouse button and the original object will be erased, leaving only the scaled object (see Figure 5-77). However, if you hold down the Option key while dragging, a scaled duplicate will be created while leaving the original in its place.

Scaling objects by dragging is good for quick stretching or shrinking, but it can be hard to control. For better control over scaling, hold down the Shift key while dragging; this constrains the direction in which the selected object is scaled. If the Shift key is held down while you stretch

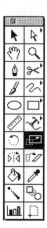

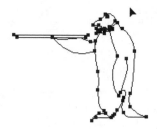

Figure 5-75.
The pointer changes to an arrowhead after clicking the focal point.

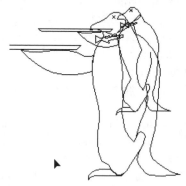

Figure 5-76.
Dragging from the second point in the direction to be scaled; both the original object outline and the scaled object are shown while dragging.

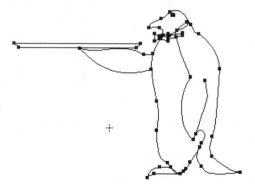

Figure 5-77.
The result of scaling the object.

or shrink something, dragging will scale the object equally along both the x and y axes (a uniform scale).

For precise control over scaling of both objects and line weights, use the Scale dialog box. Line weights cannot be scaled by dragging; you

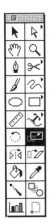

must use the Scale dialog box for this task. After clicking the scale tool in the toolbox, the pointer turns into a plus sign (+) when you move it into the active window. Position the plus sign on the spot that you want to become the focal point of the scaling operation. Hold down the Option key while clicking the point. When you depress the Option key, the (+) pointer changes into a (+...) pointer, indicating that the Scale dialog box is ready to be requested; as soon as you click the mouse button, the Scale dialog box appears (Figure 5-78).

The Scale dialog box lets you choose between uniform scaling and non-uniform scaling, and the line weights are preserved if you choose uniform scaling, unless you select the Scale line weight option.

When the dialog box appears, it contains the settings from the previous scaling operation; if this is the first use of the Scale Tool since you started up the program, the values will be set to "Uniform Scale" at 100 percent and line weights will be preserved. If you want uniform scaling, i.e. scaling performed equally along the x and y axes, make sure that the radio button in front of "Uniform :" is checked. Then point to the small box after the "Uniform:" heading, click the mouse, and enter the scaling factor number as a percentage (Figure 5-79). Numbers greater than 100 will enlarge the object and numbers less than 100 will reduce the object.

If uniform scaling is selected, you can also specify whether or not you want the line weights of the selected object scaled or preserved (when you scale by dragging, line weights are always preserved, or kept the same amount). Simply click the radio button preceding the Scale line weight option, or the line weights will be preserved. One of the features of Adobe

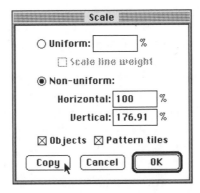

Figure 5-78.
Activate the Scale dialog box by holding down the Option key while clicking a focal point, or by double-clicking the scale tool. The scale is set up for a vertical stretch and to scale pattern tiles with the object. You can click the Copy button to scale a duplicate without changing the original.

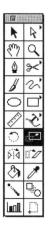

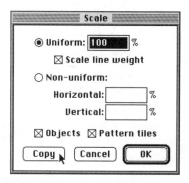

Figure 5-79.
When you select uniform scaling, you have the option to scale line weights.

Illustrator that makes it especially valuable to graphic artists is the ability to preserve line weights while scaling, which is why that is the default setting. Preserving the line weights of a drawing while enlarging or reducing it is useful when you are creating a publication where consistent line weights for illustrations are desired throughout the publication. Normal enlargement or reduction methods, such as using a stat camera, always scale line weights.

When you want line weights scaled, you must select the Scale line weight option in the Scale dialog box after selecting uniform scaling. However, if you want to scale both a drawing and its line weights to be a great deal smaller than the original size, be careful that no line weights are scaled so thin that the press can't print them properly. Adobe Illustrator offers more precision than some printing methods you can use to reproduce your drawing, so ask your printing press representative how thin a line can be preserved by the printing method you will use. For example, lines can be a single pixel wide, and your imagesetter may be able to print them, but your press might not be able to reproduce them.

If you choose the Non-uniform: option by clicking in the radio button preceding it, you will not be able to scale line weights, but you will be able to type different scaling factors for the horizontal and vertical axes. To enter the horizontal scale factor, click in the box after Horizontal:, and type the scaling factor number. Likewise, to enter the vertical scale factor, click in the box after Vertical:, and type the desired value. You enter the scale factor as a percentage of the original size. Numbers greater than 100 will enlarge the object and numbers less than 100 will reduce the object.

You can also type negative numbers to reflect and scale the drawing at the same time, which is equivalent to dragging to the left of (or above)

the focal point when scaling by dragging. As with scaling by dragging, you can therefore use the Scaling dialog box to create a reflection of the selected object along an imaginary line that passes through the focal point you established for the scaling operation.

To see how this technique can be used for reflecting, try specifying -100 percent horizontal scaling and 100 percent vertical scaling; the result will be a reflection of the image across a vertical line that passes through the focal point. If the man in the "Organizational Chart" (Plate 5) was selected, and the scale tool was clicked while holding down the Option key at the top of his head to establish a focal point, the Scale dialog box would appear, and using the numbers above and clicking the Copy button would result in two men, with the duplicate man upside down, connected to the original one head to head. You can use percentages other than 100 percent to accomplish scaling and reflecting simultaneously. However, for better control over reflecting, use the reflect tool.

If you intend to scale selected objects using their center points as the point of origin, you can scale them exclusively by means of the Scale dialog box. You invoke the Scale dialog box by double-clicking the scale tool. This way, you don't have to hold down the Option key to bring up the dialog box—whenever you double-click the scale tool, the Scale dialog box automatically appears.

When you are finished specifying the scaling options, and whether or not you want to scale pattern tiles and/or objects, click the OK button in the dialog box to perform the scaling operation; click the Cancel button to abandon your specifications and return to the unaltered active window; or click Copy to create a scaled copy while leaving the original in its place. The double line surrounding the OK button indicates that pressing the Return key can be used as a shortcut for selecting the OK option. After you have finished scaling, you can repeat the procedure as often as you want by selecting Repeat Transform from the Arrange menu or by pressing Command-D as a shortcut.

However, if you have altered the x and y axes using the Constrain angle setting in the General Preferences dialog box in the File menu (Command-K), the scaling of the selected object is relative to the altered x and y axes. For example, if you have rotated the x and y axes by 30 degrees using the Constrain angle setting (Command-K), any objects you scale with the scale tool will be drawn at a 30-degree angle. If you are unsure about the alignment of the x and y axes, you can check their settings by looking at the Constrain angle setting in the dialog box that appears after you select the Preferences and General commands from the File menu (or type Command-K as a shortcut for requesting the dialog box).

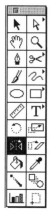

Scale Tool Summary

+ click focal point + drag

Stretches or shrinks any selected objects relative to a focal point that you first specify by clicking.

+ click focal point + Shift key + drag

Constrains the object being scaled along the x axis, the y axis, or both axes.

+ Option key + click focal point
+ double click tool

Displays the Scale dialog box for specifying precise scaling amounts, with the option of scaling line weights for a uniform scale, and another option to copy the object (create a duplicate object with the specified settings for size and position). Double-clicking the scale tool uses the center point of the object as the focal point.

+ click focal point + Option key + drag

Creates a scaled duplicate while leaving the original object in its place; useful for creating different sized copies of an object.

If you use the Scale dialog box instead of dragging, you can click the Copy button to create duplicates with precision, and repeat the same settings for subsequent scaling operations.

Command-D

Repeat the previous transformation, which may be a scaling operation, or a combination of scaling and cloning and movement.

Reflect Tool

The reflect tool is used to create mirror images of objects. Before you use the reflect tool, you must first select the path or other objects you want to reflect.

To select a grouped object to reflect, simply click the selection tool (hold down the Command key to temporarily change any tool to the selection tool), or drag a selection marquee around any object or objects you wish to select. You can also use the direct-selection tool and/or group-selection tool to select any object or objects.

Once you have selected the object that you wish to reflect, you can

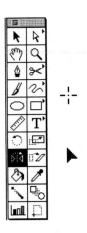

either reflect the selected object by dragging, or you can request the Reflect dialog box for specifying precise amounts of reflection.

If you want to reflect the selected object by dragging, first select the reflect tool by clicking it in the toolbox. The arrow pointer will turn into a plus sign (+) when you move it into the active window.

Point to the spot that you want to become the first point of the axis around which the selected object will be reflected and click the mouse button. The pointer will change to an arrowhead to indicate that the first axis point has been established. Then, select a second point that along with the first point will define the imaginary line that the program will use for the axis of reflection. To reflect the object across this imaginary line, simply click the mouse button. On the other hand, if you want to adjust the axis of reflection, do not click. Instead, drag the arrowhead pointer around the original focal point; the axis of reflection will change as you drag.

While dragging, both the original object you selected and the reflected counterpart are visible on the screen. When you release the mouse button, the original object is erased, leaving only the reflected object. If you hold down the Option key while dragging, a reflected duplicate will be created while the original remains unchanged in its place.

Even if rulers are displayed, reflecting objects by dragging a precise amount can be difficult. You can better control certain angles of reflection by applying constraint as you reflect the object. Hold the Shift key down while dragging to constrain the reflection axis to multiples of 45 degrees.

For precise control over the angle of reflection, use the Reflect dialog box. First click the reflect tool in the toolbox. Next, hold down the Option key, and click at the position along an imaginary line that you want to become the fixed point of origin that defines the axis around which the selected object will be reflected. As soon as you hold down the Option key, the (+) pointer changes into a (+...) pointer, indicating that the Reflect dialog box is ready to be requested; the Reflect dialog box will appear at the next click.

The Reflect dialog box contains the settings from the previous reflection. If this is the first use of the reflect tool since you started up the program, the reflection option will be set to reflect items across the horizontal axis. Specify whether you want the selected object and/or its pattern tiles reflected across a horizontal axis running through the fixed point, a vertical axis through the point, or across an angled axis by clicking in the circle preceding the desired option. If you select the option for reflecting items across an angled axis, you must then enter a number in the box that represents the angle of rotation (in degrees) of the reflection

axis about the focal point relative to the x and y axes.

When you are finished specifying the reflection options, you can either click the OK button in the dialog box to perform the reflection; click the Cancel button to abandon your specifications and return to the unaltered active window; or click Copy to create a reflected copy while leaving the original in its place. The double line surrounding the OK button indicates that pressing the Return key can be used as a shortcut for selecting the OK option. After you have finished reflecting, you can repeat the procedure as often as you want by selecting Repeat Transform from the Arrange menu or by pressing Command-D as a shortcut.

Double-click the reflect tool after you have selected the object to be reflected, to access the Reflect dialog box and use the center point of the object as the origin point for the axis of reflection. Or, to select an different origin point with the reflect tool, you can hold down the Option key and the (+) pointer changes into a (+...) pointer, to indicate that the Reflect dialog box (Figure 5-80) will appear when you click to establish an origin point for the reflection.

If you have altered the Constrain angle with the Preferences command on the Edit menu, the reflection of the selected object is aligned to the constrain angle of the x and y axes. This means that if you have rotated the x and y axes by 40 degrees using the Constrain angle setting in the General Preferences dialog box (Command-K), any items you reflect with the reflect tool will be rotated at an additional 40-degree angle. If you are unsure about the alignment of the x and y axes, you can check their settings by looking at the Constrain angle setting in the dialog box that appears when you select the Preferences and General commands from the File menu (or type Command-K as a shortcut for requesting the General Preferences dialog box).

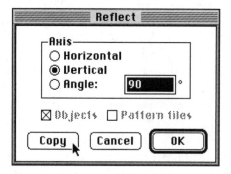

Figure 5-80.
Activate the Reflect dialog box by holding down the Option key while clicking a focal point, or by double-clicking the reflect tool.

Reflect Tool Summary

▷❙◂ + click first point on axis + click to establish next point

Reflects a mirror-image of any selected object across an imaginary reflection line defined by your points.

▷❙◂ + click first point on axis + drag to next point

Reflects a mirror-image of any selected object across a rotating reflection line defined by your dragging away from the reflection line defined by the first and second points.

▷❙◂ + click + Shift key + drag

Constrains the reflection of the selected object to horizontal (reflected across the x axis), vertical (reflected across the y axis), and increments of 45 degrees (relative to the x and y axes).

▷❙◂+ + click on axis
▷❙◂ + Option key + first point on axis

Displays the Reflect dialog box for specifying a precise reflection.

▷❙◂ + click on axis + Option key + drag

Creates a reflected duplicate while leaving the original object in place.

Command-D

Repeat the previous transformation, which may be a scaling operation, or a combination of scaling and cloning and movement.

Shear Tool

The shear tool is used to put a uniform slant on an object. The shear tool uniformly shears the selected object or objects along a horizontal, vertical, or angled axis.

Before you use the shear tool, you must first use the selection tool to select the path or other objects that you want to shear. To select more than one object to shear, either drag a selection marquee around the objects or select one object first by clicking it, and then hold down the Shift key and select the remaining objects by clicking them. Once you have selected the objects that you wish to shear, you can either use the mouse to shear the selected objects by dragging, or you can request the Shear dialog box for specifying precise amounts of shearing.

If you want to use the mouse to shear the selected object by dragging,

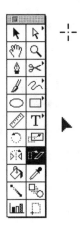

first select the shear tool by clicking its icon in the toolbox. The pointer will turn into a plus sign (+) when you move it into the active window.

Click a point to define the origin point for the axis along which the selected object will be sheared (Figure 5-81). Then start dragging from another point away from the axis in the direction of the shear. All points along the shear axis will remain fixed. The pointer will change to an arrowhead to indicate that the shear axis has been established. The object changes shape as you drag; release the mouse button when you have the shear that you want (Figure 5-82). The further away from the axis point that you start your dragging, the greater control you will have over the shearing. Drag horizontally to shear the selected object along the x axis, drag vertically to shear along the y axis, or drag diagonally to shear along both the x and y axes.

While dragging, both the original object you selected and the sheared counterpart are displayed. When you have finished shearing the selected object, release the mouse button and the original object will be erased, leaving only the sheared object. If you hold down the Option key while dragging, a sheared clone will be created while leaving the original in its place.

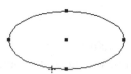

Figure 5-81.
Click to establish the axis for shearing the selected object; the axis points do not move. The axis passes through this point horizontally or vertically for shearing by dragging.

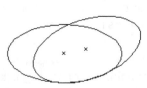

Figure 5-82.
Start dragging from another point in the direction of the shear; if you start dragging from a point far away from the axis, you have more control.

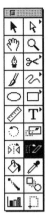

Shearing objects by dragging, even with rulers displayed, is difficult to do precisely. To get better control over shearing, hold the Shift key down while dragging; this constrains shearing to an angle that is a multiple of 45 degrees (relative to the x and y axes).

For precise control over shearing at any angle, use the Shear dialog box. First click the shear tool icon in the toolbox. The pointer will turn into a plus sign (+) when you move it into the active window. Next, hold down the Option key, and click an origin point to define the axis along which the selected object will be sheared. As soon as you hold down the Option key, the (+) pointer changes into a (+...) pointer, indicating that the Shear dialog box is ready to be requested; as soon as you click, the Shear dialog box appears (Figure 5-83).

If you intend to shear objects using their center points as the origin points for the shear axes, exclusively by means of the Shear dialog box, you can double-click the shear tool to access the shear dialog box. With this shortcut, you don't have to hold down the Option key to bring up the dialog box—whenever you double-click the shear tool, the Shear dialog box automatically appears.

When the dialog box appears it contains the settings from the previous shearing; if this is the first use of the shear tool since you started up the program, the shear angle will be set to zero and horizontal shearing will be selected.

Specify the desired angle of shearing in degrees by clicking in the Angle: box. The degree of shearing that you specify corresponds to the

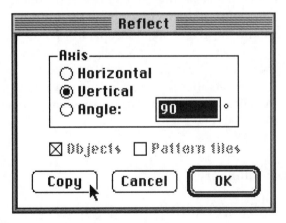

Figure 5-83.
Hold down the Option key when clicking the shear tool's axis point to use the Shear dialog box for accurate shearing (or double-click the shear tool). You can shear pattern tiles and/or the object, and use the Copy button to shear a clone and leave the original object unchanged.

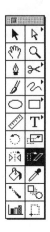

amount of slant you want to put on the selected object, relative to an axis that is perpendicular to the axis point you clicked. A positive angle performs a clockwise shear and a negative angle performs a counterclockwise shear (this is in contrast to rotation angles, where a positive angle performs a counterclockwise rotation and a negative angle performs a clockwise rotation).

Next, click either a horizontal axis shear, vertical axis shear, or angled axis shear by clicking the appropriate radio button. If you select an angled shear you must also click in the box after the words "Angled axis:" and then specify the angle (in degrees) of the shear axis around the fixed point that you established, relative to the x and y axes.

You also have the option of shearing the object only, its pattern tiles only, or both.

When you are finished specifying the shear options, you can click the OK button in the dialog box to perform the shear; click the Cancel button to abandon your specifications and return to the unaltered active window; or click Copy to create a sheared copy while leaving the original in its place. After you have finished shearing, you can repeat the procedure as often as you want by selecting Repeat Transform from the Arrange menu or by pressing Command-D as a shortcut.

If you aren't getting the results you expect, check the Constrain angle setting in the Preferences dialog box in the Edit menu. The shearing of the selected object is relative to the x and y axes. This means that if you have rotated the Constrain angle of the x and y axes by 60 degrees using the General and Preferences commands in the File menu (Command-K), any items you shear with the shear tool will be sheared at an additional 60-degree angle.

If you are unsure about the alignment of the x and y axes, you can check their settings by looking at the Constrain angle setting in the dialog box that appears after you select the General and Preferences commands on the File menu (or type Command-K as a shortcut for requesting the dialog box).

Shear Tool Summary

▷ + click an axis point + drag from a second point

Shears any selected object uniformly along an imaginary axis line that runs through the two points; the axis point, and the second point (where you start dragging) defines the shear axis.

▷ + click an axis point + Shift key + drag from a second point

Constrains the shearing of the selected object to horizontal (sheared along the x axis), vertical (sheared along the y axis), and shearing in increments of 45 degrees (relative to the x and y axes).

+ Option key + click an axis point
+ double-click tool

Displays the Shear dialog box for specifying a precise angle of shearing, with options for shearing the object and/or pattern tiles, and a Copy button to create a sheared clone, leaving the original in place. Double-clicking the shear tool uses the center point of the selected object as the axis origin point.

+ click an axis point + Option key + drag from a second point
Creates a sheared duplicate, leaving the original object in place.

Command-D
Repeat the previous transformation, which may be a shearing operation, or a combination of shearing and cloning and movement.

Paint Bucket and Eyedropper Tools

You can use the eyedropper tool to copy an object's color and its attributes (fill pattern and/or stroke color/pattern) to the Paint Style Palette, and then use the paint bucket tool to assign exactly the same paint attributes to objects in the artwork. Paint attributes include fill color/pattern (with an overprint option), and stroke color/pattern (with an overprint option), with stroke options for weight, caps, joins, miter limit and solid or dash pattern. Color selections include None, White, Black, Process, Custom, Pattern, or Gradient.

The Paint Style palette is updated to use the paint style attributes selected with the eyedropper tool, and uses those settings for drawing all new objects until you change them by either selecting the eyedropper tool and sampling another area filled and stroked with different attributes, or by changing the paint style attribute settings in the Paint Style palette (Show Paint Style from the Window menu, or selecting the Paint Style command from the Objects menu).

The eyedropper tool samples a point you click in the artwork, just as ink is drawn into an eyedropper (the empty eyedropper pointer changes to a filled eyedropper pointer), and displays the paint style attributes of that point, ready to paint them again. An object does not have to be selected first with a selection tool, before using the eyedropper tool. No

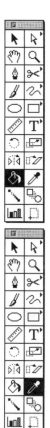

matter if the Paint Style palette is open or closed (select Show or Hide Paint Style from the Window menu to open or close the Paint Style palette), it will be updated to use the paint style attributes selected by the eyedropper tool. However, if you want the eyedropper tool to pick up, and the paint bucket tool to apply, only some of the attributes, double-click either the paint bucket tool or the eyedropper tool to display the Paintbucket/Eyedropper Options palette (Figure 5-84). Uncheck the boxes next to the attributes that you want to remain unchanged.

To examine the paint style of any portion of your artwork, first open the Paint Style palette to display the settings, and then click with the eyedropper tool at the point you wish to examine (Figure 5-85). You can continue to sample areas with the eyedropper tool, and display the settings in the Paint Style palette, without changing the art. The eyedropper tool is unaffected by whether or not objects are selected, but you can select objects before using the eyedropper tool and then change the attributes of all of them at once (see shortcuts below).

The paint bucket tool uses the current paint style attributes, which

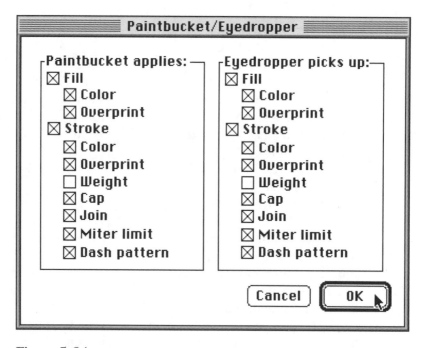

Figure 5-84.
Double-click the paint bucket tool or the eyedropper tool to display the Paintbucket/Eyedropper options palette.

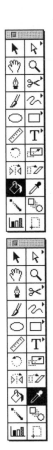

could be those of the last selected object, or of a portion of the art that the eyedropper tool has just sampled.

As a shortcut to apply the attributes of one object to another object, you can click the eyedropper tool to select it, then click to sample a point in the artwork, hold down the Option key to change to the paint bucket tool, and click the object to be repainted.

Another shortcut for changing the attributes of all selected objects at once is to first select the objects, then click to select the eyedropper tool, and click an object with the attributes you wish to apply to the selected objects. The just clicked object should display its attributes in the Paint Style palette. Next, double-click the object again to apply the same attributes to all of the selected objects.

If you select more than one object with different attributes, their common attributes are displayed in the Paint Style palette (Figure 5-86), and those not in common are displayed with question marks and the description "Mixed" or are blank.

If you are having trouble selecting objects (such as objects stroked but not filled) in artwork view, either switch to Preview (View menu), or select the outline of the object instead of inside the object. If the Paint

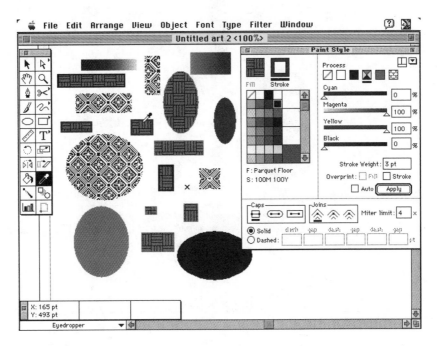

Figure 5-85.
Using the eyedropper tool to examine selected areas of the artwork.

Style palette is hidden, display it (Show Paint Style from the Window menu, or select the Paint Style command from the Objects menu) to help you select objects.

Paint Bucket and Eyedropper Tools Summary

+ double-click eyedropper tool

+ double-click paint bucket tool

Displays the Paintbucket/Eyedropper options palette (see Figure 5-84), where you specify which paint style attributes to apply with the paint bucket tool and/or pickup with the eyedropper tool.

+ click a point

Samples a point in the artwork, as if you were drawing ink into an

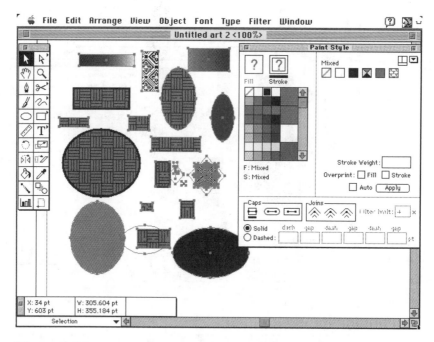

Figure 5-86.
After selecting all the objects, common attributes are shown in the Paint Style dialog box, while paint style attributes not common to all are labeled as "Mixed" or are blank.

eyedropper, and updates the Paint Style palette to use the new paint style attributes. (Use the Paint bucket/Eyedropper options palette to sample only the attributes you specify.)

 + click a point

Applies the current Paint Style attributes to the object or point clicked. (Use the Paint bucket/Eyedropper options palette to apply only the attributes you specify.)

 + Option key

Changes from the paint bucket tool to the eyedropper tool while the Option key is held down, so that you can click and sample a point quickly. When you release the Option key, the paint bucket tool is again selected and ready to paint an object, using the new paint style attributes sampled with the eyedropper tool.

 + Option key

Switch from the eyedropper tool to the paint bucket tool while the Option key is held down, so that you can click and change the paint style attributes of a point or object quickly. Continue clicking all the objects and points that you want to use the same paint style attributes, while the Option key is depressed. When you release the Option key, the eyedropper tool is again selected and ready to sample the paint style attributes of more objects.

( + drag marquee) or ( + Shift-click to select objects)

After selecting objects with the selection tool, the Paint Style palette (Show Paint Style from the Window menu) displays the paint style attributes in common for the selected objects, and those not in common are displayed with question marks and the description "Mixed" or are blank (see Figure 5-86).

( + drag marquee) or ( + Shift-click to select objects),

then  + click, then double-click

Shortcut to change the paint style attributes for all the selected objects at once, to match the attributes of the object at the point first clicked.

Gradient Tool

The gradient fill tool is used to repaint and adjust gradient fills, after they have been assigned to objects using the Paint Style palette, or using the paint bucket tool.

For example, you might create a circle and paint it with a radial gradient fill that places the highlights in the center and the shadows at the edges of the circle. You can then use the gradient fill tool to modify the fill to simulate a 3-D ball with a light source focused on the highlights.

Use the Gradient dialog box to change the gradient fill attributes, such as the direction and type (linear or radial), and the colors for the starting and ending points of the fill.

The direction determines the angle of the fill, the starting point determines the highlight areas, and the ending point determines the shadow areas. The midpoint where two colors meet can also be adjusted to reduce or increase the amount of blending between the colors. In addition to creating new gradient fills, the gradient tool can duplicate or delete gradients.

First select an object with a gradient fill to be modified, and select the gradient tool. Click a starting point for the new gradient fill, but do not let up the mouse button. Drag from the starting point to the ending point, and then let up the mouse button.

The direction in which you drag determines the direction of the gradient fill (see Figure 5-87). Holding down the Shift key while dragging constrains the angle to a 45° increment, relative to the constrain angle set in the General Preferences dialog box.

Radial gradient filled objects that are selected can simply have their starting points moved by clicking a new starting point within the object using the gradient tool.

To apply a gradient fill across more than one object, first select all the objects, and paint them with a gradient fill style, using the Paint Style palette or the paint bucket tool and/or eyedropper tool. While they are selected, use the gradient tool to click a starting point and drag to the ending point for the fill.

To apply a gradient fill to type, first select the type and convert it to outline type (Select the Create Outlines command from the Type menu).

Gradient fills are adjusted using the Gradient dialog box displayed by selecting the Show Gradient command from the Window menu, or by selecting the Gradient command from the Object menu. Double-clicking the gradient tool also displays the Gradient dialog box.

To manipulate the colors, use the Show Gradient palette (from the Window menu) or the Gradient command in the Object menu to display

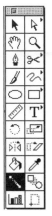

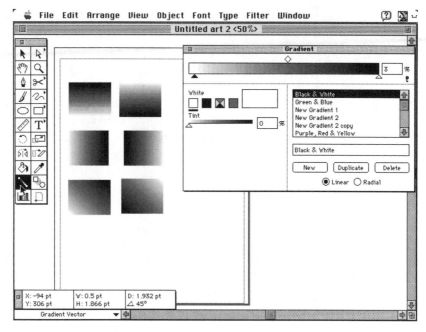

Figure 5-87.
Gradient fills are offset by the constrain angle set in the General Prefer-
ences dialog box. If you hold down the Shift key while dragging a new
direction for the gradient fill, you can further constrain the angle to an
increment of 45 degrees, offset from the constrain angle. This figure uses a
constrain angle of 0 degrees, and the Shift key was used to constrain the angles to
45 degree increments. Reading clockwise from the top left, the six rectangles
were repainted by the gradient fill tool as follows: Bottom to top, top to bottom,
right to left, top right to bottom left, bottom left to top right, and left to right.
Highlights are at the starting point, and shadows are at the end points.

the Gradient bar. Diamond and triangle markers appear at the beginning
(black triangle) and end (hollow triangle) and midpoints (diamonds) of
the gradient bar. Drag these to adjust colors. For example, to transpose
the starting and ending colors, drag the starting triangle on top of the
ending triangle, or drag the ending triangle on top of the starting triangle.
The diamond shape above the gradient bar marks the point where the
colors are at 50 percent, and you can drag it to adjust the midpoint, giving
your gradient more highlights, or more shadows.

For fills of multiple colors, a diamond marks the midpoint of each color
change, and triangles indicate the beginning and endpoints of each color.
For more information on adjusting gradient colors, see the Gradient
command section later in this chapter.

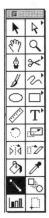

Gradient fills can use process colors, black and white, or custom colors, but not patterns. You can use two or more colors for gradient fills. However, if your gradient fill uses more than one custom color and you plan to reproduce it on a printing press, use Adobe Separator to assign different screen angles to the different custom colors before creating color separated film (one piece of film is created for each custom color), to avoid moirés. Alternatively, you can convert the custom colors to process colors using Adobe Illustrator, and avoid problems on press.

Gradient Tool Summary

+ drag across selected gradient filled object

Changes the angle of the gradient fill to follow the direction of the drag. The starting point of the drag contains the highlights (lightest color) while the ending point of the drag contains the shadows (darkest color).

+ Shift while dragging

Constrains the direction of the drag to a 45° increment, relative to the constrain angle set in the General Preferences dialog box (File menu).

+ click in a selected object with a radial fill

Changes the location of the starting point for the radial fill, and repaints the object to move the highlights to the point clicked. Useful for simulating a 3-D look by moving the highlights from the center of the object to another point within the object to simulate a change in location of a light source.

+ double-click

Double-clicking the gradient tool displays the Gradient dialog box. Alternatively, you could select the Show Gradient command from the Window menu, or select the Gradient command from the Object menu.

+ Command key

Changes to the selection tool while the Command key is depressed.

Blend Tool

Adobe Illustrator offers the unique blend tool that can automatically blend one shape (and its color, gray shade, or tint) into another. The blend tool can create a blend of intermediate steps between any two paths or objects. You can use the blend tool to blend one color into another to achieve an airbrush effect (see Plates 7 and 8, "Swan" and "Violin").

To perform a blend operation, first select the two objects or paths that define the starting and ending shapes, and after selecting the blend tool, click one point of the starting object or path and a corresponding point of the ending object or path (Figure 5-88). The program displays a dialog box asking for the number of steps, or discrete shapes, that the program should create between the starting and ending shapes (Figure 5-89). The program then creates all these shapes automatically (Figure 5-90).

The blend tool works best if both objects use the same pattern (if any), but you can use different colors, gray scales, and stroke widths. The blend tool can blend process colors, gray scales, and stroke widths to achieve special effects such as an airbrush effect or a contour with different line weights. The number of steps you specify in the Blend dialog box

Figure 5-88.
After selecting the two paths and the blend tool, click one point on the starting path and one point on the ending path.

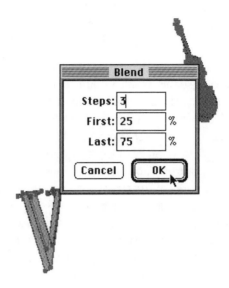

Figure 5-89.
The Blend dialog box appears after you click the second point. You can specify the number of intermediate steps and the percentages for the first and last intermediate steps.

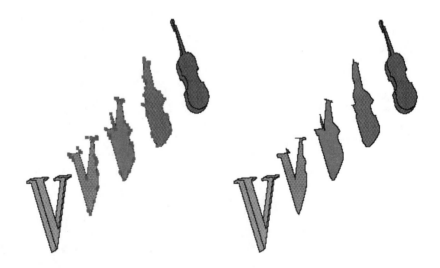

Figure 5-90.
The results of the blend operation shown first selected and then deselected in the Preview window (the objects are from the illustration in Plate 8, "Violin").

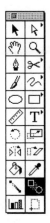

determines the color and tint blending percentages that Illustrator will use. You can also change the percentages of the first and last intermediate steps in order to fine-tune the blending or produce special effects.

The program interpolates shapes between the two points you clicked with the blend tool, and calculates percentages of color and black for the steps. The program calculates the blend based on the selected points in both paths. Before using the blend tool, you can select more than two points with the selection tool (such as two entire paths) to have more control over the results.

Paths must be ungrouped first before you can select them for blending with the selection tool. Alternatively, you can use the direct-selection tool to select any two objects that are part of the same group, or of different groups, and perform a blend between those two objects only. To blend between open paths, select an endpoint on each path. Blending can occur between two open or two closed paths, but not between an open and a closed path.

You can create up to 1000 steps; the more steps you specify, the finer the gradation will be between the starting and ending shapes. However, to avoid unneccessary complexity that may affect the printing of the file, Illustrator suggests a recommended number of steps to use for blends that corresponds to the chosen device's output resolution. For example, to create a smooth blend from 100 percent black to 100 percent white for the high-resolution imagesetter used to produce the pages in this book, Illustrator suggests 254 steps, because 256 is the maximum number of grays that can be produced on this device. (Subtract the first and last steps from 256 and you get 254.) You can choose more steps, but then you may get banding or shade-stepping, which means you will see a distinct line between colors, rather than a smooth transition. If you change the starting and ending percentages for the blend in the Blend dialog box, Illustrator will suggest an appropriate number of steps for the blend, which you can use or change. The number specified for percentage of change for the First and Last steps in the Blend dialog box must be between -100 and 200.

Use the Document Setup command in the File menu to change the output resolution setting. However, the output resolution for objects already drawn is unchanged. Only new objects drawn after you make the change use the new setting. To change the resolution of already drawn objects, first select them, and then select the Attributes command from the Object menu, and change the output resolution setting in the Attributes dialog box.

Blending works between two objects painted with process colors or custom colors, and between a PANTONE or custom color and a process

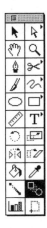

color. Process colors are used for all intermediate shapes between any two colors. However, tints are blended by percentage in the same color, whether it is a process, custom, or PANTONE color, so the steps will be painted with tints of the same custom color for a blend between tints of a custom color.

To blend a custom color with white, use a 0 percent tint of the custom color in place of white, so that colors separate onto a single piece of film for the printing press.

You can't use the blend tool with typed characters unless you first convert those characters into outlines with the Create Outline command in the Type menu (this command turns each character into a compound path). Also, you can't use a blend as a masking object (although each intermediate step could be a masking object for a set of masked objects).

You can blend two objects that have the same pattern, but not objects with different patterns unless one of the patterns is defined with artwork that is a transformation of the other pattern (the blend produces intermediate shapes with intermediate transformations of the pattern).

If you get banding or shade-stepping in your printed blends, it is because the blend is too long or there are too many steps specified. You can try one of these fixes: use lighter colors, shorten the length of dark blends, shorten the length of any blend to less than 7.5 inches, increase the percentage of change in the blend (less than 50 percent change can cause banding).

Blend Tool Summary

The blend tool creates intermediate shapes that are blends between two open or two closed paths. Blending also calculates percentages of color, gray scale, or tint and assigns them to the intermediate steps.

You select both paths (more points selected offers more control), and click a point on each path with the blend tool, then specify the number of steps in the Blend dialog box (including the percentages for the first and last steps).

⌖ + Command key

Temporarily converts the blend tool into the last selection tool used (regular, direct-selection, or group-selection tool).

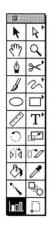

+ Space bar + drag

Temporarily converts the blend tool into the hand tool for moving the document within the active window so that you can easily select more paths for blending.

+ Command key + Space bar + click

Temporarily converts the current tool into the zoom tool for zooming into the document while using the blend tool.

+ Command key + Option key

Temporarily converts the blend tool into a selection tool by toggling between the direct-selection tool and the group-selection tool. If the last selection tool used was the direct-selection tool, the group-selection tool will be selected, or vice versa.

+ Command key + Option key + Space bar + click

Temporarily converts the current tool into the zoom tool for zooming out from the document while using the blend tool.

Graph Tool

Illustrator can automatically create a chart or graph based on numerical data. The graph tool can create column charts (grouped or stacked), line graphs, pie charts, scatter graphs, and area graphs.

The default graph tool is the grouped column chart (also known as a bar chart). To select any other type of chart or graph, use the Graphs and Style commands in the Object menu to select another style of graph, before using the graph tool. The Graph tool icon will change to the style of graph you select. The data for the charts or graphs can be entered directly, or imported from a spreadsheet, into a table for calculations.

The charts and graphs can be changed automatically, or ungrouped into objects that can be manipulated like other objects. However, be sure that you will never want to change the graph's data, style or design before you ungroup a graph, because re-grouping the graph after you ungroup it will not allow you to make any of the changes you can make while it is still grouped. After ungrouping, the graph becomes an object like any other you draw.

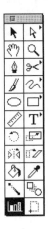

Graphs are created as grouped objects. As long as they remain grouped, you can change the type of graph (graph style), the graph's data or the graph's design, by selecting the Graphs Data commands or other options from the Object menu.

First, you use one of the graph tools to drag over an area of the drawing space to define the graph. (Use the Graphs and Style commands in the Object menu to select a style of graph, if the style you want isn't already selected, and the Graph tool icon will change to the style of graph you select. Alternatively, you can use whatever graph style is already selected, and change the style later on. The default style is grouped column (bar chart), unless you have changed it. By default, you drag from corner to corner, but you can hold down the Option key to drag from the center to a corner. If you would rather specify the dimensions in amounts, click in the top left corner of the area to be used for the graph, or hold down the Option key and click in the center of the area, and the Graph dialog box appears for typing in the width and height of the graph area. (You can use the General Preferences command in the File menu to select one of three units of measure — points/picas, inches, or centimeters — after selecting the graph tool, and before clicking with the Graph tool to display the Graph dialog box.) To resize the graph later, use the scale tool.

Next, the Graph Data window appears, and you can enter the data directly or import the data from a text file using the Import button, or you can cut and paste the data directly from a spreadsheet program. (To import data from a text file, first save the data file as text using that program, with a tab between each cell, and a carriage return between each row.) You can easily edit the rows and columns in the Graph Data window (Figure 5-91). You enter each label or value in a cell of the worksheet by clicking on the cell and typing in the entry area. Numbers are treated as data unless you type quotation marks around them (as in "1991"), in which case they are treated as text (labels).

To import a spreadsheet, you can use Copy in another application to copy numbers and text, and Paste in Illustrator's Graph Data dialog box to paste them into the data workspace.

When the data is properly entered in cells, click OK to create the graph. If the data is entered in the wrong order in the workspace, you can open the Graph Data dialog box with the Graph Data command in the Object menu, and use the Transpose option to transpose your columns and rows. Categories and legends are thus reversed in the graph.

The grouped column graph, also known as the bar chart, is used to compare one item to another, or to compare different items over a period of time. Categories are labels on the horizontal (x) axis, and values are

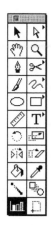

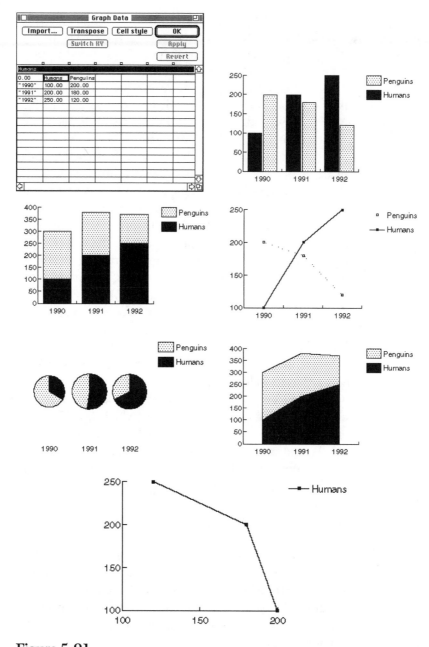

Figure 5-91.
The graph tool can be used to define the graph area, which automatically brings up the Graph Data dialog box for entering or importing the data. A graph is created automatically as a group of objects. The Graph Style command is used to select a graph type. The six graph types shown are grouped column, stacked column, line, pie, area, and scatter.

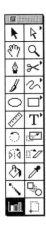

labels on the vertical (y) axis. Positive and negative numbers can be graphed. Enter category labels at the beginning of each row of the Graph Data worksheet. A label at the top of each column is used as a legend defining a data series.

Grouped column graph options include the column width and the cluster width. The cluster width is the total width of all columns in a cluster (corresponding to data in a row). Widths are measured in percentages of the space between columns or clusters; thus, 100 percent moves columns or clusters flush against each other. The default percentages are 90 percent for the column width and 80 percent for the cluster width. To change these settings, use the Graph Stye command in the Object menu.

The stacked column graph compares progress of a group of items over time, or shows the relationship of parts to the whole. Values for each category (row) are stacked one on top of another, not side by side as with a grouped column graph. Values must be all positive or all negative. The options are the same as for the grouped column graph.

With a line graph, you can compare trends over a period of time. The vertical (y) axis usually represents quantities while the horizontal (x) axis usually represents time. Each column corresponds to a line on the graph. Row labels appear on the horizontal axis, and column labels are used as legends.

Options include marking data points, which places square markers at each data point; connecting data points, which draws lines to connect the points; and edge-to-edge lines, which draws lines extending across the graph. When you connect data points, you can also use the fill lines option to paint wider lines depending on the data series. You specify the width of the line using the Fill line width option.

Pie graphs are circular with wedges indicating data segments as percentages of the total. Only one row is used to plot a pie graph, and you can't combine positive and negative numbers. If you have more than one row, separate pie graphs are created for each one.

Column labels are used as legends. The Standard Legends option puts column labels outside of the graph. The Legends in Wedges option puts labels inside the corresponding wedge. You can also specify No Legends. Use the direct-selection tool if you want to pull a wedge out from the pie graph for emphasis.

Area graphs are similar to line graphs showing two or more items and progress over time, but with a filled area representing total volume as well. Each column's values are added to the previous column's totals, making area graphs different in appearance than a line graph of the same data. You can't combine positive and negative numbers in area graphs containing

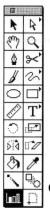

more than one column. An area graph must contain at least two rows. Column labels appear as legends.

Scatter graphs are useful for indicating patterns or trends, or whether one variable affects another. A scatter graph plots data points as paired sets of coordinates along the horizontal (x) and vertical (y) axes. Both axes measure values (there are no categories). You must have two columns of data; the first provides the values for the y-axis, and the second provides the values for the x-axis. Labels can be entered manually after creating the graph.

Graph Tools Summary

The graph tools automatically create graphs as grouped objects using data from a worksheet (entered manually or imported).

⬛ + drag from corner to corner

⬛ + Option key + drag from center to corner
   Define the grouped column graph area.

⬛ + click left-top corner

⬛ + Option key + click center
   Bring up the Graph dialog box to specify the width and height of the grouped column graph area.

⬛ + drag from corner to corner

⬛ + Option key + drag from center to corner
   Define the stacked column graph area.

⬛ + click left-top corner

⬛ + Option key + click center
   Bring up the Graph dialog box to specify the width and height of the stacked column graph area.

⬛ + drag from corner to corner

⬛ + Option key + drag from center to corner
   Define the line graph area.

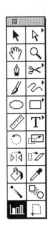

+ click left-top corner

+ Option key + click center

Bring up the Graph dialog box to specify the width and height of the line graph area.

+ drag from corner to corner

+ Option key + drag from center to corner

Define the pie graph area.

+ click left-top corner

+ Option key + click center

Bring up the Graph dialog box to specify the width and height of the pie graph area.

+ drag from corner to corner

+ Option key + drag from center to corner

Define the area graph area.

+ click left-top corner

+ Option key + click center

Bring up the Graph dialog box to specify the width and height of the area graph area.

+ drag from corner to corner

+ Option key + drag from center to corner

Define the scatter graph area.

+ click left-top corner

+ Option key + click center

Bring up the Graph dialog box to specify the width and height of the scatter graph area.

Page Tool

The page tool is used to control how Adobe Illustrator divides its drawing space (the Artboard) into pages for printing. Since very few PostScript printers are capable of printing the entire drawing space on a single piece of paper, Illustrator provides a way to define the printable area, and a way to define subdivisions for multiple pages (called *tiling*).

Illustrator provides three Artwork Board options in the Preferences dialog box: Single Full Page, Tile Full Page, and Tile Imageable Areas. When you first start up Illustrator, the program is set to Single Full Page by default, which defines a full-sized page region that is located in the center of the work area. The size of the full page depends on the type of printer you've selected in the Chooser (see the Apple menu), and the paper size setting in the Page Setup dialog box and Document Setup dialog box for that document. With Single Full Page in effect, you can print only one page, but you can set the size of that page (the Artboard) to be tabloid, legal, etc. You can work in any size drawing space; up to 120 by 120 inches, if you have enough free memory (RAM) available.

The size and shape of the printable page region is automatically changed if you change the page size specifications by choosing Document Setup or Page Setup from the File menu and altering the specifications in the Document Setup or Page Setup dialog box. It's important to remember that the Page Setup dialog box is not always the same; since the page setup capabilities are different from printer to printer, the information displayed in the Page Setup dialog box is supplied by the printer icon in the system file for the printer that is actively in use (the Chooser in the Apple menu allows you to select the active printer).

However, the placement of the printable region may not be well suited to your particular piece of artwork. In order to correct this, you can use the page tool to control how Illustrator defines the printable page area.

If your artwork is small enough to fit on a single page but the program's preset page breaks cause your artwork to be split into two or more pages, the page tool can be used to position the artwork entirely within one page region. If your artwork is too large to fit on a single page, the page tool with tiling on can be used to place the page breaks on the best places to divide your artwork. Placing the page breaks creatively can make it easier to reassemble large pieces of artwork from their component printouts.

Before you use the page tool you will probably want to use either the zoom tool to zoom out to a view that will allow you to see the entire

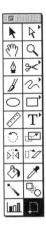

drawing space within the active window, or choose Fit In Window from the View menu (or press Command-M or double-click on the hand tool as shortcuts). You can use the page tool in the Preview view as well as with other views.

To use the page tool, click it in the toolbox. The pointer will turn into a plus sign (+) when you move it into the active window.

In order to move the page grid, first place the pointer over your artwork and hold down the mouse button; as soon as you depress the button, the program displays a dotted rectangle that corresponds to the printable area of a page (as currently defined in the Page Setup dialog box). The pointer (+) will be positioned at the lower left-hand corner of the dotted rectangle (Figure 5-92).

While holding down the mouse button, drag the rectangle (Figure 5-93) to the desired position over your artwork and release the button. The program will then draw the page grid according to your placement of the dotted rectangle (Figure 5-94).

If the artwork doesn't quite fit onto a single page, you can use the tiling feature. If you switch to the Tile Full Pages option in the Document

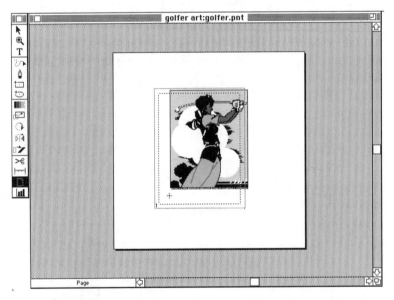

Figure 5-92.
After selecting the page tool to adjust the page boundary (in Single Full Page mode), click the lower left corner to adjust the page boundary. You can use the page tool in any view including Preview.

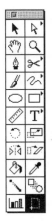

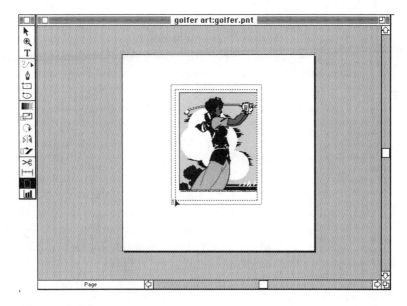

Figure 5-93.
Dragging the boundaries of the page to center the artwork for printing.

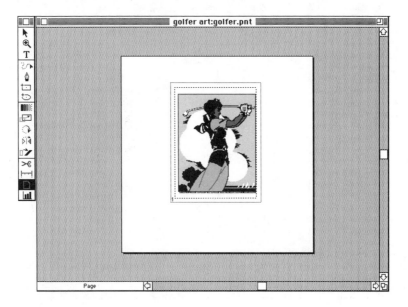

Figure 5-94.
The program draws the page boundaries according to the adjustment made by dragging the dotted lines.

Setup dialog box, more than one page can be printed, and your artwork can extend over more than one page.

If you switch to the Tile Imageable Areas option in the Document Setup dialog box, more than one page can be printed, and the pages that do print are the only the ones into which your artwork extends. With this option, a page grid made of dotted lines appears that represents the printable area of each page (Figure 5-95). These regions are related to the printable area of the page size specified in the Document Setup and Page Setup dialog boxes.

The dotted lines of the page grid are visible in all views of the active document (e.g. if you have another view of the same piece of artwork in another window, the page grid will be transferred to that view as well). The page numbering of these regions (page 5 is the center region) is used internally by the program and the numbers are not printed on the pages, although they are displayed in the Print dialog box as you are printing the document as a way to gauge the progress of the print job.

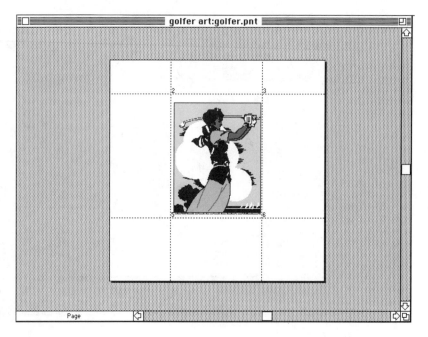

Figure 5-95.
These print area grids are displayed when you choose the Tile Imageable Areas option in the Document Setup dialog box. You can adjust them with the page tool.

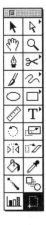

Illustrator measures the height and width of your artwork to create an imaginary rectangle called the *bounding box* around your artwork. Depending on the shape of your artwork and positioning of the bounding box, one or more blank pages may be printed because the bounding box falls on those pages, even if there is no visible artwork.

The only way to alter the size of your artwork is with the scale tool, or using the Adobe Separator program supplied with Adobe Illustrator.

This is the end of the toolbox reference section. Now that you know all about Adobe Illustrator's tools, you can turn the page to begin the menu reference section, beginning with an illustration of Adobe Illustrator's nine menus.

File Edit Arrange View

New	⌘N
Open...	⌘O
Close	⌘W
Save	⌘S
Save As...	
Place Art...	
Import Styles...	
Document Setup...	⌘⇧D
Page Setup...	
Print...	⌘P
Preferences	▶
Quit	⌘Q

Edit Arrange View

Undo Pen	⌘Z
Redo	⌘⇧Z
Cut	⌘X
Copy	⌘C
Paste	⌘V
Clear	
Select All	⌘A
Select None	⌘⇧A
Paste In Front	⌘F
Paste In Back	⌘B
Publishing	▶
Show Clipboard	

Arrange View Object

Repeat Transform	⌘D
Move...	⌘⇧M
Bring To Front	⌘=
Send To Back	⌘-
Group	⌘G
Ungroup	⌘U
Lock	⌘1
Unlock All	⌘2
Hide	⌘3
Show All	⌘4

View Object Font Type

✓Preview	⌘Y
Artwork	⌘E
Preview Selection	⌘⌥Y
Show Template	
Show Rulers	⌘R
Hide Page Tiling	
Hide Edges	⌘⇧H
Hide Guides	
Zoom In	⌘]
Zoom Out	⌘[
Actual Size	⌘H
Fit In Window	⌘M
New View...	⌘⌃V
Edit Views...	

Object Font Type F

Paint Style...	⌘I
Custom Color...	
Pattern...	
Gradient...	
Attributes...	⌘⌃A
Join...	⌘J
Average...	⌘L
Guides	▶
Masks	▶
Compound Paths	▶
Cropmarks	▶
Graphs	▶

Font Type Filter Wi

Chicago	
Courier	▶
Geneva	
✓Helvetica	▶
Helvetica Narrow	▶
Monaco	
New York	
Palatino	▶
Symbol	
Times	▶

Type Filter Window

Size	▶
Leading	▶
Alignment	▶
Tracking...	⌘⇧K
Spacing...	⌘⇧O
Character...	⌘T
Paragraph...	⌘⇧T
Link Blocks	⌘⇧G
Unlink Blocks	⌘⇧U
Make Wrap	
Release Wrap	
Fit Headline	
Create Outlines	

Filter Window

Last Filter	⌘⇧E
Colors	▶
Create	▶
Distort	▶
Objects	▶
Select	▶
Stylize	▶
Text	▶

Window

New Window	
Hide Toolbox	⌘⌃T
Show Layers	⌘⌃L
Hide Info	⌘⌃I
Show Paint Style	
Show Gradient	
Show Character	
Show Paragraph	
✓Untitled art 1 <50%>	

File ▶ | *File Menu*

File	Edit	Arrange	View
New			⌘N
Open...			⌘O
Close			⌘W
Save			⌘S
Save As...			
Place Art...			
Import Styles...			
Document Setup...			⌘⇧D
Page Setup...			
Print...			⌘P
Preferences			▶
Quit			⌘Q

The File menu is used for working with Illustrator artwork and template documents. The commands in the File menu let you create new Illustrator documents, open existing Illustrator documents, open a template document while creating a new Illustrator document, place Encapsulated PostScript files inside an existing Illustrator document, close and save Illustrator documents, set up pages for printing, print Illustrator documents, and quit the Illustrator program to return to the Macintosh's Finder. The File menu gives you access to the Macintosh's operating system from within the Illustrator program.

New...

The New command creates a new Illustrator document. Select New in the File menu (or press Command-N as a shortcut). Illustrator automatically creates a new Illustrator document without a template.

New documents are automatically given the name "Untitled art." To name a new Illustrator document, you must save the document using either the Save, Save As or Quit options in the File menu. The Adobe Illustrator program will not let you quit without first naming or agreeing not to save any unnamed documents.

Open...

The Open command opens an existing Illustrator document and an associated template (if any), or opens a template document with a new untitled Illustrator document. You can issue the Open command by either selecting Open in the File menu or by pressing Command-O as a shortcut. Illustrator 5 supports the opening of more than one file at a time.

Use the Open command when you want to work on an existing Illustrator document, or as an alternative to the New command when you want to create a new Illustrator document from an existing template.

After you select Open, the Get File dialog box appears and prompts you to select either an Illustrator document or a template (MacPaint or PICT file) from the scroll box. If you select an Illustrator document, the Illustrator program will attempt to locate the template that was used to create the Illustrator document (if there was a template). When the active window appears, it will highlight the name of the Illustrator document

File

in the window's title bar; if there is a template associated with the Illustrator document, the name of the Illustrator document will be followed by a colon (:) and then the name of the template document.

If you want to force the Illustrator program to prompt you to select a template when you open an existing Illustrator document (instead of automatically trying to retrieve a template), you can hold down the Option key while selecting Open in the File menu (or while pressing Command-O as a shortcut). Forcing Illustrator to prompt you for another template is useful when you are creating a piece of artwork that is based on more than one template.

If you select a template document from the scroll box, the program will assume that you want to create a new Illustrator document based on that template. When the new active window appears, the name of the Illustrator document will appear as "Untitled Art" followed by a colon (:) and then the name of the template document.

After you open the template and/or Illustrator document, you may not be able to see all of (or any of) the image in the active window. To bring the image into view, you should first try scrolling the image using either the scroll bars or the hand tool. If the image is too large to fit into the active window, you can use the zoom tool to zoom out from the image step by step until it fits in the window. Alternatively, you can select Fit In Window from the View menu or double-click on the hand tool to fit the entire drawing space in the window and then use the zoom tool to zoom in on the image.

Close

The Close command (Command-W) is used to close the current Illustrator document and template (if any) without quitting the program. Use the Close command when you have finished working with one document and want to work on another.

Selecting Close in the File menu is equivalent to clicking inside the small close box located in the upper left-hand corner of the window's title bar. When you issue the Close command, the file is closed and removed from the Illustrator desktop, if no changes have been made to the document since the last time it was saved. If changes have been made since the last save, a dialog box will ask if you want the changes to be saved. Click the Save button if you want to save the changes; click Don't Save to close the document without saving the changes; or click Cancel to return to the Illustrator file and cancel the Close command. The bold double line surrounding the Save button indicates that if you simply press the Return key, that button will be activated to save your changes.

If it is a new untitled document, the program will bring up the Save File dialog box and request that you give the document a name to save it with.

Save

The Save command is used to save and name a new untitled Illustrator document or to periodically save an existing document. You should remember to save your documents frequently while you are working on them as a preventative measure against a problem with the document, a system crash, or a power failure. You can issue the Save command by either selecting Save in the File menu or by pressing Command-S.

The Save command does not affect the template document since the template cannot be altered by the program. If you are saving a new untitled document for the first time, you will be presented with the Save As dialog box, which will prompt you for the name that you want to use for saving the document. For more information about the Save As dialog box see the section on the Save As command below.

If you have already saved the document (i.e., if it already has a name other than "Untitled Art"), then issuing the Save command will not bring up the Save As dialog box. Instead, the document will be saved under the current name, on the same volume (folder, disk drive, or other storage device) that it was opened from, and the saved document will replace the previous version of the document.

Save As...

The Save As command is used to either save the active Illustrator document under a different name, or on a different volume (a volume can be a folder, disk drive, or other storage device). You also have a choice of whether to use a preview bit map for IBM or Macintosh programs, and whether to use a color or black and white preview for Macintosh programs. Illustrator uses the Encapsulated PostScript format when it saves files. You can save the file in different formats for compatibility with previous versions of Illustrator.

To issue the Save As command, you must select Save As in the File menu; this command brings up the Save As dialog box that lets you specify how you want the Illustrator document in the active window to be saved.

If you want to save the document under a different name, you simply

File

type in the new name in the box that appears below the words "Save illustration as:" in the dialog box. You can then either save the file in the current folder that is displayed at the top of the dialog box, or you can select a different file folder and/or disk drive. To select a different folder, point to the folder name and scroll down the list of folders (if any) that will appear under the current folder. If the file is stored on the disk without being placed in a folder, the icon and name of the disk will appear where the folder appears at the top of the dialog box.

If you want to save the file on a different disk drive, point to the Drive button and click the mouse button; each click will display a different disk drive until all the drives connected to the system (including AppleShare and other network drives) have been displayed; after that the list recycles with each new click. If only one drive is connected, the Drive button will be grayed-out and cannot be used. If a drive with removable disks is selected, the Eject button appears normal and pressing it would eject the disk from its drive so that another disk could be inserted.

Adobe Illustrator normally saves documents as Encapsulated Post-Script files for use with Adobe Illustrator, with None (Omit EPSF Header) set for the Preview bitmap. These documents occupy the least amount of disk space and can be edited and viewed with Illustrator. However, other applications may not be able to display the image (a gray box appears in the other applications, although the image should print correctly).

The Preview bitmap option lets you save a preview bitmap of the image for display purposes with other applications. You can choose among several options: Black and White Macintosh (the least amount of space occupied), Color Macintosh, and IBM PC. The None (With EPSF Header) setting, and the other preview settings, make the file an Encapsulated PostScript file that can be placed in any other application that accepts such files.

You can use Illustrator-created artwork with a variety of page layout and presentation programs on the Macintosh and on IBM-compatible PCs and PS/2 computers, as long as you save a copy of the artwork with an Encapsulated PostScript File (EPSF) Header. To select any one of the Encapsulated PostScript formats, click the pop-up menu for the Preview option.

When you have finished selecting the Save As options you desire, click the Save button. If you want to return to the Adobe Illustrator program without saving your work, press the Cancel button to send the dialog box away and return to the program.

File **Place Art**

The Place Art command can place a complete Encapsulated PostScript file into an Adobe Illustrator document. Encapsulated PostScript (EPS) is a standard format for transferring PostScript graphics to and from PostScript drawing and page makeup programs, and from scanner programs and clip art libraries.

The contents of the EPS file occupy a box in your drawing space, and an image may also appear in the box that represents the graphics. You can move, scale, rotate, reflect, or shear the box just as any other piece of artwork. However, you can't adjust any of the anchor points, segments, or paths of the EPS graphics, nor can you apply paint or stroke colors or gray shades.

When you use the Preview Illustration command, you will see either a gray box or an image of the EPS graphics, depending on the type of EPS file saved by the other application. Adobe Illustrator also lets you save Illustrator artwork as EPS files with the Save As command.

Import Styles

The Import Styles command is used to import style characteristics from another document into your current file. You can import custom colors, patterns, gradients, and graph designs, and the new one will overwrite the existing one if they have the same names.

Document Setup

The Document Setup command (Command-D) is used to select the page-oriented (as opposed to printer-oriented) options that affect how the page will be printed. Selecting the Document Setup command allows you to specify the artboard size and orientation. In addition to selecting a unit of measure for rulers, and a page view (Tile imageable areas, Tile full pages, or Single full page), you can also set the View options for placed images and patterns to increase drawing speed, and the resolution for output.

The Preview and print patterns option determines whether the

File

program should print patterns and display them with the Preview command. The Show placed images option, when on, displays EPS artwork that has been placed in the document with the Place Art command.

The Split long paths option, usually turned off, lets you split complex shapes and patterns into two or more separate paths automatically on saving or printing the document, to help eliminate printing delays and errors and save memory.

When the option is turned on, you must enter an Output resolution, or use the default resolution already entered for the device you are printing to. The resolution is used to determine how Illustrator should split paths.

If the path length of a complex shape exceeds the printer's memory, Illustrator breaks the shape into pieces shown by lines in the Artwork view.

The higher the resolution, the more frequently a path will be split. Pattern-filled paths are often split because they contain a lot of information. Also, the lower a path's flatness setting (determined by the output resolution setting), the more likely it is that the path will be split. If the printer resolution is greater than the output resolution, the flatness setting will be greater than 1. If the flatness setting is calculated to be less than one, it is set to 1. For example, if the printer resolution is 2400dpi and the output resolution is 800 dpi, the flatness setting is 3. If the printer resolution is 2400dpi and the output resolution is 2400 dpi, the flatness setting is 1. You can reduce the output resolution setting and also use the Split long paths option if you are getting limitcheck errors.

Note that once a path is split, in any further editing operations you must treat the shape as two or more paths rather than as a single path. It makes sense to save the original document without the option on, then turn on the option to save a copy for printing on a particular output device, leaving the original with unsplit paths.

You can alternatively use the Attributes command in the Object menu to specify output resolution.

Illustrator provides three Artwork Board options in the Document Setup dialog box: Single full page, Tile full pages, and Tile imageable areas.

Single full page is the default option, which defines a full-sized page region that is located in the center of the work area. The size of the full page depends on the type of printer you've selected in the Chooser, and the paper size setting in the Page Setup dialog box for that document. With Single full page in effect, you can print only one page.

With the Tile full pages option more than one page can be printed,

File ▶

and your artwork can extend over more than one page.

With the Tile imageable areas option in the Preferences dialog box, more than one page can be printed, and the pages that do print are the only ones into which your artwork extends. With this option, a page grid made of dotted lines appears representing the printable area of each page.

Checking the Use Page Setup box will automatically set the artboard size to match the page size you set in the Page Setup dialog box.

Page Setup

The Page Setup command is used to select the page-oriented (as opposed to printer-oriented) options that affect how the page will be printed. Selecting the Page Setup command in the File menu brings up the Page Setup dialog box, allowing you to specify the paper size, either vertical (portrait) or horizontal (landscape) page orientation, a percentage of reduction or enlargement, and other printer options available for the selected printer.

Unlike most of the other dialog boxes in the Adobe Illustrator program, the Page Setup dialog box and the related Print dialog box are provided by the Macintosh's operating system, not the program. Although the Page Setup dialog boxes for different printers appear similar, there are some important differences, described here in greater detail. For more information about printing, see the section on the Print command.

The options you specify in the Page Setup dialog box are only applied to the Illustrator document displayed in the window that was active when you selected the Page Setup command. Any options you specify will be saved with the Illustrator document. Since the options you select only affect the document in the active window, you will need to select Page Setup and specify the options for other documents separately, after you have activated each of the windows that display those documents.

Because the Page Setup options are saved with the document, and the options and dialog boxes vary for different printers, Adobe Illustrator will not automatically change all the Page Setup options if you change printers. If you use a different printer than the one you specified in the Page Setup dialog box, Adobe Illustrator will use the default options provided by the new printer's system resource file instead of the options that were saved with the document. Therefore, if you change printers with the Chooser, check the Document Setup and Page Setup dialog boxes to make sure that the options you desire are selected.

LaserWriter Page Setup

If you are using the LaserWriter for printing, you will see a Page Setup dialog box. The LaserWriter's Page Setup dialog box is revised from time to time by Apple, and the current version number is displayed on the top right of the dialog box near the OK button. Select the desired paper size. You can also specify a reduction for your document with the Page Setup dialog box. However, this reduction does not affect the size of the actual document or the artwork in the document. The only way to actually change the size of the artwork in a document is to use the scale tool.

You can also specify the orientation of the printout: vertical (also known as portrait), or horizontal (also known as landscape). Vertical (portrait) is the standard way pages are printed. When horizontal (landscape) orientation is selected, the artwork is printed sideways, which is an ideal choice for printing a short, wide image that would not fit on the page in the vertical orientation.

If you want to control how the page orientation affects the Illustrator document, you can use the page tool to preview how the page will be set up and use Document setup to change the way Illustrator defines the artboard, but the Page Setup dialog box options define the area for printing. Changes made in the Page Setup dialog box will be reflected in the grid controlled by the page tool. You can select either the vertical orientation icon or the horizontal orientation icon by simply pointing to it and clicking the mouse button. The selected icon will appear black.

Print

The Print command is used to select the printer-oriented (as opposed to page-oriented) options that affect how the page will be printed. Before printing you should familiarize yourself with the Document Setup and Page Setup options described above and make sure that the proper options are selected in the Document Setup and Page Setup dialog boxes. Selecting the Print command in the File menu (or pressing Command-P as a shortcut) brings up the Print dialog box. If you want to print without bringing up the Print dialog box (because you have already set the printer options the way you want), hold down the Option key while issuing the Print command.

The Print dialog box allows you to specify the number of copies to be printed, the range of pages to be printed, how the paper is handled by the printer, and other options that may be available for a particular printer.

File

Although the Print dialog boxes for different printers look similar, there are some important differences. The exact dialog box that will be presented depends on what printer is currently installed in the system and selected for use, and which version of the system software is used. Printers can be color printers, or black and white printers.

To select a printer (if there is more than one installed in your system and connected to your Macintosh), use the Chooser desk accessory. It's usually a good idea to check the Chooser before printing to make sure the correct printer has been chosen. Also, if you have changed printers, you should check the Page Setup settings before printing, using the Page Setup command in the File menu.

Keep in mind that Adobe Illustrator is designed to work with PostScript printers. If you are using an ImageWriter or other dot-matrix or laser printer that uses the Macintosh's native QuickDraw graphics language instead of PostScript, the results will not be as good as they would be with a PostScript printer. Be sure to check your printer's documentation to find out if it uses PostScript. Some printers provide for PostScript as an option; if so, check to find out if that option is installed in your printer.

If you don't own a PostScript printer, you can make drafts on your StyleWriter (or similar printer) and take your Illustrator document to a service bureau or other location that has a PostScript printer connected to a Macintosh for getting the final printout.

LaserWriter Printing

If you are using the LaserWriter printer (and it is properly attached, chosen, and set-up), issuing the Print command will bring up a Laser-Writer Print dialog box. The LaserWriter Print utility (and dialog box) is revised periodically by the printer manufacturer, and the current version number is displayed at the top right of the dialog box near the OK button.

When you have selected the Print options that you want, you can initiate the printing process by clicking the Print button.

If you don't want to print, click on the Cancel button to return to the Adobe Illustrator program.

After you press the Return key or click the Print button, a dialog box will be displayed, indicating that the connection to the printer is being established and, if necessary, that the Macintosh is initializing the printer. Once the printing process has started, another dialog

File

box is displayed, indicating the progress of the print operation.

If you want to stop the printing process while either of the two above dialog boxes are displayed, hold down the Command key while typing a period (.); this will cancel the printing. The printer may not stop right away due to the fact that the print buffer must be depleted before the Cancel command actually takes effect; using a print spooler can further prolong the time it takes to stop printing.

Preferences

You can select the Preferences command from the Edit menu, and sub-commands for General, Color Matching, Hyphenation Options, and Plug-ins.

General Preferences (Command-K) affect tool behavior, such as the Constrain angle, Corner radius for rectangles, Freehand tolerance, and Auto trace gap, as well as checkboxes to turn on or off the Snap to point, Transform pattern tiles, Scale line weight, Area select, and Use precise cursors options.

You can also set the ruler units, indent/shift units, and Greek text limit. Keyboard increments can be set for the Cursor key, Size/leading of type, Baseline shift, and Tracking. Also, you can set the number of undo levels (no limit except RAM) and the Paste remembers layers option.

Press Command-K to select the General Preferences dialog box. The Preferences command displays a dialog box (Figure 5-96) that contains all of the general preference settings for your session with Adobe Illustrator.

You can turn on or off the Snap to point feature, which causes an object to attach itself to an anchor point whenever the the object is moved within two pixels of that anchor point. The Snap to point feature makes it possible to place one point on top of another without having to zoom into the drawing to see much more detail.

The Transform pattern tiles option determines whether pattern tiles will be transformed or moved along with an object that is undergoing a transformation or a move. This option is automatically turned on if you choose to transform pattern files in any of the transformation or move dialog boxes. Ordinarily patterns are not moved or transformed with an object.

The Scale line weight option makes the scaling of line weights the default setting for uniform scale operations (the Scale dialog box offers an option of scaling line weights). When this option is off, line weights are preserved as the default when you uniformly scale one or more

File

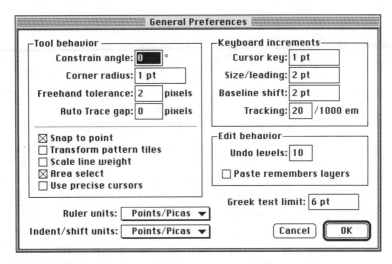

Figure 5-96.
*The General Preferences dialog box is displayed when you select Preferences
and General from the File menu.*

objects; when this option is on, line weights are scaled by default.

The Area select option is turned on by default, so that when you select
a filled object, clicking anywhere inside the object selects the object. Turn
it off if you only want to be able to select the object by clicking a path
segment or anchor point. Turning the Area select option off is helpful
when you have two overlapping filled objects, and you want to select only
one of them.

The Constrain angle lets you rotate the x and y axes of the
document. With a setting of zero degrees (the default), the x and y
axes are set parallel to the sides of your display, vertically and
horizontally. When you draw, move, or transform an object while
holding down the Shift key, the drawing, movement, or transformation occurs relative to the x and y axes at 45-degree increments. You
can set the Constrain angle to change the x and y axes relative to its
original position as vertical and horizontal, and the new axes will
affect transformations and movements in any other documents you open
or create during that session (until you quit the program). The new axes
are rotated counterclockwise from the horizontal origin if you specify a
positive angle, or clockwise if you specify a negative angle.

The new constrain angle does not affect freehand drawing, blending,
or automatic tracing. It affects all transformations and constrained
movements, drawing with the rectangle and oval tools, and constrained
drawing with the pen tool. Always specify the constrain angle before

drawing, because you can't apply a new constraint to an existing object without transforming the object.

If you want to reset the axes to the original horizontal and vertical position parallel to the sides of your display, change the Constrain angle to zero. Changes made to the x and y axes are not saved with a document; the next time you open the document (during another program session) the axes will be reset to their original position parallel to the sides of the document.

The Corner radius setting specifies the radius of the circles used to form rounded corners of rectangles. If you specify a corner radius, that radius is applied to all new squares or rectangles you draw, until you change it again in the Rectangle dialog box or in the Preferences dialog box. Always specify the corner radius before drawing the rectangle, because you can't apply a new corner radius to an existing rectangle. You specify the amount of movement in the current measurement used for the ruler units (inches, centimeters, or picas/points).

If the radius you specify is too large for the rectangle (more than one-half the size of either the height or width, whichever is smaller), then the program uses the radius for the largest oval that can fit in the corner of the rectangle. Specify a radius of zero for ordinary square-cornered rectangles.

The Freehand tolerance setting determines how sensitive the freehand tool will be to sudden quirks and changes in your hand movement. The freehand tool responds to shakiness or other slight variations in your drawing motion, creating bumps.

You can set the freehand tolerance level to reduce (or increase) the number of bumps. The default setting for the freehand tolerance level is two pixels, which means that a variation of two pixels will not create a bump. The larger the number of pixels, the more bumps the program will ignore, providing for smoother lines.

The Auto trace over gap is also measured in pixels, and determines the largest gap that the auto trace tool will jump across in an effort to continue tracing a shape. Scanned images and bit-mapped graphics sometimes have gaps that are visible when you enlarge your view with the zoom tool. The auto trace tool will ignore gaps that are equal to or less than the number of pixels you specify for the distance.

The Ruler units can be set to centimeters, inches, or picas and points. These units are used in the rulers, which change along with the zoom tool to show greater or lesser magnification. They are also used in dialog boxes.

The Keyboard increments settings are used to set increments to move when you use keyboard shortcuts. Cursor key setting describes the distance a selected object will move when you press one of the cursor control keys. You can press the cursor keys as many times as you want to move selected objects, and change direction at will. You can also set increments for Size/leading for type, for Baseline shift, and for Tracking. You specify the amount of movement in the current measurement used for the ruler units (inches, centimeters, or picas/points).

The Edit behavior options include a box to set the number of undo/redo levels (no limit except available RAM), and whether or not Paste remembers layers. Turn the Paste remembers layers option on if you want pasted objects to retain their layer levels; otherwise, they are placed in front of any selected objects in the current layer.

Preferences: Color Matching

Selecting Color matching brings up the color matching dialog box, for adjusting colors of ink, how colors are displayed on the monitor, and the Gamma setting. You can also turn on or off CIE calibration, or simply check the Use Defaults button.

Adobe Illustrator provides a way to adjust the display (monitor) and ink system of your Macintosh II so that colors more closely match the printed colors. You make these adjustments by referring to a sample progressive color bar from your printer. Progressive color bars are printed on color separations on the right edge by the Adobe Separator program. The printer prints color bars on the press. Color bars and other marks are trimmed off before a print job is finished.

It is helpful to get a color sample with a color bar printed on the paper stock, from the same printer that will be printing the color artwork or publication, so that you can match a specific paper's ink coverage.

A progressive color bar shows cyan, yellow, magenta, and the following combinations: magenta and yellow, cyan and yellow, cyan and magenta, and then all three colors, followed by black.

Although Adobe Illustrator can display colors on a monitor set in the Control Panel to 16 colors, you get better results in matching the printed version by using a monitor set to 256 or more colors. Best results are obtained by setting the monitor to the "Millions" of colors setting (16.7 million colors), which you can do only if you have the 24-bit (or 32-bit) display capability on your Macintosh. You set the number of colors by opening the Monitors Control panel, and selecting the desired option.

After running the monitor for about 20 minutes (so that it warms up), choose Preferences and Color Matching from the File menu and the Color matching dialog box showing swatches of the four process colors, white, and the same combinations of CM and Y found on the color bar

(Figure 5-97) will appear. You can hold your printer's color bar up to the display and compare it to the colors in this dialog box.

If one or more colors in the dialog box do not match the printed colors closely enough, click the color swatch and the Progressive Colors dialog box appears, so that you can change the color. You can move the tiny white dot across the color wheel to change the hue and saturation, and scroll through brightness levels, to get the right color. Or you can specify a color exactly by typing its hue, saturation, and brightness values or its red, green, and blue values (Figure 5-98).

Turn off the CIE calibration if you can't get the Progressive Colors dialog box to appear when you click a color swatch. Turn on the CIE calibration to access the Ink, Monitor, and Gamma settings. The Ink options include matching inks for selected PostScript color printers, as well as Toyo inks and Standard Web Offset (SWOP) inks for both coated and uncoated papers. The Monitor setting includes a scrolling list of many brands and models of monitors, as well as an NTSC standard setting.

Since ambient light and general room conditions can vary over the course of a day, you may need to adjust the monitor a few times in order

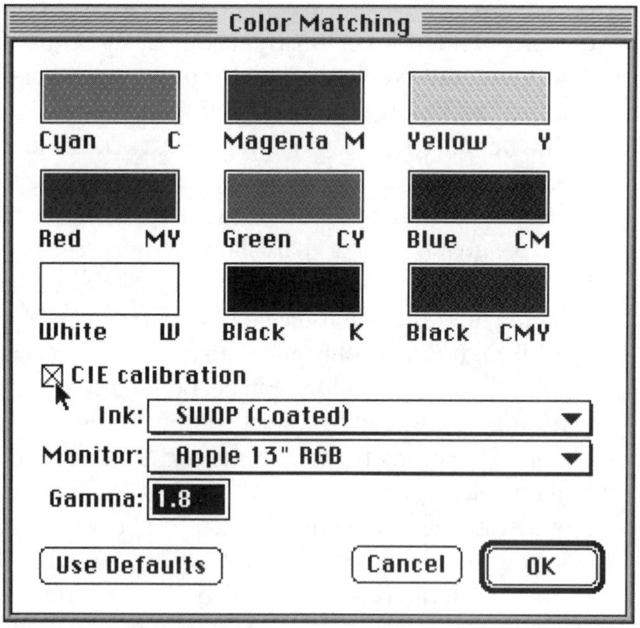

Figure 5-97.
The Color Matching dialog box.

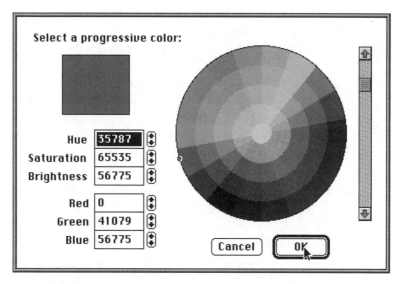

File N!

to get a close match to the printed version. However, the monitor can never be as close in matching the final printed version as a PostScript color printer can be, since a color printer also uses ink and paper.

Preferences: Hyphenation Options and Plug-ins

Selecting Hyphenation Options brings up the Hyphenation Options dialog box, where you can enter (add or delete) hyphenation exceptions, and choose from several languages.

Plug-ins brings up the Get File dialog box so that you can choose a different plug-ins folder to install only the plug-in filters from the chosen folder.

Quit

The Quit command ends your current session with Adobe Illustrator and returns you to the Macintosh desktop. You can issue the Quit command by either selecting Quit in the File menu or by pressing Command-Q as a shortcut.

If you have not made any changes to the Illustrator document since

Figure 5-98.
The Progressive Colors dialog box.

the last time you saved it (changing the Page Setup options would count as a change), the program will end your session, close any documents, and automatically return you to the Macintosh desktop.

However, if you have made any changes to the Illustrator document, the program will ask whether or not you would like to save any changes you've made. If you click the "Save" button, Adobe Illustrator will save any open documents and then close them before returning to the Macintosh desktop.

If there are any new Illustrator documents (i.e. any that are named "Untitled Art"), the Save As dialog box will be displayed so that you can name each untitled document before quitting. If you select the "Don't Save" button by clicking on it, that document will be closed without any changes being saved.

If you select the Cancel button, the Quit command will be canceled and you will return to the Adobe Illustrator program.

Edit Menu

The Edit menu is used for selecting various commands used to edit your Adobe Illustrator documents. The commands on the Edit menu allow you to undo the last action made by you or the computer; redo actions that were undone; cut, copy, and paste objects to and from the clipboard; clear (delete) artwork objects from the document; select all or none of the objects in a document; paste objects in front of or behind other objects; show or hide the contents of the Clipboard; and use the Macintosh System Software 7.0 or greater's Publish and Subscribe features, by invoking Illustrator's Publishing commands, which let you share documents with other users on a network, and update those documents.

Undo and Redo

The Undo command can be used to undo the last several operations (exactly how many operations you can undo/redo depends on how many levels of undo you have set in the General Preferences dialog box). To choose the Undo command, select Undo in the Edit menu or press Command-Z as a shortcut. After you select Undo, you can choose the Redo command if you want to redo an operation.

The Redo command can be used to undo the last Undo commands. To choose the Redo command, select Redo in the Edit menu (it is right

Edit

below the Undo command) or press Command-Shift-Z as a shortcut.

The Undo command is not always available. (For example, it is not available if you have just opened a new file.) If the Undo command is not available, it will appear grayed-out. If the Undo command is available, it will be listed in the menu followed by the action that will be undone if the command is chosen.

The Redo command is not always available. If the Redo command is not available, it will appear grayed-out. The Redo command is only available after the Undo command has been chosen. If the Redo command is available, it will be listed in the menu followed by the action that will be redone if the command is chosen. You can undo the Redo command by selecting Undo again.

The number of Undo/Redo operations you can do is limited by available RAM and the number of Undo/Redo levels you set in the General Preferences dialog box (select Preferences and General from the File menu).

Cut

The Cut command removes all the selected objects from the document and places them in the Clipboard for temporary storage, ready for a Paste command. The objects are stored in the Clipboard until something else is copied or cut to the Clipboard with the Copy or Cut command.

You can choose the Cut command by either choosing Cut in the Edit menu or by pressing Command-X as a shortcut. Issuing the Cut command replaces whatever else was contained in the Clipboard with the selected objects. After you choose the Cut command, you can check the contents of the Clipboard by issuing the Show Clipboard command in the Edit menu.

In order to permanently store objects that are temporarily placed in the Clipboard, you must either paste them to an Adobe Illustrator document using the Paste, Paste In Front, or Paste In Back commands, or transfer them to the Scrapbook by selecting the Scrapbook from the Apple menu and selecting the Paste command (Command-V).

If you quit Illustrator or switch to another application program after a cut operation, the image is saved as a PostScript language file (provided enough memory is available to save the Clipboard). You can thus move the contents of the Clipboard into another Illustrator file or to a file created with another application

If you want to undo a cut that you have made, select Undo Cut from the Edit menu or press Command-Z as a shortcut. In order to retrieve an object that was cut and placed in the Clipboard, click inside the window where you want the object to go and then choose one of the Paste commands (Paste, Paste In Front, or Paste In Back); the object will be pasted into the document according to the chosen Paste command.

Use the Paste Remembers Layers option in the General Preferences dialog box if you want objects to retain their layer level when they are cut and pasted. See the Layers discussion in the Window menu section, for information about pasting objects between layers.

Copy

The Copy command is similar to the Cut command described above except that it places a copy of the selected objects in the Clipboard without removing them. To choose the Copy command, either choose Copy in the Edit menu or press Command-C as a shortcut.

Issuing the Copy command copies all the selected objects in the active window and places them in the Clipboard for temporary storage (this replaces whatever else was contained in the Clipboard). You can then Paste the objects to the Scrapbook if you want to store them there.

To retrieve an object that was copied or cut and placed in the Clipboard, click inside the window where you want the object to go and then choose one of the Paste commands described below (Paste, Paste In Front, or Paste In Back); the object will be pasted into the document.

The Copy command can also be used to generate a PICT-format image of the Preview view of the selected artwork. First select the objects you want to copy, or use the Select All command (Command-A) in the Edit menu to select the entire artwork document. To create a PICT preview of the selected artwork, hold down the Option key while issuing the Copy command.

Use the Paste Remembers Layers option in the General Preferences dialog box if you want objects to retain their layer level when they are cut and pasted. See the Layers discussion in the Window menu section, for information about pasting objects between layers.

Paste

The Paste command retrieves objects that are temporarily stored in the Clipboard and places them in the document. You can choose the Paste command by either selecting Paste in the Edit menu or by pressing Command-V as a shortcut.

Only Adobe Illustrator artwork objects that were cut or copied can be pasted directly into an Adobe Illustrator document, with the exception of type into a type block.

When you choose the Paste command, any objects that are in the Clipboard will be pasted into the center of the active window and will be placed on top of all the other objects in the document. Even though pasting places all the objects in the Clipboard on top of everything else in the document, the relative painting order of the objects being pasted stays the same. If you want to place the pasted object in back of all or some of the objects, or if you want the objects pasted at the same locations they were cut or copied from, use one of the other Paste commands (either Paste In Front or Paste In Back).

When you paste objects from the Clipboard into an Illustrator document using Paste, the objects that are pasted will be selected and all the other objects will be deselected. Since the Paste command does not remove the contents of the Clipboard, you can continue to Paste the same objects into the document or into other documents.

Use the Paste Remembers Layers option in the General Preferences dialog box if you want objects to retain their layer level when they are cut and pasted. See the Layers discussion in the Window menu section, for information about pasting objects between layers.

Clear

The Clear command deletes any objects that are selected. You can choose the Clear command by selecting Clear in the Edit menu or by pressing either the Delete key (Backspace key on the Macintosh Plus) or the Clear key as shortcuts. For more information on how to select the objects that you want to delete, refer to the section about the selection tool.

To delete all of the objects in an Adobe Illustrator document, first click in the document's window, then choose Select All in the Edit menu (or press Command-A as a shortcut), and then choose Clear in the Edit menu (or press the Delete/Backspace key or Clear key as a shortcut). This action will delete everything in the document, and all the objects in the window will disappear.

Select All and Select None

The Select All command selects all of the objects (points, lines, curves, etc.) that are contained in the document that is displayed in the active window. You can choose the Select All command by either choosing Select All in the Edit menu or by pressing Command-A as a shortcut.

After selecting all objects, if you now want to deselect all the objects, simply click in any blank area in the document, use the Select None command in the Edit menu, or use the Command-Shift-A shortcut.

If you want to deselect one of the selected objects, point to the object you want to deselect and hold down the Shift key while clicking the mouse button; alternatively you can hold down the Shift key and drag the selection marquee around the object to deselect it (be careful not to accidentally include another object in the marquee).

If you want to deselect more than one of the selected objects, you can continue the deselection process by holding down the Shift key while pointing to the next object you want to deselect and either click on the object or drag the selection marquee around it.

Be sure that the objects you want deselected are actually selected in the first place; if you try deselecting an object that is not already selected, it will be added to the group of already selected objects instead.

Also keep in mind that selecting or deselecting objects has no effect on the order in which they are painted by the program (the stacking order).

Use the Paste in Front, Paste in Back, Send to Front or Send to Back commands to change the stacking order. See the Layers discussion in the Window menu section, for information about moving objects between layers.

Paste In Front

The Paste In Front command is used for pasting objects stored in the Clipboard in front of the objects that are selected in an Adobe Illustrator document. You can choose the Paste In Front command by either selecting Paste In Front in the Edit menu or by pressing Command-F as a shortcut. Only Adobe Illustrator artwork objects that were cut or copied onto the Clipboard can be pasted directly into an Adobe Illustrator document.

When you choose the Paste In Front command, any objects that are in the Clipboard will be pasted in front of all the selected objects in the current layer in the document, and behind the objects in the current layer in the document that are not selected, if the Paste Remembers Layers option is turned off in the General Preferences dialog box.

Even though pasting the group of objects in the Clipboard changes the order in which that group is painted by the program, the relative

Edit

painting order of the objects being pasted stays the same. If you want to place the pasted object in back of all or some of the objects, use the Paste In Back command described next.

When you paste objects from the Clipboard into an Adobe Illustrator document using the Paste In Front command, the objects that are pasted will be selected and all the other objects will be deselected. It will also paste in front of everything if nothing is selected. Issuing the Paste In Front command does not remove the contents of the Clipboard.

The Paste In Front command is handy for placing duplicate objects on top of each other for special effects, such as placing an object that was outlined over an object that was filled with a shade of gray or color. Since pasting does not remove the contents of the Clipboard, all you need to do to create a duplicate of an object is to select it, copy it to the Clipboard, and choose the Paste In Front command.

Use the Paste Remembers Layers option in the General Preferences dialog box if you want objects to retain their layer level when they are cut and pasted. See the Layers discussion in the Window menu section, for information about pasting objects between layers.

Paste In Back

The Paste In Back command is used for pasting objects, stored in the Clipboard, behind the objects that are selected in an Adobe Illustrator document.

You can choose the Paste In Back command by either selecting Paste In Back in the Edit menu or by pressing Command-B as a shortcut. Only Adobe Illustrator artwork objects that were cut or copied onto the Clipboard can be pasted directly into an Adobe Illustrator document.

When you choose the Paste In Back command, any objects that are in the Clipboard will be pasted in back of all the selected objects that are in the current layer of teh document, and in front of the objects in the current layer of the document that are not selected, if the Paste Remembers Layers option is turned off in the General Preferences dialog box. Even though pasting the group of objects in the Clipboard changes the order in which that group is painted by the program, the relative painting order of the objects being pasted stays the same. If you want to place the pasted object in front of all or some of the objects, use the Paste In Front command described above.

When you paste objects from the Clipboard into an Adobe Illustrator document using the Paste In Back command, the objects that are pasted will be selected and all the other objects will be deselected. It will also paste in back of everything if nothing is selected. Issuing the Paste In Back command does not remove the contents of the Clipboard.

Use the Paste Remembers Layers option in the General Preferences dialog box if you want objects to reatin their layer level when they are cut and pasted. See the Layers discussion in the Window menu section, for information about pasting objects between layers.

Publishing

The Publishing commands are used with the Macintosh System Software 7.0 or greater's Publish and Subscribe features. By invoking Illustrator's Publishing commands, you can share documents with other users on a network, and update those documents. You can copy and update material from one document to other documents. First select the material that you want to be published; this material is called a Publisher, and is saved as a separate file (called an Edition) when you use the Create Publisher command, and name and save the Edition. You can save the Edition as a PICT file only, or as a Pict and EPS file.

When you open another Illustrator document file on your Macintosh or someone else launches Illustrator on their Macintosh on the network, using the Publishing and Subscribe To commands invokes the Subscribe to dialog box, which prompts the user to select an Edition to place. The placed Edition is called a Subscriber, and it appears with special gray borders (see next paragraph) and an x through it, which are only visible when the Subscriber object is selected.

When you publish a selection (called an Edition), the published selection is highlighted with special gray borders. You can hide these borders using the Publishing and Hide Borders commands in the Edit menu, but first you must deselect the objects. To make the borders appear again, select the Publishing and Show Borders commands in the Edit menu.

Note that the Show and Hide Borders commands show and hide borders for all objects that have been published, even though the objects may be published in different Editions. However, if you select only the object(s) that you want to show or hide borders before you use the Show and Hide Borders commands, then only the selected objects will be affected by the command.

When you make changes to published objects, the changes are reflected in each copy of the object in subscribed documents. To see the latest Edition's save time and date, use the Publishing and Publisher Options commands in the Edit menu to bring up the Publisher Options dialog box. Here you can also unpublish a selection of published Editions by selecting the Cancel Publisher button, or you can move the published Edition to a new folder/disk/server, using the Publisher Options command.

When you need to update Editions right away, the Send Editions options in the Publisher options dialog box can be set to On Saves. Use the Manually option if you do not want updates to be sent automatically, and click the Send Edition Now button to update an Edition.

You can also use the Publisher options dialog box to change the Edition from PICT only to PICT and EPS format, or vice versa. Use PICT and EPS format for Adobe Illustrator and Adobe PhotoShop and other applications that support EPS format, otherwise, use the PICT only format.

Show and Hide Clipboard

The Show Clipboard command displays the current contents of the Clipboard. The Clipboard is a temporary storage area used by Macintosh applications for objects stored by the Cut and Copy commands. Objects stored in the Clipboard can be retrieved using the Paste commands. The Clipboard is common to virtually all Macintosh applications and can be used to easily move small amounts of data between applications.

Although many types of data can be stored in the Clipboard, only three types are relevant to Adobe Illustrator: Illustrator artwork objects, text, and PICT data. Only Illustrator artwork objects can be pasted directly into any window.

Illustrator text elements can be cut or copied into the Clipboard from an Illustrator document and pasted into another Illustrator document. However, text from another program, from the Note Pad, or from the Scrapbook, cannot be pasted into an Illustrator document.

PICT-formatted graphic images cannot be pasted into any Illustrator window (templates cannot be altered with Illustrator), but PICT images of the artwork's Preview view can be copied into the Clipboard by holding down the Option key while you choose the Copy command.

The Hide Clipboard command, displayed in place of Show Clipboard when the Clipboard is visible, is used to hide the Clipboard after it has been displayed with Show Clipboard. To choose the Hide Clipboard command, either select Hide Clipboard, or click in the small close box located in the upper left-hand corner of the Clipboard window's title bar. The Clipboard can also be hidden by clicking in any other window besides the Clipboard window.

Arrange ▶ *Arrange Menu*

Arrange ▶ View	Object
Repeat Transform	⌘D
Move...	⌘⇧M
Bring To Front	⌘=
Send To Back	⌘–
Group	⌘G
Ungroup	⌘U
Lock	⌘1
Unlock All	⌘2
Hide	⌘3
Show All	⌘4

The Arrange menu is used for manipulating, modifying, and arranging artwork objects. The commands on the Arrange menu allow you to repeat the transformation (scaling, rotating, reflecting, shearing, or moving) of an object or group of objects, bring an object to the front of or send it behind other objects, move an object a precise amount, combine objects into a unified group or ungroup them, lock objects so that they can't be selected, unlock all objects, hide selected objects, and show all objects.

Repeat Transform

The Repeat Transform command repeats the last transformation of an object or group of objects. You can choose the Repeat Transform command by either selecting Repeat Transform in the Arrange menu or by pressing Command-D as a shortcut.

A transformation refers to the action of scaling, rotating, reflecting, shearing, or moving. If your last transformation created a transformed duplicate (because you held down the Option key while performing the transformation), the Repeat Transform command will both transform and create a duplicate for the object again each time that you choose the command.

Repeating transformations a number of times can be used to create special effects. For example, objects can be rotated around a central point (e.g. spokes on a wheel, petals on a daisy, etc.) by using the rotate tool and Rotate dialog box to specify a precise amount of rotation for an object, clicking on the Copy button in the dialog box, and issuing the Repeat Transform command to repeat the rotation and duplication. The Repeat Transform command can be chosen repeatedly (to create any number of transformed duplicate objects) until you ultimately run out of memory in your computer.

Move

The Move command is used for moving objects using the precision of the Move dialog box. You can choose the Move command by either

Arrange

selecting Move in the Edit menu or by pressing the Option key and clicking the current selection tool.

The Move dialog box lets you move an object a specific distance and direction relative to the current orientation of the x and y axes, which is set by the Constrain Angle option in the General Preferences dialog box. For example, if the Constrain Angle option is set to 20 degrees, specifying a 30-degree move actually moves the object along a line that is 50 degrees from the window's horizontal axis (30 degrees from the Constrain Angle x and y axes).

A horizontal distance moves the object to the right; a vertical distance moves it up. If you enter the distance and angle, the horizontal and vertical entries are automatically calculated; if you enter the horizontal and vertical distances, the angle is automatically calculated. Positive angles specify an angle that is clockwise from the point of origin; negative angles specify an angle that is counterclockwise.

The Move dialog box always displays the direction and distance of the last move operation or measurement using the measure tool. The unit of measure is set in the General Preferences dialog box. You can move a copy of an object, and you can choose whether or not to move the pattern tiles only, the object only, or the pattern tiles as well as the object.

If you use the measure tool to measure the distance you want to move an object (or a copy of the object), and then immediately select the Move dialog box, the results of the measurement are automatically used to fill in the Horizontal, Vertical, Distance and Angle boxes, so that you can easily make the move.

Bring To Front

The Bring To Front command is used for placing selected objects in the frontmost position in an Adobe Illustrator document. You can choose the Bring To Front command by either selecting Bring To Front in the Edit menu or by pressing the Command key and the equal (=) sign key as a shortcut. When you choose the Bring To Front command, any objects that are selected are placed in front of all other objects in the document. However, if the object is part of a group, masked artwork, compound paths, text wraparounds, graphs, etc., then it is moved to the front of the group, rather than to the front of the layer.

See the Layers discussion in the Window menu section, for information about moving objects between layers.

Arrange▸ Send To Back

The Send To Back command is used for placing selected objects behind all other objects in an Adobe Illustrator document. You can choose the Send To Back command by either selecting Send To Back in the Edit menu or by pressing the Command key and the dash (-) key as a shortcut. When you choose the Send To Back command, any objects that are selected are placed in back of all other objects in the document. However, if the object is part of a group, masked artwork, compound paths, text wraparounds, graphs, etc., then it is moved to the back of the group, rather than to the back of the layer.

See the Layers discussion in the Window menu section, for information about moving objects between layers.

Group

The Group command consolidates a number of artwork objects into a single object. To choose the Group command, either select Group in the Arrange menu or press Command-G as a shortcut. Issuing the Group command converts all the objects that are selected in the document into a single composite object.

To select the objects that you want to group together you can either: 1) drag the selection marquee around the objects; 2) select the objects one-by-one by first clicking on an object and then holding down the Shift key while you click on the other objects you want included in the group; 3) select all the objects in the document for grouping by issuing the Select All command found in the Edit menu; or 4) choose the Select All command and then deselect the objects that you don't want in the group.

Keep in mind that only complete paths can be grouped; therefore if any of the objects you have selected for grouping includes a partially selected path, the entire path will become part of the group. After you have selected the objects that you want grouped together you can choose the Group command to combine all the selected objects into a single grouped object.

Once a number of objects are grouped together with the Group command, they can be selected, deleted, moved, scaled, rotated, reflected, sheared, cut, copied, pasted, moved between layers, or painted as a single unit. You can select individual points or paths in a group by using the direct-selection tool. The group-selection tool can be used to find out if an object is part of a group, and to find all the objects that are also members of the same group. See the selection tools discussion earlier

Arrange

in Chapter 5 for additional information about using these selection tools.

Combining objects into a group does not change the relative painting order of the objects in the group, but it does change the painting order of the group as a whole. When objects are grouped together, the program paints them starting with the top object in the group. If you want to change the painting order of objects within a group, you must first ungroup the objects using the Ungroup command, and then use the Paste In Front and Paste In Back commands (in the Edit menu), or Bring To Front and Send To Back commands (in the Arrange menu) to change the order in which the component objects are painted.

Grouped objects can be combined with other groups and/or objects to create a larger grouped object. Grouped objects cannot be changed with the pen tool unless they are ungrouped with the Ungroup command. Because grouped objects are more resistant to changes than ungrouped objects, grouping objects is a convenient way to "freeze" a path or object once you are finished drawing it, to prevent accidental changes. You can also lock an object so that it can't be selected — see the Lock command, or Hide an object—see the Hide command.

Ungroup

The Ungroup command breaks a grouped object down into its original component parts. You can choose the Ungroup command by either selecting Ungroup in the Arrange menu or by pressing Command-U.

If any of the original components were also grouped objects, the Ungroup command will leave the component groups intact. If you want to break any of these component groups down into their original parts, you must repeat the Ungroup command after selecting the component group.

Issuing the Ungroup command has no effect on which objects are selected or on what order the program paints the objects that were contained in the group.

Lock and Unlock All

Objects can be locked so that they can no longer be selected unless they are unlocked. First select the object or objects to be locked, then choose the Lock command from the Arrange menu or press Command-1. If you hold down the Option key, all unselected objects are locked, leaving only selected objects unlocked.

When objects overlap each other, it is useful to be able to lock certain objects so that they no longer get in the way of selecting other objects. You can lock only entire paths; if you select only a segment, the entire path is locked anyway.

Locked objects are saved with the document in their locked state. To unlock, use the Unlock All command, which unlocks all locked objects at once. You can choose the Unlock command from the Arrange menu or press Command-2.

Hide and Show All

Objects can be hidden from view with the Hide command. After selecting the object or objects to hide from view, you choose the Hide command from the Arrange menu or press Command-3.

Hiding objects can be useful if objects are too close together or overlapping, and you need to work on other objects that are partially or fully obscured.

You can hide only paths; if you select only a segment, the entire path is hidden anyway.

A hidden object can't be selected and it doesn't appear in print or in the Preview view.

Hiding is not saved with the document; therefore, all objects are shown when you open a document. You can also show all objects by choosing the Show All Command from the Arrange menu, or press Command-4.

View Menu

The View menu contains various commands that allow you to alter your view of the Adobe Illustrator document in the active window.

The View commands let you see a preview of the printed artwork, show or hide the template, the Adobe Illustrator artwork only, or preview a selection of the artwork only.

You can control the size at which the document is viewed, and control whether or not the rulers, guide objects, page tiling and selection edges and anchor points of selected objects are displayed in the active window. You can also create multiple views of a document (up to 25 views), showing, for example, detail of various areas in artwork and preview views, and these views are named and listed at the end of the View menu, so that you can select them by name.

View **Preview**

The Preview command creates an approximate view of what Adobe Illustrator artwork will look like when it is printed. Select Preview from the View menu (Command-Y), and the program changes its view of the document and uses the current Paint Style and Type settings to display an approximation of what your artwork would look like if it were printed. You can modify the image of the artwork directly in this Preview view, as well as in the Artwork view.

You can also alter your view of the image, such as by using the scroll bars, hand tool, zoom tool, and page tool. However, if you have open windows that represent more than one view of a document (created with the New Window command in the Window menu), the windows that contain previews of the artwork will be updated automatically when changes are made in other views of the document.

Previews of gray-scales and color shades are not accurate, and only serve as a very rough approximation of the final output. Preview is very useful for checking the order in which objects are painted by the program.

To change the colors used in the Preview view, use the Preferences and Color Matching commands in the File menu to display the Color Matching dialog box to show the cyan, yellow, magenta, and black combinations for comparison to printed color bars. To change these colors, click on any color swatch to display the Progressive Colors dialog box to adjust that color for the display.

Artwork

The Artwork command displays the Adobe Illustrator document and the template beneath it (if any) in the active window, unless the Hide Template option in the View menu is selected. If the Hide Template option is selected, then only the artwork is displayed. The Artwork view is what is displayed when you first open a document, and it is the view that you will probably use most of the time for creating and working on your artwork. Select it from the View menu, or as a shortcut use Command-E.

Preview Selection

Since the Preview command takes a long time to finish when you are previewing complex shapes, you can use the Preview Selection command to preview only the selected object or objects. You can do this by first selecting the object or objects, then choosing the Preview Selection command or typing Command-Option-Y. If you preview selected artwork as you work, you can see how a picture is affected by each new path you draw without having to resort to using the Preview command. You can create a new view or window to represent the preview and simultaneously display both the Preview window and the Artwork window (also see the New Window command in the Window menu and the New View command in the View menu for details).

Show Template and Hide Template

The Show Template and Hide Template commands display or hide the template document in the active window. The Hide Template view is useful for inspecting the artwork without the distraction of the template image. Although the template is usually grayed in the Artwork and Preview views, hiding the template allows you to view the art as it will be printed, with no template visible.

Show Rulers

The Show Rulers command displays two rulers, one along the right-hand side and one along the bottom of the active window. Show Rulers only appears as a menu option if the rulers are not currently displayed in the active window; if the rulers are already displayed, the Hide Rulers command occupies this position in the menu instead. To display or hide the rulers, you can use Command-R to turn the rulers on and off.

The rulers are useful for precision work where measurements or sizes are important. Every window or view can have its own set of rulers. When you first create a document or first start the program and open an existing document, the rulers will not be displayed. To display the rulers, select Show Rulers in the View menu (Command-R).

The rulers use one of three different units of measurement: centimeters, inches, or picas and points (one point = 1/72 of an inch, one pica = 12 points or 1/6th of an inch). In Figure 5-99 the rulers are numbered in picas at actual size, with tick marks corresponding to 4-point intervals and numbered subdivisions at 4-pica intervals. As the magnification or reduction of the view changes, the numbering system on the ruler also changes (Figure 5-100).

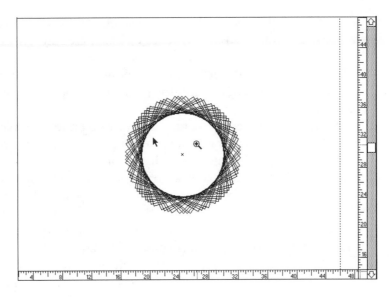

Figure 5-99.
*The rulers are displayed by the Show Rulers (Command-R) command. This
view is actual size.*

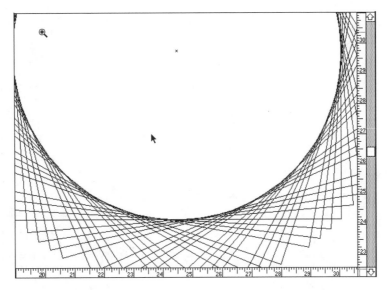

Figure 5-100.
*The ruler unit marks change as you zoom into or out from a document to
provide precise measuring.*

When the rulers are displayed you will notice that as you move the mouse, the pointer's position is indicated by a dotted line on each of the rulers. The ruler origin point for the rulers (i.e., the zero point for each ruler) is tied to the document, not the window, so if you scroll, move, or zoom around in the document, the numbers on the rulers will change to reflect the document's ruler origin.

When the document is created, the ruler origin for the rulers is the lower left-hand corner. If you want to change the ruler origin, move the arrow cursor over the lower right-hand corner of the active window, where the rulers intersect, and a set of dotted cross-hairs appears (Figure 5-101). Hold down the mouse button and the pointer changes into a plus sign (+) when you move it into the active window. Drag the cross-hairs over the point that you want to become the new origin for the rulers and release the mouse button (Figures 5-102 and 5-103).

For color separation purposes, you should be aware that this point also becomes the PostScript origin point for the measurements of the bounding box. The bounding box describes the smallest rectangle that defines the outside dimensions of the entire illustration, and controls where trim marks and registration targets appear in the color separation produced by the Adobe Separator program. You may want to reset the

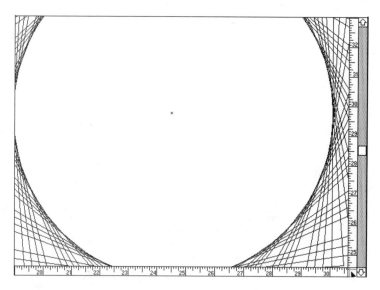

Figure 5-101.
Clicking the intersection point that defines the ruler origin (where zero appears on each ruler).

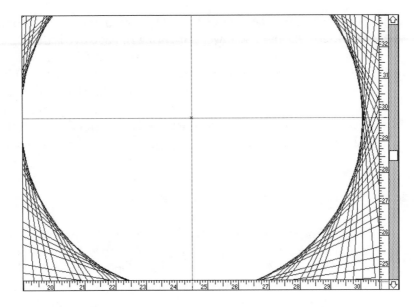

Figure 5-102.
Dragging the ruler origin to be in the center of the circle.

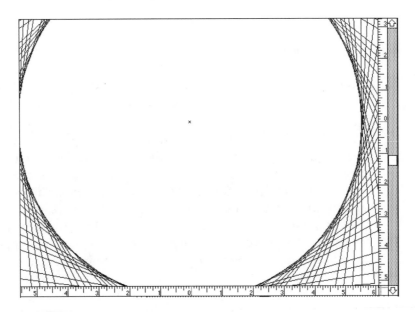

Figure 5-103.
The ruler's zero points now define the center of the circle.

ruler origin point before saving the illustration document for producing color separations. The lower-left corner of page five is the logical ruler origin for specifying the bounding box in the Adobe Separator program.

To remove the rulers from view, you can either choose Hide Rulers in the View menu or press Command-R as a shortcut. The Hide Rulers command only appears as a menu option if the rulers are currently displayed in the active window; if the rulers are not displayed, the Show Rulers command will occupy this position in the menu instead.

Hide Page Tiling and Show Page Tiling

Page Tiling options (tile imageable areas, tile full pages and single full page) determine the display of page boundaries on the artboard. The Hide Page Tiling and Show Page Tiling commands on the View menu turn on and off the display of page boundaries. Turn them off so that they do not interfere with viewing of the artwork. Turn them on so that you can see the partition lines for imagable areas of the artwork.

Page boundaries are used to determine how pages will be printed. Change the page tiling options and page size using the Document Setup and Page Setup commands in the File menu.

Hide Edges and Show Edges

You can hide and show selection elements' edges—such as anchor points (Artwork and Preview views), paths (Artwork view) and selection edges (Preview view) — so that they don't appear in the Artwork or Preview views. Sometimes selection elements (which might be part of a group) are in the way of objects beneath them. You can hide such edges by selecting the Hide Edges command in the View menu. Selected objects can still be moved, transformed, or otherwise manipulated, because they remain selected until you unselect them. You can then show them again by choosing the Show Edges command, which replaces the Hide Unpainted Objects command in the View menu. As a shortcut, you can use Command-Shift-H to turn the display of edges on and off.

Hide Guides and Show Guides

Guide objects are path objects created temporarily from any object by selecting the object and using the Make Guides command in the Object menu (Command-5). You can also create ruler guides by clicking in a vertical or horizontal ruler and dragging the dotted ruler guide into position on the artboard (also hold down the Option key to switch the ruler guide's direction). The object or ruler guide is displayed as a dotted line and can be used as a guide to place other objects.

You can then Lock the Guide object or objects by selecting Guides and Lock from the Object menu. However, all guides in the document will be locked. To lock only a selected guide or guides, first select only the guide object(s) you wish to lock, and use the Lock command in the Arrange menu (Command-1).

To release a guide or guides locked with the Lock command, use the Unlock All command in the Arrange menu (Command-2). To release a guide or guides locked with the Guides and Lock commands in the Object menu, use the Guides and Lock command again in the Object menu to remove the check mark next to the Lock command.

When you release the guide object or objects, they are again made visible objects in the artwork document, and can be moved, transformed, deleted, and so on.

To hide guide objects temporarily so that they don't appear in the Artwork or Preview views, select the Hide Guides command in the View menu. You can then show them again by choosing the Show Guides command, which replaces the Hide Guides command in the View menu.

Zoom In and Zoom Out

You can always zoom in and out using the zoom tool. The zoom tool zooms in closer to a point on the page by default when you click at a point while using the zoom tool, or you can press the Option key while using the zoom tool to zoom out and away from the page. To access the zoom-in tool while using another tool, hold down the Spacebar and Command key. You can access the zoom-out tool by holding down the Spacebar, Command and Option keys. (For zooming in text mode, press Command-Spacebar; for zooming out of text in text mode, press Command-Option-Spacebar.)

You can also use the Zoom In command (Command-]) and the Zoom Out command (Command-[) in the View menu to magnify and reduce your view of the image in the viewing window, no matter which tool you are using. The view of the image in teh viewing window remains centered when you use the Zoom In and Zoom Out commands. Using the zoom tool allows you to select a point to be the centerpoint for the zooming. You can also drag a selection marquee around the area you want to zoom into or out of with the zoom tool; hold down the Shift key as you drag with the zoom tool, and the zoom level will be constrained to preset zoom levels.

When you use the zoom tool and the Zoom In and Zoom Out commands, you do not change the magnification level of the document, you only change your view of the image. If you switch to another view of the artwork after zooming in or out with the zoom tool or Zoom In and Zoom out commands, the document is again displayed at the viewing size you saved and named it at.

Actual Size

The Actual Size command displays the document in the active window at the actual size of the Adobe Illustrator document (maximum size 10 feet by 10 feet). At actual size one screen pixel is equivalent to one point (1/72 of an inch).

You can choose the Actual Size command by either selecting Actual Size in the View menu, pressing Command-H, or double-clicking on the zoom tool in the toolbox. Issuing the Actual Size command also centers the document (and accompanying template, if any) in the active window.

Fit In Window

The Fit In Window command displays the entire artboard (up to 10-feet by 10-feet drawing space) containing the document, centered in the active window. Select Fit In Window in the View menu, press Command-M, or double-click on the hand tool in the toolbox. The Fit In Window command also centers the document (and accompanying template, if any) in the active window.

New View

The New View command displays the New View dialog box, which allows you to name and save up to 25 different views of your artwork, which are listed at the end of the View menu. You can access these views by selecting them from the View menu by name, or by using Command-Shift-number key (numbers 1-25) shortcuts. To rename or delete the views, use the Edit Views command.

Object Edit Views

The Edit Views command displays the Edit Views dialog box, where you can select a named view in the scrollbox, and delete or rename it. Since you cannot change an existing view and then save those settings, first delete the existing view if you no longer need it, or rename it, then create a new view using the new settings, and save the new view using the same old name as the deleted (or renamed) view.

Object Menu

Object	Font	Type	F
Paint Style...	⌘I		
Custom Color...			
Pattern...			
Gradient...			
Attributes...	⌘^A		
Join...	⌘J		
Average...	⌘L		
Guides	▶		
Masks	▶		
Compound Paths	▶		
Cropmarks	▶		
Graphs	▶		

The Object menu contains the Paint Style and other commands that let you specify attributes that determine how the artwork or text will be painted. There are various kinds of color you can assign to artwork: a mix of the process colors (cyan, yellow, and magenta), premixed colors (such as PANTONE MATCHING SYSTEM (PMS) colors, FOCOLTONE COLOR SYSTEM colors, TRUMATCH color swatching system colors, and TOYO ink colors), and custom colors. Learning to use these Object menu commands is critical to creating Adobe Illustrator artwork in color. In addition, Adobe Illustrator offers the ability to make custom patterns, gradients, and mix custom colors (or rename PMS colors) from the Paint Style palette. You also create and release guides for aligning objects, masks, compound paths, cropmarks for marking the image area of the page, and graphs. You can also join two endpoints, average two or more anchor points, or average and join two endpoints at the same time, to link the two paths at a point midway between the two endpoints.

Paint Style

The Paint Style command brings up the Paint Style dialog box (see also the Show Paint Style palette command in the Window menu), which lets you control how regions are filled and how paths are stroked. You can specify no fill and no stroke, or white, 100 percent black or a percentage of black (for grays), percentages of process colors (cyan, yellow, and magenta), or a custom color, such as PMS, FOCOLTONE COLOR SYSTEM, TRUMATCH color swatching system, or TOYO ink color, or a pattern for both fill and stroke for type and for objects. If you have created custom patterns, you can also assign them to fills and strokes in

Object ▷

the Paint Style dialog box. Gradients can be used to stroke objects and type. If you have created custom gradients, you can also assign them to fills for objects and type in the Paint Style dialog box. If you are planning to produce color separations from the file, you will want to use the Overprint option for fills and/or strokes.

In addition, for strokes you can specify either solid or dashed lines, the pattern for dashed lines, the stroke line weight, the type of line cap and join, and the miter limit on miter joins.

To choose the Paint Style command, you can either select Paint Style in the Object menu or press Command-I as a shortcut. Choosing the Paint Style command brings up the Paint Style dialog box (Figure 5-104). You can use the Style command to examine or change the painting attributes of a particular object by selecting the object and then choosing the Style command, which displays the Paint Style settings for that object.

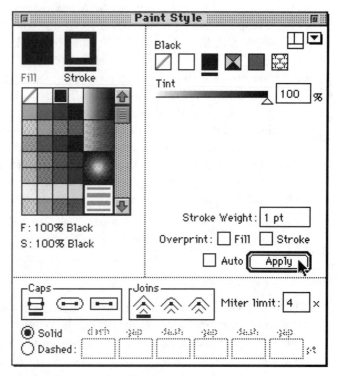

Figure 5-104.
The Paint Style dialog box with black fill and black stroke set to 100 percent. Since a stroke is specified, you can also specify the stroke line weight, solid or dashed lines, the pattern for dashed lines, the type of line cap and join, and the miter limit for miter joins.

Object

Adobe Illustrator uses the settings of the Paint Style dialog box to produce the final image that is output to the printer, displayed on the screen with the Preview and Preview Selection commands, or output by the Adobe Separator program.

PostScript automatically masks objects that overlap one another, so that the painted fill and stroke of an object that is underneath another filled and stroked object does not print. It is like painting with non-transparent pieces of paper for each shape. If you ever have any doubt that two shapes overlap, choose the Preview option and a magnification level that allows you to see what will happen when the illustration is printed.

Adobe Illustrator lets you assign custom colors to paths in an image whether or not you are using a color display. Printing presses use cyan, magenta, and yellow (CMY) primary subtractive colors in inks that can be applied to a white surface and combined with black ink. This color model, referred to as CMYK (for cyan, magenta, yellow, and black), is available in the Paint Style dialog box (Figure 5-105) for the fill and stroke of type and paths. The program automatically displays CMYK assignments using the proper RGB values, so that you don't have to make wild guesses about how the colors will appear. Adobe Illustrator also lets you adjust this conversion for your particular display, so that colors will appear the same under different lighting conditions, and to adjust the display to match the ink colors in a sample or test of the final printed result. (see Preferences and Color Matching commands in the File menu).

You can also assign more than 700 PANTONE printing inks which are available with all printing presses. The premixed PANTONE colors are chosen by consulting the PANTONE MATCHING SYSTEM, developed by Pantone, Inc. Unlike process colors, which can be mixed by yourself to make different shades of color, PANTONE colors can't be mixed—you simply select one that looks right. The PANTONE Process Color System allows you to assign more than 3000 CMYK combinations that can be used to simulate Pantone ink colors.

Other custom color ink systems include TOYO (1050 colors from the Toyo 88 Color Finder 1050, and 624 colors from the Toyo 91 Process Color Finder), FOCOLTONE (763 CMYK colors selected to avoid prepress trapping and register problems), and TRUMATCH (2000 computer created colors that cover the visible spectrum of the CMYK gamut in even steps).

PANTONE and other custom colors are specified by clicking the Custom Color selection option to display a scrolling list of color names (Figure 5-106). To see the list of PANTONE colors, you must also have open a document with PANTONE colors already specified; Adobe Systems provides Illustrator document containing all of the PANTONE

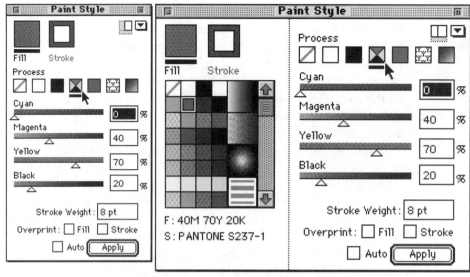

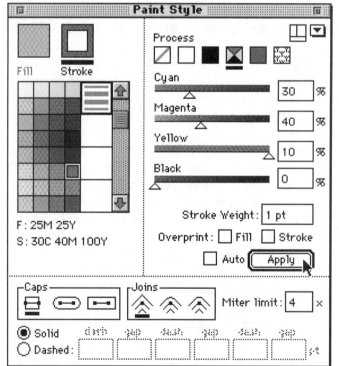

Figure 5-105.

The Paint Style dialog box showing percentages of process colors used for the path's fill and stroke. You can select one of several palette display choices, including the three shown here, and change the palette display style at any time using the down arrow control located at the top right.

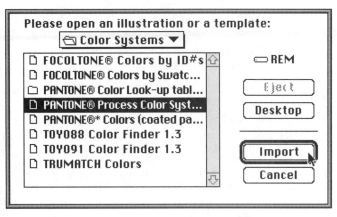

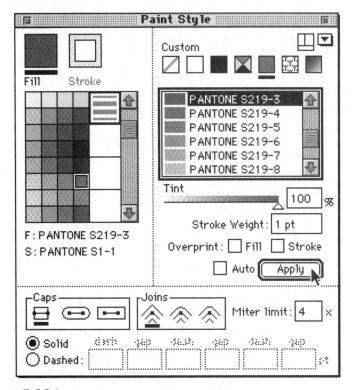

Figure 5-106.

After importing a PANTONE color document using the Import Styles command (or opening another artwork document containing PANTONE color assignments), the Paint Style dialog box shows PANTONE colors that can be assigned to any open document. PANTONE or other custom-mixed colors can be assigned to fill and stroke, and you can specify a percentage tint of a PANTONE color.

Object

colors. You can open this document and leave it open while coloring objects in other documents. As you assign a PANTONE color to an object in a document, that particular color name is saved with the document, appearing whenever you open that document.

Use the Import Styles command with the Startup file to load in all the custom colors, patterns and gradient fills you want to make available in the Paint Style palette of every new artwork document file. Delete unused ones to save file storage space, or create a custom set of colors patterns and gradient fills to use for a particular job, such as a corporate identity portfolio (containing brochures, letterhead, data sheets, price lists, etc.) that will be published on a network.

Colors do not usually mix when they overlap. The overprint option (available separately for fill and stroke) allows color underneath an object to mix with the color of the object, thus creating a color somewhere between the two for the overlapping area. An overprinting stroke mixes its color with the color beneath it, preventing any separation between the two objects in print even if the registration is slightly off.

Use the Overprint option whenever you want to make a selected object or objects transparent.

When a colored object is overprinted, the process colors that are common to it and the objects behind it are not affected and print normally; only the colors that are not in common are mixed. You don't need to use the overprint feature for 100 percent black because Adobe Illustrator automatically overprints black. However, tints of black must be overprinted if used for trapping.

Adobe Illustrator paints objects according to how they are ordered in the document. The program starts painting the backmost object in the backmost layer in the document and then paints objects successively until the foremost object in the foremost layer is painted. Since the ink that Illustrator paints with is opaque (unless you turn on overprint), each layer of ink completely covers any layers under it.

If you want to change the order in which objects are painted (which is often necessary for the artwork to look right), you can use the Paste In Front and Paste In Back commands (Edit menu), or the Send To Back and Bring To Front commands (Arrange menu). The Group command in the Arrange menu is also handy for controlling the order in which objects are painted. Moving objects between layers also can affect the painting order.

When Adobe Illustrator paints your document for previewing, separating, or printing, all the objects in your artwork, including the type, are treated as paths and can therefore have fills and strokes painted. Paths consisting of a single point (such as center points) are not painted. Type

Object

characters are treated as if each character were a closed path, so you can specify whether the type should be filled with black or any color or pattern, stroked with black or any color or pattern, or both.

If you fill an open path with two distinct endpoints, the program will treat the open path as if it were a closed path by connecting the two endpoints with an imaginary straight line; it will then fill the area inside the imaginary closed path (Figure 5-107).

If you specify a stroke for a path, the path is drawn as a series of connected curve and line segments. The thickness (line weight), color (white, black, gray, process color, custom color, or custom pattern), and dash pattern of the line can be examined or specified in the Paint Style dialog box. If you specify that an object should be filled and stroked, then the object will be filled first, and then the stroke will be placed over the fill (the filled area will be covered by one-half the specified line weight).

When you first start the Adobe Illustrator program, and display the Paint Style palette (Show Paint Style in the Window menu), the Paint Style dialog box displays the following default settings: "Fill" is set to 100 percent Black (the selected areas will be filled with 100 percent black ink), "Stroke" is set to none (there will be no stroke

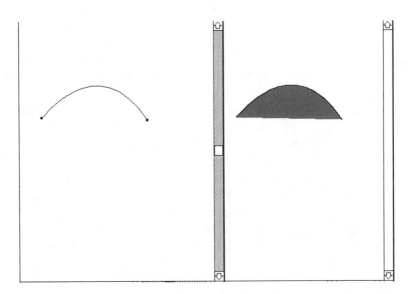

Figure 5-107.
When you paint an open path, the program draws an imaginary straight line to close the path and paints the object. The Preview window shows the result of painting the fill with 50 percent black and the stroke with 100 percent black.

Object

delineating the paths), "Weight:" and stroke styles are grayed-out (since Stroke is set to none), and "Overprint" is off.

If you specify a colored (white, black, process color, custom color, or custom pattern) stroke, the default stroke "Weight:" is set to 1 point, default "Miter Limit:" is set to 4, a mitered line join and butt caps are automatically selected, the "Dash pattern" is set to solid, and "Overprint" is left off.

If you select a single path, or an object consisting of a single path, then choose the Paint Style command (Command-I); the settings for that path or object are displayed in the dialog box. If you select more than one object and then choose the Style command, only the settings common to all the selected objects are displayed in the dialog box, and any settings that were not the same for all the selected objects have question marks or are left unspecified.

If you select an object that you don't realize is grouped with another object, and some of the settings differ, then those settings will appear blank in the Paint Style dialog box. You could Ungroup the selected objects (Command-U), select only one object at a time, and use Command-I for the Paint Style dialog box to see all the settings, but you can instead simply use the direct-selection or group-selection tools to select the desired object, and use Command-I for the Paint Style dialog box to see all the settings.

The first set of options in the Paint Style dialog box are Fill options that specify what color ink, if any, will be used to fill the selected objects. If you click the None swatch, the area will not be filled and will be transparent.

Click the White swatch, and opaque (not transparent) white ink will be used to fill the selected objects. Painting areas with white ink can provide a handy way to erase things; this is analogous to using white paper tape over typing errors, only better because the edges of the "painted" tape never cause shadows on the page, which is a problem with paper tape. For example, the Nurse (Plate 2) has a wide, white tape strip along the outside of each of the four sides, to create the white border around the art. The border tapes are filled with 100 percent white paint.

Clicking the Black button displays the number 100 in the box following the tint bar, indicating that the area will be filled with 100 percent black ink. If you want to fill the selected objects with a shade of gray, enter the desired shade (as a percentage of black) into the box instead of the number 100. If you specify less than three percent black as a fill or stroke, it could fade away and disappear on press, or actually be printed at around five percent due to various press factors.

Click the Process Color button, and the process color percent boxes

Object

appear below the process color selection option. To specify colors for a four-color process (black, cyan, magenta, and yellow), click in the appropriate boxes and type in percentages between 0 and 100 that represent the amount of each of the four colors that you want the selected objects to be filled with. If your printer does not feature color printing capabilities, the program converts the specified color mix into an equivalent shade of gray while printing, and retains the specified colors.

The Custom Color selection scrolling list box will be empty if you do not have any custom colors available, or the Illustrator Startup document does not include any custom colors, and you have not already opened a document containing custom or PMS color assignments.

The Pattern selection scrolling list box will also be empty unless you have already defined custom patterns, or the Illustrator Startup document includes custom patterns. You can select PMS or custom colors, custom patterns, or gradient fills, rather than none, black, white, or process colors.

The second set of options in the Paint Style dialog box are Stroke options. The color selections are exactly the same as with the Fill options, except you cannot stroke objects with gradients. You can fill objects and type with gradient fills. (See also the gradient fill tool section of this chapter.)

The Stroke Weight option for strokes in the Paint Style dialog box specifies the line weight (thickness) that the selected paths will be stroked with. The Stroke Weight option is grayed-out when the stroke is set to none. To change the stroke of selected paths, click in the box after the words "Stroke Weight:" and enter a number that represents how many points of thickness (one point = 1/72 inch) you want the lines to be. Line weights can be less than 1 point, but very fine lines will appear thicker when printed on the LaserWriter than when printed on a high-resolution device such as the Linotronic 300. If you specify the finest line weight that a 2400 dpi priter can print, you will get a line 1 pixel wide that a printing press might not be able to reproduce. Line weights of objects are not scaled unless you specify a uniform scale and click the Scale line weight option and Objects box in the Scale dialog box.

The "Caps" choices affect the endpoints of open paths and dashed lines. The "Joins" choices affect the corners of paths that are stroked (it has no effect on nonstroked paths or points where paths intersect).

The default setting for caps is the butt cap (at the top). If you don't change it, the butt line cap uses squared-off ends perpendicular to the path. The middle choice, round cap, creates a half-moon cap in which the diameter equals the line width. The projecting cap (bottom) offers square ends that extend half of the line width beyond the end of the line.

Object

The default join is a miter join (at top), in which the edges of the intersecting strokes are extended until they meet in a point. The middle choice is the round join, which connects corners in a circular arc with a diameter equal to the line width. You would use both round caps and round joins because round joins do not fit well with squared-off butt caps. The bottom choice is the bevel join, which connects corners with triangular ends.

Miter joins can be modified by the "Miter limit:" ratio, which is active if you select the miter join choice. When two lines intersect at a sharp angle, a miter corner extends a spike that is controlled by the miter limit ratio. The higher the ratio, the sharper the corner. You can select a ratio between 1 and 500, with 4 corresponding to a pointed join of up to 4 times the line weight, and 1 corresponding to a bevel (squared-off) corner.

You can also specify a solid line or a dashed line pattern for the stroke. The solid pattern is usually checked (by default). If you want a dashed line, click the Dashed button, which activates six boxes for entering the length, in points, that you want the first dash to be. Then click in the next box and type the length, in points, that you want the first gap to be. Fill in the other four boxes if you want the dash and gap length pattern to vary. Whatever lengths are typed will be repeated and used for the dash pattern of the line. Remember that the type of line cap you select also affects the dash pattern, and that if you select round or projecting caps you should widen the gap width to accommodate caps that stick out an amount equal to half the current line weight setting.

Once you have set the paint attributes the way that you want, you can click the Apply button or Auto checkbox, and the specified attributes in the document are changed. To close the Paint Style palette, use the Command-I shortcut, use the close box to send the dialog box away, or select the Hide Paint Style command in the WIndow menu. To cancel any attribute changes that you have just specified, turn off the Auto option if it is on, use the Undo command in the Edit menu (Command-Z) to undo the Paint style change, and close the Paint Style dialog box to leave your document unchanged.

Custom Color

You can create custom mixes of process colors that can also be listed by name along with the PANTONE and other custom colors in the Custom color scroll box of the Paint Style dialog box. You can also rename a PMS

Object

color to have a more familiar name when assigning it to documents from the Paint Style dialog box.

First, create the custom color by selecting the Custom color selection option and clicking the New box in the Paint Style menu, or by double-clicking on an existing custom color in the Custom color scroll box. You can simply create a custom name for a PMS color, or mix process colors into custom colors that you can use by name.

You can also import custom colors from other documents using the Import Styles command in the File menu. The Custom Color dialog box (see Figures 3-32 through 3-34 in Chapter 3) also allows you to Select all unused custom colors in a document, and then you can delete them to reduce the size of the file. When you choose a custom color, you can use a tint percentage of that custom color, or use it in a gradient fill. (See the gradient fill tool section for more information on using custom colors in Gradient fills.) Create a custom name for a PMS color in this dialog box, or mix percentages of process colors or other custom colors to define new custom colors.

To make it easy to call up custom and PMS colors, create a Startup document that contains all of the regular custom and PMS colors that you use. As long as this document is open, you can assign those colors to objects in any other documents.

Pattern

Adobe Illustrator lets you fill and stroke paths with a custom pattern. You can even stroke and fill type with a custom pattern. A pattern can be transformed with the shape, transformed separately, or remain the same while the shape is transformed.

A pattern is available for a document if it has been defined in that document or in another document that is open at the same time. A custom pattern is always stored with the document in which it was defined and in any document that uses the pattern as a fill or stroke. You can see the list of custom patterns stored with the documents that are currently open by choosing the Paint Style dialog box and clicking the Pattern selection button for either the fill or stroke (Figure 5-108).

You can also see the pattern list by choosing the Pattern command from the Object menu (Figure 5-109). Any pattern in the list can be used in any open document. If you intend to use a lot of patterns, it helps to define them in one document which can be left open while opening other documents and applying patterns. When you are through applying

Object

patterns in a document, you can select all unused patterns and then delete them from that document to conserve file storage space.

To create a pattern, draw an element of the pattern in a document (see Figures 4-33 and 4-34 in Chapter 4), and paint the element as you would like it to appear in the pattern. Then clone the element several times and place the clones in appropriate places. Next, define the pattern tile with a rectangle. The pattern tile exposes the part of the pattern that will be repeated. The rectangle must have perpendicular corners (be sure that the corner radius is zero in the General Preferences dialog box). You can draw the rectangle with the rectangle tool or with the pen tool as long as the constrain angle set in the General Preferences dialog box is set to zero.

The pattern tile rectangle must be behind the other objects in the pattern. Whatever fill you apply to the rectangle becomes the pattern's

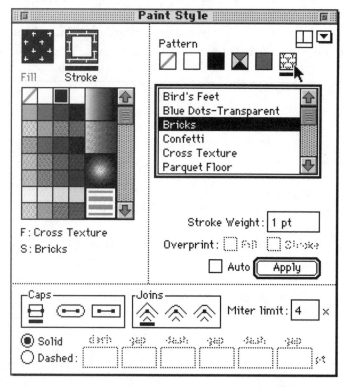

Figure 5-108.
The Paint Style dialog box lets you assign previously defined custom patterns to the fill and stroke of a path.

background — if you specify no fill, the background will have no fill. You should always specify no stroke for the pattern tile rectangle unless you want the pattern tile lines to be visible in the pattern.

A placed EPS image can't be used as a pattern element, nor can a masked group be used as a pattern element. Another pattern can't act as the fill for either the pattern tile rectangle or for the pattern elements because a pattern can't be defined as containing another pattern. You can create a pattern using another pattern by using the Paste button in the Pattern dialog box to paste the other pattern into the artwork for the new pattern. Any defined pattern can be pasted into another document and treated as regular artwork by using this Paste button.

With both the pattern tile and the elements selected, you can define the pattern by choosing Pattern from the Object menu, and click the New button. The name New Pattern 1 appears in the pattern list and in the change name field, and you can rename it by typing over this name. A preview of the pattern appears in the Pattern dialog box.

To assign a pattern to an object's fill or stroke, click the Pattern button in the Paint Style dialog box (in the fill or stroke area), and click on the

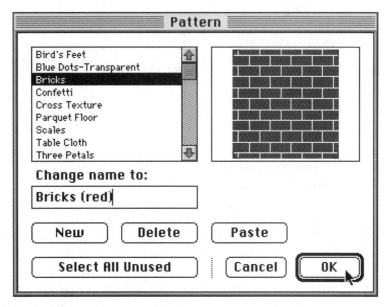

Figure 5-109.
The list of defined custom patterns also appears in the Patterns dialog box, where you can define new patterns, redefine or rename existing ones, select and delete unused ones to save file storage space, and more.

Object

name of a pattern. The pattern is displayed when you choose the Preview or Preview Selection options.

The pattern is like another layer that starts at the current ruler origin, which is usually at the lower left corner of the artboard. You can change the ruler origin (the point where zero appears on both rulers) by moving the ruler intersection square to the new position (see the Show Rulers command in the View menu (Command-R)).

You can transform an object painted with a pattern fill and the pattern can either be transformed in the same fashion, or left alone. A pattern can also be transformed without transforming the object. The rotate, scale, reflect, shear, and blend tools and Move dialog box can be used to transform or move a selected object or selected text element's pattern fill or stroke, including transforming or moving the selected objects or not. (To invoke the Move dialog box, select the Move command from the Arrange menu (Command-Shift-M), or hold down the Option key and click the current Selection tool in the toolbox.)

When transforming (including moving and cloning with the Option key) an object with a pattern, if you drag to move or transform (and you haven't checked the Transform pattern tiles box in the General Preferences dialog box, or in the transformation tool's dialog box), the pattern is not moved or transformed with the object. If, however, you previously checked this option in the General Preferences dialog box or in the transformation tool's dialog boxes, the pattern tiles are moved or transformed with the object when you drag to move or transform. (Whenever you turn this option on or off in the General Preferences dialog box, it automatically updates the transformation tools' dialog boxes, to your latest choice.)

When you transform a pattern, the operation doesn't change the definition of the pattern, nor does it change the pattern as it is used in other parts of the document or other documents.

You can blend two objects that have the same pattern, but not objects with different patterns unless one of the patterns is defined with artwork that is a transformation of the other pattern.

Use patterns to stroke only very simple paths, or you may not be able to print the pattern stroked paths. Patterns slow down printing and displaying patterns slows down performance. Do not use patterns to paint compound paths, and do not use very many different patterns extensively in your artwork file, unless you are prepared to wait for very slow printing, or have the document not print.

Object ▶. Gradient

The Gradient command in the Object menu is used to create gradient fills that you apply to selected objects using the Paint Style palette. Type must be converted (with the Create Outlines command in the Type menu) to an object before a gradient fill can be applied.

Select the object to fill and then select Gradient from the Object menu, or select Show Gradient from the Window menu, or double-click a gradient name in the Paint Style palette, to display the Gradient palette, where you can create, duplicate, delete, and edit gradients.

Gradient fills supplied with Adobe Illustrator, or ones you save for use as startup documents, can also be imported into an open artwork document using the Import Styles command in the File menu, just as you would import documents containing Patterns and Custom colors.

After specifiying or creating a gradient fill and assigning the gradient to an object, you can use the gradient tool to modify the fill. For example, after filling several objects with gradient fills, you can apply the fill across all the objects, specifying where the fill begins and ends using the gradient fill tool. See the gradient fill tool section of this chapter for more information.

To copy a color from one end of a gradient fill to another point along the fill, hold down the Option key and drag the starting or ending triangle (located below the gradient bar) to its new location (See Figure 5-87). Use this technique to create repeating patterns for gradients.

You can create a fill of two or more colors, and adjust the start, end, and midpoint of each color, and see the results in the Gradient bar, all before applying the new fill to an object.

You can even copy a color used in the artwork to a gradient fill, by clicking at the desired point to create a new triangle (or clicking an existing triangle) below the gradient bar, and then selecting the eyedropper tool and holding down the Control key while clicking the color in the artwork.

To avoid printing problems with gradients you plan to color separate, do not use more than one custom color in the gradient fill. If you do use more than one custom color, use Adobe Separator to assign different screen angles to each color to avoid moirés, or convert the custom colors to process colors.

If your document is extremely complex to print, and you are using gradients, patterns and/or blends extensively, you may experience

Object

printing problems with gradients. To avoid banding and shade-stepping in gradients, try reducing the length of the object using a gradient fill to less than 7.5 inches, use lighter colors or reduce the number of steps of color, or increase the percentage of change in color to 50 percent or more. See the gradient tool section for more information on gradients.

Attributes

The Attributes command (Command-Control-A) is used to invoke the Attributes dialog box, which contains the Note: box that allows you to enter a text comment (of up to 240 characters) that is inserted into the PostScript text file when the program saves the artwork. The Note option is handy for tagging an object, so that you can find it in the PostScript file. The note appears as a comment with the "%AI__Note" prefix in the PostScript file. For further information about PostScript, see Chapter 6.

Use the Attributes command to show or hide the centerpoints of selected objects, and to reverse path direction for paths within compound paths (see compound path discussion later in this chapter).

The Attributes dialog box also lets you specify a change to the output resolution used to print your file. Changing the Output Resolution setting determines the Flatness setting. Flatness refers to how smoothly curves will be drawn (how many straight line segments to use to define a curve), and it affects the printed artwork. The flatness value is measured in terms of pixels in the output device and corresponds to the distance of any point on the printed curve from any point on the theoretically ideal curve. The value used will always be at least one; smaller values are rounded up to one automatically, to increase the chances that the file will print, because lengthening the segments by reducing the output resolution decreases memory requirements. You can set the value to be higher than the minimum value of one. Printing and previewing will be faster, but the curves in the artwork will not be as smooth. Increasing the flatness value also helps when printing or previewing long paths which can be slow to draw.

If you get the PostScript limitcheck error when you try to print the file, select all or portions of the art, use Command-Control-A (or select the Attributes command from the Object menu) to display the Attributes dialog box, and decrease the output resolution. Continue decreasing resolution to increase the flatness until the file prints without error.

Object . **Join**

The Join command is used to connect two open endpoints in order to close a open path or to connect the endpoints of two open paths. The Join command either connects two endpoints that are apart from each other with a straight line or it combines two endpoints that are directly on top of one another into a single anchor point.

You can select Join from the Arrange menu or press Command-J as a shortcut. Two endpoints must already be selected. To select two endpoints that are on top of each other, drag the selection marquee over the points. The two endpoints can't belong to a grouped object; you must ungroup the object with the Ungroup command before joining the two endpoints.

When you select two endpoints on top of each other, the Join command displays a dialog box to let you specify the point to be a corner point or a smooth point. The program replaces the points with a single anchor point.

If you are having trouble selecting only two endpoints, try switching to another selection tool, or turning off the Snap to Point option in the General Preferences dialog box (Command-K), or check that they are endpoints of open paths.

The Join command draws a straight line segment between two endpoints that are apart from one another, leaving both the line and the two endpoints selected. If you selected the two endpoints of an open path when you selected the Join command, the path will be closed with a straight line. If you selected the endpoints of two different paths when you selected the Join command, the two paths will be connected (either with a straight line or by combining the two points) and will become one longer path. Joining points that are on top of each other is handy for connecting objects that were cut apart with the scissors tool.

To join and average two paths at the same time, select the paths, and press Command-Option-J. The two endpoints will be joined at the midpoint of their original positions.

Average

The Average command moves two or more anchor points to the average location of the points, and you can specify along one or both of the x and

Object

y axes. You can choose the Average command by either selecting Average in the Arrange menu or by pressing Command-L as a shortcut. You can only choose the Average command if there are two or more anchor points selected.

If you have chosen the Average command with two or more anchor points selected, a dialog box appears (Figure 5-110) for choosing which axis, or both axes, should be used to constrain the averaging.

By averaging with both axes, the selected anchor points move to the location midway along both axes. The paths and shapes connected to the points change shape, as they always do when any of their anchor points are moved.

The Average command only moves anchor points on top of each other; it does not connect them, merge them, or join them. If you want to connect anchor points, you have to use the Join command described above to connect them (two anchor points can be connected at a time). Averaging anchor points is used mainly for moving points, paths, or other objects next to each other.

To join and average two paths at the same time, select the paths, and press Command-Option-J. The two endpoints will be joined at the midpoint of their original positions.

Making Guides, Releasing Guides and Locking Guides

Guides are helpful for aligning graphics and text objects. Guides do not appear in Preview mode or in print, but show up as dotted lines in the Artwork view. The movement of objects can be constrained to a guide

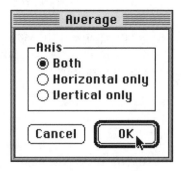

Figure 5-110.
The Average dialog box lets you specify which axis or both axes for performing the average operation. Two anchor points are selected for averaging.

Object

if the Snap to point option in the General Preferences dialog box is turned on. Objects snap to any part of the guide object, not just to an anchor point (as with any other object).

Guide objects are path objects created temporarily from any object by selecting the object and then using the Make Guides command in the Object menu (Command-5).

Ruler guides can be created either by dragging a dotted line from the ruler onto the artboard (also hold down the Option key to switch the ruler guide's direction).

The object or ruler guide is displayed as a dotted line and can be used as a guide to place other objects.

You can then Lock the Guide object or objects by selecting Guides and Lock from the Object menu (Command-7). However, all guides in the document will be locked. To lock only a selected guide or guides, first select only the guide object(s) you wish to lock, and use the Lock command in the Arrange menu (Command-1).

To release a guide or guides locked with the Lock command, use the Unlock All command in the Arrange menu (Command-2). To release a guide or guides locked with the Guides and Lock commands in the Object menu, use the Guides and Lock command again in the Object menu to first remove the check mark next to the Lock command.

Release the unlocked guide or guides by selecting them and then selecting the Guides and Release commands in the Object menu, or use the Command-6 shortcut. When you release the guide object or objects, they are again made visible objects in the artwork document, and can be moved, transformed, deleted, and so on.

To hide guide objects temporarily so that they don't appear in the Artwork or Preview views, select the Hide Guides command in the View menu. You can then show them again by choosing the Show Guides command, which replaces the Hide Guides command in the View menu.

Make Masks and Release Masks

The Mask commands let you set an object as a masking object, so that it is filled with whatever artwork lies in front of it, or release a masking object. The masking object defines the boundaries and treats everything it touches (that is pasted in front of it) as part of a pattern for itself.

To create a masking object, select an ungrouped path (a single path is preferred to a compound path) that you want to use as a mask. Place it on top of the object(s) you want to mask. Select the mask and the

`Object`

objects you want to mask, and then choose Masks and Make from the Object menu. The mask is assigned new fill and stroke values (None).

If the mask and masked object(s) are on different layers, intermediate layers between the mask and masked object(s) become part of the masked artwork. Use the group-selection tool to examine what objects are part of the masked object(s). To modify the mask and masked objects, first use the selection tools to select them.

The Mask and Release commmands turn off a selected mask, but you must assign it new fill and stroke attributes to make it visible again, because the fill and stroke attributes are still both set to None.

Make Compound Paths and Release Compound Paths

Illustrator lets you draw two paths that intersect to form a "hole" in which the underlying layer shows through. Such paths are called *compound* paths.

You create compound paths by drawing two paths so that the intersection of the paths forms the hole (see Figure 4-18 in Chapter 4). Then select the two paths and choose Compound Paths and Make from the Object menu (Command-8).

In general, where compound paths overlap, a hole appears exposing the underlying compound path; where they don't overlap, the frontmost path is the only one that appears.

Compound paths act like grouped objects. If you want to select part of a compound path, use the direct-selection tool. Once you create a compound path, you can transform and change them as you can any group of objects. You can also combine two compound paths into a single compound path.

You can blend between components of a compound path, but you can't blend between one compound path and another compound path (you must first release the compound paths).

When you create a compound path, all the objects in the compound path take on the paint attributes of the backmost object. The other objects' paint attributes are updated when you convert the objects into a compound path.

You can convert a compound path into a regular path with the Compound Pahts and Release commands in the Object menu (Command-9), but the former paint attributes are not restored.

You can use the Reverse Path Direction option (select Attributes from the Object menu) to reverse selected paths, possibly changing whether or not the path is filled or transparent, depending on how Illustrator fills the paths.

Set and Release Cropmarks

Crop marks indicate the boundaries of the image area of a page. Crop marks print when you print from Illustrator or from Adobe Separator (when creating color separations or color prints). To set crop marks, first draw a rectangle to define the image area, then select the rectangle and use the Cropmarks and Make commands in the Object menu. Cropmarks replace the selected rectangle.

If you have set the page size to use the Single Full Page option in the General Preferences dialog box, you can use the Make Cropmarks command without drawing a rectangle, (it uses the page boundaries with cropmarks automatically set around the page boundary).

Use the cropmarks filter to set additional cropmarks on the page to be used by a printer to divide up and trim the printed page.

Once you set the crop marks, you can't select them to delete them unless you first use the Release Cropmarks command to release them (turning them back into a rectangle). If you set new crop marks, the old ones are automatically replaced.

Graphs

The Graphs command is used to change graph attribute options, such as style, data, design, column and marker. See the Graph tool section for more information.

Font Menu

The Font menu enables you to easily set type fonts to use for selected text characters and selected text objects, including the type style (such as Regular, Oblique (italic), Bold and Bold Oblique). Use the shortcut Command-Shift-F to access the Character palette to change additional type attributes, or use the Type menu commands.

The fonts that are listed will depend on what fonts you have installed in your Macintosh System. See your Macintosh System 7 and font manuals for more information. Adobe Illustrator includes 40 Adobe Type 1 fonts you can install and use.

Type Menu

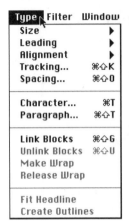

The Type menu is used for altering type characteristics, changing the font and spacing specifications, setting tracking or kerning amounts, linking and unlinking text elements, wrapping text around graphics, fitting headlines, and creating outlines (paths) with type created with the type tool. For a more detailed description of the type tools, see the section on the type tools earlier in this chapter.

Text entered into a document with any of the type tools can be styled in many different ways using the Type menu options. You can adjust leading (vertical spacing between lines of text), kerning (spacing between two characters), and tracking and spacing (adjusting the spacing between characters in a selection). Characters can be shifted vertically (baseline shift) and scaled horizontally, indents can be set, and paragraphs aligned to the left, right, centered, or justified, including an option to justify only the last line. Paragraphs can have left and right indents, and a first line indent specified. You can control letterspacing and word spacing, leading before each paragraph, hanging punctuation, and hyphenation (or choose auto hyphenation). In addition, by specifying fill and stroke attributes in the Paint Style dialog box, color or shades of gray can be applied to filled characters and you can specify the color and thickness of the stroke.

Type attributes can be set before typing text and changed after typing text, and you can set attributes for several blocks of type simultaneously (if they are all selected with one of the type tools).

Size

The Size command in the Type menu is used to quickly gain access to a variety of type sizes, to check the type size set at a selected point in a text block, or to select a desired size from the scrolling menu of sizes to resize a selected text block. A checkmark is displayed next to the current type size.

If the size is set to Other, select Other (or use Command-Shift-S) to display the Character palette showing the current size, which can be

Type

changed by typing a new size in the Size box.

Alternatively, you can select the Character command in the Type menu (Command-T) to display the Character palette.

To quickly increase the size of selected type, in increments set in the Size/leading text box (in the General Preferences dialog box (Command-K)), press Command-Shift-> (greater than sign), and decrease the selected type by the same increments by pressing Command-Shift-< (less than sign).

The smallest point size you can use is .1 point, and the largest is 1296 points.

Leading

Leading, which is the amount of space between the lines of type, is measured from baseline to baseline. The smallest amount of leading you can have is .1 point and the largest is 1296 points. A negative leading moves the baseline above the baseline of the line of type above. Auto leading sets the leading at 120% of the font size.

Use the Leading command in the Type menu to quickly gain access to a variety of leading sizes, to check the leading set at a selected point in a text block, or to select a desired leading from the scrolling menu of sizes to change the leading for a selected text block. A checkmark is displayed next to the current leading setting.

If the leading is set to Other, select Other to display the Character palette showing the current leading, which can be changed by typing a new leading amount in the Leading box.

Alternatively, you can select the Character command in the Type menu (Command-T) to display the Character palette.

To quickly increase the leading of selected type, in increments set in the Size/leading text box (in the General Preferences dialog box (Command-K)), press Option-Down Arrow, and decrease the selected leading by the same increments by pressing Option-Up Arrow.

Alignment

Alignment controls how lines of type are set in paragraphs. The choices are left, right, centered, or justified (and a justify last line option). Each paragraph (or line ending with Return) can have its own alignment setting.

Type

Left alignment aligns text along the left margin of a text column, with the right margin set to ragged. Right alignment aligns text along the right margin, with the left margin set to ragged. Justified aligns text to both left and right margins. Centered aligns text to the center of the text column, leaving both the left and right margins ragged. Only rectangle type and area type can be justified. Point type and type set along a path can't be justified. Another option, Justify Last Line, sets the last line of a justified paragraph to fill the column width.

To quickly change the alignment of a selected paragraph, use Command-Shift-L for left alignment, Command-Shift-R for right alignment, Command-Shift-C for center-alignment, or Command-Shift-J for justified alignment. To justify the selected last line of a paragraph of justified type, use Command-Shift-B.

Tracking/Kerning

Illustrator offers *tracking*, which is a method of inserting uniform spacing between more than two characters to space them further apart, and *kerning*, which adjusts the space between only two characters, on either side of an insertion point.

If you click an insertion point in the text, you will see the Kern command in the Type menu.

If you have selected a range of text, such as a paragraph or text block, you will see the Tracking command in the Type menu.

You can select the Tracking or Kerning commands from the Type menu, or as a shortcut, you can press Command-Shift-K, to display the Character palette. In the character palette, you can specify a negative number for tracking to move characters closer together, or a positive number move characters further apart. Tracking is measured in 1/1000 of an em space, which is relative to the current font size.

Kerning controls the spacing between two characters, and the kerning option lets you adjust this space between two characters, on either side of an insertion point. A positive value moves characters farther apart, and a negative value moves them closer together. Kerning values are measured in units of 1/1000 of an em space, which is relative to the current font size. The character spacing is built into a font by the font designer and can vary at different point sizes. Usually, 100 kerning units between two 10-point characters is equivalent to one point.

Fonts that contain information about kerning certain pairs of characters can be kerned automatically if the Auto-Kerning option is turned on in the Character palette. Auto-kerning can also increase the file size and slow down displaying and printing.

To quickly change the tracking of selected text, or to quickly change the kerning of characters on either side of an insertion point you click, press Option-Left Arrow, and the spacing is reduced, moving the characters closer together.

To quickly move characters apart by tracking selected text, or to increase space between two characters on either side of an insertion point you click, press Option-Right Arrow, and the spacing is increased, moving the characters further apart.

The increments used for tracking and kerning depend on the increments you set in the General Preferences dialog box. To adjust the Tracking/Kerning increments by 5 times the value set in the General Preferences dialog box, hold down the Command key as well as the Option key and Left Arrow when moving selected characters closer together, or hold down the Command key as well as the Option key and Right Arrow when moving selected characters further apart.

Use the Show Info command in the Window menu to display the Info palette to see the total kerning value for the two characters on either side of an insertion point you have clicked.

Spacing Options

Spacing is the measure of space between characters or words in justified or unjustified (aligned) text. You can select the Spacing command in the Type menu, or type Command-Shift-0 to display the Paragraph palette. Alternatively, you can select the Paragraph command in the Type menu (Command-Shift-T), or the Show Paragraph command in the Window menu to display the Paragraph palette.

The Word spacing and Letter spacing controls in the Paragraph palette let you apply new spacing settings for entire paragraphs you select before changing the word spacing and letterspacing settings. The minimum and maximum fields are available only for justified text. To change the spacing for only some of the text in a paragraph, use the Tracking controls.

Or, you can examine the spacing settings for a paragraph by first clicking an insertion point in the paragraph and then invoking the paragraph palette.

Change the word spacing (space between words) or letterspacing, which is the space between characters, for justified or unjustified type. Illustrator uses the values that are set for the minimum, maximum, and desired word spacing and letterspacing when justifying text. The values are measured as percentages of the width of a space. The default values for word spacing for justified text are 100 percent minimum, 100 percent desired and 200 percent maximum. Letterspacing defaults are 0 percent minimum, 0 percent desired and 5 percent maximum. The values must be between 0 and 1000 percent. Experiment to see which values look best for your typefont at a specific size, alignment style, etc.

Character

Type settings can be chosen directly from the Font menu and Type menu options, or you can set all characteristics in one of two dialog boxes by choosing the Character command (see Figure 4-27 in Chapter 4). The options for font, style, size, spacing, leading, tracking, kerning, and alignment are described with those Type menu options.

The Character command in the Type menu (Command-T) invokes the Character palette, where you can examine or select a font, style, size, leading (or use auto leading), kerning (or auto kerning) and a baseline shift and/or horizontal scale for a selection of text. You can also set the characteristics to use for new text here all at once, before typing the text. (See the text tools section for more information.)

The horizontal scale percentage specifies the proportion between the height and width of the type. Unscaled characters have a proportion of 100 percent. You can change this percentage to be higher than 100 percent to expand the characters, or lower to condense the characters. If you transform the characters non-uniformly, the horizontal scale amount is affected, and you can change the horizontal scale amount to 100 percent to return the characters to their original proportions.

The baseline shift feature controls the distance between the characters and the baseline and is used to raise or lower the selected type, to create superscripts and subscripts, or to move type above or below a path without changing its direction.

To apply the character attributes to a selected type element, press Tab or Return. On the other hand, if you want to cancel any attribute changes that you have specified, click the title button for that attribute to return to the default value, and leave your document unchanged.

Remember, if you have changed the x and y axes by setting the Constrain angle in the General Preferences dialog box (File menu) to a value other than zero degrees, the placement of text blocks will be relative to the x and y axes. If you are placing type and it looks a bit slanted or askew, check the alignment of the x and y axes by looking at the General Preferences dialog box. You can use this feature to type several text blocks in sequence at a certain angle.

Paragraph

Type and Paragraph settings can be chosen directly from the Type menu options, or you can set all characteristics in one of two dialog boxes by choosing the Paragraph command (see Figure 4-27 in Chapter 4). The options for font, style, size, spacing, leading, tracking, kerning, and alignment are described with those Type menu options.

The Paragraph command in the Type menu (Command-Shift-T) invokes the Paragraph palette, where you can change the alignment for a selection of text. You can also set left, right, and first line indents, leading before paragraphs, hyphenation options, and word and letterspacing values. You can set these characteristics to use for new text here, before you type the text. (See the text tools section for more information.)

Indentation controls the amount of space between the text element (or path that contains the text) and the edge of the characters in each line of the text. Indents are measured in ruler units (as set in the General Preferences dialog box). You can indent from the left or right side of the text element or path, with an additional indent for the first line of each paragraph. A negative indent moves the type outside the margin of the text element or path. Indents can be specified only for area type and rectangle type.

The hanging punctuation option controls whether punctuation marks such as periods, commas, quotation marks, apostrophes, hyhens, colons, semicolons, em dashes, and en dashes fall inside or outside the margins.

The leading before a paragraph option sets the amount of space between the first line of a paragraph and the preceding paragraph. Each paragraph is defined with an ending Return (carriage return character).

You can select the auto hyphenate option, or you can specify hyphenation controls to use, for a number of letters after the beginning of a word, and for the number of letters before the end of a word, including a setting to limit the number of consecutive hyphens to the value you specify.

To apply the paragraph attributes to a selected type element, press Tab or Return. On the other hand, if you want to cancel any attribute changes that you have specified, click the title button for that attribute to return to the default value, and leave your document unchanged.

Link Blocks and Unlink Blocks

You can link text objects created with the area-type tool or the type tool, whether or not they are the same shape or size, by selecting the objects with the selection tool and choosing Link Blocks from the Type menu (Command-Shift-G). A single text element, either imported or typed in manually, can then fill several columns or irregularly-shaped objects.

Text flows from one object to another based on the stacking order of the objects. The most recently created object is the frontmost object, and text flows from the object created first to the object created last.

After linking objects, you can select any object with the group-selection tool. You can change the stacking order by selecting one or more objects and using the Send to Back and Bring to Front commands in the Arrange menu.

To unlink selected linked text blocks, use the Unlink Blocks command in the Type menu, or use the Command-Shift-U shortcut. After unlinking objects, you must cut and paste the type to remove it from the text block. To delete a text object without also deleting the type it contains, first create a new path, link it with the text object, and then delete the old path.

Transforming or editing selections of text does not affect the linking of the text objects.

See the type tools section for more information.

Make Wrap and Release Wrap

Text within an area can be made to wrap around an irregularly shaped object within the area. The object within the area must be in front of the object containing the text (use the Bring to Front command in the Arrange menu).

To wrap text around an object, select the text object and the graphic object using the selection tool, and choose Make Wrap from the Type menu. The Release Wrap command separates the text object from the graphic object. You can create an unfilled, unstroked object to use for a precise text wrap to fit a particular shape, then place another graphic object in front.

`Filter` Fit Headlines

The Fit Headline command lets you fit type across the full width of a text path in an text area or text rectangle. This command was designed to work with Adobe Multiple Master fonts, adjusting the font weight and tracking when spreading type. With other fonts, the Fit Headline command adjusts only the tracking to spread the type across the full width of the text object.

Note that if you subsequently adjust the tracking for the type, you may need to use the Fit Headline command again to spread the type again.

Create Outlines

The outlines of individual characters of text can be edited like regular curves and lines, after using the Create Outlines command in the Type menu to converts a text element into a set of paths which you can then manipulate with the selection tools. The Create Outlines command converts every character in a text block into an outline, so to convert a single character, either create it alone in its text block, or create it alone as point type.

Outlines of characters can be modified to create logos, display type, or a variety of special effects. You can also use letters as masks, just like any other compound path. You must convert an entire text element to outlines; you can't convert just one character unless you type or Paste that character as a separate text element. You can also fill outline type with a pattern or blend. See those sections, and the type tool section, for more information.

Filter Menu

The Filter menu contains the list of currently available plug-in filters you can use in your currently open artwork documents.

Using plug-in filters saves you time and allows you to achieve professional results more easily, and include special effects in your artwork.

Filters are supplied with Illustrator, and additional plug-in filters can be obtained from Adobe or third parties, including user groups and commercial sources. If you want to create filters for Adobe Illustrator, and provide them to others, contact Adobe's Technical Support Department.

Window

Filter folders are installed into documents using the Preferences and Plug-ins commands in the File menu.

You can add additional filters to folders by dragging the filter files into the Plug-Ins folder within the Adobe Illustrator 5 application folder.

To remove filters, drag them out of the Plug-Ins folder. When you add or remove filters you must restart Illustrator to have the filters appear in the Filter menu.

Several categories of plug-in filters ship with Adobe Illustrator, including Colors, Create, Distort, Objects, Pathfinder, Select, Stylize and Text. Each category contains several plug-in filters. The category names appear in the Filter menu, and submenus show all available filters in each category.

Colors filters include Adjust Colors, Blend Front to Back, Blend Horizontally, Blend Vertically, Desaturate, Desaturate More, Invert Colors, Saturate and Saturate More.

Create filters include Fill & Stroke for Mask, Mosaic, Polygon, Spiral, Star, and Trim Marks. These filters create objects and special effects.

Distort filters include Free Distort, Roughen, Scribble, Tweak and Twirl. These filters change an object to create special effects.

Objects filters include Add Anchor Points, Align Objects, Distribute Horizontally, Distribute Vertically, Get Info, Move Each, Rotate Each and Scale Each. These filters can adjust the position, shape or size of objects.

PathFinder filters include Unite, Intersect, Exclude, Back Minus Front, Front Minus Back, Divide Fill, Divide Stroke, Crop Fill, Crop Stroke, Merge Fill, Merge Stroke, Mix Hard, and Mix Soft. These filters create compound paths by combining, isolating, and subdividing paths, and create new paths formed at the intersection of objects. You can't load Pathfinder filters if your computer doesn't have a math coprocessor installed.

Select filters include Same Fill Color, Same Paint Style, Same Stroke Color, Same Stroke Weight, Select Inverse, Select Masks, and Select Stray Points. These filters improve selection choices for ungrouped objects with matching attributes, and select stray single points.

Stylize filters include Add Arrowheads, Bloat, Calligraphy, Drop Shadow, Punk, and Round Corners. Use these filters to add special effects and elements to objects.

Text Filters include Export (selected text) and Find (with replace option).

For convenience, the last used filter is always displayed at the top of the Filter menu, or you can select it using the Command-Shift-E shortcut. If you have not yet used a filter, then this option is grayed out.

Window ⧏ *Window Menu*

Window ⧏
New Window

Hide Toolbox ⌘⌃T
Show Layers ⌘⌃L
Hide Info   ⌘⌃I
Show Paint Style
Show Gradient
Show Character
Show Paragraph

✓Untitled art 1 <50%>

The Window menu contains options for showing or hiding the Adobe Illustrator toolbox palette, showing or hiding the Layers palette, Info palette, Paint Style palette, Gradient palette, Character and Paragraph palettes, creating multiple views of a document (New Window command), and switching the active window to other documents.

You can have several documents open at once with Adobe Illustrator. The Window menu can grow with the names of many documents as you open documents without closing others.

New Window

The New Window command creates a new window that displays another view of the Adobe Illustrator document. The command creates a new active window that is identical to the window that was active when the command was chosen.

The new window and the old window are automatically numbered by the program and the numbers are placed after the document and template document names. Any other new views of the same document that are created are consecutively numbered in the order in which they were opened. If you close one of the views of a document, the remaining view windows of that document will be automatically renumbered, removing the closed window from the sequence. Select the Window by name from the end of the Window menu.

The new window can be manipulated independently of the active window. Any changes made to the document from the active window affect the document and are subsequently displayed in all views of that document.

Creating new views of a document can be helpful for such purposes as viewing a preview and a regular view of the artwork, for viewing different areas of the artwork, or for viewing the artwork at different magnifications simultaneously. You can switch the active window to any window by selecting its name from the end of the Window menu.

Creating new views is especially useful when you are using a large display. Using multiple windows with different views can slow down the system if you have limited memory.

Window ## Hide and Show Toolbox

The Hide Toolbox command (Command-Shift-T) removes the toolbox from view. Hiding the toolbox lets you see more of the artwork on the screen at one time. You can choose the Hide Toolbox command by selecting Hide Toolbox in the Window menu, or clicking in the small close box that is located at the top of the toolbox.

When the toolbox is hidden you can still use the tool that was selected when you hid the toolbox. You can also use the selection tool by holding down the Command key; the hand tool by holding down the space bar; and the zoom tool by either holding down the space bar and Command key to zoom in or by holding down the space bar, Command key, and Option key to zoom out. If you want to use any of the other tools, you must first bring the toolbox back onto the screen by issuing the Show Toolbox command.

The Show Toolbox command (Command-Shift-T) displays the toolbox after it has been removed from view by Hide Toolbox. If you have more than one screen available, you can drag the toolbox onto another screen, so that it does not obscure the artwork.

You can choose the Show Toolbox command by selecting Show Toolbox in the Window menu (it occupies the same menu slot as Hide Toolbox). When the toolbox is displayed, it can't be moved behind another window; if you try to place another window on top of the toolbox, the toolbox will force itself on top of the window. However, you can place other palettes on top of the toolbox.

You can reset an individual set of tools to its original, default set of tools by holding down the Shift key and clicking inside the slot for that set of tools.

Hide and Show Layers

The Show Layers command in the Window menu (Command-Shift-L) displays the Layers palette. You can choose the Show Layers command by selecting Show Layers in the Window menu (it occupies the same menu slot as Hide Layers).

The Hide Layers command (Command-Shift-L) removes the Layers palette from view, or you can simply click the close box at the top left of the Layers palette.

Hiding the Layers palette lets you see more of the artwork on the screen at one time. If you have more than one screen, you can simply drag the Layers palette onto another screen.

The Layers palette contains the Layers commands that allow you to create new layers, delete layers, view and change layer options separately for each layer, and select options such as Hide Others, Artwork Others and Lock Others, and Paste Remembers Layers, and turn these options on or off. See Figure 1-11 for more information on Layering options.

Hide and Show Info

The Show Info command in the Window menu (Command-Shift-I) displays the Info palette, which can be used to measure objects, or display type attributes, such as measuring the kerning value set between two characters. You can choose the Show Info command by selecting Show Info in the Window menu (it occupies the same menu slot as Hide Info).

The Hide Info command (Command-Shift-I) removes the Info palette from view, or you can simply click the close box at the top left of the Info palette.

Hiding the Info palette lets you see more of the artwork on the screen at one time. If you have more than one screen, you can simply drag the Info palette onto another screen.

Hide and Show Paint Style

The Show Paint Style command displays the Paint Style palette, as discussed in the Object menu section of this chapter. You can choose the Show Paint Style command by selecting Show Paint Style in the Window menu (it occupies the same menu slot as Hide Paint Style).

The Hide Paint Style command removes the Paint Style palette from view, or you can click the close box at the top left of the Paint Style palette.

Hiding the Paint Style palette lets you see more of the artwork on the screen at one time. If you have more than one screen, you can simply drag the Paint Style palette onto another screen.

Hide and Show Gradient

The Show Gradient command displays the Gradient palette, as discussed in the Gradient command and Object menu section of this chapter. You can choose the Show Gradient command by selecting Show Gradient in the Window menu (it occupies the same menu slot as Hide Gradient). The Hide Gradient command removes the Gradient palette from view, or you can simply click the close box at the top left of the Gradient palette.

Hiding the Gradient palette lets you see more of the artwork on the screen at one time. If you have more than one screen, you can simply drag the Gradient palette onto another screen.

Hide and Show Character

The Show Character command displays the Character palette, as discussed in the Character command and Type menu section of this chapter. You can choose the Show Character command by selecting Show Character in the Window menu (it occupies the same menu slot as Hide Character).

The Hide Character command removes the Character palette from view, or you can simply click the close box at the top left of the Character palette.

Hiding the Character palette lets you see more of the artwork on the screen at one time. If you have more than one screen, you can simply drag the Character palette onto another screen.

Hide and Show Paragraph

The Show Paragraph command displays the Paragraph palette, as discussed in the Paragraph command and Type menu section of this chapter. You can choose the Show Paragraph command by selecting Show Paragraph in the Window menu (it occupies the same menu slot as Hide Paragraph).

The Hide Paragraph command removes the Paragraph palette from view, or you can simply click the close box at the top left of the Paragraph palette.

Hiding the Paragraph palette lets you see more of the artwork on the screen at one time. If you have more than one screen, you can simply drag the Paragraph palette onto another screen.

Adobe Separator

Adobe Separator™ 5.0

Adobe Illustrator files can be separated by the Adobe Separator program, supplied with Adobe Illustrator. The program can produce four-color and custom separations, and provides choices for various options including the page size, orientation, type of emulsion, positive or negative, and the halftone screen ruling in lines per inch. Adobe Systems provides PostScript Printer Description (PPD) files for various printers and imagesetters, so that separations are produced with the best possible control settings. The PPD folder is located in the Adobe Separator folder, along with other utilities, such as a Densitometer Control Chart, a Riders folder, a Third Party Utilities folder including a RidersMaker filter, and filters such as Artwork View Speedup.

When you start Adobe Separator, a dialog box asks for the name of an Encapsulated PostScript file (see Figures 4-19 and 4-20 in Chapter 4). Illustrations saved by Adobe Illustrator are PostScript files, and you can also select PostScript files from other applications.

Adobe Separator offers the capability to preview the Illustrator image, but this capability works only with Illustrator files that have been saved with a preview format. Use the Color Macintosh format for the best results with the Separator preview capability.

After choosing the PostScript file, the program asks for a PostScript Printer Description file. The PPD file contains specific device information for Adobe Separator including the resolution, available page sizes, color support, and acceptable screen rulings. You should always use the appropriate PPD file for the device you are using. See the Read ME-PPD files document shipped with Adobe Illustrator for help in obtaining new PPDs.

After clicking OK for the PPD file, Adobe Separator displays a preview image and various output settings and choices, including the name of the output device corresponding to the chosen PPD file. You can switch PPD and PostScript files for convenience in producing multiple separations. The program displays a dotted line representing the dimensions of the artwork's bounding box. The bounding box is defined in PostScript units (points) and represents the outside dimensions of an illustration (the smallest rectangle that could be dragged over all printing pieces of the artwork). You can adjust this bounding box by dragging on the dotted line from any edge or corner, or by specifying new dimensions in the Separator setup box. Trim marks, color bars, and registration symbols are printed by Adobe Separator just outside the bounding box.

Page sizes are listed by name and by dimensions, which define the printable area for the separation (including space for trim marks). The page orientation can be set to Portrait or Landscape. The emulsion type depends on your printer's requirements; film separations are usually set to have emulsion side down. You can also choose to print a positive or negative image (usually set to negative for film separations). The halftone screen ruling defines the number of halftone dots per inch, referred to as lines per inch (lpi). You can specify a bleed (between 0 points and 72 points) to apply to the artwork, and you can set a transfer adjustment that allows you to adjust output to compensate for discrepancies between the tint values you specified in the artwork file, and the values your imagesetter can print. If the imagesetter is calibrated daily, and the chemicals are fresh, you do not need to set the transfer adjustment.

Adobe Separator lets you print all of the process color separations in one operation, or separately, or as a color comp to a color printer. The Print All Separations option in the File menu (Command-P) lets you print separations for all four process colors and one for each custom color. Alternatively, custom colors and PMS colors can be converted into percentages of process colors automatically and included in the separations for the four process colors.

To convert a custom or PMS color to appropriate process color percentages, select the color's name in the list of custom and PANTONE colors, and the color's name will be dimmed, to indicate that it will automatically be converted from the custom or PMS color into process color percentages; to reverse the process (reverse previously converted custom or PMS colors), select the process colors, then click the custom color name, which is no longer dimmed.

Adobe Separator's Get Info command in the File menu compiles a list of information about the file which can be printed, such as typefaces, styles, pattern files used, and EPS files placed in the document.

6

PostScript and Adobe Illustrator

The PostScript language has emerged as the leading graphics language in use today due to the endorsement by many major computer companies including Apple and IBM. PostScript is the foundation on which Adobe built Adobe Illustrator. The program uses PostScript for such purposes as drawing images on the Macintosh video screen, communicating with printers and typesetting machines, and as a format for saving artwork documents. Knowing PostScript will allow advanced users to understand Adobe Illustrator documents and create special PostScript effects.

What is PostScript?

PostScript is a computer language that is used for describing the appearance of graphics and text on a page. Adobe Illustrator documents are PostScript programs saved as ordinary text files. PostScript is used to write programs for computers or printers, or to create special graphic effects.

PostScript describes text and graphics in a standard format that can be understood by other computers, printers, and other output devices. Printers (such as laser printers and typesetting machines) interpret PostScript page descriptions and create bit-mapped representations of the pages for printing. Video displays use PostScript to accurately interpret page descriptions, convert the result into a bit-mapped image, and display the image on the computer screen.

Since graphics and text together convey more information per page than text alone, there is a major trend in computer technology away from the text-only computer screens that have dominated computing since its inception and toward the heavy use of graphic information in both computer documents and operating systems (such as the Macintosh Finder, Microsoft Windows, and IBM's Presentation Manager). Data processing and information processing on desktop computers is rapidly becoming document processing, and the documents being processed are using much more graphics to help convey information. PostScript has emerged as the standard language for describing the text and graphics that are on the pages of computer documents.

PostScript allows pages to be described very concisely, which means that PostScript files take up less memory than many other types of page descriptions, including the typical bit-mapped descriptions. For example, a page on the Apple LaserWriter has a printable area of 8-by-10.9 inches for a total of 87.2 square inches; at the LaserWriter's resolution of 300 dots per linear inch (which equals 90,000 dots per square inch) an 87.2 square inch LaserWriter page would have 7,848,000 dots in it. To store this document as a bit-mapped document with no gray-scale (where one dot is represented by one bit of memory) would require 7,848,000 bits of memory, which is just shy of one megabyte. Considering that the standard Macintosh floppy disk only stores 800K, a full-page bit-mapped image would not fit on a floppy disk, and you'd be forced to use a hard disk. If you've ever used a scanner to digitize a page of graphics, you know that the image files are usually enormous (sometimes over two megabytes). However, a PostScript description of a page usually takes up much less memory.

Not only does PostScript offer a compact way to describe pages, but the PostScript description is also not tied to a particular device. In computer jargon this is referred to as *device-independence*. What device-independence means in practical terms is that PostScript files created on the Macintosh with Adobe Illustrator (or any other application that works with PostScript) can be used on certain computer systems from IBM and other vendors, and these PostScript files can be printed on many different PostScript printers and typesetting machines from a wide array of vendors such as Apple, IBM, DEC, Varityper, and Linotype. The advantages of PostScript, and its endorsement by both Apple and IBM, has led to its current status as the major industry standard among computer graphics languages.

PostScript was created with graphic arts in mind, and it uses a way of describing images that is modeled after graphic arts. In PostScript an image is created by putting certain types of computer-generated "ink" in specified areas. The ink can be in various forms such as lines, shapes, or spots of ink in a bit-mapped photograph. The computer-generated ink can be black, white, any shade of gray, or any shade of color. PostScript starts building a page by taking a white page and placing the ink in specified areas according to the PostScript description of the page. As ink is placed on the page, any new ink completely covers any ink it is placed on top of; in other words, every type of ink on the page is opaque and keeps its color, rather than being transparent and bleeding colors together.

Some of PostScript's capabilities include the ability to construct arbitrary shapes from straight lines and curves. Shapes may be convex, concave, contain disconnected sections and holes, and can even intersect with themselves. PostScript includes painting commands for further describing shapes; the paint commands allow PostScript to do such things as assign any thickness of line to outline a shape, fill the shape with any color, or use the shape as a clipping path to crop any other graphics or images.

PostScript features a general coordinate system that allows all types of graphics to be transformed mathematically in all the possible linear transformations such as scaling, rotating, reflecting, skewing, and translating. PostScript also has commands that allow it to be used to describe text alone, or text integrated with graphics. The language allows you to specify typefaces, type styles, and type sizes. It treats text as graphic shapes that can be manipulated and operated on by any of PostScript's graphics commands such as painting, scaling, rotating, reflecting, or slanting. PostScript also has commands for working with digitized images that are either scanned or created artificially with a computer. Digitized images of any resolution can be conveyed in PostScript and the language provides methods for assigning gray-scale and color values to the images.

The main commands used for placing images on a page are fill, stroke, image, and show. The fill command places a filled area on the page. When PostScript calculates how to fill a path, it uses the "Winding number rule." According to this system, the way in which Adobe Illustrator determines whether a particular location is inside the path (for the purpose of filling the area) is to draw an imaginary ray from that location that extends to infinity (beyond the edge of the document), and then examine each place that the path of the object being filled crosses that ray. Then, starting with a value of zero, a value of one is added to the total each time the path crosses the ray from the left, and a value of one is subtracted from the total each time the path crosses the ray from the right. After the program either adds or subtracts a unit for all the places that the path crosses the ray, it can determine whether or not to fill the area by examining the total. If right-hand intersections equaled left-hand intersections, then the total would be zero — a zero total indicates that the original location was outside the object because the ray extending from that location entered and exited the object (by crossing the path) the same number of times. If a value other than zero remained as a total, then Adobe Illustrator decides that the original location was inside the object and fills the area with the specified type of ink.

The stroke command draws lines on the page, the image command is used for placing a gray-scale halftone digitized image on the page, and the show command places characters on the page. Just as Adobe Illustrator uses paths to create artwork, PostScript uses the concept of the "current path" as a way to draw things on the page. Commands used to describe how the path should be drawn include newpath, moveto, lineto, curveto, arc, and closepath. In addition to the current path, PostScript also features a "current clipping path" that represents an outline of the area on the page that will be

displayed or printed. Usually the clipping path is the entire printable area on a page. Anything that is drawn outside that area is cut off and discarded. However, by using the PostScript clip command, you can shrink the size of the area that will be displayed or printed down to any desired size or shape. Clipping the artwork can be useful for placing it in a particular layout, or for creating special graphics effects.

In order to draw pages the same way on different types of devices, PostScript uses two different types of coordinate systems, device space and user space, for locating items on a page.

Device space is the area that can be displayed or printed on a particular output device. On the Apple LaserWriter Plus, for example, the device space is an 8-by-10.9-inch area with 300 dots per linear inch for a total of about 7,848,000 dots. The characteristics of the device space such as image resolution and the shape of the dots used to create images are idiosyncratic to the particular device. PostScript's device space provides an x-axis and y-axis coordinate system that allows any dot to be located. The device space is only a consideration for the PostScript interpreter program in a printer; PostScript programs only need to concern themselves with the user space.

The user space provides a standard ideal coordinate system that is always the same for every page, regardless of the characteristics and idiosyncrasies of the output device (printer, typesetting machine, video display, etc.). The PostScript interpreter in the printer automatically converts the items in the user space into points to be printed or displayed in the device space. PostScript starts each user space out as a default user space and sets the point of origin in the lower left-hand corner of the output page, and the length of a unit of space along either the x-axis or y-axis to a default value of 1/72nd of an inch (approximately 1 point). A PostScript program can then modify the user space by using the coordinate transformation commands: translate, rotate, and scale. Translate lets you change the point of origin, rotate lets you turn the axes relative to the point of origin, and scale lets you change the length of a unit of space.

PostScript programs are usually created by other programs such as Adobe Illustrator. However, it is possible to use PostScript to create special graphic effects that are not feasible to draw with Adobe Illustrator program alone, such as wrapping text or graphics around models of solid objects.

PostScript and Output Devices

A PostScript page description can be rendered on a wide variety of output devices such as printers, typesetting machines, and video monitors. The PostScript page description is interpreted by a special controller known as a raster image processor (RIP) that is connected to the output device. The RIP converts the compact PostScript page description into a very large number of dots that are then printed on a specific printer or displayed on a particular video monitor.

Although the primary use of PostScript is to describe pages for printing, it should be noted that Adobe Illustrator uses PostScript for drawing your artwork on the Macintosh screen. This is an example of how PostScript is used for displaying images on video monitors. Adobe System's implementation of this technology indicates that PostScript may start gaining ground as a video screen description language as well as a printed page description language. The advantage to desktop publishing of using PostScript as a screen description language as well as a printer language is that what you see on the screen will probably more closely correspond to what is printed on the page. This discrepancy can be especially bothersome when working with certain graphics and page-layout programs. The discrepancy is caused by the fact that most Macintosh applications use a graphics description language called Quick-Draw to control the video display; when a document is printed on a PostScript printer, the Macintosh's native QuickDraw is translated into PostScript as part of the printing process. Inherent differences between QuickDraw and PostScript cause a certain amount of precision to be lost in the translation.

In order to solve the problem of the discrepancies between QuickDraw and PostScript, Adobe Illustrator uses PostScript to draw artwork on the screen, uses PostScript as the format in which it saves the artwork, and sends a PostScript file directly to the printer. The advantage of this method is that less precision is lost between the way that the image is displayed on the screen and described to the printer. Also, since the artwork file is saved in the PostScript format, no translation is needed between QuickDraw and PostScript, which improves the speed and performance of the printing process.

Since Adobe Illustrator files are saved as pure PostScript text files, you can use the standard PostScript language to understand and modify the Illustrator files.

Adobe Illustrator files can also be printed on PostScript Level 2 devices. PostScript Level 2 is the first major new release of the PostScript interpreter software since PostScript was introduced more than five years ago. Level 2 consolidates extensions to the current version of the language (mostly in the realm of color printing) and adds new features including improved forms handling, a device-independent color model, a composite font format for fonts containing thousands of characters, and a host of performance improvements. Included in Level 2 are graphics and text operators that operate faster and are more convenient to use; data compression techniques including CCITT Group 3 and 4, run-length encoding, JPEG, ASCII/85, and ASCII/HEX; and Adobe Type Manager (ATM) font rendering technology to render fonts faster and with higher quality at small point sizes and low resolutions. A new forms feature lets you define a form to cache between pages so that only changes to each form need to be interpreted for each page, to increase printing speed. New pattern operators describe an image for tiling, and patterns can be saved in a pattern cache. Adobe also improved memory management and eliminated arbitrary memory limitations, making it easier to render complex images.

Adobe had previously extended PostScript to accommodate the CMYK color model with black generation and undercolor removal functions, screen and transfer functions for separate color components, and a colorimage operator for rendering color sampled images. These extensions have been rolled into Level 2.

Besides these and other performance benefits, the major technological breakthrough with PostScript Level 2 is device-independent color. This feature promises to make it easier for users to create and exchange color documents with no variation in how those colors are printed or displayed, so that users can get true color fidelity with different devices. The need is to have a truly device independent color model that lets you transfer color documents across networks and to remote sites, to print the same colors on a variety of different printers, and to have true fidelity with what you see on the screen and what you print.

Learning PostScript: The Basics

If you plan on doing any special effects with Adobe Illustrator documents (other than what you can achieve with the Illustrator tools and menu items), you will need to know the PostScript programming language. In order to help you learn PostScript we have included a brief overview that will give you some basic PostScript skills. If you want to learn more about the PostScript language, you can either take a PostScript programming class (available at some colleges and universities), or you can read the *PostScript Language Tutorial and Cookbook* and the *PostScript Language Reference Manual*, both published by Addison-Wesley and available from Adobe Systems. The *PostScript Language Tutorial and Cookbook* provides an introduction and explanation to PostScript as well as some handy tips and techniques for improving your PostScript programming skills. The *PostScript Language Reference Manual* is a more technically oriented book, and the second edition covers PostScript Level 2.

This chapter presents some of the basic principles, structures, and commands you'll need to know in order to understand the way PostScript programs operate. It assumes that you are already familiar with some other programming language or that you are a fairly experienced computer user.

PostScript is a stack-oriented language, keeping its working values, definitions, and intermediary results in a set of ordered lists, known as *stacks*. The language is more like Forth than like BASIC or Pascal. In general, values and objects are either used immediately or pushed onto a stack. When the program needs data or encounters a command to retrieve a value, it pops a value back off the top of the stack again.

PostScript is also an extensible (or "threaded") language, meaning that you can define routines in terms of basic PostScript operations and then use these new terms as part of further definitions. When the LaserWriter, or other PostScript printer, interprets your PostScript program, it follows each new term back through your definitions until it reaches a description made up of primitive operations that it knows how to perform.

As a complement to the threaded-stack structure of the language, most PostScript operations are written in postfix notation — you first list the objects you want to use, and you then say what you want to do with them. For example, to add 3 and 4, you write:

```
3 4 add
```

rather than

```
3 + 4
```

In other words, you use a postfix form rather than the infix form you would use in BASIC or ordinary math. This procedure makes it possible for PostScript to evaluate objects according to a set of simple rules, although it does make the programs harder for beginners to read and write.

In general, PostScript works its way through a program as follows. As the computer reads each set of symbols, PostScript figures out where the breaks are between the words and assigns each group to a logical unit called a *token*. As soon as a token becomes available, PostScript looks to see what type of object it represents.

If the token is a number, PostScript saves it for later use by pushing it onto the operand stack. It does the same for definitions. Likewise for specially marked command routines intended for later use.

If, on the other hand, the token is a name, PostScript checks to see if it represents an executable routine or a primitive operation. If it does, the language executes the statement, pulling as many values off the stack as the operation requests and returning any results back onto the stack.

The basic scheme is first to define any new terms and push them onto the stack. Then you supply the values you want the program to work with. Finally, you give the commands that will retrieve the values, do the required arithmetic and logic, and print out the result. In practice, it's slightly more complicated, and you usually alternate between adding values to the stack and popping them back off.

PostScript actually has four distinct stacks: *operand, execution, dictionary,* and *graphic states.* A different class of operations affects each stack.

The operand stack is much like a piece of scratch paper or the running total on a calculator. If an operation needs input values, it pops the required number of values from the operand stack. Similarly, any results produced go back on the stack for later use. This holds true for both arithmetic operations and those that handle text.

The execution stack is where PostScript stores away your program. Normally, you don't explicitly work with this stack but let PostScript do the stack management as it works its way through your program.

The dictionary stack lets you create new definitions and save libraries of procedures. PostScript searches this stack for your definitions, then for built-in operations, and flags any terms that it can't find in either.

Finally, the graphics-state stack is a holding area for sets of parameters that define how the PostScript language interfaces to a specific printer or interprets the exact graphic commands in your program. PostScript can keep track of several sets of parameters, which makes it possible to temporarily alter graphics characteristics in order to draw certain objects and then return to the original mode.

A Simple PostScript Example

You have now read enough theory to start with some practical examples, beginning with the simplest useful PostScript routine:

```
copypage
```

This is a one-line program that tells a PostScript printer to produce a printout of the current page. Because you haven't declared anything to write on the page and the printer assumes a blank white page to begin with, this routine will simply eject an empty sheet of paper.

Suppose you want two blank pages. The routine then becomes:

```
2 {copypage} repeat
```

The PostScript interpreter, as it reads this line, first encounters the 2. Remember, PostScript pushes values it encounters in the input stream onto the operand stack until they are needed. So the 2 is pushed onto that stack.

Then the interpreter finds {copypage}. Curly brackets (braces) tell the interpreter that it should save the enclosed commands, rather than execute them. The program treats deferred commands as a special form of text input — as operands to be saved on the operand stack until they're called for. That's what happens to the {copypage} command.

Proceeding along, the PostScript interpreter then finds the repeat command. Repeat is a word that it understands as an executable command that takes two operands. Going back to the stack, repeat treats the object on the top of the stack as a sequence of commands to execute and the next object on the stack as the number of repetitions to be made.

The object on the top of the stack is copypage, which still prints out the current page. The next object is the repeat factor, which in this case is 2. The LaserWriter responds by printing two blank pages.

To add some text to the page you'll have to gather up some more PostScript tools. To print text, you'll need to use fonts, arrays, and a positioning command.

Before the PostScript interpreter can place text within a page image, it has to know what style and size you want to use. For this example, use Times Roman.

The first token in the statement is:

```
/Times-Roman
```

which is the name of the font, preceded by a slash. The slash tells the PostScript interpreter that Times-Roman is a name that it should put on the operand stack, rather than interpreting it. Otherwise, the interpreter would look at the name Times-Roman, decide that it wasn't a built-in command or a word already defined, and flag it as an error.

With Times-Roman on the stack, you can then issue a command to select it for use. Your line then becomes:

```
/Times-Roman findfont
```

The findfont command tells the interpreter to locate the dictionary of information about the font whose name is on top of the operand stack and push all the information about that font onto the operand stack.

Fonts are generally stored in a reference size, rather than in the actual size of letters. PostScript uses a one-point font as the reference ($1/72$-inch high), which it can do because it is able to smoothly scale fonts up in size without creating jagged lines.

The operator called scalefont takes the scale factor from the top of the operand stack and the font information from underneath it. You have set the font name, but you need the number. To put a number on the stack, you include it in a command as a separate token. Putting these elements together, the command is now:

```
/Times-Roman findfont 12 scalefont
```

Finally, with the font specified, you add one more command to make it the current font until further notice.

The first line now reads:

```
/Times-Roman findfont 12 scalefont setfont
```

Now that you have a font, the next step is to specify where on the page you want the typing to start. The most basic positioning command in

PostScript is moveto, which tells the LaserWriter which point on the page to use as the starting point for further graphics or text commands.

Naturally enough, since a page is two-dimensional, moveto takes two numeric values as its input. In stack-language form, the two values must already be on the stack when you execute the moveto command. The command line to start at halfway up the page, about an inch from the left margin, is:

```
72 396 moveto
```

(0,0 is at the bottom left of the page and there are 72 units to an inch).

In PostScript, the operator to place text on the page image is show, which takes a string for input, places the characters on the image, and advances the current location point as it goes. The string input, as you've probably guessed, must first be placed on the operand stack.

Strings in PostScript are made up of sequences of characters. You can create these sequences with operators, or as literal elements. First you'll learn to create arrays with literals. You set strings off by enclosing them with parentheses. Therefore your text string is:

```
(this page intentionally not left blank)
```

The command to place the text on the page is:

```
(this page intentionally not left blank) show
```

That gets the print on the image, which, as you already know, is put on the paper with showpage.

You now have a complete Postscript program. To print your single line on the page, you run the program:

```
/Times-Roman findfont 12 scalefont setfont
72 396 moveto
(this page intentionally not left blank) show
showpage
```

You can now understand that PostScript is a stack-oriented language, and you have worked a little bit with the stacks. You have written a short program and seen the very basics of how to get an image on a page. On the way, you've encountered commands, deferred commands, arithmetic, strings, arrays, and graphics. And you've gotten the printer to actually print a page.

Next, a closer look at the PostScript graphics commands and what you can do with them. Then, back to text in more detail.

PostScript Graphics Commands

Using a collection of saved values called "the current graphics state" for the defaults, PostScript creates on a page an image that depends on your commands. Those graphics commands, like all other PostScript commands, are written in postfix form, with the operators following the values they work on.

In the examples that follow, lines that start with the percent sign are program comments. In these examples the comments usually appear first, followed by the command lines to which the comments refer.

The first operation in most PostScript graphics routines is to save the current graphics state. This operation allows us to change the state as you please without worrying about losing the standard values other routines might need. When you're done, you restore the original graphics state. The first and last operational lines of the program, then, are usually:

```
%save the graphics state
gsave
```

```
%restore the saved state
grestore
```

Further on, you'll change some of the graphics-state values, but right now you should consider the blank page you have to work with. The PostScript page is a two-dimensional space with the origin (0,0) point at the bottom left, and a default scale of 72 units to the inch. If you want to switch the drawing point to two inches over and four up, for example, you write:

```
144 288 moveto
```

On the LaserWriter, the page is assumed all white unless you place a mark upon it.

The most common way to make graphic designs on a PostScript page is to create a "path" of connected lines or curves, which you can then make visible, fill, replicate, or used as a template for filling with colors and shades of gray. This is, in fact, exactly what Adobe Illustrator does when it creates a piece of artwork. To create a simple drawing of a house, for example, you might in turn create paths representing the walls, doors, windows, and roof. Tell the PostScript interpreter you want to start a path with the newpath command. Your sequence thus far becomes:

```
gsave
144 288 moveto
newpath
grestore
```

If you were to add a showpage command at this point, you'd still get a blank page. Moving to a position or defining a path doesn't actually draw the image. To actually draw the image, you create a path and either use the stroke command (to follow the outline of the path, much like inking in a drawing with a pen) or the fill command (to color in any area completely enclosed by the current path). You may recognize that the concept of either stroking or filling paths is identical to Adobe Illustrator. You now have all the elements to draw a small bar across the paper.

```
%save the state
%move to the initial position
gsave
144 288 moveto

%set up a path,
%draw a line,
%ink it in,
%output the page

newpath
288 288 lineto
stroke
showpage
grestore
```

Now, expand the program to draw a simple box and color it black. Tell it exactly where to move for the first point on the box, specify relative movements for three of the sides, and tell the interpreter to close up the path to make the fourth side. When you have completed the outline, tell the interpreter to fill in the square.

```
%set initial position
gsave
288 288 moveto

%set up a path,
%move up, over, down
%complete path,
%fill it in
newpath
0 144 rlineto
144 0 rlineto
0 -144 rlineto
closepath
fill

%print out
showpage
grestore
```

Notice that you didn't say explicitly what to fill the box with. PostScript specifies that the fill operator gets the fill color or pattern from the current graphics state, and on the LaserWriter the initial default fill pattern is black.

Can you add a round peg to your square hole? PostScript uses simple arcs and more complex Bézier curves (a class of curves connecting four points). We show arcs in this example, although Adobe Illustrator relies mostly on the Bézier curves.

To make a circle, you start a new path, specify the origin point, give the radius, and finish with the starting and ending angles. A one-inch circle in the middle of a standard page becomes:

```
%save
%create a path
%specify the arc
%ink it in
gsave
newpath
288 360 72 0 360 arc
stroke
```

```
%show page, restore
showpage
grestore
```

To make this an outline, follow the arc command with stroke; to make the circle solid, follow it with fill.

You don't have to choose just a white interior or a solid black fill. By setting the color parameter in the graphics state, you can choose any gradation in between. To set a middle-darkness gray, for example, before executing a fill you write:

```
0.5 setgray
```

It may seem incongruous that leaving the image white requires a color value of 1 and filling with black needs a 0, but if you remember that PostScript is a general solution that is also designed for working with color printers, having more brightness carry the higher value makes sense.

If you want to outline your arc rather than fill it, you also have a wide variety of choices for the stroke pattern and size. In much the same way you can set the brush shape and pattern in MacPaint, you can set the stroke width and the shape of the corners. Stroke width is another value saved in the graphics state, but you can change it with the setlinewidth command. For example, consider the following statement.

```
5 setlinewidth
```

It says to set the width to five units wide. The units start out as points, but you can change them and even make the vertical and horizontal units different.

Line endings and corners are set by the setlinecap and setlinejoin parameters, also part of the graphics state.

Line caps (the end of lines) can be butt (squared off, ending right at the end of the stroke), rounded (semicircular arc with the diameter the same as line width, centered at the end of the stroke), or projecting square (squared off, projecting beyond the end of the stroke by half the line width).

Similarly, line joins can be mitered (extended until they meet at an angle), rounded (circular arc with center at intersection), or beveled (flattened connections). The same choices for Caps and Joins are offered in the Illustrator Paint Style dialog box.

Make a series of three half-boxes, each with a different stroke width, line cap, and join. Because you are going to make three identical figures, you'll use PostScript's ability to define a word by pushing a name and deferred procedure onto the stack, followed by the def operator to define the name you specified as invoking the procedure.

```
%define a procedure to start a
%path, move right 1", up 1",
%ink in the result, then move
%over 1"

/halfbox
{newpath
72 0 rlineto
0 72 rlineto
stroke
72 0 rlineto}
def

%save the state,
%move to the initial position

gsave
144 144 moveto

%set but caps and mitered joins
%set 2 unit line width
%move to an initial position,
%invoke the procedure

0 setlinecap
0 setlinejoin
2 setlinewidth
100 350 moveto
halfbox

%set rounded caps and rounded joins
%set 5 unit line
%invoke the procedure
```

```
1 setlinecap
1 setlinejoin
5 setlinewidth
halfbox

%set projecting caps and bevelled joins
%set 10 unit line
%invoke the procedure

2 setlinecap
2 setlinejoin
10 setlinewidth
halfbox

%print the result,
%reset the state

showpage
grestore
```

For the last example, draw an arrow, followed by a closing message. Write:

```
%because you are including text
%you need to set a font

gsave
/Times-Roman findfont
12 scalefont
setfont

%start off at the middle of the page
%and mark the start of the figure

newpath
288 500 moveto
%draw a vertical two-inch line
%with no change in horizontal
%position
```

```
0 -144 rlineto
currentpoint
stroke
newpath
moveto

%make the triangular head by
%moving a half inch up and right,
%an inch left, and then closing the
%path. Fill in the result.
36 36 rlineto
0 -72 rlineto
closepath
currentpoint
fill
moveto

%put our text in, make a copy
(That's all, folks) dup

% find the width, throw out
% the height, divide the result
% by two, and make it negative

stringwidth pop 2 div neg

% set -18 points for vertical,
%put the x and y in right order
%on stack, move relative

-18 exch rmoveto

% now save our string, which
% should be on top of stack

show

%finally, you print the page
%and restore the state
```

```
showpage
grestore
```

Text and PostScript

The ability to work with and manipulate text is one of the strong suits of the PostScript language. To PostScript, text is a special class of graphics shapes, and also a set of special codes. All the graphics commands that apply to other shapes in PostScript also apply to text. In addition, text has special commands and procedures.

As stated earlier, PostScript is a stack-oriented language. Operations get their inputs from this variable-length list of values; results or other items not immediately needed are pushed back onto the stack until popped back off. PostScript actually has four stacks, but the one you should be most concerned with is the operand stack.

PostScript uses the postfix form of notation, with the input values expressed first, followed by the operation that acts on them ("3 4 add" rather than "add 3 and 4" or "3 + 4"). Programs don't need a special overall format, but lines starting with a percent sign (%) are treated as comments.

You have already seen how producing a printed line on the page entails picking a font, making it the right size, establishing a position on the page, specifying the string to be printed, and then telling the printer to output the page. The simple program was:

```
% pick a font
/Times-Roman findfont
% scale it to 12 point,
% set it as the current font
12 scalefont setfont
%move over 1 inch, up about 5
72 396 moveto
% image the text at that point
(this page intentionally) show
(not left blank) show
% print out the page
showpage
```

Now, take a look at some of the more special ways PostScript can handle text. You'll start by performing transformations on the Times Roman font included in the LaserWriter.

First, make a copy of the Times Roman font, calling it Yourfont. Remember that operators and commands get their values from the stack:

```
% put a name on the stack
/Yourfont
% tell PostScript to retrieve a copy of
% Times Roman and put it on the operand stack too
/Times-Roman findfont
% define that copy as Yourfont
def
```

You're now ready to start making variations.

Use the makefont command, which scales and slants a font using a six-element ordered group of numbers called a matrix. We can skip over the mechanics of matrix multiplication and follow some simple plug-in formulas for using makefont matrices.

For a start, make a version of Yourfont that's much taller than normal (much more narrow than usual for its height).

To scale a font, you plug in the scale factor in the x (horizontal) direction as the first value, the scale factor in the y (vertical) direction as the fourth value, and leave the others as zero. Your code thus becomes:

```
% define Yourfont as a copy of Times-Roman
/Yourfont /Times-Roman findfont def
% put a copy on the stack, followed
% by the matrix, then create the new font
Yourfont [12 0 0 36 0 0] makefont
% make that new font the current font
setfont
% move to position on the page, write
216 432 moveto
(Tall fonts and) show
% wait to print until the next part
```

In addition to making the font larger or smaller, you can also slant the letters. Again, you use the makefont command, but this time the matrix is a bit more complex. To get a slant to the right, for example, you want the top of the letter to sit further over to the right than the bottom of the letter does, with the horizontal skew proportional to vertical distance (halfway up, the letter should be displaced half as far over as at the top, and so on).

The mathematical function gives that proportionality factor for x as a function of y and the specified angle is the tangent. To slant a letter, you put the tangent, multiplied by the horizontal-scale factor, in the matrix's third position.

There is one small additional complicating factor: PostScript doesn't have the tangent function built in, but instead expects you to find it by dividing the sine by the cosine. So, continuing on with the example, your code becomes:

```
% put a copy of the font on the stack
Yourfont
% follow it with our matrix
% with the the third position filled with the
% sine of 30 degrees divided by the cosine of 30
% degrees, multiplied by 24 points
[24 0 30 sin 30 cos div 24 mul 24 0 0]

% create the new font, set it as current
makefont setfont
% continue imaging text at our current position
(slanted fonts) show
% print the page
showpage
```

Next, see how you can get PostScript to make text fit into a specified space. You might need to do that, for example, to create justified columns in a report or to label a chart.

The basic strategy will be to measure the length of a text phrase, then subtract the length from the intended measure. Follow that by dividing the remaining distance among the spaces in the line, which you'll then add to the image. Because you want to use several values more than once (and PostScript operations take parameters from the top of the stack), you'll have to use several exchange operations to reorder the pending values on the stack.

```
% save the environment
gsave
% set up a 12-point font
/Times-Roman findfont 12 scalefont setfont
% move in 4 inches, up 8
```

```
288 572 moveto
% put two copies of the string on the stack
(All the news that fits in print) dup

% make another copy, use it to count length,
% which uses up the copy and leaves the length
dup stringwidth

% get rid of change in vertical position
% because you just want an even horizontal edge
pop
% exchange the length and the extra copy of the string
% you left on the stack with the first "dup"
exch

% now, you need to set up the stack to count
% the spaces in a line. First, you
% put a zero on the stack for a counter
0
% pull the string up above the 0 on the stack
exch
% start a procedure to do for each element
% of the string, but mark it for deferred execution;
% the procedure will count how many spaces you have in
% the string
{
% set a flag if the element is a space (code 32)
32 eq
% leave a procedure on the stack to add 1
% to top of stack, which should be our counter
% when this operation is executed
{ 1
add}
% do the add to counter procedure if
% the flag was set true
if
% end of the procedure for each member
}
% tell PostScript to execute the test and
% possibly add to counter procedure for
```

```
% each element of the string (which is on the
% stack)
forall
% now exchange so the length is
% on top of the count
exch
% now subtract the leftover space
% from a desired length of 4 inches (72 X 4)
288 exch sub
% do the division, computing length
% to add at each space
exch div
% you now have the excess space that must
% be added at each space position sitting
% on the top of the stack. You don't want
% any extra vertical increment,
% but you need a y-axis value on the stack to
% be taken off by widthshow
0
% widthshow needs the string at the top of
% the stack, and it's now 3 down,
% so pull the third element to the top and
% roll all the others down
3 -1 roll
% show the string (from the stack),
% adding the increment whenever a space
% (character code 32) is encountered
32 exch widthshow
% show the page, restore the environment
showpage grestore
```

If you were actually writing a program to justify lines of text, you might optimize the process so the stack would need less rearranging. For simple text, however, the LaserWriter's built-in computer (or any other Post-Script device's RIP) is much faster than the print mechanism anyway, so optimizing isn't always worth the trouble. Instead, it's more worthwhile to write programs in logical order, with ample comments, so that they can be read and understood by others.

In this section you discovered a few ways to shape your own alphabets and how to make text fit in a defined space. Those processes are a small fraction of what PostScript can do with text, but they serve as an introduction. PostScript can literally write in circles, spirals, up and down steep angles, and even backward and forward. Illustrator provides most of the capabilities you need in its type tools, which let you fit text within an area or set text along the shape of a path.

Matrices in Space

PostScript keeps track of shapes and points as grid locations, but the grid may be different for the individual characters, for the page description, and for the output device. You can also set up temporary grids with new origins (0,0 position) or at an angle to the existing lines. Many of the PostScript operators are concerned with making a transformation from one grid to another.

One effective way to go between grids is by using matrix multiplication. PostScript makes extensive use of these multipliers, from mapping the character space into the user space, to mapping the user space onto the output device itself. Like many of the details of PostScript, you can start off without worrying at all about matrix mathematics and let PostScript automatically calculate the essential values. However, if you're curious or ready for more advanced operations, this is how graphic matrices work.

Starting with any point value in two dimensions, extend that (X, Y) pair to a triplet matrix of [x y 1]. You can then accomplish the three basic graphic transformations by multiplying by the appropriate three-by-three matrix. For those of you who haven't learned matrix multiplication or have forgotten it along the way, multiplying the matrix:

```
A   B   0
C   D   0   by  [X   Y    1]
E   F   1
```

yields a new three-element matrix with:

```
first term  = (X*A)+(Y*C)+(1*E)
second term = (X*B)+(Y*D)+(1+F)
third term  = (1*0)+(1*0)=(1*1).
```

To translate (move position sideways), you set the matrix to:

```
1  0   0
0  1   0
dx dy  1
```

which multiplied by [X Y 1] yields

```
[(X*1)+(Y*0)+(1*dx)  (X*0)+(Y*1)+(1*dy)
(1*0)+(1*0)+(1*1)]
```

simplifying to

```
X' = X + dx, Y' = Y + dy, 1 = 1
```

To scale (move up or down in size), the matrix becomes:

```
Sx 0   0
0  Sy  0
0  0   1
```

which multiplied by [X Y 1] yields

```
[(X*Sx)+(Y*0)+(1*0)  (X*0)+(Y*Sy)+(1*0)
(1*0)+(1*0)+(1*1)]
```

simplifying to

```
X' = X * Sx, Y' = Y + Sy, 1 = 1
```

Finally, to rotate the axes at an angle, the matrix is:

```
cos(a)  -sin(a) 0
sin(a)  cos(a)     0
0       0          1
```

which multiplied by [X Y 1] yields

```
[(X*cos(a))+(Y*sin(a))+(1*0)
(X*-sin(a))+(Y*cos(a))+(1*0)  (1*0)+(1*0)+(1*1)]
```

simplifying to

```
X' = X * cos(a) + y * sin(a)
Y' = X * -sin(a) + Y * cos(a)
1 = 1
```

Although these matrix operations seem tedious by hand, they're reasonably easy for a computer. More complex transformations can be constructed using combinations of displacement, scale, and rotation in the proper sequence.

If you'd like to try your hand at PostScript programming, you'll need access to a LaserWriter or another PostScript printer connected to an AppleTalk or serial connection. You can write the PostScript programs on just about any word processing program. To send the program to the printer that is connected to your computer via AppleTalk, use the SendPS program included on some PostScript printer disks, or use a program such as Lasertalk (Adobe/Emerald Software).

If you want to send your program to a printer connected via the serial port, you can use a communications package such as MacTerminal or MicroPhone. Set your communications parameters to 8 data bits, 1 stop bit, no parity, and the X-ON/X-OFF protocol. You can use 1200 bps (set the Mode control on the LaserWriter to 1), 9600 bps (Mode 2), or AppleTalk (Mode 3). Send the LaserWriter a Control-D to stop any current job, a Control-T to have it report the job's status, and the Executive command to tell it to echo back your input. Then, enter your PostScript programs.

The EPSF Riders File

The Adobe Illustrator EPSF Riders file, stored in the Riders folder, is a special Encapsulated PostScript File (EPSF) that lets you add PostScript statement fragments to an Adobe Illustrator document. The file contains PostScript code and comments that explain how to insert custom PostScript language code into four different sections of an Adobe Illustrator document. If you move this file out of the Riders folder and into the folder containing the Adobe Illustrator program, Illustrator inserts the code automatically so that you do not have to open any Illustrator documents.

If you don't plan to use the Riders file, leave it in the Riders folder or the Adobe Illustrator program will run slower. Also, see the RidersMaker file, in the Third Party Folder. RidersMaker is a plug-in interface for building "Adobe Ilustrator EPSF Riders" PostScript files for use with Adobe Illustrator 5.0.

If you want to add code fragments to Illustrator documents, edit the Adobe Illustrator EPSF Riders file to contain the fragments (or modify the sample fragments already included in the file), and then move the file into the same folder as the Adobe Illustrator program. (Before editing the file, be sure to make a copy of the original file in case you need it.) If you are *not* adding code fragments, do not move it into the same folder with the Adobe Illustrator program because the EPSF Riders information can slow down the program's performance. When not using it, the file can remain in the Riders folder within the Misc folder.

Modifications to this file should be performed only by those who are fluent in the Adobe PostScript language. If you are not an experienced PostScript language user, you probably should not modify this file.

Whatever code fragments you put between the lines beginning with double comment symbols (%%) in the Adobe Illustrator EPSF Riders file are inserted into the artwork document file. The inserted lines are bracketed between the %AI3BeginRider and %AI3EndRider comment lines in the artwork document. Adobe Illustrator knows to ignore these code fragments (called riders) when opening and displaying the artwork document. The riders affect the printing of documents or their use on other systems besides the Macintosh or other programs besides Illustrator.

The Adobe Illustrator EPSF Riders file includes fragments that may be useful as they are, requiring very little modification. It contains an error handler and several sample PostScript language code fragments to set the default flatness, screen frequency, and screen angle of your print job. It also contains a simple example of how you can annotate each printed page. Except for the error handler, all code fragments are commented out to disable them. To enable a particular fragment, just remove the % and • characters from the beginning of each code line of the fragment.

Note that even though these code fragments are disabled by comments, they are still written out to all files with headers; therefore, you may wish to remove everything that you don't need from between the lines with double comment symbols (%%) in the Adobe Illustrator EPSF Riders file.

There is no other program for the Macintosh that offers this combination of precise drawing tools, automatic charting and graphing, and extensive type manipulation and text layout features along with the capability to completely customize the image description to fit your needs. There is no other technology like PostScript that provides a seemingly impossible mix of features: complete device independence and extensive device customization. Adobe Illustrator is the key that unlocks the power behind PostScript. We hope it provides inspiration as well.

The Illustrator 88 Artwork Document

An Adobe Illustrator artwork document is a PostScript program that describes the appearance of a piece of artwork that you create with the Adobe Illustrator program. An artwork document is saved as a text file that can be opened and edited using a standard word processing program such as Microsoft Word, or Claris MacWrite, or T/Maker's WriteNow. The document communicates a description of the artwork to PostScript output devices such as the Macintosh screen, printers, and typesetting machines; and to graphics software such as the Illustrator program itself.

Illustrator versions 3 and 5 use a new format that conforms to the standards of Adobe's specifications for Encapsulated Post-Script (EPS) files, which can be used by many different application programs on many different computer platforms, including

Macintosh and IBM-compatible computers. However, a previous version of Illustrator, Adobe Illustrator 88, used a different PostScript format that is recognized by some desktop publishing programs. The 88 format is offered as an option in the Save As dialog box, and it is described in this appendix.

Adobe Illustrator 88 artwork document files consist of a prologue and data. The prologue defines the procedures that are used by Illustrator to describe the artwork. The data part of the artwork document consists of calls to the procedures defined in the prologue and the associated target groups of data about the components of the artwork such as coordinates and positions of all the lines and curves, their associated line weights, gray-scale or color values, paint and type specifications, and page breaks.

The procedures in the prologue relate to many of the functions that are available within Illustrator, with the notable exception that transformations such as scaling, rotating, reflecting, and skewing are performed within the Adobe Illustrator program itself and only the information about the resultant transformation is contained in the artwork document. Although commands for performing the transformations are available within PostScript, saving the transformed objects saves time during printing since the PostScript interpreter in the printer (the RIP) doesn't have to be burdened with the task of the transformation, which can be a relatively slow process.

Adobe Illustrator (versions 3 and 5) usually saves an artwork document in the standard Encapsulated PostScript (EPS) format. It may optionally contain a reduced resolution image of the artwork in addition to its PostScript description, in either the Macintosh format or the IBM PC-compatible format. This image is a 72 dot-per-inch representation of the artwork in either the Macintosh's QuickDraw (PICT) format or in TIFF (Tag Image File Format) for IBM PC-compatible computers. The representation of the artwork can be used by another program such as a page layout program for placement of the artwork in a layout, or for scaling or cropping the image. The page layout program can use the bit-mapped representation of the image to provide a displayed preview without requiring the program to understand PostScript.

The PostScript portion of Encapsulated PostScript (EPS) documents created by Adobe Illustrator follows the bit-mapped representation of the artwork and conforms to the Adobe PostScript Document Structuring Conventions, version 2.0, the Adobe Encapsulated PostScript File Format For Apple Macintosh and IBM PC Application, version 1.2, the Aldus Encapsulated PostScript File Format for PageMaker Import for PC Windows and Macintosh Applications, version 1.2, and the Altsys Encapsulated PostScript File Format for Apple Macintosh and PC-Windows Applications, version 1.2.

Another convention used by EPS artwork document formats is not to include the PostScript command showpage (or copypage) at the end of the document as is often the case in other PostScript documents. The showpage command causes the PostScript output device to print (or display) the page and clear the page from the printer's memory after the page is printed. The copypage command is similar to the showpage command except that the image of the page is left unchanged in the printer's memory after the page has been printed.

Since artwork document files are usually created for the purpose of becoming a component in another document (such as a page layout), printing the page at the end of the artwork is not usually desirable because it would interfere with the normal printing process of that page by causing it to be printed prematurely. Adobe Illustrator temporarily appends a showpage command to the end of the document as part of the program's normal printing process that is invoked by either selecting Print in the File menu or by typing Command-P as a shortcut. If you want to print an artwork document from outside of Adobe Illustrator, you can add the showpage command to the end of the document while you are editing it, or you can use the SendPS program or a similar program, which has an option for temporarily appending the showpage command to a PostScript file for the purpose of printing.

The Illustrator 88 Artwork Document Structure

The Adobe Illustrator 88 format is a standard text file. One of the advantages of using this format is that people can easily read and modify an artwork document with just about any word processing program.

To understand the document structure, refer to the following listing of the contents of the artwork document, which is in PostScript, and to the mouse drawing that results from executing the PostScript code. Following the artwork document listing is an explanation of what the various elements in the document mean.

Artwork Document Listing

```
%!PS-Adobe-2.0 EPSF-1.2
%%Creator:Adobe Illustrator(TM) 1.0
%%For:Fred Davis
%%Title:Mouse art
%%CreationDate:4/25/87 1:39 PM
%%DocumentProcSets:Adobe_Illustrator_1.0 0 0
%%DocumentSuppliedProcSets:Adobe_Illustrator_1.0 0 0
%%DocumentFonts:Courier
%%BoundingBox:27 -366 526 -55
%%TemplateBox:0 -720 576 0
%%EndComments
%%BeginProcSet:Adobe_Illustrator_1.0 0 0
% Copyright (C) 1987 Adobe Systems Incorporated.
% All Rights Reserved.
% Adobe Illustrator is a trademark of Adobe Systems
Incorporated.
/Adobe_Illustrator_1.0 dup 100 dict def load begin
/Version 0 def
/Revision 0 def
% definition operators
/bdef {bind def} bind def
/ldef {load def} bdef
/xdef {exch def} bdef
% graphic state operators
/_K {3 index add neg dup 0 lt {pop 0} if 3 1 roll}
bdef
/_k /setcmybcolor where
{/setcmybcolor get}{{1 sub 4 1 roll _K _K _K
setrgbcolor pop} bind} ifelse def
/g {/_b xdef /p {_b setgray} def} bdef
/G {/_B xdef /P {_B setgray} def} bdef
/k {/_b xdef /_y xdef /_m xdef /_c xdef /p {_c _m _y
_b _k} def} bdef
/K {/_B xdef /_Y xdef /_M xdef /_C xdef /P {_C _M _Y
_B _k} def} bdef
/d /setdash ldef
/_i currentflat def
```

```
/i {dup 0 eq {pop _i} if setflat} bdef
/j /setlinejoin ldef
/J /setlinecap ldef
/M /setmiterlimit ldef
/w /setlinewidth ldef
% path construction operators
/_R {.25 sub round .25 add} bdef
/_r {transform _R exch _R exch itransform} bdef
/c {_r curveto} bdef
/C /c ldef
/v {currentpoint 6 2 roll _r curveto} bdef
/V /v ldef
/y {_r 2 copy curveto} bdef
/Y /y ldef
/l {_r lineto} bdef
/L /l ldef
/m {_r moveto} bdef
% error operators
/_e [] def
/_E {_e length 0 ne {gsave 0 g 0 G 0 i 0 J 0 j 1 w 10
M [] 0 d
/Courier 20 0 0 1 z [0.966 0.259 -0.259 0.966
_e 0 get _e 2 get add 2 div _e 1 get _e 3 get add 2
div] e _f t T grestore} if} bdef
/_fill {{fill} stopped
{/_e [pathbbox] def /_f (ERROR: can't fill, increase
flatness)
def n _E} if}
bdef
/_stroke {{stroke} stopped
{/_e [pathbbox] def /_f (ERROR: can't stroke, increase
flatness) def n _E} if} bdef
% path painting operators
/n /newpath ldef
/N /n ldef
/F {p _fill} bdef
/f {closepath F} bdef
/S {P _stroke} bdef
/s {closepath S} bdef
```

```
/B {gsave F grestore S} bdef
/b {closepath B} bdef
% text block construction and painting operators
/_s /ashow ldef
/_S {(?) exch {2 copy 0 exch put pop dup false
charpath currentpoint _g setmatrix
_stroke _G setmatrix moveto 3 copy pop rmoveto} forall
pop pop pop n} bdef
/_A {_a moveto _t exch 0 exch} bdef
/_L {0 _l neg translate _G currentmatrix pop} bdef
/_w {dup stringwidth exch 3 -1 roll length 1 sub _t
mul add exch} bdef
/_z [{0 0} {dup _w exch neg 2 div exch neg 2 div} {dup
_w exch neg exch neg}] bdef
/z {_z exch get /_a xdef /_t xdef /_l xdef exch
findfont exch scalefont setfont} bdef
/_g matrix def
/_G matrix def
/_D {_g currentmatrix pop gsave concat _G
currentmatrix pop} bdef
/e {_D p /t {_A _s _L} def} bdef
/r {_D P /t {_A _S _L} def} bdef
/a {_D /t {dup p _A _s P _A _S _L} def} bdef
/o {_D /t {pop _L} def} bdef
/T {grestore} bdef
% group construction operators
/u {} bdef
/U {} bdef
% font construction operators
/Z {findfont begin currentdict dup length dict begin
{1 index /FID ne {def} {pop pop} ifelse} forall /
FontName exch def dup length 0 ne
{/Encoding Encoding 256 array copy def 0 exch {dup
type /nametype eq
{Encoding 2 index 2 index put pop 1 add} {exch pop}
ifelse} forall} if pop
currentdict dup end end /FontName get exch definefont
pop} bdef
end
```

```
%%EndProcSet
%%EndProlog
%%BeginSetup
Adobe_Illustrator_1.0 begin
n
%%EndSetup
0 g
0 G
1 i
0 J
0 j
0.2 w
10 M
[]0 d
%%Note:
163.75 -161.25 m
156.75 -165.75 152.75 -171.25 160.75 -174.25 C
344.25 -249.75 l
360.25 -251.75 361.75 -254.25 377.75 -242.75 c
393.75 -231.25 459.75 -185.75 y
464.811 -180.343 457.938 -177.323 452.25 -174.75 c
447.156 -172.445 243.25 -91.75 y
232.625 -88.125 224.25 -88.25 216.25 -93.25 c
208.25 -98.25 104.569 -169.953 102.25 -173.25 c
99.875 -176.625 97.75 -182.75 118.25 -189.25 c
138.75 -195.75 365.25 -291.25 371.75 -294.25 c
378.25 -297.25 393.75 -307.25 421.75 -284.75 c
449.75 -262.25 507.75 -217.75 y
513.25 -212.75 513.75 -206.75 502.75 -200.75 c
491.75 -194.75 457.625 -177.25 y
S
101 -176.625 m
98.5 -209.625 99.25 -239.25 99.25 -242.25 C
99.75 -251.5 102.625 -251.25 113.75 -255.25 c
130.714 -261.349 376.25 -345.25 y
384.75 -347.25 399.75 -351.5 420.75 -335.75 c
444.19 -318.169 516.75 -260.25 y
523.625 -253.312 521.25 -247.75 520.25 -242.25 c
519.25 -236.75 515.75 -216.25 y
```

```
514.75 -210.875 509.875 -206.375 y
S
103 -251.25 m
98.5 -253.75 102.25 -254.75 107.25 -256.75 c
112.25 -258.75 377.75 -348.25 y
389.75 -352 401 -350 410.75 -344.75 c
419.421 -340.08 519.75 -260.25 y
521.875 -258.187 520.937 -253.937 y
S
521.187 -256.937 m
518.25 -275.312 510.255 -279.244 507.25 -282.25 c
503.75 -285.75 416.75 -351.5 y
404 -362 388.75 -363.75 374.75 -359.25 c
360.75 -354.75 116.25 -269.25 y
106.375 -265.25 101.5 -264.625 101 -253.125 c
S
85 -181 m
83 -167.5 l
96 -159.75 l
199.75 -160 l
86.5 -167.75 l
88.5 -182.5 l
85 -181 l
s
89.899 -182.811 m
88.014 -168.234 l
101.639 -160.26 l
105.642 -160.525 l
91.75 -168.5 l
93.634 -184.403 l
89.899 -182.811 l
s
95.076 -185.032 m
93.036 -169.254 l
107.784 -160.622 l
112.117 -160.909 l
97.079 -169.541 l
99.119 -186.755 l
95.076 -185.032 l
s
100.392 -187.333 m
```

```
98.309 -170.254 l
114.274 -160.91 l
118.464 -161.221 l
102.686 -170.565 l
103.02 -172.323 l
S
90.25 -163 m
71.5 -161 48 -168 42.25 -115.5 c
36.5 -63 35.75 -57 y
S
83.5 -172 m
70 -170.75 41 -174 35.5 -124.5 c
29.668 -72.009 29 -66 y
S
147.125 -154.25 m
145.125 -155.875 145.125 -156.25 144.25 -158.5 C
158.25 -157.5 162.25 -157.75 163.75 -158.75 c
165.25 -159.75 216.492 -180.796 217.75 -180.25 C
220.562 -182.187 296.375 -127.562 296.375 -126.062 c
S
144.25 -158.625 m
144.5 -160.375 144.875 -161 y
S
104.25 -176.25 m
152.75 -170.75 l
S
226.75 -90.75 m
248.75 -99.75 l
S
218.312 -177.125 m
217.875 -179.75 l
S
294.19 -126.316 m
283.092 -134.798 234.443 -168.174 221.228 -175.821 C
218.228 -177.446 217.009 -176.519 214.384 -176.144 C
202.719 -171.863 166.924 -157.366 165.25 -156.25 c
163.991 -155.41 159.772 -155.025 150.615 -155.595 C
145.365 -156.22 145.838 -155.079 148.588 -152.829 C
166.414 -141.471 215.09 -106.17 220 -105 c
223.715 -104.114 243.875 -101.625 246 -103 C
294.299 -123.469 L
```

```
295.486 -124.219 295.253 -125.441 294.19 -126.316 C
S
294.687 -123.75 m
295.564 -124.353 296.125 -124.812 296.375 -126.062 C
S
296.375 -126.125 m
296.5 -127 296.625 -128.437 y
S
144.125 -159.375 m
142.375 -160.375 141.187 -160.812 142.312 -161.062 C
156.312 -160.062 162.25 -160.25 163.75 -161.25 c
165.25 -162.25 214.75 -182.25 217.75 -182.75 c
220.75 -183.25 298.149 -128.899 297.812 -127.437 c
297.625 -126.625 296.875 -126.687 296.5 -126.5 c
S
368.25 -255.25 m
392.25 -293.25 l
S
465.25 -186.25 m
505.25 -207.25 l
S
322.5 -220.75 m
338.5 -210.75 l
340.25 -209.5 343.5 -209 346.25 -210 c
351.45 -211.891 371 -219.5 y
373 -221 372.25 -222.25 370.25 -224 c
365.984 -227.732 353.75 -235.25 y
352 -236.25 349.5 -236.5 346.75 -235.5 c
341.844 -233.716 322.5 -226 y
319.5 -225 318.75 -223.25 322.5 -220.75 C
s
321.25 -224.75 m
338.75 -213.5 l
340.5 -212.25 343.75 -211.75 346.5 -212.75 c
351.7 -214.641 371.25 -222.25 y
S
339.687 -220.375 m
335.687 -220.75 332.125 -222.125 331.875 -224.5 c
```

```
331.625 -226.875 332.375 -230 338.25 -231.875 c
344.125 -233.75 347.936 -233.396 351.375 -232.25 c
354 -231.375 353.462 -229.617 354.5 -228.75 c
356.463 -227.107 359.564 -227.437 361.5 -225.625 c
365.411 -221.963 354.219 -216.578 348.5 -215.625 c
347 -215.375 346.319 -215.056 344 -215.875 c
342.024 -216.572 341.375 -217.125 341 -218.125 c
340.625 -219.125 341.125 -221.5 340.25 -219.25 c
339.375 -217 339.125 -215.25 338.25 -215.25 C
337.875 -216.75 337.937 -219.75 339.687 -220.375 C
338.812 -220.375 339.687 -220.375 y
s
167.25 -155.25 m
245.125 -103.875 l
S
217.812 -180.375 m
217.125 -181.812 217.875 -182.562 y
S
%%Trailer
_E end
```

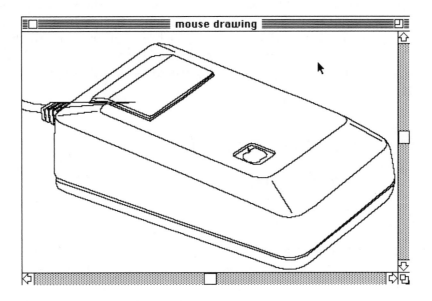

The Document Structure Explained

As stated earlier, the Illustrator 88 document consists of two major sections, a prologue followed by a script. The prologue contains a set of specific definitions that are used by the script. These definitions describe Illustrator output functions in PostScript language primitives.

The script describes the component graphic elements that are used to create the artwork. The description consists of references to the definitions made in the prologue, interspersed with operands and the data required by those operations. Below is an overview of the artwork document's component sections and subsections, and the order in which they appear in the document. Following the overview is a more detailed description of the prologue definitions and the component descriptions within script.

The following section, which describes an Adobe Illustrator 88 artwork document, focuses primarily on the document's overall structure as defined by a set of PostScript comments. Comments can be recognized by the percentage sign (%) that precedes them. Comments are usually ignored by a PostScript interpreter. However, they convey structural information about the document to other programs that operate on the document. Some comments serve primarily to mark the boundaries between the various parts of the document (the prologue and the script). Others provide information such as a bounding box that encloses all the marks painted as a result of executing the document and the set of fonts that may need to be downloaded to a PostScript printer before the document can be printed.

The Prologue of an 88 Artwork Document

The document's prologue section is subdivided into header and definition subsections.

Prologue Header Subsection

```
%!PS-Adobe-2.0 EPSF-1.2
```

This is the first line in the document and indicates that the document conforms to version 2.0 of the Adobe PostScript Document Structuring Conventions and version 1.2 of the Encapsulated PostScript Document Format.

```
%%Creator:Adobe Illustrator(TM) version serial
```

This indicates that the document was created by the specified version of Adobe Illustrator optionally serialized with the specified serial value. The version value and the optional serial value consist of arbitrary text delimited by white space.

```
%%For:name organization
```

This indicates that the document was created by a version of Adobe Illustrator personalized for the specified name and organization. The name and organization values consist of arbitrary text, including white space. Organization is terminated by a new-line character.

```
%%Title:name
```

This indicates the title of the document. The name value consists of arbitrary text (such as the filename) terminated by a newline.

```
%%Creation Date:date time
```

This indicates the date and time at which the document was created. The date and time values consist of arbitrary text, including white space. Time is terminated by a newline.

```
%%DocumentProcSets:Adobe_Illustrator_version
level revision
```

This indicates that the document requires the specified prologue procedure set. The version, level, and revision values consist of arbitrary text delimited by white space.

```
%%DocumentSuppliedProcSets:Adobe_Illustrator_version
level revision
```

This indicates that the document supplies the specified prologue procedure set. The version, level, and revision values consist of arbitrary text delimited by white space.

```
%%DocumentFonts:font...
```

This indicates that the document uses the specified fonts. These fonts may need to be downloaded to the PostScript printer before the document is sent. The font values consist of PostScript font names delimited by white space.

```
%%+font...
```

When following the `%%DocumentFonts` comment, this comment indicates that the document uses the specified fonts, in addition to those given by the `%%DocumentFonts` comment. The font values consist of PostScript font names delimited by white space.

```
%%BoundingBox:llx lly urx ury
```

This indicates the bounding box (the smallest rectangle that encloses all the marks painted as a result of executing (for example, printing) the document). All four values are integers: lower left x, lower left y, upper right x, and upper right y. The coordinates (llx, lly) and (urx, ury) are the lower left and upper right corners of the bounding box, respectively. The coordinates are specified in the default user coordinate system in which the unit length along both of the axes is $1/72$ of an inch, the positive x axis extends horizontally to the right, and the positive y axis extends vertically upwards (and negative x extends left, negative y extends down). The value urx - llx, which must be an integer, provides an upper bound on the width of the illustration. The value ury - lly, which must be an integer, provides an upper bound on the height of the illustration.

```
%%TemplateBox:llx lly urx ury
```

This indicates the bounding box that encloses all the samples in the document's template. All four values are integers: lower left x, lower left y, upper right x, and upper right y. The coordinates (llx, lly) and (urx, ury) are the coordinates of the lower left and upper right corners of the bounding box, respectively. The coordinates are specified in the default user coordinate system in which the unit length along both axes is $1/72$ of an inch: Illustrator assumes that the size of each sample is $1/72$ -by-$1/72$- inch. The value urx - llx, which must be an integer, equals the number of rows of samples. If the document has no template, llx equals urx and lly equals ury.

When Illustrator opens the document, the illustration is placed on the drawing area in such a way that the coordinate ((llx +urx)/2), ((lly +ury)/2) is centered in the drawing area. (Use these coordinates; lower left, center and upper right, to determine adjustments to make to the bounding box when using the Adobe Separator program, to adjust the page size to print trim marks, etc., outside a larger-size bounding box.)

```
%%EndComments
```

This explicitly ends the prologue header subsection and marks the beginning of the prologue definition subsection.

Prologue Definition Subsection

```
%%BeginProcSet:Adobe_Illustrator_version level
revision prologue definitions
%%EndProcSet
```

The %%BeginProcSet and %%EndProcSet comments explicitly delimit the prologue definitions of the document. These definitions are used by the script section to match the Adobe Illustrator output functions to the capabilities and primitives that PostScript supports. The entire prologue is packaged as a single procedure set identified by the version, level, and revision values, each of which is delimited by white space.

```
%%EndProlog
```

The %%EndProlog remark explicitly ends the prologue section and marks the beginning of the script section.

The Script Section

The document's script section is subdivided into setup, body, and trailer subsections.

Script Setup Subsection

```
%%BeginSetup
script setup
%%End Setup
```

The `%%BeginSetup` and `%%EndSetup` comments explicitly delimit the script setup, which performs various graphics state and error recovery initialization and font reencoding operations required by the document's prologue and script.

Script Body Subsection

```
script body
```

The script body describes the set of component graphic elements that define the illustration. The script consists of references to definitions made in the prologue, interspersed with operands and data required by those operations.

```
%%Trailer
```

The `%%Trailer` remark explicitly ends the script body subsection of the document and marks the beginning of the script trailer subsection.

Script Trailer Subsection

```
script trailer
```

The script trailer performs various cleanup and error recovery operations required by the document's prologue and script.

Illustrator Document Prologue Definitions

This section specifies and defines the operations provided by the prologue of an Adobe Illustrator 88 document. These operations are used within the script to match Adobe Illustrator's output functions to the capabilities and primitives provided by PostScript.

Graphic State Operations

The prologue maintains a graphics state that establishes a context in which its graphic operations execute. The graphics state inherits most of its functionality from the underlying graphics state supplied by the PostScript interpreter. Many of the prologue's graphics state operations have a one-for-one mapping into a single PostScript primitive, and hence, they simply provide a set of abbreviated primitive names or aliases.

The primary difference between the prologue's graphics state and that of PostScript is in the handling of color state and font metric information. The prologue maintains two separate current color parameters: a filling color and a stroking color. These two parameters determine the color of subsequently filled and stroked shapes, respectively (see g, G, k, and K). They are provided to match Adobe Illustrator's capability of filling and stroking a single path with different colors.

The font metric information included in the graphics state, in addition to the current font, consists of the spacing (also called kerning) adjustment to the x width of each character, the leading distance between each successive line of text, and a specification of the alignment method that aligns each line of text. These parameters are provided to support the Illustrator operators.

Several of PostScript's graphic state parameters are not directly accessible through prologue operators. These parameters include the current transformation matrix, the clipping path, the halftone screen, the transfer function, and the output device. Values for these parameters are inherited by the prologue when the prologue is executed by a specific physical device (such as an Apple LaserWriter laser printer or a Linotype Linotronic 300 imagesetter) and remain unchanged throughout the execution of the rest of the document. (This statement may not be strictly true if the document's script contains embedded documents. However, the graphics state may be restored and all printer virtual memory recovered by embedding the document itself within a save/restore context.)

```
d array offset d -
```

This sets the dash pattern parameter in the graphics state which determines the dash pattern of subsequently stroked paths (see s and S). The array and offset parameter values have meaning identical to those of the PostScript setdash operator. That is, if array is empty, normal unbroken stroked lines are produced. If array is not empty, dashed lines, whose pattern (in user space) is given by the elements of array, which must all be nonnegative, but not all zero, are produced. The offset parameter, which must be nonnegative, is interpreted as a distance (in user space) into the dash pattern at which the pattern should be started.

```
g gray g -
```

This sets the current filling color parameter in the graphics state which determines the color of subsequently filled paths (see f and F). The gray parameter value has a meaning identical to that of the PostScript setgray operator. That is, the filling color is set to a gray shade corresponding to gray, which must be a number between 0 and 1, where 0 corresponds to black, 1 corresponds to white, and intermediate values correspond to intermediate shades of gray. If no shade is specified, the default fill shade of black is used. The specified gray shade remains in effect for all fills until another setgray operator changes it.

```
G gray G -
```

This sets the current stroking color parameter in the graphics state which determines the color of subsequently stroked paths (see s and S). The gray parameter value has a meaning identical to that of the PostScript setgray operator. That is, the stroking color is set to a gray shade corresponding to gray, which must be a number between 0 and 1, where 0 corresponds to black, 1 corresponds to white, and intermediate values correspond to intermediate shades of gray. If no shade is specified, the default stroke shade of black is used. The specified gray shade remains in effect for all strokes until another setgray operator changes it.

```
i flat i -
```

This sets the current flatness parameter in the graphics state, which determines the accuracy with which curved path segments are to be rendered on the output device. A positive flat parameter value has a meaning identical to that of the PostScript setflat operator. That is, its value gives the maximum error tolerance (measured in output device pixels) of a straight line segment approximation of any portion of a curve. If flat is 0, the flatness is set to the flatness value in effect when the document's prologue section is executed, which normally equals the device's default, built-in flatness.

```
j join j -
```

This sets the current line join parameter in the graphics state, which determines the shape to be placed at the corners of stroked paths (see s and S). The join parameter value has a meaning identical to that of the PostScript setlinejoin operator. That is, the value 0 establishes miter joins, 1 establishes round joins, and 2 establishes bevel joins.

```
J cap J -
```

This sets the current line cap parameter in the graphics state, which determines the shape to be placed at the ends of open stroked paths and at the ends of dashed line segments (see s and S). The cap parameter value has a meaning identical to that of the PostScript setlinecap operator. That is, the value 0 establishes butt caps, 1 establishes round caps, and 2 establishes projecting caps.

```
k cyan magenta yellow black k -
```

This sets the current filling color parameter in the graphics state, which determines the color of subsequently filled paths (see f and F). The cyan, magenta, yellow, and black parameter values have meaning identical to those of the PostScript setcmybcolor operator (contact Adobe Systems Technical Support for a definition of this operator). That is, each value must be a number between 0 and 1, where 0 corresponds to no contribution at all of that color, 1 corresponds to maximum intensity of that color, and intermediate values correspond to intermediate intensities.

   If the setcmybcolor operator is not known in any of the dictionaries on the current dictionary stack when the document's prologue section is executed, then the current filling or stroking color parameter is set to the color obtained by the following operation:

```
red green blue setrgbcolor
```

where:

```
red = 1 - min(1, cyan + black)
green = 1 - min(1, magenta + black)
blue = 1 - min(1, yellow + black)
```

That is, the black component is added to each of the other three components, and the resulting values are converted to a color specified by the red-green-blue color model.

On most existing black-and-white PostScript printers, the setrgbcolor operator is implemented as if the following operation were performed:

```
gray setgray
```

In this case, gray is an NTSC (video standard) weighed average of the three color components given by the following:

```
gray = .3* red + .59* green+.11* blue
```

Of course, page composition systems and other printing managers may produce color separations on black-and-white printers by redefining the setcmybcolor and setgray operators and establishing the appropriate halftone screens and transfer functions before sending the document.

```
K cyan magenta yellow black K -
```

This sets the current stroking color parameter in the graphics state, which determines the color of subsequently stroked paths (see s and S). The cyan, magenta, yellow, and black parameter values have meaning identical to those of the PostScript setcmybcolor operator. That is, each value must be a number between 0 and 1, where 0 corresponds to no contribution at all of that color, 1 corresponds to maximum intensity of that color, and intermediate values correspond to intermediate intensities of that color.

See the k operator for a discussion of the setcmybcolor operator.

```
M miter M -
```

This sets the current miter limit parameter, which determines when the objectionably long spikes produced at the corners of sharply angled stroked paths by mitered joins should be cut off with bevels (see j). The miter parameter value has a meaning identical to that of the PostScript setmiterlimit operator. That is, miter specifies the maximum desired ratio between the miter length at the corner and the line width.

```
w width w -
```

This sets the current line width parameter in the graphics state, which determines the thickness of stroked lines (see s and S). The width parameter value has a meaning identical to that of the PostScript setlinewidth operator. That is, all points whose perpendicular distance from the current path (in user space) is less than or equal to one-half of width are painted. As usual, a value of 0 is permitted: it is interpreted as the thinnest line that can be rendered on the output device.

```
z font scale leading kerning alignment z -
```

This sets the current font parameter in the graphics state, which establishes the font dictionary to be used by subsequent text-block painting operators (see a, e, o, and r). The positive scale factor (z) is applied to the font dictionary given by the literal name font, producing a new font whose characters are scaled by the positive number scale (in both x and y). The resulting font is established as the current font.

This operator also sets the current leading, spacing, and alignment method parameters in the graphics state. The spacing parameter, given by the number kerning, specifies a spacing value (in user space) that is added to the x width of each character in the scaled font, thus modifying the horizontal spacing between the characters. The leading parameter, given by the nonnegative leading, specifies the vertical spacing (in user space) between successive lines of text composing the text block. The alignment method parameter, given by the integer alignment, specifies how the lines of text are aligned with one another. That is, an alignment value of 0 specifies align left (flush left, ragged right), 1 specifies align center (ragged left and right), and 2 specifies align right (ragged left, flush right).

```
Z array newfont font Z -
```

This creates a newly encoded font, whose name is given by the literal name newfont, that is a copy of an existing font, whose name is given by font, except that portions of the new font's encoding vector have been modified as specified by the array parameter value. Array is an array of encoding numbers and literal character names organized as follows:

```
[code1 name11 name12...name1m1
code2 name21 name22....name2m2
....
coden namen1 namen2...namenmn]
```

where codei for $1 <= i <= n$ are encoding numbers between 0 and 255, and nameij for $1 <= i <= n$, $1 <= mi$ are literal character names. The encoding vector of the new font is identical to that of the existing font except that the element at index codei + j equals nameij for $1 <= i <= n$, $1 <= j <= mi$. It is assumed that all of the encoding numbers codei + j are distinct. In addition, n may be equal to 0, in which case array is an empty array, and the encoding vector of the new font is identical to that of the existing font.

Path Construction Operations

A path is built up by executing one or more path construction operations that append a sequence of connected straight or curved line segments onto the path. Once a path is completely built up, it is painted with one of the path painting operations.

Only one path may be built up at a time. This path is called the current path. The current path is initially empty and is reset to empty by all of the path painting operations.

The trailing endpoint of the most recently appended segment is referred to as the current point. All of the path construction operations that append a segment start at the current point. Each segment is specified by a set of coordinates specified in user space. A new path is begun by executing a special operation that establishes a current point on an otherwise empty path.

As the path is built up, each point that joins two segments is marked a smooth point or a corner point. If the point is marked smooth, then the point and the two associated Bézier direction points of the segments that the point connects are assumed to be colinear. If the point is marked corner, then no constraint is assumed. (A straight line segment can be thought of as a degenerate Bézier curve whose direction points are coincident with its endpoints).

```
c x1 y1 x2 y2 x3 y3 c -
```

This adds a Bézier curve segment to the current path between the current point and the point (x3, y3), using (x1, y1) and then (x2, y2) as the Bézier direction points; (x3, y3) then becomes the current point. The new current point is marked a smooth point.

```
C x1 y1 x2 y2 x3 y3 C -
```

This adds a Bézier curve segment to the current path between the current point and the point (x3, y3), using (x1, y1) and then (x2, y2) as the Bézier direction points; (x3, y3) then becomes the current point. The new current point is marked a corner point.

```
l x y l -
```

This appends a straight line segment to the current path. The line extends from the current point to the point (x, y); (x, y) then becomes the current point. The new current point is marked a smooth point.

```
L x y L -
```

This appends a straight line segment to the current path. The line extends from the current point to the point (x, y); (x, y) then becomes the current point. The new current point is marked a corner point.

```
m x y m -
```

This starts a new current path by setting the current point to (x, y) without adding any segment to the path. Initially, the path must be empty and have no current point.

```
v x2 y2 x3 y3 v -
```

This adds a Bézier curve segment to the current path between the current point and the point (x3, y3), using the current point and then (x2, y2) as the Bézier direction points; (x3, y3) then becomes the current point. The new current point is marked a smooth point.

```
V x2 y2 x3 y3 V -
```

This adds a Bézier curve segment to the current path between the current point and the point (x3, y3), using the current point and then (x2, y2) as the Bézier direction points; (x3, y3) then becomes the current point. The new current point is marked a corner point.

```
y x1 y1 x3 y3 y -
```

This adds a Bézier curve segment to the current path between the current point and the point (x3, y3), using (x1, y1) and then (x3, y3) as the Bézier direction points; (x3, y3) then becomes the current point. The new current point is marked a smooth point.

```
Y x1 y1 x3 y3 Y-
```

This adds a Bézier curve segment to the current path between the current point and the point (x3, y3), using (x1, y1) and then (x3, y3) as the Bézier direction points; (x3, y3) then becomes the current point. The new current point is marked a corner point.

Path Painting Operations

The prologue provides a set of painting operations that can convert the current path to represent marks on the current page. All of these operations are based on combinations of the underlying PostScript primitives closepath, fill, and stroke.

The results of these painting operations are controlled by the prologue's current graphics state.

All of the painting operations assume that the current path has been previously built-up by a sequence of path construction operations. After the painting operation is completed, the current path is initialized to be empty.

```
b - b-
```

This indicates that the current path should be closed and then first filled (see f and F) with the current filling color and then stroked (see s and S) with the current stroking color. The stroke line width (see w) is set by the current line width parameter.

```
B - B -
```

This indicates that the current path should be first filled (see f and F) with the current filling color and then stroked (see s and S) with the current stroking color. The stroke line width (see w) is set by the current line width parameter.

```
f - f -
```

This closes the current path and then paints (fills) the area enclosed by the current path with the current filling color. The inside of the current path is determined by the normal PostScript nonzero winding number rule. Any previous contents of that area on the current page are obscured.

```
F - F -
```

This paints (fills) the area enclosed by the current path with the current filling color. The inside of the current path is determined by the normal PostScript nonzero winding number rule. Any previous contents of that area on the current page are obscured.

```
n - n -
```

This closes the current path and then neither fills (see f and F) nor strokes (see s and S) the path.

```
N - N -
```

This neither fills (see f and F) nor strokes (see s and S) the current path.

```
s - s -
```

This closes the current path and then paints (strokes) a line following the path with the current stroking color. This line is centered on the path, has sides parallel to the path segments, and has a width given by the current line width parameter (see w).

The joints between connected path segments are painted with the current line join (see j). The ends of the line's dash segments, if any, are painted with the current line cap (see J). The line is either solid or broken according to the current dash pattern (see d).

```
S - S -
```

This paints (strokes) a line following the path with the current stroking color. This line is centered on the path, has sides parallel to the path segments, and has a width given by the current line width parameter (see w).

The joints between connected path segments are painted with the current line join (see j). The ends of the path and the ends of the line's dash segments, if any, are painted with the current line cap (see J). The line is either solid or broken according to the current dash pattern (see d).

Text Block Painting Operations

The prologue provides a set of text block painting operations that paint the successive lines of text composing the text block, using the current font, spacing (also called kerning), leading, and alignment method parameters in the graphics state.

```
a matrix a -
```

This indicates the start of a text block whose character outlines should be neither filled (see e) nor stroked (see r). Matrix specifies a matrix that is concatenated with the current transformation matrix to define a new user space whose coordinates are transformed into the former user space according to matrix. This new space establishes an origin for the first line of text.

```
e matrix e -
```

This indicates the start of a text block whose character outlines should be filled with the current filling color. Matrix specifies a matrix that is concatenated with the current transformation matrix to define a new user space whose coordinates are transformed into the former user space according to matrix. This new space establishes an origin for the first line of text.

```
o matrix o -
```

This indicates the start of a text block whose character outlines should be first filled (see e) with the current filling color and then stroked (see r) with the current stroking color. Matrix specifies a matrix that is concatenated with the current transformation matrix to define a new user space whose coordinates are transformed into the former user space according to matrix. This new space establishes an origin for the first line of text.

```
r matrix r -
```

This indicates the start of a text block whose character outlines should be stroked with the current stroking color. The stroked line is centered on the character's outline, has sides parallel to the outline's segments, and has a width given by the current line width parameter (see w). The joints between connected outline segments are painted with the current line join (see j). The ends of the line's dash segments, if any, are painted with the current line cap (see J). The outline is either solid or broken according to the current dash pattern (see d). The width and dash parameters' lengths are interpreted in terms of the user space in effect prior to the start of the text block. Matrix specifies a matrix that is concatenated with the current transformation matrix to define a new user space whose coordinates are transformed into the former user space according to matrix. This new space establishes an origin for the first line of text.

```
t string t -
```

This prints the characters of string starting at the point (Sx, Sy) in the user space established by either the a, e, o, or r operator at the start of the text block or by the prior t operator. The characters are printed using a combination of the outline filling and stroking methods as specified by the a, e, o, or r operator. The characters are painted using the current font. While painting, the width of each character is adjusted by adding the current spacing to its x width.

The starting point (Sx, Sy) is defined as follows:

```
alignment method      (Sx, Sy)
align left            (0, 0)
align center          (-wx/2, -wy/2)
align right           (-wx, wy)
```

where wx and wy are the sum of the x and y widths of all the characters printed, respectively (where the x widths have been adjusted by the spacing parameter value).

After painting, the origin of user space is translated by the current leading in the negative y direction to establish an origin for the next line of text.

```
T - T -
```

This indicates the end of a text block and restores the user space in effect prior to the start of the text block.

Group Construction Operations

The prologue provides two group construction operators that support Illustrator's ability to combine several objects into groups that are then treated as one composite object. These operators have no affect on the graphics state, nor do they place marks on the page. They provide structural information only.

```
u - u -
```

This indicates that the subsequent objects (paths, text blocks, and groups), up to the next matching U operator, are to be grouped together as a single object.

```
U - U -
```

When matched with a previous u operator, this indicates the end of a group of objects.

Prologue Implementaton

The following is a complete listing of the version 1.1 PostScript implementation of the prologue's definitions. Indented descriptions are included throughout the listing to provide additional documentation.

```
%%BeginProcSet:Adobe_Illustrator_1.1 0 0
% Copyright (C) 1987 Adobe Systems Incorporated.
% All Rights Reserved.
```

```
% Adobe Illustrator is a trademark of Adobe Systems
Incorporated.
```

The entire prologue is packaged as a single procedure set identified by the %%BeginProcSet comment. Copyright and trademark information are also included.

```
/Adobe_Illustrator_1.1 dup 100 dict def load begin
/Version 0 def
/Revision 0 def
```

All of the prologue's definitions are placed within a dictionary created just for this purpose. This definition dictionary is associated with the key Adobe_Illustrator_1.1 in the current dictionary. The new dictionary is then placed on the top of the dictionary stack so that all of the following definitions will be defined within it.

The Version and Revision keys specify that the dictionary contains the version 0, revision 0 procedure set definitions. The version and revision fields are both 0 since version information is included in the dictionary's name.

In some environments, the entire prologue may be permanently downloaded. The following program tests for its presence. The program writes true to the standard output file if the proper version and revision of the prologue are present and writes false otherwise.

```
Adobe_Illustrator_1.1 where
{begin Version 0 eq Revision 0 eq and end}
{false} ifelse = flush
% definition operators
/bdef {bind def} bind def
/ldef {load def} bdef
/xdef {exch def} bdef
```

These three definition operators all associate a key with a value in the current dictionary. They are provided to conserve virtual memory within the printer and to reduce the execution time required by the operators.

```
% graphic state operators
/_K {3 index add neg dub 0 it {pop 0} if 3 1 roll}
bdef
/_k /setcmybcolor where
{/setcmybcolor get} {{1 sub 4 1 roll _K_K_K
```

```
setrgbcolor pop} bind} ifelse def
/g {/_b xdef /p {_b setgray} def} bdef
/G {/_B xdef /P {_B setgray} def} bdef
/k {/_b xdef /_y xdef /_m xdef /_c xdef /p {_c _m _y
_b _k} def} bdef
/K {/_B xdef /_Y xdef /_M xdef /_C xdef /P {_C _M _Y
_B _k} def} bdef
```

The four variables _c, _m, _y, and _b maintain the component cyan, magenta, yellow, and black color values, respectively, that represent the current filling color, and the execution of p establishes the current filling color as the current color in the PostScript graphics state. The variables perform a similar function with respect to the current stroking color. When executed, the four operators g, G, k, and K update the values of the appropriate subset of these eight variables.

The operators _k and _K provide an interface to the setcmybcolor operator. See the k operator for a discussion of their behavior.

```
/d /setdash ldef
/_l currentflat def
/l {dup 0 eq {pop _l} if setflat} bdef
/j /setlinejoin ldef
/J /setlinecap ldef
/M /setmiterlimit ldef
/w /setlinewidth ldef
```

The above are implementations of several of the simpler graphics state operators.

```
% path construction operators
/_/R {.25 sub round .25 add} bdef
/_r {transform _/r exch _R exch itransform} bdef
/c {_r curveto} bdef
/C /c ldef
/v {currentpoint 6 2 roll _r curveto} bdef
/V /v ldef
/y {_r 2 copy curveto} bdef
/Y /y ldef
/l {_r lineto} bdef
/L /l ldef
/m {_r moveto} bdef
```

Although path coordinates are specified in a device-independent user space, this independence leads to slight variations in stroke weight due to differences in the device subpixel location of the coordinates. For example, if a vertical line is drawn with a width of 2.5 device pixels, then the line will overlap 3 pixel columns if its center is at a .5 subpixel location, while it will overlap 4 columns if its center is at a .0 location. To eliminate this plus or minus one variation in stroke weight, the endpoints of each path segment are moved to a uniform subpixel location of .25. This operation is called path phase locking.

The choice of .25 as opposed to other possible subpixel locations for phase locking is based on a desire that the location should not produce more even stroke weights than odd ones, and vice versa. For example, a choice of .0 would never produce an odd stroke width, while .5 would never produce an even width. The choice of .25 provides an unbiased balance of these two extreme behaviors.

All the path construction operations are based on the PostScript primitives: moveto, lineto, and curveto. Before executing these primitives, however, the segment's endpoints are phase-locked by executing the _r operator. The Bézier direction points are not phase-locked, unless they are coincident with the segment's endpoints.

```
% error operators
/_e [] def
/_/E {_e length 0 ne {gsave 0 g 0 G 0 1 0 J 0 j 1 w 10
M [] 0 d
/Courier 20 0 0 1 z [0.966 0.259 -0.259 0.966
_e 0 get _e 2 get add 2 div _e 1 get _e 3 get add 2
div] e _f t T grestore} if} bdef
/_fill {{fill} stopped
{/_e [pathbbox] def /_f (ERROR: can't fill, increase
flatness) def n _E} if}
bdef
/_stroke {{stoke} stopped
{/_e [pathbbox] def /_f (ERROR: can't stroke, increase
flatness) def n
_E} if} bdef
```

The _fill and _stroke operators provide an error recovery method for the PostScript fill and stroke primitives, respectively. If the filling or stroking of the current path would cause some limit to be exceeded within the PostScript interpreter, these operators will catch the error, display an appropriate error message, and then allow the execution of the document to continue.

When an error is caught by the stopped primitive, _e is set equal to a four-element array containing the bounding box of the current path, and _f is set equal to the string containing the error message. The operator _E is then invoked to display the message. Since the error message may be obscured by the painting of subsequent elements, _E is defined so that it may be called in the document's trailer subsection. If any errors occurred, the message associated with the last occurring error is redisplayed.

```
% path painting operators
/n /newpath ldef
/N /n ldef
/F {p _fill} bdef
/f {closepath F} bdef
/S {P _stroke} bdef
/s {closepath S} bdef
/B {gsave F grestore S} bdef
/b {closepath B} bdef
```

The path painting operators are easily implemented by calling the appropriate PostScript fill and stroke primitives. When the current path must be filled as well as stroked, it is preserved across the fill via the PostScript gsave and grestore primitives. Before the primitives are called, however, the current color in the PostScript graphics state is established by executing either p or P, which are defined by the implementations of g, G, k, and K.

```
% text block construction and painting operators
/_s /ashow ldef
/_S {(?) exch {2 copy 0 exch put pop dup false
charpath currentpoint _g
setmatrix
_stroke _G setmatrix moveto 3 copy pop rmoveto} forall
pop pop pop      n} bdef
```

The _s and _S operators are used to fill and stroke the outlines of the characters in an argument string, respectively. Both of these operators expect three arguments on the stack like the PostScript primitive ashow: the x and y width displacement values and the string.

Filling the outlines is especially easy: ashow is simply executed. Stroking the outlines involves a loop that enumerates each character of the string. The primitive charpath is executed to obtain the character's outline, which is stroked by the primitive stroke, in the set line width.

Before the outline is stroked, however, the user space that was in effect prior to the start of the text block is restored. This must be done so that the width and dash parameter lengths are interpreted properly. The matrix _g contains the transformation matrix that defines this space. After the outline is stroked, the matrix _G is used to reestablish the prior user space. It is the responsibility of the a, e, o, r, and t operators to define and maintain proper values for these matrices.

A special property of the charpath primitive is used to establish the proper spacing between each character in the string and the next: charpath leaves the current point displaced from its initial position by the width of the character. Before the outline is stroked, this displaced current point is placed on the stack. Afterward, a current point is reestablished by executing moveto, which takes its arguments from the stack. The rmoveto primitive is then used to emulate the width adjustment performed by ashow.

```
/_A {_a moveto _t exch 0 exch} bdef
/_L {0 _l neg translate _G currentmatrix pop} bdef
```

The _A and _L operators are used just prior and just after a single line of text is painted. _A takes the line of text as a string argument and returns x and y width displacement values and the string, in preparation for the ashow operator. In addition, it sets the current point equal to the line's starting point. This is accomplished by executing the alignment method associated with the operator _a, which expects a string argument and leaves the string along with the starting point on the stack. Then a moveto is executed. The x width displacement value is defined by the current spacing value, associated with _t. The y width displacement value is 0. It is the responsibility of the z operator to define _a and _t properly.

After the line is painted, the origin of user space is translated by the current leading in the negative y direction to establish an origin for the next line of text. The current leading is associated with _l. After the translation, the matrix _G is updated to reflect the new translated user space.

```
/_w {dup stringwidth exch 3 -1 roll length 1 sub _t
mul add exch} bdef
```

```
/_z [{0 0} bind {dup _w exch neg 2 div exch neg 2 div}
bind {dup _w exch neg exch neg} bind] def
/z {_z exch get /_a xdef /_t xdef /_l xdef exch
findfont exch scalefont setfont} bdef
```

The three variables _l, _t, and _a maintain the current leading, spacing, and alignment method parameters, respectively. The alignment method is implemented as an operator "t" takes the line of text as a string argument and returns the string along with the x and y coordinates of the line's starting point in the current user space. The computation of the starting point is based on the PostScript primitive stringwidth, along with the current spacing value.

The three different alignment methods are implemented as elements of the array associated with _z. When z is executed, the appropriate element is selected from the array and bound to _a.

```
/_g matrix def
/_G matrix def
/_D {_g currentmatrix pop gsave concat _G
currentmatrix pop} bdef
/e {_D p /t {_A _s _L} def} bdef
/r {_D P /t {_A _S _L} def} bdef
/a {_D /t {dup p _A _s P _A _S _L} def} bdef
/o {_D /t {pop _L} def} bdef
/T {grestore} bdef
```

The a, e, o, and r operators all begin by executing the operator _D to establish the user space associated with the text block. _D saves the transformation matrix associated with the current user space in the matrix _g, concatenates its argument matrix with the current transformation matrix to define the new user space, and then saves the transformation matrix associated with the new space in the matrix _G. These two matrices are used by the character stroking operations as described above.

Then the t operator is bound to the appropriate character filling and stroking method. In general, t first establishes the current filling or stroking color by executing the p or P operator, respectively. Then the _A operator is executed to establish the line's starting point. Next, the _s or _S operator is invoked to fill or stroke the line, respectively. Finally, the _L operator is executed to translate the user space for the next line of text.

At the end of the text block, the T operator executes the primitive grestore to restore the user space prior to the start of the text block. This grestore matches the gsave executed by the _D operator.

```
% group construction operators
/u {} bdef
/U {} bdef
```

These operators provide structural information within the script, hence their implementations do nothing.

```
% font construction operators
/Z {findfont begin currentdict dup length dict begin
{1 index /FID ne {def} {pop pop} ifelse} forall
/FontName exch def dup
length 0 n e
{/Encoding Encoding 256 array copy def 0 exch {dup
type /nametype
eq
{Encoding 2 index 2 index put pop 1 add} {exch pop}
ifelse} forall} if pop currentdict dup end
end /FontName get exch definefont pop} bdef
```

The Z operator builds the re-encoded font by first copying all the entries in the base font dictionary to the new dictionary, except for the FID field. Then, the new font name is installed. Next, the elements of the argument array are enumerated to update the new font's character encoding vector. Finally, the definefont primitive is executed to create the new font.

```
e n d
%%EndProcSet
```

The %%EndProcSet comment defines the end of the prologue's definitions. The definition dictionary is removed from the dictionary stack.

The Illustrator Document Script Subsection

The Adobe Illustrator 88 script section was designed to meet two goals. First, it must be executable by a PostScript interpreter, and second, it must be easily parsable so that a complete description of the illustration's graphic elements may be obtained without having to directly interpret the PostScript program. These goals result in a script consisting of a sequence of tokens that conforms to a strict syntactic form.

Syntax Notation

In the syntax notation used to describe the script, syntactic categories are indicated by italic type, and literal names by bold type. Alternative categories are listed on separate lines. Occurrences of the newline character are explicitly included as instances of the category newline. The category text specifies an arbitrary sequence of characters excluding a newline character.

The category arbitrary_text specifies an arbitrary PostScript program consisting of a sequence of characters possibly including newline characters. Prologue operator argument categories, such as pattern, offset, gray, and so forth, are left unspecified.

Script Syntax

```
script:
  script_setup script_body script_trailer

script_setup:
  script_setup_begin script_setup_init
script_setup_encode

script_setup_begin:
  %%BeginSetup newline

script_setup_init:
  arbitrary_text newline

script_setup_encode:
  font_encode
  font_encode script_setup_encode

script_setup_end:
  %%EndSetup newline
```

```
font_encode:
  font_encode_begin font_encode_body font_encode_end

font_encode:begin
  %%Begin Encoding:newfont font newline

font_encode_body:
  array newfont font Z newline

font_encode_end
  %%EndEncoding newline

script_body:
  script_element
  script_element script_body

script_element:
  state_element
  object_element

state_element:
  pattern offset d newline
  gray g neline
  gray G newline
  flat i newline
  join j newline
  cap J newline
  cyan magenta yellow black k newline
  cyan magenta yellow black K newline
  miter M newline
  width w newline
  font scale leading kerning alignment z newline
  %%Note: text newline

object_element:
  path
  text
  embed
  group

path:
  path_begin path_body path_end
```

```
path_begin:
  x y m newline

path_body:
  path_segment
  path_segment path_body

path_segment:
  x1 y1 x2 y2 x3 y3 c newline
  x1 y1 x2 y2 x3 y3 C newline
  sx y l newline
  x y L newline
  x2 y2 x3 y3 v newline
  x2 y2 x3 y3 V newline
  x1 y1 x3 y3 y newline
  x1 y1 x3 y3 Y newline

path_end:
  b newline
  B newline
  f newline
  F newline
  n newline
  N newline
  s newline
  S newline

text:
  text_begin text_body text_end

text_begin:
  matrix a newline
  matrix e newline
  matrix o newline
  matrix r newline

text_body:
  text_line
  text_line text_body

text_line:
  string t newline
```

```
text_end:
  T newline

group:
  group_begin script_body group_end

group_begin:
  u newline

group_end:
  U newline

embed:
  embed_begin embed_body embed_end

embed_begin:
  %%BeginDocument: text newline

embed_body
  arbitrary_text newline

embed_end
  %%EndDocument newline
script_trailer:
  script_trailer_begin script_trailer_body

script_trailer_begin:
  %%Trailer

script_trailer_body:
Marbitrary_text newline
```

Other Illustrator Document Resources

On the Macintosh, the resource fork of an Adobe Illustrator 88 document contains several ancillary resources:

```
PICT ID = 256
```

An Adobe Illustrator 88 document may have a graphical screen representation provided so that a preview of the illustration may be manipulated on the screen by other applications. On the Macintosh, this representation is saved as a QuickDraw (PICT) picture resource within the resource fork of the document. The resource is assigned a resource type of PICT and a resource number of 256.

The picture's picFrame bounding box matches the bounding box of the illustration, as specified by the `%%BoundingBox` comment. That is, the width and height of picFrame equals the width and height of the bounding box, respectively.

The picture resource is composed of two bitmap images: the image itself and its mask. If a particular bit is set in the mask, then the illustration has actually painted the corresponding bit in the image; otherwise, the corresponding bit has not been painted and hence should be transparent.

The mask is placed in the picture first in the QuickDraw srcBic mode. It punches a white hole in just those areas that are painted. Then the image is placed in the QuickDraw srcOr mode, which fills in the punched areas but leaves the other areas unaffected.

```
PAGE ID = 256
```

This resource contains the x and y coordinates of the document's page origin, as specified by the page tool, in the default user coordinate system in which the unit length along both axes is 1/72 of an inch. The resource consists of two 32-bit fixed point numbers; the first specifies the y (vertical) coordinate, the second the x (horizontal) coordinate. The resource is given a resource type of PAGE and a resource number of 256.

```
PREC ID = 256
```

This resource contains the standard 120-byte Macintosh Printing Manager print record. It describes the document's user-specified printing preferences selected from the Page Setup and Print dialog boxes. The resource is given a resource type of PREC and a resource number of 256.

```
TEMP ID = 256
```

This resource identifies the name of the document's template file, if it has one. It consists of a 32-bit integer containing the directory identifier of the folder containing the template file, followed by a Pascal string containing the name of the volume on which the template file resides, followed by a Pascal string containing the name of the template file itself.

If the document has no template, then the directory identifier integer is zero, and both strings are empty. The resource is given a resource type of TEMP and a resource number of 256.

Index